The International Library of Environmental, Agricultural and Food Ethics

Volume 29

Series Editors

Michiel Korthals, Wageningen University, Wageningen, The Netherlands
Paul B. Thompson, Michigan State University, East Lansing, USA

The ethics of food and agriculture is confronted with enormous challenges. Scientific developments in the food sciences promise to be dramatic; the concept of life sciences, that comprises the integral connection between the biological sciences, the medical sciences and the agricultural sciences, got a broad start with the genetic revolution. In the mean time, society, i.e., consumers, producers, farmers, policymakers, etc, raised lots of intriguing questions about the implications and presuppositions of this revolution, taking into account not only scientific developments, but societal as well. If so many things with respect to food and our food diet will change, will our food still be safe? Will it be produced under animal friendly conditions of husbandry and what will our definition of animal welfare be under these conditions? Will food production be sustainable and environmentally healthy? Will production consider the interest of the worst off and the small farmers? How will globalisation and liberalization of markets influence local and regional food production and consumption patterns? How will all these developments influence the rural areas and what values and policies are ethically sound?

All these questions raise fundamental and broad ethical issues and require enormous ethical theorizing to be approached fruitfully. Ethical reflection on criteria of animal welfare, sustainability, liveability of the rural areas, biotechnology, policies and all the interconnections is inevitable.

Library of Environmental, Agricultural and Food Ethics contributes to a sound, pluralistic and argumentative food and agricultural ethics. It brings together the most important and relevant voices in the field; by providing a platform for theoretical and practical contributors with respect to research and education on all levels.

More information about this series at http://www.springer.com/series/6215

Munamato Chemhuru

Editor

African Environmental Ethics

A Critical Reader

 Springer

Editor
Munamato Chemhuru
Department of Philosophy
University of Johannesburg
Johannesburg, South Africa

Department of Philosophy and Religious
Studies
Great Zimbabwe University
Masvingo, Zimbabwe

ISSN 1570-3010 ISSN 2215-1737 (electronic)
The International Library of Environmental, Agricultural and Food Ethics
ISBN 978-3-030-18806-1 ISBN 978-3-030-18807-8 (eBook)
https://doi.org/10.1007/978-3-030-18807-8

This Springer imprint is published by the registered company Springer Nature Switzerland AG
The registered company address is: Gewerbestrasse 11, 6330 Cham, Switzerland

Acknowledgements

I am greatly indebted to a number of people whose contributions and insights have led to the success of this project. In particular, I would like to thank the University of Johannesburg's Department of Philosophy and Faculty of Humanities for awarding me the Global Excellence Stature (GES) postdoctoral research fellowship in 2017. Great Zimbabwe University also offered me a sabbatical leave during the year 2017. This book project was initiated during this period while on sabbatical leave, pursuing the postdoctoral research fellowship with the University of Johannesburg.

Also, while at the University of Johannesburg, I organised a workshop through assistance from the Philosophy Department and the Humanities Faculty where I invited authors to this volume for a workshop where all the chapters were presented and got useful feedback. I wish to thank all the participants to this workshop which has culminated in the production of this book. I also got useful advice from Prof. H. P. P. [Hennie] Lötter and members of the U. J. Philosophy reading group in environmental ethics.

I am also greatly indebted to Prof. Thaddeus Metz of the University of Johannesburg for the continued moral support and academic guidance. His academic guidance has been very helpful to my academic career and the success of this book project.

I also wish to thank all the contributors to this volume for their invaluable contributions, patience and support. I am also grateful to Christopher Wilby and Manjula Saravanan, the Series Editors to this volume, Michiel Korthals and Paul B. Thompson and other colleagues at Springer for showing confidence in our work and for their patience and support and to Great Zimbabwe University, especially my colleagues in the Philosophy Department, for their support, which is always appreciated.

Finally, I would like to acknowledge with gratitude, the support and love from my family.

Masvingo, Zimbabwe   Munamato Chemhuru
2019

Contents

Editor and Contributors

About the Editor

Munamato Chemhuru obtained his doctoral degree in philosophy from the University of Johannesburg in 2016. Upon completion of his doctoral degree in philosophy, he was awarded a commendation bursary for outstanding performance in doctoral studies by the University of Johannesburg's Faculty of Humanities. In 2017, he was awarded the prestigious Global Excellence Stature (GES) postdoctoral research fellowship that he pursued with the University of Johannesburg's Department of Philosophy and Faculty of Humanities. After completion of his postdoctoral research fellowship, he was appointed as Senior Research Associate in philosophy by the Faculty of Humanities at the University of Johannesburg from 2018 to 2020. He is Senior Lecturer in philosophy at Great Zimbabwe University. His current research focuses on various applied ethical issues in African philosophy stemming from concepts such as African communitarian philosophy and the idea of Ubuntu. He has published research articles in some central philosophy journals like Amoye: *Journal of African Philosophy and Studies*, *Caribbean Journal of Philosophy*, *Journal on African Philosophy*, *Africana Journal of African Studies*, *Philosophia Africana*, *South African Journal of Philosophy*, *Politikon*, *Theoria* and *Phronimon*. He also has a chapter in an edited book published by Lexington Books in 2014. He has also presented conference papers at local and international conferences in Zimbabwe, South Africa, Tanzania, Ghana, Senegal, Kenya and Greece.

Contributors

Afia Ban holds a Master of Theology—Columbia Theological Seminary USA (2017), a bachelor of theology—Trinity Theological Seminary Ghana (2014) and a diploma in basic education—St. Monica's College of Education Ghana (2008). She is an ordained minister of religion with the Presbyterian Church of Ghana.

Michelle Louise Clarke is a Ph.D. student at SOAS University of London. Her research interests centre around African philosophy and environmental ethics. Her thesis engages with ecocritical discourse within African speculative fiction. She obtained a research masters (MRes) from Lancaster University, and her background in the field of environment and development means she has carried out varied fieldwork projects, such as assessing the impacts of climate change on hibiscus growers in Uganda and researching the use of oral history in land disputes cases in Ghana.

Ernst M. Conradie is Senior Professor in the Department of Religion and Theology, University of the Western Cape, where he teaches systematic theology and ethics. His research is mainly in the field of Christian ecotheology, and he is the author of several monographs and edited volumes in this area, including *Redeeming Sin? Social Diagnostics amid Ecological Destruction* that will appear later this year with Lexington Books.

Patrick Giddy studied philosophy at the University of Cape Town (BA, Ph.D., 1994) and Stellenbosch (MA), and theology at Blackfriars College, Oxford. He lectured in philosophy for some years at the University of Lesotho before moving to the University of KwaZulu-Natal, Durban, where he is currently a senior research associate. Current areas of research include religion in a scientific and secular culture and virtue ethics; the most consulted article on his ResearchGate page has been "Virtues in a Post-Traditional Society" *Acta Academica* 2014: 18–34. The article "Human Agency and Weakness of Will: a neo-Thomist approach" (*South African Journal of Philosophy* 35, 2016: 197–209) reflects my research on contemporary Thomism.

Ephraim Taurai Gwaravanda holds a DLitt et Phil in philosophy from the University of South Africa (UNISA). He was awarded a postdoctoral research fellowship in the Faculty of Education at the University of Johannesburg in 2017. He is also a senior lecturer in philosophy at Great Zimbabwe University, where he teaches logic, philosophy of law and metaphysics. His research interests are in environmental philosophy, philosophy of education and African philosophy.

Kai Horsthemke teaches philosophy of education at KU Eichstätt-Ingolstadt in Germany. He is also Visiting Professor in the School of Education at the University of the Witwatersrand, South Africa, and Fellow at the Oxford Centre for Animal Ethics, UK. He has published extensively since 2004, on African philosophy, indigenous knowledge systems and animal ethics. He is the author of *The moral status and rights of animals* (Porcupine Press 2010) and *Animals and African ethics* (Palgrave MacMillan 2015).

Kalu Ikechukwu Kalu is Doctoral Researcher in environmental ethics, at Philosophisches Seminar der Christian-Albrechts-Universität zu Kiel, Deutschland. Kalu holds a bachelor of philosophy from Pontifical Urban University—Rome, a master of applied ethics major in corporate responsibility and sustainable development of Norwegian University of Science and Technology (NTNU) Trondheim—Norway as a European Union student within the framework of Erasmus Mundus. Kalu's areas of interest are in corporate compliance and ethics, corporate responsibility and concept of sustainability.

Garikai Madavo is a Ph.D. student in philosophy at the University of Johannesburg. His main research interests are in ethics. Currently, he is working on a doctoral thesis titled "Dignity and Equality in Civic Reintegration of Ex-criminal Offenders". In this volume of African Environmental Ethics, his proposed contribution seeks to re-articulate African agricultural ethics.

Nompumelelo Zinhle Manzini is Sessional Lecturer for the WITS Philosophy Department. She completed her master's degree in philosophy (WITS), as a Mandela Rhodes Scholar (2016). Her MA dissertation argued that certain African conceptions of personhood are gendered, ableist and anti-queer. Her areas of interest include critical race theory, disabilities studies, queer theory, Black feminism, personhood and African philosophy.

Dennis Masaka is a holder of a Ph.D. in philosophy and a senior lecturer in the field of philosophy at Great Zimbabwe University in Zimbabwe. He has papers published by reputable journals such as *Philosophical Papers*, *Journal of Black Studies*, *Centre for Advanced Studies of African Society (CASAS)*, *African Study Monographs*, *South African Journal of Philosophy* and *Journal of Negro Education*. His areas of interest include philosophy of liberation, African philosophy and African environmental ethics.

Thaddeus Metz is Distinguished Professor at the University of Johannesburg (2015–2019), where he is affiliated with the Department of Philosophy. Author of more than 200 books, articles and chapters, he is particularly known for having analytically articulated an African moral theory, applied it to a variety of ethical and political controversies, compared it to East Asian and Western moral perspectives, and defended it as preferable to them. His book, *A Relational Moral Theory: African Contributions to Global Ethics*, is under contract with Oxford University Press.

Motsamai Molefe obtained his doctoral degree in philosophy from the University of Johannesburg. He has an interest in African philosophy, moral philosophy and applied ethics. He is Guest Co-editor of *Theoria* 65 (4). Currently, he is teaching in the Department of Philosophy at the University of Witwatersrand in Johannesburg, South Africa. He has published extensively in the area of African philosophy.

Stephen Nkansah Morgan is a Ph.D. candidate in ethics studies at the University of KwaZulu-Natal. His current area of research is in animal and environmental ethics. He holds a bachelor of arts degree in philosophy with classics and a master of philosophy. He taught philosophy at various levels at the University of Ghana. He also has research interests in African philosophy and moral philosophy.

John Mweshi (Ph.D.) is currently Lecturer and Researcher in the Department of Philosophy and Applied Ethics at the University of Zambia. He specialises in environmental philosophy (ethics) and environmental policy and conflict analysis. He also teaches in other areas such as development and administrative ethics. Of late, he has also ventured into contemporary African philosophy and related themes.

Philomena Aku Ojomo is Lecturer at Lagos State University in Nigeria. She has published in the area of African environmental ethics.

Beatrice D. Okyere-Manu (Ph.D.) is Lecturer in applied ethics in the School of Religion, Philosophy and Classics at the University of KwaZulu-Natal. She is the programme director for applied ethics. Her research interests cover the following areas in applied ethics: ethical issues affecting African women, indigenous knowledge in African culture, environmental ethics and professional ethics.

Konrad Ott is Professor and Chair of Philosophy and Environmental Ethics, Philosophisches Seminar der Christian-Albrechts-Universität zu Kiel, Deutschland. He is a third-generation Frankfurt School scholar of critical theory and former student of Habermas. He has a series of publications on the intersection of discourse ethics and environmental ethics to his credit, and moreover, he is publically serving on various applied environmental ethics consortiums and projects in Germany.

Angela Roothaan (Ph.D.) works as Assistant Professor of philosophy at the Free University Amsterdam. She published widely on philosophy of nature, spirituality, spirits and modern culture, with an increasing focus on intercultural and African philosophy. Presently, she works on a project titled *Philosophy of Spirit Ontologies —A Study in Intercultural Philosophy*, in which the relations between humans and animals in shamanist ontologies will be investigated.

Margaret Ssebunya (Ph.D.) is Ugandan Postdoctoral Scholar in the School of Religion, Philosophy and Classics at the University of KwaZulu-Natal. She holds a Ph.D. in ethics studies from UKZN. Her interests include environmental ethics, leadership ethics, feminist ethics as well as ethics and indigenous knowledge systems.

Aïda C. Terblanché-Greeff is Temporary Lecturer at the School of Philosophy, North-West University, South Africa. She teaches thinking skills; history of philosophy; socio-economic ethics; aesthetics; and Know and Understand the World of Health. She also has various degrees which include B.A. humanities (philosophy and psychology); B.A. Hons. (psychology); and M.D.M (development and management: disaster studies). Her areas of research interest are time orientation; Ubuntu; environmental ethics; social self-construal; disaster risk reduction and management; aesthetics; and subjective attitudes towards death.

Jessica van Jaarsveld is a Ph.D. student at the University of Johannesburg. Her work is in its early phases, but focuses on using Martha Nussbaum's capabilities approach as the basis for an environmental ethic. Her MA and honours in philosophy and BA in politics, philosophy and economics were all completed at UJ, though her studies included a UJ-sponsored exchange programme for a semester at Sciences Po University in Paris. In 2016, she won second place in the John Broadbent prize for excellence in philosophical writing at the University of Johannesburg.

Chapter 1
Introducing African Environmental Ethics

Munamato Chemhuru

Abstract This critical reader addresses African environmental ethics in a unique way by drawing from a variety of authors with diverse perspectives on underexplored and often neglected issues in African philosophy and ethics. Central issues in contemporary African environmental ethics are addressed such as: The moral status of nature, *Ubuntu* and the Environment, African conceptions of animal moral status and rights, African conceptions of environmental justice, African relationalism, theocentric and teleological environmentalism. The book goes beyond the generalised focus on African metaphysics and African ethics by exploring further how these views might be understood differently in order to conceptualise plausible African environmental ethical perspectives.

The title of the book might come as a surprise to some because of the misconceptions surrounding the existence and nature of African Philosophy despite "strong arguments hav[ing] been advanced to demonstrate the actual existence of African philosophy" (Ramose 2003: 3). As a result, African ethics, and ultimately African environmental ethics, have been determined by the fate and direction of African philosophy in Africa especially after the second half of the twenty first century. The history of African Philosophy seems to give the impression, at least to many scholars outside Africa, that there is no elaborate African ethics except for the various African myths, cultural and religious practices that have been transmitted from generation to generation. Kai Horsthemke makes a similar observation as he avers that, "until recently very little has been written on the subject. Most of what was known about African ethics was extracted from anthropological and sociological writings on African religions and cultures as well as transcriptions of oral accounts, or it was gleaned from ethnographic collections of myths, tales, folklore and proverbs" (Horsthemke 2015: 1). While there has not been much in terms of unified and coherent accounts on African Ethics, recently there has been a considerable body of

M. Chemhuru (✉)
University of Johannesburg, Johannesburg, South Africa
e-mail: munamatochemhuru@gmail.com

Great Zimbabwe University, Masvingo, Zimbabwe

© Springer Nature Switzerland AG 2019
M. Chemhuru (ed.), *African Environmental Ethics*, The International Library of Environmental, Agricultural and Food Ethics 29,
https://doi.org/10.1007/978-3-030-18807-8_1

literature addressing fundamental issues on African ethics, such as collections edited by Murove (2009) and, Imafidon and Bewaji (2014).

The book addresses African environmental ethics in a unique way by drawing from a variety of authors with diverse perspectives on under-explored and often neglected issues in African philosophy and ethics. Central issues in contemporary African environmental ethics are addressed such as: The moral status of nature, *Ubuntu* and the Environment, African conceptions of animal rights, African conceptions of environmental justice, African relational environmentalism, African theocentric and teleological environmentalism. The book goes beyond the generalized focus on African metaphysics and African ethics as it explores how these views might be understood differently in order to conceptualize plausible African environmental ethical perspectives. Also, against the background where environmental problems such as pollution, climate change, extinction of *flora* and *fauna*, and global warming have for a long while been plain to see in terms of their consequences on humanity and nature itself (see While 1974: 1–7), it becomes useful to examine how African conceptions of environmental ethics could be understood in order to confront some of these problems facing the world owing to its recognition of the bond between human beings and the environment (see Murove 2004: 195). A number of contributors to this volume maintain African thought about nature to be fundamentally different from Western approaches, and so might augment some fresh insights into the global efforts to deal with the environmental crisis.

The question of moral status, i.e., of which things matter morally for their own sake, lies at the core of any environmental ethical thinking. Yet this question has traditionally been understood from varied perspectives ranging from individualist and sometimes pluralist and holist perspectives (Chemhuru 2016: 184). At the same time, so far there has not been consensus in terms of which of these perspectives could inform a plausible view of moral status, or whether some other approach is best. The first part of the book therefore focuses on the questions of *Moral Status and the African Environment*. It divides into four different chapters which all address the critical questions surrounding African conceptions of moral status. While the question of moral status has also traditionally been examined and understood with reference to inherently anthropocentric approaches that give importance to human beings alone, and especially from non-African philosophical traditions, this first part addresses the idea of moral status from an African philosophical perspective and tries to establish grounds on which such moral status could understood.

In Chap. 2, Thaddeus Metz critically analyses how unified an African relational and specifically communal, view of moral status could inform environmental ethical thinking in African philosophy, contrary to the dominant individualistic and holistic approaches in traditional Western philosophy. In Chap. 3, Munamato Chemhuru dissects the question of whether moral status could be limited to human beings and living beings alone with a view to consider the grounds for granting moral status to non-living beings as well. Chapter 4 by Patrick Giddy considers non-anthropocentric approaches to environmental ethics that draw attention to the overarching eco-system and equalize the functional roles of both human and non-human beings. Drawing on Aristotelian/Thomist metaphysics, congruent with the African traditional idea of "vital force", Giddy argues that organisms—human or otherwise—are *not* merely functional elements in the ecosystem but historically viable co-determinants thereof. In Chap. 5, Motsamai Molefe concludes the first part by arguing that the best account of the foundations of morality in the African tradition should be include some relevant spiritual property or 'ethical supernaturalism', contrary to the dominant humanistic view on African ethics that are mainly informed by analytic methods in contemporary Anglo-American philosophy.

In the light of the African conceptions of moral status, the environmental ethical import in African traditional environmentalism cannot be overemphasised. Godfrey Tangwa makes the observation that "the pre-colonial traditional African metaphysical outlook can be described as eco-bio-communitarian, implying recognition and acceptance of interdependence and peaceful coexistence between earth, plants, animals, and humans" (Tangwa 2004: 389). In 1980, a Zimbabwean couple, Stanlake Samkange and Tommie Marie Samkange had set the tone for the search for such a systematic African indigenous epistemology through *Hunhuism* or *Ubuntuism* (Samkange and Samkange 1980). Although the African philosophy of *ubuntu* has received much attention in the last few decades, not much has been done in terms of appraising it from an environmental ethical perspective. In pursuit of this kind of an epistemology, part two, *Ubuntu and the Environment*, brings the African philosophy of *ubuntu* into conversation with central issues in African environmental ethics. In Chap. 6, Ephraim Taurai Gwaravanda explores some conceptions and misconceptions about *ubuntu* with a view to refine the generalised conceptions of *ubuntu* across the diverse African cultures and communities. In the same spirit, Aïda Terblanché-Greeff looks at the import of *ubuntu* for environmental ethics in Chap. 7. She challenges non-African communities like the West to consider harnessing the philosophy of ubuntu in order to confront the reality of climate change that is facing the world. The section ends with Nompumelelo Zinhle Manzini emphasizing the non-anthropocentric nature of what she refers to as 'Southern Environmental Ethics' in Chap. 8.

The quest for any sound environmental ethical thinking shows that anthropocentric and individualistic approaches to environmental ethics are unpersuasive. As alternative to anthropocentric thinking, prudential appeals to sustainability, future generations, sentiency and biology (see Warren 1987: 434) are not all that convincing in so far as they do not take into account the entire ecosystem. This calls for environmentalists to "go a step further and also include plants, inanimate nature, or entire ecosystems" (Roser and Seidel 2017: 14) into the whole web of interconnectivity and realm of ethical concern. In the same vein, in part three that focuses on *African Ecocentric Environmental Ethics*, the centrality of the ecosystem as the basis of environmental ethical thinking comes at the fore of African environmental ethics. In Chap. 9, Ernst Conradie examines the way an African environmental ethics could be informed by an ecocentric approach to environmentalism, while Chap. 10 by Garikai Madavo is more focused on how the metaphysics of the African Rain-maker also contributes to the African ecosystem and ultimately the African environment at large. This part of the book concludes with a contribution by Michelle Clarke who examines in Chap. 11 the importance of the ocean in African and global environmental ethics in general.

The link between justice and environmental degradation is increasingly becoming another area of serious concern for environmental philosophers (see Roser and Seidel 2017: 1–16). Yet these questions on *Environmental Justice in African Philosophy* remain underexplored in recent debates on African Environmental Ethics. Part four therefore seeks to explore, in different respects, the ways in which environmental justice could be approached in order to achieve global justice and harmonious relationships in African environmental ethical living. In Chap. 12, Margaret Ssebunya, Stephen Nkansah Morgan and Beatrice Okyere-Manu identify a fundamental gap on what an Afrian model of environmental justice ought to look like by considering the possibilities of equitable distribution of environmental resources and environmental burdens in Africa. John Mweshi attempts in Chap. 13, to understand the question of environmental ethics and justice within the framework of the African emphasis on harmonious relations. In Chap. 14, Jessica du Plessis concludes the second part of the book by situating Martha Nussbaum's eighth capability within the context of African environmental ethics. Overall, this second part of the book sets the tone for African environmental ethicists to seriously consider what African and non-African communities should do in respect of the distribution of environmental benefits and burdens as well as what actions could be taken to deal with environmental offenders.

Considering the continued and unabated uses of various animals and their products in Africa and elsewhere, *Questions of Animal Rights in African Philosophy* remain at the centre of African environmental ethics because of humanity's failure to draw a line between the moral status, inherent value and moral rights of living beings from those of non-living beings (Warren 1987: 433). These issues are brought to the fore in this fifth part of the volume. In Chap. 15, Dennis Masaka advocates for a moderate view of anthropocentric environmentalism that could guarantee the moral status of non-human animals, while in Chap. 16 Kai Horsthemke sees the need to move from anthropocentrism and speciesism and search for non-anthropocentric and non-speciesist orientations of environmentalism in the African philosophical traditions. In Chap. 17, Angela Roothaan ends the section with a call for the decolonization of human-animal relations in Africa by appealing to alternative ontologies from the African context.

The sixth and last part of the volume, *Issues of Environmental Pollution in Africa*, addresses applied, concrete and contemporary issues about environmental pollution in Africa with nuanced focus on the Niger Delta in Nigeria and the problem of solid waste collection in Ghana. In Chap. 18, Kalu Ikechukwu Kalu and Konrad Ott are worried about the unsustainable use and pollution from oil and gas in the Niger Delta, while Philomena Aku Ojomo and Ademola Kazeem Fayemi bring Aldo Leopold's Land Ethic into conversation with these critical issues of pollution within the Niger Delta in Chap. 19. In the end, Chap. 20 by Afia Ban reflects on the problem of solid waste collection in Ghana with the aim of proposing a theology of stewardship that ought to bind human beings with the environment in general.

Overall, we do not want to pretend that this *Critical Reader* in *African Environmental Ethics* is exhaustive of all central issues in African environmental ethics.

However, it is our belief that the contributions in this volume articulate pertinent issues in African environmental ethics that can help humanity to rethink the contribution of African thought and philosophy to their existential conditions and reality. Although this volume could be accused for being less representative than it could be, it is our hope that it sets the tone for the search of a balanced African environmental ethics.

References

Chemhuru, M. 2016. The Import of African Ontology for Environmental Ethics. D Litt et Phil (Philosophy). [Unpublished]: University of Johannesburg.

Horsthemke, K. (2015). *Animals and African Ethics*. New York: Palgrave Macmillan.

Imafidon, E., and J.A.I. Bewaji (eds.). 2014. *Ontologized Ethics: New Essays in African Meta-Ethics*. Lanham: Lexington Books.

Murove, M.F. 2004. An African Commitment to Ecological Conservation: The Shona Concepts of *Ukama* and *Ubuntu*. *The Mankind Quarterly* XLV (2): 195–215.

Murove, M.F. (ed.). 2009. *African Ethics: An Anthology of Comparative and Applied Ethics*. Pietermaritzburg: University of KwaZulu-Natal Press.

Ramose, M.B. 2003. The Struggle for Reason in Africa. In *The African Philosophy Reader*, ed. H. Pieter Coetzee and P.J. Abraham Roux, 1–9. London: Routledge.

Roser, D., and C. Seidel. 2017. *Climate Justice: An Introduction*. London: Routledge.

Samkange, S., and T.M. Samkange. 1980. *Hunhuism or Ubuntuism: A Zimbabwean Indigenous Political Philosophy*. Salisbury: Graham Publishing.

Tangwa, G.B. 2004. Some African Reflections on Biomedical and Environmental Ethics. In *A Companion to African Philosophy*, ed. Kwasi Wiredu, 385–395. Malden: Blackwell Publishers.

Warren, M.A. 1987. Difficulties with the Strong Animal Rights Position. *Between the Species* 2 (4): 433–441.

While, L. 1974. The Historical Roots of Our Ecological Crisis. In *Ecology and Religion in History*, ed. David Spring and Eileen Spring. New York: Harper and Row.

Part I
Moral Status and the African Environment

Chapter 2
An African Theory of Moral Status: A Relational Alternative to Individualism and Holism

Thaddeus Metz

Abstract The dominant conceptions of moral status in the English-speaking literature are either holist or individualist, neither of which accounts well for widespread
judgments that: animals and humans both have moral status that is of the same
kind but different in degree; even a severely mentally incapacitated human being
has a greater moral status than an animal with identical internal properties; and a
newborn infant has a greater moral status than a mid-to-late stage foetus. Holists
accord no moral status to any of these beings, assigning it only to groups to which
they belong, while individualists such as welfarists grant an equal moral status to
humans and many animals, and Kantians accord no moral status either to animals
or severely mentally incapacitated humans. I argue that an underexplored, modal-
relational perspective does a better job of accounting for degrees of moral status.
According to modal-relationalism, something has moral status insofar as it capable
of having a certain causal or intensional connection with another being. I articulate a
novel instance of modal-relationalism grounded on salient sub-Saharan moral views,
roughly according to which the greater a being's capacity to be part of a communal
relationship with us, the greater its moral status. I then demonstrate that this new,
African-based theory entails and plausibly explains the above judgments, amongst
others, in a unified way.

2.1 Introducing African Relationality

English-speaking philosophical accounts of moral status are typically either holist
or individualist. For example, claiming that a being warrants moral consideration
in light of its capacity for reason or pleasure implies that moral status is a function
of something internal to an individual. In contrast, views that ascribe moral status
to ecosystems and to species are holist accounts, deeming moral status to inhere in
groups of certain kinds. Much of the contemporary debate about moral status is about

T. Metz (✉)
University of Johannesburg, Johannesburg, South Africa
e-mail: tmetz@uj.ac.za

© Springer Nature Switzerland AG 2019
M. Chemhuru (ed.), *African Environmental Ethics*, The International
Library of Environmental, Agricultural and Food Ethics 29,
https://doi.org/10.1007/978-3-030-18807-8_2

whether it is adequately captured by either individualism or holism alone, and about which specific versions of these general perspectives are most attractive.

There is, however, a third perspective on moral status available, one that grounds moral status on *relational properties*. My aim in this article is to develop a new relational theory of moral status, and to bring out its often appealing implications in a wide variety of contexts.[1] While I do not have the space to argue that it is more justified than all the views that currently dominate English-speaking discussion, I do mean to demonstrate that it should be taken just as seriously. Of particular interest is that the theory promises to solve some long-standing conundrums that continue to plague Anglo-American discussion of moral status, e.g., of why animals and humans might both have moral status that is of the same kind but different in degree, of why even a severely mentally incapacitated human being might have a greater moral status than an animal with identical internal abilities, and of why a newborn infant might have a greater moral status than a mid-to-late stage foetus.

I call the theory I develop "African", since it is grounded on what is the most central strand of sub-Saharan ethical thought, which places relationality at the core of morality. One will find individualism and holism in African moral philosophy,[2] but the relational theory I articulate fits with much more of the field. One will also find some relational ideas in Western philosophy, particularly in the ethic of care, but it is far from a prominent contender, probably in part because it and similar views are overly parochial. My goal is to spell out a relational account of moral status that is in informed by sub-Saharan ethical reflection, avoids major problems facing the relational accounts that one currently finds in the literature, and plausibly accounts for many intuitions about moral status.

I begin by defining what I mean by "moral status" and differentiating between individualist, holist and relational theories of it (2). In the next section, I sketch the existing relational theories of moral status, and argue that they all face the same objection, that they exclude beings from having moral status that clearly have it (3). This criticism will pave the way towards developing a new relational account that is not vulnerable to it (4). I propose the view that, roughly, the more a being is capable of being part of a certain communal relationship, the greater its moral status. I contrast this modal theory with other relational accounts, deeming it to be a *prima facie* improvement over them, and I explain the sense in which it counts as "African". Then, I apply the African, modal-relational theory to many cases, noting respects in which it easily entails and reasonably explains a variety of firm judgments about moral status, including several that have evaded theoretical capture up to now by the most prominent, Kantian and utilitarian traditions (5). I conclude that, in

---

[1]I first very briefly suggested this account of moral status in Metz (2010a: 57–58), and I have discussed related ideas of dignity in Metz (2010b: 91–95), reasons for beneficence in Metz (2010c: 61–67), and legal personhood in Metz (2010d).

[2]For an example of individualism in African philosophy, see Bujo (2001), who is naturally read as holding that a being's spiritual nature is what constitutes moral status, and for an apparent example of holism, see Odera Oruka and Juma (1994: 125–126).

light of the African theory's ability to account for many widely shared intuitions, it warrants no less attention than individualist and holist accounts as a promising form of monism (6).

2.2   The Concept of Moral Status

A *conception* of moral status is a theory of it, i.e., a comprehensive and basic principle that purports to entail that, and explain in virtue of what, things either have moral status or lack it. A conception of moral status aims to account for the "underlying structure" of the myriad things with moral status by invoking as few properties as possible. Individualism, holism and relationalism are (abstract) conceptions of moral status. In contrast, the *concept* of moral status is what all these competing conceptions are about; it is that which makes a given theory one of moral status as opposed to something else such as right action or good character.

The concept of moral status is the idea of something being the object of a "direct" duty, i.e., owed a duty in its own right, or is the idea of something that can be wronged. Contrast this idea with that of an object of an "indirect" duty, where an agent has a moral reason to treat it a certain way but not ultimately because of facts about it. For a standard example, I could have a duty not to destroy a football, where this duty would be indirect, something owed not to the ball, which cannot be wronged, but to its owner.

The way I understand moral status, it in principle admits of degrees. Some philosophers do not understand the concept this way (Gruen 2003; cf. DeGrazia 2008), but there are strong reasons for siding with those who think otherwise (such as Miller 1988; VanDeVeer 1995; Warren 2003).[3] For one, the existence of degrees of moral status best explains many intuitions about forced trade-offs amongst the urgent interests of different beings. Suppose, for example, that you are driving a bus and have no alternative but to run over either a mouse or a normal, adult human being. The right thing to do would be to run over the mouse, which seems *best* explained by the idea that its moral status is not as great. For another, differential moral status also accounts best for uncontroversial judgments about how to treat beings that have already been killed or otherwise died. If an animal has died for whatever reason, many find it permissible not to let its body go to waste, but such a practice applied to humans would be horrific. In any event, I shall work with a sense of "moral status" that is not an all or nothing matter; I suppose that something can have either full moral status, which normal, adult human beings are typically thought to have, or partial moral status.

An individualist account of moral status is the view that properties intrinsic to an entity ground the capacity to be wronged or to be the object a direct duty. An intrinsic property, as understood here, is a property that is internal to an individual and that

---

[3]The rest of this paragraph borrows from Metz (2010d: 308–309), which includes some evidence beyond that mentioned here.

includes no essential connection to any other being. Influential forms of individualism include the views that moral status is solely a function of: being the agent (egoism), possessing a soul (monotheism), being alive, or at least a living organism (biocentrism), exhibiting the capacity for autonomy or rationality (Kantianism[4]), being able to recollect the past and satisfy desires for future states of affairs (subject of a life theory), and having the capacity for preference realization/frustration or for pleasure/pain (welfarism). All these properties can be purely internal to an individual.

A holist account of moral status, as I construe it here, is the view that the bearers of moral status are groups, where a group is a discrete collection of entities that are near, similar to or interdependent with one another. Leopold's (1968) land ethic is a clear version of holism, as are accounts that accord moral status to species, and not merely to their individual members.

A relational account of moral status is the view that it is constituted by some kind of interactive property between one entity and another. It therefore stands "in between" individualism and holism. Similar to individualism, a relational account implies that moral status can inhere in things as they exist apart from their membership in groups. A relational theory implies that something can warrant moral consideration even if it is not a member of a group, or, more carefully, for a reason other than the fact that it is a member. Similar to holism, though, a relational account accords no moral status to organisms on the basis of their intrinsic properties. A relational theory implies that a being warrants moral consideration only if, and because, it exhibits some kind of intensional (attitudinal) or causal (behavioural) property with regard to another being. Below I contend that the most promising kind of relationalism is one according to which something has moral status insofar as it has a certain relation to human beings in particular.

One might reasonably wonder what the difference is between holism and relationalism, for, after all, is not a group just a kind of relationship? As I understand "group", something could constitute a group without it being a "relationship" in the relevant sense. For example, the species of elephants is a group, but there is not any *interaction* between elephants in Kenya and those in India, and hence no relationship. Furthermore, there could be a "relation" between organisms that do not constitute a group, say, a person whom tourists pay to ride them on an elephant. In short, relationships require interaction of some kind between organisms, while groups do not, and groups require some kind of discreteness, while relationships do not. To be sure, there are *some* groups that are constituted by relationships, e.g., ecosystems and biotic communities within them, but the properties of being a group and of being a relationship are nonetheless conceptually and metaphysically distinct and ground differing accounts of moral status.

---

[4]Kant himself might hold a view that would count as "relational", for he deems moral status to be grounded on the capacity to act according to maxims that can be universalized without frustrating purposes, or, allegedly equivalently, the capacity to act in accordance with the absolute value of rational nature wherever it is encountered.

2.3 Critical Review of Relational Ethics

The relational theory that I shall develop is much less parochial than existing accounts in the literature. My favoured view is much better able than these others to count as having a moral status those things that intuitively have it. In this section, I show that existing Western and African relational accounts are counterintuitive for being arbitrary, or partial in the wrong ways, and then, in the following section, I develop an alternative view that avoids this problem.

In the Western tradition, talk of grounding morality on relationality immediately brings to mind the ethic of care. On the classic model from Noddings (1984), a being has moral status to the extent that it does or would respond to a person who cares for it. That is, a being has moral status only insofar as there is or would be reciprocation, a back and forth, between a person caring and the one cared for. In Noddings' words,

> If the other toward whom we shall act is capable of responding as cared-for and there are no objective conditions that prevent our receiving this response—if, that is, our caring can be completed in the other—then we must meet that other as one-caring….When we are in relation or when the other has addressed us, we must respond as one-caring. The imperative in relation is categorical. When relation has not yet been established….the imperative is more like that of the hypothetical: I must if I wish to (or am able to) move into relation. (Noddings 1984: 86)

Beings who are not already interacting with a person, or who are interacting but cannot or will not respond to her caring behaviour, counterintuitively cannot be an object of a direct duty that she has towards them. Excluded are, for example, animals in the wild that have no interaction with us but foreseeably can be harmed by our actions. More significantly, human strangers with whom one lacks any interaction and who would not demonstrate appreciation or some other response to help are not owed duties of aid, including the distant who could be easily rescued from starvation (Noddings 1984: 86). Also beyond the pale of direct duty are any severely mentally incapacitated humans and Alzheimer's patients who cannot respond to caring behaviour, supposing, as per the early Noddings, that "our obligation to summon the caring attitude is limited by the possibility of reciprocity" (1984: 149).

More recent versions of the ethic of care usually do not restrict moral status in the way that Noddings' original account does (e.g., Noddings 1992: 110–12; Donovan and Adams 2007). However, they fail to articulate an alternative conception of moral status with any rigor and specificity. Similar remarks apply to recent work in African moral philosophy. However, in that literature there are some suggestive ideas that can form the basis of a promising new theory of moral status, and I therefore turn to them now.

Central to much sub-Saharan moral thought is the maxim usually translated as either "A person is a person through other persons" or "I am because we are".[5] To most non-African readers, these phrases will indicate nothing normative, and instead will bring to mind merely some empirical banalities about the causal dependence of a

---

[5]For classic statements of these ubiquitous sayings, see Mbiti (1969: 108–109) and Menkiti (1979). My explications of the basics of African morality borrow from Metz (2010b: 83–84).

child on her parents or on society more generally. However, such statements express a controversial moral claim.[6] In typical African reflection, talk of "personhood" (as in the second instance of "person" in the quote above) is inherently moralized, such that to be a person is to be virtuous or to exhibit good character. That is, one can be more or less of a person, self or human being, where the more one is, the better. One's ultimate goal should be to become a full person, a real self or a genuine human being. And the phrases say that obtaining humanness—"*ubuntu*", as it is famously known amongst Zulu and Xhosa speakers in southern Africa–is entirely constituted by relating to others in certain ways. Such a purely relational account of self-realization contrasts with characteristically Greek conceptions of it that include "individualist" or "self-regarding" elements such as organizing one's mental faculties (Plato's *Republic*) or contemplating basic features of the universe (Aristotle's *Nicomachean Ethics*).

Exactly which sort of relationship is the key to virtue? The well-documented recurrent answer is, roughly, a *communal* one, as can be gleaned from this brief survey of the views of some prominent African intellectuals. First off, note the following summary of the moral aspects of John Mbiti's famous post-war survey and analysis of African religious and philosophical worldviews: "What is right is what connects people together; what separates people is wrong" (Verhoef and Michel 1997: 397). Next, consider these remarks from South African black consciousness leader Steve Biko, in an essay that explores facets of culture that are widely shared by Africans:

> We regard our living together not as an unfortunate mishap warranting endless competition among us but as a deliberate act of God to make us a community of brothers and sisters jointly involved in the quest for a composite answer to the varied problems of life. Hence....our action is usually joint community oriented action rather than the individualism which is the hallmark of the capitalist approach. (Biko 1971: 46)

And, finally, consider a recent summary of the nature of indigenous African society and its characteristic morality by the foremost professional African philosopher in the world, the Ghanaian Kwasi Wiredu: "(T)here can be little doubt that traditional African society was communitarian, unless it be a matter of exceptions that prove the rule....Communalism is an embodiment of the values of traditional Africa" (2008: 333, 336).

It is as yet unclear how a communal relationship is precisely to be understood, a concern that I address later (see Sect. 2.4). For now, I note that the above influential thinkers, along with many other theorists of African morality,[7] maintain that it is typical of traditional sub-Saharans to conceive of morality in terms of community, and that this major strand of African ethical reflection applied to the issue of moral status naturally suggests two conceptions of it. First, there is the idea that a communal relationship *itself* is the bearer of moral status. Awareness of this view is occasioned by the following remark from Desmond Tutu, renowned chair of South Africa's Truth and Reconciliation Commission, about what, for many sub-Saharans, has fundamental moral value: "Harmony, friendliness, community are great goods.

---

[6] As is made particularly clear in Wiredu (1992) and Gyekye (1997: 49–52).

[7] For a few more representative examples, see Shutte (2001: 16–33), Murove (2004) and Mkhize (2008).

Social harmony is for us the *summum bonum*—the greatest good. Anything that sub-verts or undermines this sought-after good is to be avoided like the plague" (1999: 35).[8] It is natural to identify the greatest good, a harmonious relationship, with that which has moral status (though I do not claim that this is Tutu's view).

It is implausible to think that moral status inheres *solely* in existing relationships of any sort, as that view implies that any being that is not part of the relevant relationship entirely lacks moral status. This would include not merely Robinson Crusoes, but also people who interact with others on the "wrong" basis, namely, at least for Tutu, in a roughly unfriendly or discordant way. Such individuals would plausibly have less "personhood" in African thinking, for recall that to be a full person in this tradition means that one has exhibited moral excellence. However, even if one has not been an upright moral agent, one should still count as a moral patient, someone owed moral treatment of certain kinds in her own right.

Equally vulnerable to this criticism is the view that persons are the bearers of moral status, but only if, and because, they are parts of an existing communal relationship. Whereas the view inspired by Tutu's comment is that a communal *relationship* is the sole bearer of moral status, the present view is that a person can bear moral status but only *in virtue* of being in a certain communal relationship with others. This view is brought to mind by some comments of Nigerian Ifeanyi Menkiti (though I do not claim that it is his view), in one of the most widely read texts in African moral philosophy:

> (W)hereas most Western views of man abstract this or that feature of the lone individual and then proceed to make it the defining or essential characteristic which entities aspiring to the description "man" must have, the African view of man denies that persons can be defined by focusing on this or that physical or psychological characteristic of the lone individual….(I)n the African view it is the community which defines the person as person, not some isolated static quality of rationality, will, or memory. (1979: 171, 172)

Menkiti is in first instance speaking of "man" in the sense of "humanness" ("*ubuntu*") or "morally virtuous individual". However, when Menkiti contrasts the African view with the Western one that prizes the capacity for rationality, will or memory, he is slipping into discussion of moral status, for these attributes are classic contenders for moral status, not for virtue, in the Western tradition. In any event, someone friendly to a relational ethic might think that persons are bearers of moral status, but only insofar as they are components of a community. But, again, the prob-lem facing this view is that if one is not part of a community of the relevant sort, then one counterintuitively lacks a moral status. There are hermits who live utterly on their own and individuals who are locked up in solitary confinement, but they are surely worthy of moral consideration for their own sakes.

So far, I have canvassed three different ways that a relational ethic might ground moral status, and all have suffered from the problem of failing to entail that certain beings that intuitively have moral status in fact do. If something has moral status only

---

[8]For a similar comment from a moral-anthropological survey, see Silberbauer (1991: 20), and for philosophical analysis and defence of the idea that a relationship *qua* relationship can provide a reason for (beneficent) action, see Metz (2010c: esp. 67–72).

if it would reciprocate in some way upon being cared for, only if it is a communal relationship itself, or only if it is part of a community, then too many beings that uncontroversially have moral status will be excluded.

2.4 A Modal-Relational Account of Moral Status

In order to avoid the problem of arbitrariness or parochialism, my suggestion is to keep the characteristically African idea that morality is a function of communal relationship but to focus on a novel relational property. My proposal is that a being has moral status roughly insofar as it is *capable* of being part of a communal relationship of a certain kind. A large majority of existing relational theories of morality appeal to *actual* relationships, but my suggestion is instead to appeal to *modal* ones. I first spell out the nature of the communal relationship, ground a conception of moral status on the capacity for it, and then bring out its largely sub-Saharan pedigree. I apply the theory only in the following section.

What is a morally attractive sort of communal relationship? Elsewhere in the context of formulating a principle of right action grounded on African mores, I have articulated and defended the following analysis of community: a relationship in which people identify with each other and exhibit solidarity with one another (Metz 2007). To identify with each other is largely for people to think of themselves as members of the same group, i.e., to conceive of themselves as a "we", as well as for them to engage in joint projects, coordinating their behaviour to realize shared ends. For people to fail to identify with each other could involve outright division between them, i.e., people not only thinking of themselves as an "I" in opposition to a "you" or a "they", but also aiming to undermine one another's ends. To exhibit solidarity with one another is mainly for people to engage in mutual aid, to act for the sake of one another. To act for the sake of another is, in the first instance, to seek to improve some other organisms' quality of life for non-instrumental motives. Solidarity is also a matter of people's attitudes such as affections and emotions being invested in others, e.g., by feeling good consequent to when their lives flourish and bad when they flounder. For people to fail to exhibit solidarity would be for them to be either indifferent to one another's good[9] or downright hostile and cruel.

An equivalent way of phrasing my preferred analysis of community is in terms of relationships in which people share a way of life and care for one another's quality of life. Note that the combination of sharing a way of life and caring for others'

---

[9]Some suggest that factors besides sentience or even well-being more generally can ground a being's moral status. For instance, Nussbaum (2006) has recently argued that the capacity to be a good member of its kind grounds moral status to no less a degree than the capacity to live a good life. However, even she maintains that in order for the former, perfectionist good to matter morally, it must inhere in a being with the latter, welfarist good. With Nussbaum, I suggest that exhibiting solidarity with a being can involve acting for its perfectionist good, but if and only if it also has a welfarist good. Such a qualification most easily enables one to exclude, say, knives from being objects of moral status.

quality of life (or of identifying, and exhibiting solidarity, with others) is basically a relationship that English-speakers call "friendship" or a broad sense of "love". Hence, one way to put my favoured conception of moral status is this: the more a being is capable of being part of a friendly or loving relationship with normal humans, the greater its moral status.

By the present view, a being that is capable of being both the *subject and object* of such a relationship has *full* moral status, whereas a being that is capable of being merely the *object* of such behaviour has *partial* moral status. Being a subject involves identifying with others and exhibiting solidarity with them oneself. A being can be a subject of the relevant communal relationship insofar as it can think of himself as a "we", seek out shared ends, sympathize with others and act for their sake. In contrast, a being can be the object of a friendly relationship insofar as characteristic human beings could think of it as part of a "we", share its goals, sympathize with it and harm or benefit it. Note that having the capacity to be an object of such a relationship does not imply that a being would or even could *respond* to any friendly engagement by another.

This modal view is neither that a communal relationship itself has moral status, nor that only those who are in such a relationship have it, but is rather that those who could be part of it have it.[10] To be "capable" of being part of a communal relationship means being able *in principle,* i.e., without changes to a thing's nature. Contingent obstacles to being a subject or object of a communal relationship are not constitutive of a thing's "capacity" to be a part of it in the relevant sense.

Examples of contingent inabilities to be the object of a communal relationship, irrelevant to a being's moral status, include the facts that the being is: unknown, the object of false beliefs and the object of fear or disgust on the part of an individual. While these might hinder a being's actually becoming the object of identity and solidarity with one of us, they are not relevant to determining its moral status, for it nonetheless could become such an object in light of its nature and ours. A being that "cannot" be the object of a communal relationship in the relevant sense would, for instance, be one that utterly lacks the ability to have a better or worse life, say, a rock.

Examples of contingent inabilities to be the subject of a communal relationship include: being asleep, having drunk too much alcohol, electing not to sympathize, being too sick to help others and being ignorant of what would benefit others. While these might hinder a being's actually becoming the subject of identity and solidarity, they are not relevant to determining its moral status, for it nonetheless could become such a subject in light of its nature. A being that "cannot" be the subject of a communal relationship in the relevant sense would be one that is, say, genetically unable to act for the sake of others.

I mean two things when I say that the *greater* the capacity for communal relationship (of identity and solidarity), the *greater* a being's moral status. In the first

---

[10]There are a very small handful of other modal views in the literature, restricting moral status either to the capacity to be caring (Jaworska 2007) or to the capacity to be an object of sympathy (Mercer 1972: 129–133).

place, I am indicating, as I have said, that being capable of both subject and object of a communal relationship constitutes a higher status than merely being the object. In the second place, though, I mean that large, and not merely incremental, differences in degrees of ability to be either a subject or an object of a communal relationship constitute differences in moral status. So, for example, if, by virtue of the nature of human beings, dogs and mice, humans were *much* more able to identify with and exhibit solidarity with dogs than with mice (upon full empirical information about both), then dogs would have a greater moral status than mice. The qualification about "much" is important. Of those who believe in degrees of moral status, most implicitly think of it in a way that can be captured well, I submit, with an orbit metaphor. Supposing that dogs were only marginally more capable than, say, cats of entering into the relevant communal relationship with us, cats would intuitively get "pulled into" the same moral status orbit that dogs have.

Before explaining why this theory of moral status counts as "African", I note two friendly amendments to it that one might be inclined to suggest, but that I do not accept. First, a reader could fairly wonder whether, instead of focusing on the *capacity* for community as the relevant property, I should rather focus on the *potential* for it. Both a tree and a first trimester human foetus lack the capacity for community, but the latter exhibits the potential for community, whereas the former does not. I deem capacity to be the crucial feature precisely because of my prior stance on the abortion debate; my intuitions are the common ones that abortion is permissible in the early stages of pregnancy but that infanticide is wrong. Those who believe that abortion is no less wrong than infanticide, and who find a relational theory attractive, probably should appeal to potential and develop a theory that differs from mine.

Second, a critic may reasonably question my appeal to community *with normal human beings* as the relevant property, and instead propose community *with some other being or other*. For what is probably the most powerful example of the latter, imagine an intelligent alien creature who could be both the subject and object of friendly relationships with members of its own species, but not with us, for whatever reason. To reply in depth, I would need to consider the case in some detail, carefully paying attention both to the respects in which this species would be incapable of community with us and to the reasons why. What I can say, though, is that if I had to choose between rescuing a member of another species that were capable of friendly relationships with us and one that were not, I would judge myself to have more moral reason to save the former, which might be best explained by its having a greater moral status. In addition, in the following section I explain how my African theory can—attractively—deem "abnormal" rational beings, viz., ones incapable of various aspects of community with us, to have less moral status than us but more moral status than animals.

Thinking of moral status in terms of the capacity for relationships of identity and solidarity coheres well with a principle of right action prescribing respect for such relationships, which captures several salient (not essential) facets of behaviour and thought south of the Sahara desert.[11] For example, sub-Saharans often think that

---

[11] As I have argued in detail in Metz (2007).

society should be akin to family; they tend to believe in the moral importance of greetings, even to strangers; they typically refer to people outside the nuclear family with titles such as "sister" and "mama"; they frequently believe that ritual and tradition have a certain degree of moral significance; they tend to think that there is some obligation to wed and procreate; they usually do not believe that retribution is a proper aim of criminal justice, inclining towards reconciliation; they commonly think that there is a strong duty for the rich to aid the poor; and they often value consensus in decision-making, seeking unanimous agreement and not resting content with majority rule. I have the space merely to suggest that these recurrent (not invariant) practices are plausibly entailed and well explained by the prescription to respect people insofar as they can share a way of life and care for one another's quality of life. I am not suggesting that this principle has been believed by even a majority of Africans; my point is rather that it promises to capture in a *theory* several salient aspects of a communal way of life that have been widespread in the sub-Saharan region, and hence that it and its companion account of moral status qualify as "African".

Some might question, though, whether the present account of moral status is rightly called "African". After all, plenty of Westerners are fans of friendship, and the account is reminiscent of the ethic of care as well as some elements of Aristotle's ethic. Why associate it with the region south of the Sahara desert?

In reply, for something reasonably to count as "African", it need not be utterly unique to the continent of Africa. It need merely be salient there in a way that it is not most other places. Baseball is American, even though the Japanese and Cubans play it, and the combination of markets, industrialization and Constitutional democracy is Western, despite the fact that one will find it in places such as South Africa and Australia. Similarly, the present conception of moral status draws on ideas that are prominent in sub-Saharan moral thought and that differ from the views that dominate Western philosophy, which are individualist and holist. It is similar to the ethic of care, but, even here, a caring relationship would be (roughly) equivalent only to the solidarity element of community. The facet of identifying with others is more distinct, as many traditional African peoples and contemporary African ethicists deem sharing a way of life to have moral importance beyond the mere sharing of feelings, time or resources, as per the ethic of care. Moreover, even if one were to find an interpretation of care that were the same as my understanding of communal relationship, it would still be sensible to call it "African" since it is *much more common* in African philosophy than in at least Western philosophy to think of moral properties in essentially communal-relational terms.

Although I believe it apt to call the theory of moral status I have constructed "African" since it is grounded on features of folkways and worldviews that are salient amongst the black peoples of the continent, it ultimately matters little what it is called. What matters most is how well it accounts for comparatively firm judgments about what has moral status and to what degree. A good explanation for the parochialism of other relational theories is that they make an actual relationship a necessary condition for moral status. The present, modal view does not, instead appealing to the capacity for relationship, and for this reason does much better at accommodating our intuitions, or so I now argue.

2.5 Applying and Defending the Modal-Relational Account

Here I consider what the sub-Saharan account of moral status from the previous section entails in a variety of contexts, bringing out its many strengths and putative weaknesses in relation to dominant Western approaches. I first apply the theory to human beings, then to non-human animals, and finally to other things.

When it comes to normal, adult human beings, exemplary instances of beings with full moral status, it follows from the African moral theory that they have it. This theory implies that full moral status inheres in beings that can be both subjects and objects of harmonious relationships, and typical humans not only are capable of being identified with and being cared for, but also can identify with others and care for them. So far, the theory on the face of it does as well as Kantianism and utilitarianism at *entailing* the moral status of human beings.

Furthermore, there are reasons to think that the African account of human moral status is *explanatorily* more attractive than at least some of the Western individualisms. Utilitarians deny that dignity is a genuine moral category; while they readily think in terms of a being warranting moral consideration, they do not believe that any being has a superlative intrinsic value respect for which grounds basic human rights. However, many of those who believe that human beings have a moral status also think that they have a dignity, and the African theory can account for that intuition. It is naturally extended to say that humans have a dignity in virtue of their full ability to participate in communal relationships. If one is driving a bus and must run over either a mouse or a human being, the Africanist could plausibly contend that the reason to run over the mouse is that it lacks a dignity the human being has in virtue of the latter's capacity to love and be loved by us.

Friends of Kant's and Kantian views, of course, are also friends of dignity. Although Kant himself maintained that the capacity for moral reason is definitive of dignity and hence of moral status (1797: Ak. 423, 434–435), contemporary Kantians usually ground it on a being's more general capacity for reasoned deliberation or self-governance. The African theory is an attractive alternative to Kant's view and is competitive with regard to recent forms of Kantianism. Kant himself cashed out the ability to act morally in terms of a capacity to act on the basis of representations that are beyond space and time in a noumenal realm, which involves a less than compelling metaphysics that the African theory does not invoke. And unlike contemporary Kantianism, the African moral theory entails that a rational being that can, say, neither think of himself as a "we" nor act for the sake of others lacks a full moral status, which many (though, I accept, not all) will find intuitive. The suggestion is not that individuals who have acted wrongly have a lower moral status, but rather that individuals who are utterly incapable of any other-regard do. In contrast, the Kantian (though not Kant) is committed to the view that a rational being capable only of self-regard has a dignity equal to one capable also of other-regard.

Let us consider the case of the purely self-regarding rational agent in more detail. Although the African theory probably cannot claim an advantage relative to the Kantian with respect to this sort of case, I submit that the former is not much, if any, worse off than the latter. First off, note that the African theory need not entail that autistic humans, or at least "higher" functioning ones such as the well-known Temple Grandin, lack a dignity or full moral status. While these individuals are comparatively incapable of empathetic awareness and sympathetic emotion, the evidence indicates that they are capable of additional forms of other-regarding behaviour (Kennett 2002). They are able to coordinate their actions with others, to do what is likely to make others better off, to act for the sake of others and so on. Given the orbital account of degrees of moral status I suggested above, the African theory entails that many autistic individuals have a dignity equivalent to what we have.

However, the African theory does appear to entail that severely mentally incapacitated human beings and extreme psychopaths lack a dignity comparable to ours, for they are incapable of being subjects of a communal relationship. The Kantian, of course, is also committed to the view that severely mentally incapacitated human beings lack a dignity and indeed a moral status altogether. So, the nub of controversy between the Kantian view and the African one is the extreme psychopath. Now, even though the extreme psychopath has the capacity only for being an object of a communal relationship, that capacity is *much greater* than that had by other beings such as mice and dogs, and hence the African view entails that, even though he lacks a dignity equal to ours, his moral status is greater than that of animals. Compared with animals, normal human beings are more able to include "deformed" humans such as psychopaths, as well as the mentally incapacitated, in a "we", cooperate with them, act in ways likely to improve their quality of life, exhibit sympathetic emotions with them, and act for their sake. We do much more for the psychopathic and the mentally incapacitated than we do animals, which is evidence of a greater ability to make them an object of a friendly relationship. And even with respect to psychopaths, we readily feel for them and are disinclined to punish them (while remaining firm about their confinement, to protect others) when we learn that the large majority of them suffered horrific abuse as children.

The African moral theory is interesting and worthy of consideration for being able to ascribe a "middle" moral status, i.e., neither highest nor lowest, to both the extreme psychopathic and the severely mentally incapacitated. Neither Kant nor the Kantian would grant any moral status to the severely mentally incapacitated; the Kantian would ascribe full moral status—indeed, a dignity–to the psychopathic; and the utilitarian would naturally grant full moral status to both, as they are capable of pleasure or preference satisfaction.[12] The African theory presents a plausible

---

[12]Some utilitarians argue that people's "global" desires, with regard to their lives as a whole, are more important than "local" ones, giving them priority over the severely mentally incapacitated in cases of conflict. But what if a normal person, such as Galen Strawson, lacked such desires?

alternative of granting to both more moral status than animals but less than normal humans.

Furthermore, the African account is to be credited with providing a reasonable explanation of why members of two different species that have the same internal properties, viz., animals and severely mentally incapacitated humans, might nonetheless have a different moral status. It provides a genuine reason to doubt the influential "argument from marginal cases" (e.g., Singer 1993; Dombrowski 1997), the rationale that at least some animals are entitled to as much moral status as humans, since the two are biologically similar. The African theory entails that even if there is no *intrinsic* difference between two beings, there could be a *modal-relational* difference between them, *qua* capacity to have a life that is shared with, and cared for by, normal human beings, that grounds differential degrees of moral status. The idea that humans have a greater moral status than animals is a persistent intuition, and invoking the property of degree of capacity for communal relationship is a more attractive way to account for it than is the speciesist one of the bare fact of human life.

The last category of human being that I address is the very young. According to the African theory, zygotes, blastocysts and embryos lack moral status, and, if they would warrant protection, it would be only on indirect grounds. They cannot be subjects of a friendly relationship, for they lack the abilities for conceptualization, intentional action, emotion and the like that are constitutive of it. Furthermore, they cannot even be objects of such a relationship, since they are not yet organisms capable of engaging in goal-directed activity and of being better or worse off.

Of course, the embryo is alive, and so there may be a sense in which it would be "better" if it were to stay alive, but not in the relevant sense of being "better off", i.e., having an improved quality of life. And while it is true that some people, particularly pregnant women, are inclined to think of themselves as a "we" with extraordinarily young human beings, the tendency for us to identify with them increases substantially as they develop. Typical humans much more readily think of themselves as a "we" with mid-to-late stage foetuses and newborns than they do with a mere clump of rudimentary cells, upon a clear awareness of their nature. Furthermore, foetuses, at a certain point, are organisms with the capacity to feel pain and hence to be an object of solidarity. Although they still cannot be subjects of a relationship of identity and solidarity, they can be objects of them to some meaningful degree. Similar remarks go for newborn infants. So, the African theory appears to entail that human beings younger than two months old—when the very large majority of abortions take place—lack a moral status, but that they acquire a moral status upon becoming a mid-to-late stage foetus.

Comparing mid-to-late stage foetuses and newborns now, the former would have less moral status than the latter, if normal humans could more easily make the latter the objects of a friendly relationship, upon information about both kinds of beings.[13] Newborns and foetuses, while sometimes identical in biological terms, are not identical in respect of essential functions, and partly for this reason are not identical in respect of capacity to be the object of identity and solidarity with characteristic

---

[13] This line of reasoning is inspired by some remarks from Slote (2007: 17–19).

human beings. Babies cry, look people in the eyes, ingest food through their mouths, are out in the world, have desires and engage in goal-directed behaviour, which enables them to be more readily conceived as a "we", sympathized with, and helped by normal humans. The point is not that newborns are more similar to us than are foetuses, but rather that the latter are, *by their nature, cloistered* in such a way as to make communal relationship with them much more difficult. If that empirical claim were indeed true, then it would follow from the African theory that newborns have a greater moral status than foetuses.

Again, the African theory is to be credited for promising to account for a long-standing and widely shared intuition that has not been firmly captured up to now, namely, that moral status increases along with the development of a being from embryo to foetus to newborn. Utilitarianism cannot entail or explain that intuition, for once a foetus is capable of pain or preferences, there is no difference in moral status between it and a newborn, such that, notoriously, if abortion is routinely permissible, infanticide often is, too. Kantians also have difficulty accommodating the differential moral status of foetuses and infants, as either they both lack moral status for being non-rational, or they both have moral status for exhibiting the potential for rationality. Only a *relational* theory of the present sort has any real chance of differentiating between these beings.[14] And *nothing else could*, given their intrinsic similarity.

I now turn from focusing on human beings to saying more about animals. In my view, a glaring weakness amongst dominant theories of moral status is that they cannot entail all the following: (1) both humans and animals have moral status; (2) humans have a greater moral status than animals; (3) both humans and animals have moral status for a unitary reason. On (1), I find it incontrovertible that at least some animals have a moral status, and even those who question the existence of animal *rights* and defend practices such as eating animals and experimenting on them invariably admit at some point that they do (e.g., Frey 1983). The best explanation of why it is wrong to put a live cat in a microwave merely for the thrill ultimately has to do with facts about the cat, not solely the agent or other persons; Kant's ethic and contemporary Kantianism are simply mistaken.

Although utilitarianism accounts for (1), it fails with respect to (2). It entails that many animals have the same moral status as human beings, for both kinds are capable of pleasure and pain, or of preference satisfaction and frustration. And Regan's (2004) subject of a life criterion, according to which a being has moral status roughly insofar as it has propositional attitudes towards the past and the future, as well as Taylor's (1986) biocentric view, which prescribes respect for all living organisms, are also well known for entailing the equal moral status of humans and many animals, something that I, and I presume most readers, find counterintuitive (see Sect. 2.2).

Finally, there are accounts of moral status that entail (1) and (2) but that are pluralistic and hence fail (3). For instance, Stone (1985) and Warren (2003) are known for thinking that several features ground moral status of differing degrees, ranging from rationality to sentience to (actual) relationships to landscapes to species.

---

[14]Note how the African theory differs from the classic ethic of care with regard to foetuses and infants, which grounds their moral status on their *responsiveness* to care (Noddings 1984: 87–89).

However, all things being equal, a view is more desirable, the greater its unity and simplicity, meaning that a monistic theory is preferable.

The African theory promises to account well for (1), (2) and (3); it appeals to a singular property to ground moral status that entails differing degrees of it between humans and animals, and between various classes of animals as well. As I have explained, since normal humans are capable of being both subjects and objects of harmonious relationships, they have full moral status. There is evidence that some animals, such as chimpanzees and gorillas, are capable of being subjects to an extent, at least insofar as they can coordinate their behaviour, exhibit sympathy and act consequent to it (e.g., de Waal 1996), and so they would have the highest moral status in the animal kingdom. Below them would be animals that are utterly incapable of being subjects of a friendly relationship, but would have a substantial ability to be objects of one, namely, most other warm-blooded creatures. Further down would be animals that are capable of a better or worse life and so could be objects of a friendly relationship, but would be less able to be objects than other animals due to either their comparative lack of sentience or the dispositions of human nature, say, molluscs.

I now address beings other than humans and animals, and, not coincidentally, respond to two major objections that are likely to be made to this African theory of moral status. To some readers, the glaring weaknesses of this view are that it is, first, anthropocentric and, second, unable to account properly for ecological concerns. I take up both objections in turn, before concluding.

The theory might appear to be anthropocentric in that it cashes out moral status in terms of certain human capacities. To be able to be an object of a communal relationship, on this view, is analyzed in terms of a capacity to relate to normal human beings in a certain way. And so there is an irreducible appeal to humanity in its conception of moral status.

However, the African view is not anthropocentric in the most clearly questionable forms. First, it does not entail that natural objects have merely an instrumental value for human beings, for it entails that many animals have moral status, i.e., are the proper object of ethical concern in their own right. Second, the view is not speciesist, for it does not imply that human life *qua* human has a basic moral value. The theory is capacity-based, making it an empirical matter to determine not only which beings have the capacity to identify with and exhibit solidarity towards others (which chimpanzees and gorillas may well have), but also which beings can be the objects of such a relationship with us.

Even so, some friends of an environmental perspective will find the African theory unsatisfactory. For one, it entails that plants—even Redwoods–lack a moral status,[15] so that any duties with regard to them will be indirect. Although there is a sense in which a tree can "flourish" (as Stone 1972 helped make clear), that is a matter of being able to be a good instance of its kind, and not being able to live a good

---

[15]Although some scientists have suggested that trees "talk" to each other, this is not the relevant sort of relationality by the present account of moral status. For one, there is still no suggestion that trees are capable of other-regard, i.e., that they are aware of others as distinct from them, and, for another, we remain unable to help trees since they lack any quality of life (even though they do have a life that can be stronger or weaker—see footnote 9).

life, which is necessary to be an object of solidarity (cf. footnote 9). For another, groups such as species and ecosystems obviously are incapable of being subjects of friendship, and also cannot be objects of it, as they are not beings with goals and lives that can be better or worse off.

In reply, here is some reason to think that such ecological concerns might be plausibly captured without ascribing moral status to plants and groups. To put it tersely, not all final value is moral value. As Robert Nozick points out (1989: 163–164, 170–171), scientific theories and the game of chess are organic unities and for that reason plausibly have a value that is not merely instrumental, but it is implausible to think that they are ever the direct object of moral obligations. Even if the African theory of moral status denies it to plants and groups, there could be other respects in which these things are finally (not merely instrumentally) valuable and warrant respect and protection, even at some cost to beings capable of communal relationship, supposing, as is plausible, that morality is not invariably overriding.

Consider how an agent (or at least one not yet in the grip of a theory) would likely feel if she destroyed a Redwood, landscape or an ecosystem. I submit that if she would feel guilt, she would most likely feel guilt with respect to the animals or humans, including future generations, affected by this behaviour, and she would probably not feel *guilt* with respect to the tree, landscape or the ecosystem *as such*. She would be more likely to feel *shame* with respect to the way her behaviour has affected those things, but guilt is a much more reliable marker of moral status than is shame. People often feel shame about their unattractive appearance, or their impoverished condition, or their having been the victim of wrongdoing, conditions unrelated to their having violated moral norms. There is, therefore, *prima facie* reason to exclude plants and groups from the domain of moral consideration in their own right, and to continue to try to account for their non-instrumental value in other terms.

2.6 Conclusion

Those deeply committed to holism and individualism, or even a combination of them, may well not be convinced by this discussion. Diehard holists will reject the idea that anything other than a group can ground moral status, while pure individualists will reject the recurrent suggestion that two beings that are internally identical (foetus v neonate, severely mentally incapacitated human v animal) could differ in their moral status. However, my aim has not been to convince anyone to change her mind, or even to provide a complete justification for doing so. My goals have instead been the more limited ones of articulating a new, modal-relational account of moral status grounded on sub-Saharan moral philosophy, demonstrating that it avoids the severe parochialism facing existing relational accounts, and showing that it accounts better than standard Western theories for a variety of widely shared intuitions about what has moral status and to what degree. Many of these intuitions are captured by neither holism nor individualism and have lacked a firm philosophical foundation up to now. Of importance here is the African theory's promise to underwrite the ideas that humans and animals have a moral status because of the same property that differs in degree, that severely mentally incapacitated humans have a greater moral status than animals with the same internal properties, and that a human's moral status increases as it develops from the embryonic to foetal to neo-natal stages. It is too early to conclude that one has most reason to believe the African theory of moral status, particularly in light of criticisms that I have not yet had the space to address,[16] but I submit that the field would be misguided to ignore this unique and promising view in future debate.

Acknowledgements This chapter first appeared as an article in *Ethical Theory and Moral Practice* vol. 15, no. 3 (2012): 387–402, and is reprinted with only minor modifications and with the permission of Springer. For helpful comments on a prior draft of this essay, I thank Kevin Behrens, Kai Horsthemke, Neil Van Leeuwen, two (particularly thoughtful and helpful) anonymous referees for *Ethical Theory and Moral Practice* and a further two anonymous referees for Springer. I have also benefited from audience feedback at: the 2008 Annual Conference of the Philosophical Society of Southern Africa held at Monash University; a Philosophy Department Seminar at the University of Johannesburg; the 15th Annual Conference of the International Society for African Philosophy and Studies held at the University of Cheikh Anta Diop; and a Symposium on Nonhuman Animals organized by the Hunterstoun Centre at the University of Fort Hare.

References

Biko, S. 1971. Some African Cultural Concepts. In *I Write What I Like,* ed. S. Biko, 44–53. Johannesburg: Picador Africa, 2004.

Bujo, B. 2001. *Foundations of an African Ethic.* New York: Crossroad Publishers.

de Waal, F. 1996. *Good Natured.* Cambridge, MA: Harvard University Press.

DeGrazia, D. 2008. Moral Status as a Matter of Degree? *Southern Journal of Philosophy* 46: 181–198.

Dombrowski, D. 1997. *Babies and Beasts.* Chicago: University of Illinois Press.

Donovan, J., and C. Adams (eds.). 2007. *The Feminist Care Tradition in Animal Ethics.* New York: Columbia University Press.

Frey, R.G. 1983. *Rights, Killing and Suffering.* Oxford: Basil Blackwell.

Gruen, L. (2003). The Moral Status of Animals. In *Stanford Encyclopedia of Philosophy,* ed. Zalta, E. http://plato.stanford.edu/entries/moral-animal/. Accessed 14 April 2019.

Gyekye, K. 1997. *Tradition and Modernity: Philosophical Reflections on the African Experience.* New York: Oxford University Press.

Jaworska, A. 2007. Caring and Full Moral Standing. *Ethics* 117: 460–497.

Kant, I. 1797. *The Metaphysics of Morals.* Trans. M. MacGregor. Repr. New York: Cambridge University Press, 1991.

Kennett, J. 2002. Empathy and Moral Agency. *Philosophical Quarterly* 52: 340–357.

Leopold, A. 1968. *A Sand County Almanac,* 2nd ed. New York: Oxford University Press.

Mbiti, J. 1969. *African Religions and Philosophy.* Oxford: Heinemann Educational Books.

---

[16]Does the African theory entail: that cuter animals have a greater moral status than ugly ones, that a late-term human foetus has a lower moral status than a chimpanzee, that a stereotypical Mother Teresa has a greater moral status than us, or that someone actually part of a communal relationship with us has a greater moral status than someone who merely could? And, if so, are these implications counterintuitive?

Menkiti, I. 1979. Person and Community in African Traditional Thought. In *African Philosophy*, 3rd ed., ed. R. Wright, 171–181, Repr. New York: University Press of America, 1984.

Mercer, P. 1972. *Sympathy and Ethics*. Oxford: Clarendon Press.

Metz, T. 2007. Toward an African Moral Theory. *Journal of Political Philosophy*. 15: 321–341. Revised edition in *Themes, Issues and Problems in African Philosophy*, ed. I. Ukpokolo, 97–119. London: Palgrave Macmillan, 2017.

Metz, T. 2010a. African and Western Moral Theories in a Bioethical Context. *Developing World Bioethics* 10: 49–58.

Metz, T. 2010b. Human Dignity, Capital Punishment, and an African Moral Theory. *Journal of Human Rights* 9: 81–99.

Metz, T. 2010c. For the Sake of the Friendship. *Theoria* 57: 54–76.

Metz, T. 2010d. Animal Rights and the Interpretation of the South African Constitution. *Southern African Public Law* 25: 301–311.

Miller, H. 1988. Science, Ethics, and Moral Status. http://parismount.blogspot.co.za/2012/03/copyright-1988-harlan-b.html. Accessed 14 April 2019.

Mkhize, N. 2008. *Ubuntu* and Harmony. In *Persons in Community*, ed. R. Nicolson, 35–44. Pietermaritzburg: University of KwaZulu-Natal Press.

Murove, M.F. 2004. An African Commitment to Ecological Conservation. *Mankind Quarterly* 45: 195–215.

Noddings, N. 1984. *Caring*. Berkeley: University of California Press.

Noddings, N. 1992. *The Challenge to Care in Schools*. New York: Teachers College Press.

Nozick, R. 1989. *The Examined Life*. New York: Simon & Schuster Inc.

Nussbaum, M. 2006. The Moral Status of Animals. *Chronical of Higher Education* 52 (22): B6–8.

Odera Oruka, H., and C. Juma. 1994. Ecophilosophy and Parental Earth Ethics. In *Philosophy, Humanity and Ecology*, ed. H. Odera Oruka, 115–129. Nairobi: ACTS Press.

Regan, T. 2004. *The Case for Animal Rights*, 2nd ed. Berkeley: University of California Press.

Shutte, A. 2001. *Ubuntu*. Cape Town: Cluster Publications.

Silberbauer, G. 1991. Ethics in Small-scale Societies. In *A Companion to Ethics*, ed. P. Singer, 14–28. Oxford: Basil Blackwell.

Singer, P. 1993. *Practical Ethics*, 2nd ed. New York: Cambridge University Press.

Slote, M. 2007. *The Ethics of Care and Empathy*. New York: Routledge.

Stone, C. 1972. Should Trees Have Standing? *Southern California Law Review* 45: 450–501.

Stone, C. 1985. Should Trees Have Standing? Revisited. *Southern California Law Review* 59: 1–154.

Taylor, P. 1986. *Respect for Nature*. Princeton: Princeton University Press.

Tutu, D. 1999. *No Future without Forgiveness*. New York: Random House.

VanDeVeer, D. 1995. Interspecific Justice and Intrinsic Value. *Electronic Journal of Analytic Philosophy*. http://ejap.louisiana.edu/EJAP/1995.spring/vandeveer.1995.spring.html. Accessed 14 April 2019.

Verhoef, H., and C. Michel. 1997. Studying Morality within the African Context. *Journal of Moral Education* 26: 389–407.

Warren, M.A. 2003. Moral Status. In *A Companion to Applied Ethics*, ed. R.G. Frey and C. Wellman, 439–450. Malden, MA: Blackwell.

Wiredu, K. 1992. The African Concept of Personhood. In *African-American Perspectives on Biomedical Ethics*, ed. H.E. Flack and E.E. Pellegrino, 104–117. Washington D.C.: Georgetown University Press.

Wiredu, K. 2008. Social Philosophy in Postcolonial Africa. *South African Journal of Philosophy* 27: 332–339.

Chapter 3
The Moral Status of Nature: An African Understanding

Munamato Chemhuru

Abstract The idea of moral status has been examined in various applied ethical discourses such as medical ethics and environmental ethics. However, little has so far been done in terms of appraising these fundamental disciplines from an African philosophical perspective. I venture into this fairly novel area of African environmental ethics as I seek to examine an African understanding of the moral status of nature. As I take a pluralist approach to the idea of moral status of nature in African environmental philosophy, I seek to argue that both living and non-living beings in the environment ought to be granted moral status. I make use of the teleological view of existence to provide various reasons why nature should be considered as having moral or ethical standing such that human beings should have ethical obligations that are independent of their duties and obligations towards fellow human beings. Overall, I seek to espouse a uniquely African view of the moral status on nature, one that fundamentally differs from other views dominant much of Western philosophical thinking.

3.1 Introduction

In this chapter, I focus on the African hierarchy of ontology and its significance for environmental ethics, but with particular focus on the moral status of nature. By 'moral status', I mean the ethical standing that could be accorded to a being or object such that it could be given ethical consideration and respect. Although the question of moral status has traditionally been understood from either the individualistic or the holistic view (Metz 2012: 387), I take a pluralist approach to the question of moral status in African environmental ethics.

The central argument that I develop in this chapter is that the teleological understanding of existence positively contributes to a plausible African conception of

M. Chemhuru (✉)
Great Zimbabwe University, Masvingo, Zimbabwe
e-mail: munamatochemhuru@gmail.com

University of Johannesburg, Johannesburg, South Africa

© Springer Nature Switzerland AG 2019
M. Chemhuru (ed.), *African Environmental Ethics*, The International
Library of Environmental, Agricultural and Food Ethics 29,
https://doi.org/10.1007/978-3-030-18807-8_3

moral status of nature. In this respect, I address one important question that weaves throughout the discourse of environmental ethics. This is the question of whether the natural environment consisting of both non human living beings and non living beings ought to have moral or ethical standing such that human beings should have ethical obligations that are independent of their duties and obligations towards fellow human beings. Although I have partly addressed this question elsewhere when I argued that duties to God and the ancestors could plausibly ground duties to the environment (Chemhuru 2016: 130–183), in this chapter I go further than this position and critically examine the question of whether nature has moral status. By 'nature', I will be focussed on both living beings such as non human animals and plants and non living beings such as the air, water, and soils. In addressing the question of moral status with regard to these beings, I intend to offer an attractive African ontology-based view of environmental ethics that stems from the understanding of the human community and the person as they relate with various aspects of nature.

My response to the question of whether nature has moral status is in the affirmative. In asserting this position, my argument is largely informed by African ontological conceptions of being as well as some teleological arguments for existence. While Ojomo has attempted to offer a view of moral status that is based on life and *telos* as well, she has limited her focus on living beings alone (see Ojomo 2010: 53.). This is why I seek to surpass such an understanding of moral status as I also offer a defence for the position that human beings ought to be understood to have ethical obligations towards non human beings. This justification is based on a number of reasons such as *telos*, vitality, inherent value of non human beings and sentience. I also seek to establish that these beings must have a purpose that is independent to that of human beings.

Overall, in this chapter, I argue that environmental ethical thinking in sub-Saharan Africa could be meaningfully informed by teleological and normative conceptions of existence in African philosophy where nature ought to be understood to have purpose and moral status. First, I interrogate the teleological connection between human beings and the natural environment. I seek to establish that there must be a teleological connection between human beings and nature such that nature ought to be given respect on that teleological basis. Having established that teleological foundation as partly the basis for respect of nature, I also proceed to espouse the view that non human living beings such as animals and plants and non living beings such as air, water and soils must have ethical standing. I submit this view in the two respective section focusing on 'the moral status of non human living beings' and the last one on 'the moral status of non living beings'. Ultimately, I intend to conclude that nature must have moral status.

3.2   The Teleological Link Between the Human Community and the Environment

In order to appreciate what I will discuss in this chapter with relation to the moral status of nature, I see the need to first address the question of whether there ought to be any teleological connection between the human community and the natural environment. I address this question in this section where I mainly focus on 'the teleological connection between human beings and nature. The focus on such a link would make an easier transition from *telos* to moral status when I focus on the moral status of nature in the next two sections after this one. I seek to validate my argument that teleological conceptions of existence in African ontology could credibly support the recognition of the inherent value and moral status of the natural world as a whole (see also Odera Oruka and Juma 1994: 117.). Overall, I argue that there is a teleological connection between the human community and nature. This teleological interconnection is useful here because my understanding of the moral status of nature is largely informed and shaped by the way I see the teleological relationship between the human community and the natural environment. This natural environment consists of both living and non living beings.

First, it is important to realise that the teleological framework of being is closely linked to a conception of the moral status of the environment. There must be some fundamental teleological connection between human beings and nature such that nature must have purpose and eventually moral status. In order to establish this teleological connection and argue that nature has both purpose and moral status, I take a pluralist approach to the teleological grounds for moral status in African ontology. This pluralist approach is based on a variety of teleological appeals to moral status such as appeal to African biocentrism or vitalism, sentience, subject of a life, well-being and degree of vital force. Notwithstanding that these views may not necessarily cohere well together and their different implications on moral status, I argue that they all contribute in various ways, to a plausibly acceptable view teleological environmental ethics in African ontology.

Although it may not be so explicit, the way environmental ethics is broadly understood as concerned with relations between human beings and various aspects of nature must be a strong reason to believe that there must be teleological connections between human beings and the environment. This view is based on the purposive *ends* for being that I see to be shared between the human community and the natural environment. Also, these teleological connections partly comes from the fact that human beings exist *in* human communities and *in* the natural environment as well. Although this view may sound to be fairly anthropocentric, which is a view that I do not intend to legitimise in African philosophy, it is shaped by the understanding that the teleological and ethical basis for respecting nature is because it is where human beings find their habitat in, and also that nature itself ought to live and flourish and achieve its purpose for existing and well-being. Interpreted teleologically, this view could be taken to imply that one ultimate purpose of nature is to live well.

In addition to living well, nature itself must have an additional purpose of supporting the well-being and survival of both human beings and non human living creatures. At the same time, another purpose of conscious human beings could be taken to be the need to safeguard the well-being and purpose of nature. In this case, the nature of the environment as a being is such that it exists for the well-being of not only human beings that live in it, but also for the well-being of particular non human animals and non animate beings that constitute it. So, in order for the individual human beings and the environment to achieve their respective individual goals and purposes for existence in life as I have discussed elsewhere (Chemhuru 2016: 130–160), human beings ought to have obligations to do so in a manner that takes into consideration the purposes and goals other human communities, non human communities and the natural environment as well.

Apart from well-being as one useful value for understanding *telos* in African philosophy, there is also the appeal to life. This view is commonly expressed as the vitalist dimension to existence. In African ontology, the human being must be teleologically understood as a purposive being that ought to achieve its *ends* or purposes in life but without necessarily disadvantaging other beings that also have independent lives and goals to those of human beings. This view is also informed partly by what I see as the direct moral duties that human persons must have towards other human beings, non human living beings and the natural environment as I will discuss in the next two sections. First, it is important to realise that both the human communities depend on various aspects of nature for their livelihood. Accordingly, although it could be one anthropocentric basis for treating the environment well, it must follow that nature must have a purpose of furthering the life or vitality of human beings. This could be taken as one anthropocentric reason why nature has a purpose of furthering life in general, while at the same time human beings have a purpose to safeguard the well-being of nature. This is because human beings and nature can be positively or negatively affected by individual human actions. However, it must be reasonable to appreciate that not everything that human beings do will always affect the environment negatively. For example, it is acceptable that an action like taking a single dog and taming it and keeping it isolated at home in a fenced yard for the rest of its life does not necessarily affect nature negatively. However, following the African bio-centric view of environmental ethics, as commonly expressed in the vitalist view of existence, such an action remains suspect in light of the fact that a dog is an animate being that has vital force and its own *telos* for being such that it ought to be treated in a dignified way. This is because such a dog also ought to achieve its teleological goals for life such as survival, harmonious living and well being, all of which are independent of those of human beings.

The teleological connection between human beings and nature remains at the core of my understanding of what must be an African ontology-based and teleologically oriented environmental ethics. In this kind of environmental ethics, the teleological view of existence, which is the basis for moral status of nature in the next two sections is not shaped by the idea that the environment belongs to the human community as implicit in some radical anthropocentric views. It is based on the understanding that, human beings and the natural environment are teleological counterparts. They are teleological counterparts in so far as they all ought to attain some meaning and purpose for existing. Accordingly, the nature of existence of the human being and nature must be understood as being based on possession of life, co-existence and realisation of their independent purposes for existing. This is why I take as useful Bujo's contention that in African environmental philosophy, "total realisation of the self is impossible as long as one does not peacefully co-exist with minerals, plants and animals" (Bujo 1998: 208). The reason why this view is acceptable is that human beings must treat with respect, as they co-exist with these beings which also in some way possess life and vital forces in their own right such that they have independent purposes to those of human beings.

This view above is equally a bio-centric, vitalist and teleological view which I suspect is compatible with my understanding of African ontology-based and teleologically oriented environmental ethics. Ojomo espouses almost a similar view of teleological environmental ethics although hers is limited to a fairly bio-centric view of existence. For her, "all life forms are *moral patients*–entities to which we should accord moral standing… it is its *telos* (purpose) that gives each individual organism inherent worth and all living organism possess this worth *equally*[1] because all individual living beings have telos" (Ojomo 2010: 53). While I accept Ojomo's argument for moral status that is based on *telos*, my teleological view of moral status goes beyond her focus on living beings alone as I include even non living beings such as rocks, soils and the air as also capable of having purpose for existing. This is on the basis that these beings must have their purpose for being although it may not be equated to that of human beings. Following this view, I argue that ethical obligations that human beings have towards the environment should be informed, ideally by relating well with aspects of the natural environment such as non human animals, plants, the air, soil, rocks and water bodies. These components are not only 'moral counterparts' to the human community, but that they also have their teleological ends which can either be enhanced or negatively affected. In this case, as I borrow from the Aristotelian view of *telos*, I depart from his functional understanding of the purpose of being. I find the Aristotelian view to be strongly anthropocentric as it puts emphasis on the function of a being (see also Aristotle: NE, Book 1: 1059a.). Such a view is incompatible with my understanding of African teleologically oriented environmental ethics where components such as rocks, the soil and the air are considered as also having their respective purposes for being. The basis upon which these beings must have purpose is centred on some of the following reasons: First, the fact that we do not know the exact purpose/s of non living beings such as rocks does not necessarily mean that they do not have such purpose/s. Also, some of the living beings that are naturally taken as having purpose for being such as human beings, non human animals and functional things like knives cannot sometimes achieve their respective purposes without some of these non living beings. In the case of rocks for example, they can even be used to sharpen a knife so that it achieves its purpose of

---

[1] I have italicised Ojomo's use of the word 'equally' in this context because, while I agree with her argument for according moral status on the basis of purpose, my point of departure is on her attempt to grant equal moral status to all living beings.

cutting well, while human being could also use them to build their shelter and live a meaningful and purposive life. For these reasons, I contend that this could be the basis why all beings must be taken as having some purpose for being.

Also implicit in the bio-centric, vitalist and teleological views which are mainly characteristic of African environmental ethics is the appeal to sentience. Generally understood, sentience could be taken to refer to the ability of any being to feel and experience pleasure, pain or consciousness (see also Varner 2001: 192.). The aspect of sentience is important because it is capable of determining whether a given being will achieve its purpose for existing or not. Because of its emphasis on pleasure, pain and consciousness, all of which can determine whether a life or being can be better or worse, sentience must be closely linked to teleology. Although he does not focus on African environmentalism in particular, Taylor also gives us a generally acceptable understanding of what sentience-based environmental ethics entail which I suspect could be reasonably taken as a useful in determining the teleological *end* of any being in African ontology-based environmental ethics. For him, "quite independently of the duties we owe to our fellow humans, we are morally required to do or refrain from doing certain acts in so far as those acts bring benefit or harm to wild living things in the natural world" (Taylor 1986: 10). As I interpret this view from an African philosophical standpoint, I argue that this is also a useful vitalist and welfarist criterion for determining moral status, although it must be understood in the context of the African hierarchy of existence. Following my vitalist, sentience-based and welfarist view of African environmental ethics, while all beings that live life should be given moral status, I admit that it is not possible to grant all beings equal moral status, and hence the appeal to sentience is sometimes justifiable. This is because all beings do not occupy the same level of existence in the African hierarchy of existence. In such a hierarchy, forces or non animate beings such as rocks do not have sentience and are therefore taken as lower forces that have lesser purpose compared to other animate beings that have sentience and welfare.

Closely related but different from the sentience-based view of environmental ethics is the idea of *beingness* or simply ontological status which I also take as the other view informing the teleological understanding of African environmental ethics. This view is compatible with the consideration of non human beings especially non animate beings in African environmental ethics. By 'ontological status', I mean the *beingness* of a thing or its general existence as a being. Since my discussion is not limited to the ontological and teleological status of living things alone as implicit in the sentience-based view above, according to this view there are other non living beings or non animate beings such as the soil, air and rocks whose *beingness* must be safeguarded by human beings because their *beingness* or existence is independent to them. Although I take a pluralist view to the dimensions *telos* in African ontology, I go beyond these bio-centric and sentience-based views as I envisage African ontology-based communitarian environmental ethics that is based on *beingness*. This view takes into consideration even non sentient beings, phenomenon and objects like rocks, water, air and soils as having purpose like I have argued here. The basis for sustaining such a view is what I discuss as the need to take into consideration the *beingness* and purpose for being of which I suspect is teleologically oriented towards environmental ethical thinking.

Most attempts in the general discourse of environmental ethics limit human environmental ethical obligations to living things in the natural environment. However, my conception of environmental ethics extends beyond this bio-centric view of environmental ethics because of its pluralist approach to conceptions of *telos* and moral status as well. It considers both the living beings and non living beings as all having purpose for existence such that they could also be understood to have moral status. This is because some of the actions that human person may do to the natural environment, could either affect its biological, vitalist dimension, its sentience, its well-being, its *beingness* and eventually its *telos*. In view of this, Tangwa argues that "as human beings, we carry the whole weight of moral responsibility and obligations for the world on our shoulders" (Tangwa 2006: 388). This understanding of the ethical role of human persons towards the natural environment could be justified by the view that, despite the varying degrees of vital force and purpose as argued here, nature must have moral status. This view is what I now proceed to discuss and justify in the next two sections where I focus on the moral status of non human living beings and non living beings respectively.

3.3 The Moral Status of Non Human Living Beings

In the previous section I have provided a background to the teleological link between human beings and nature as a whole. I find such teleological connection to be useful to an understanding of the question of moral status which I now proceed to focus on. In this section I make a follow-up to that teleological connection and intend to proceed to give a detailed analysis and critical examination of the moral status of non human living beings. I use the phrase 'non human living beings' to mean all beings that are not necessarily human, but that exist or live life such as wild and domesticated animals as well as plants which all exist as living beings or things in general.

I focus on the moral status of non human living beings as being strongly informed by the African ontological and teleological views of existence. Working on the teleological orientation of existence, I critically examine the extent to which the moral status of non human living beings is grounded on *telos* of these beings. Following such an ontological and teleological understanding of being, I argue that in order to determine the moral status of either an animal or a plant that exists and live life, it is first important to understand what an animal or plant is, as well as whether its existence or non existence is of any purposive function.

Within the African ontological hierarchy, non human animals and plants are vital forces by virtue of possession of life. Despite being commonly referred to as 'lower forces' these non human animals and plants that possess life have their own vital force such that they complement the teleological dimension of existence. These are beings that also live their own independent lives to those of human beings. Some of these beings such as animals could also even have independent goals, hopes and desires to those of human beings that human beings themselves may not necessarily be aware of. This could explain why different animal species also mate and produce offspring and look after them just like what human beings do. Similarly other trees and flowers also live, grow and blossom and in the end produce flowers and fruits that eventually add on to the beauty of life. All these could plausibly be taken as some of their purposes for existence. On that basis, I therefore take non-human animals and plants as having moral status.

Consequently I grapple with the problem of whether non human beings such as animals and plants that exist could have moral status or ethical standing such that human beings could be deemed to have direct ethical obligations towards them. I argue that it is plausible to take this position in the confirmatory. This is because of my suspicion that the human community and the non human living beings are somewhat integrated. They are incorporated in so far as both human beings and non human living beings such as animals and plants are not only biological or subjects of life, but also moral and teleological counterparts. By 'moral and teleological counterparts', I do not intend to mean that non human living beings should be held to be equally morally accountable to human beings or that they should have the same or equivalent purposive goals for existing. In fact, I contend that human beings and those components of the environment such as non-human animals and plant species are somewhat 'moral counterparts' in so far as these components have life and moral status just as human beings. They are also 'teleological counterparts' because all non human living beings have been made in such a way that they are disposed to attain some purpose for existence.

An important feature of African ontology-based environmental ethics is its emphasis on the bio-centric aspect where moral status is given on the basis of biological status or by virtue of having life. Izibili characterises a largely bio-centric view of environmental ethics which I see as being useful to the African view of environmental ethics in the following:

> Generally speaking, the principle of the value of life requires that one respects life, that one does not unthinkingly destroy or alter forms of life. Living beings are to be regarded as having [intrinsic] life only. This expression is meant to remind us that this is value that is supposed to inhere, or belong directly to living beings. (Izibili 2005: 386)

My view in light of Izibili's position concerning all living beings is that African environmental ethics is mainly life-centred. This is despite the fact that in African ontology, moral status is determined by the hierarchy of existence such that not all living beings could have equal moral status. Notwithstanding the consideration of moral status on the basis of level and hierarchy of existence, the African understanding of existence must not be understood as being solely limited to the human person alone. This is because of its potential to take into account other beings that live life such as non human animals and plants. Focussing on 'ecology and ethical responsibility from an African perspective', Bujo espouses a similar life-centred view of environmental ethics in which "… the African person can only be understood in reference to his/her basic attitude to life… [hence for that reason]… life is seen as a basic form of reality" (Bujo 1998: 208–9). Implicit in both Izibili's and Bujo's understanding of African bio-centric environmental ethics is the notion that the moral status of non human living beings such as animals and plants is strongly informed by the ontological and biological status of such a being. This is what I conceive as the African bio-centric and vitalist view of African environmental ethics that I see to be strongly grounded on the teleological view of existence. According to this bio-centric, vitalist and teleological view of environmental ethics, since non human living beings are biological objects that exist and live life, it means that they must be vital forces since they also have purposes for existence such as the need to live life, harmonious living, well-being, balance and continued. According to this view, teleology flows from the vitalist view of existence of these non human living beings in African ontology. It must be such that all vital forces, including non human living beings such as plants and animals have different and independent purposes for which they are made and also that these forces complement the vital force of other beings. This is why it is important to consider the relationship between all beings as being anchored on the vitalist and teleological foundation.

Also, according to the above vitalist view, it is apparent that the basis for moral status of these non human living beings is mainly the life aspect. This life aspect, which I also take as a purpose for being is one purpose which I also take to be more primary that other purposes such as well-being, balance and harmony. This could be explained by the fact that life is so basic that without it first, other purposes cannot be conceptualised. In other words, life comes first before well-being, balance and harmony. However, this does not suffice to mean that the other purposes are not important towards consideration of moral status.

From the above view, environmental ethics becomes life-centred in so far as "it sees everything that has life as possessing inherent value" (Nnamani 2005: 398). While this view is quite reasonable, it should not be overly taken to imply that African ontology-based and teleologically oriented environmental ethics would grant equal moral status to all beings just because they live life and because life is one of those purposes which are more primary. This explains why for example, a non human living being like a lion should be taken as having greater moral status than a shrub of grass despite all of them having life or being alive. In this case, a being such as a lion must have greater moral status than the other being on the basis of intensity of its vital force. By intensity of vital force or life force, I mean the degree of importance in terms of life and purpose. The more a being has life, sentience and ability to have influence in other beings as in the case of the lion, the greater its ontological status and as a result its purpose becomes more intense than that of a shrub of grass. This is despite the fact that both the lion and the shrub of grass all must live life and continue to survive such that they achieve balance, well-being and harmony as some of their essential purpose for being.

An African ontology-based bio-centric view of environmental ethics which I advance here is what I see as a reasonable African life-centred view of environmental ethics. This view considers the moral standing of all objects of life as being worth considering in the environmental ethical discussions despite some variations of moral status of these beings like I have indicated in the above example of the lion and a shrub of grass. This view of environmental ethics is strongly informed by the African understanding of existence and its bearing on a bio-centric view of environmental ethics. According to this view, objects of life such as animate and plant species must be treated with care because they are also purposive beings that must survive and live a meaningful life. They as well contribute to the meaningful life as they also enhance life in various ways. For example, one other view, although it could be charged for being anthropocentric could be that, among all non human living beings some lower forces such as plants have a purpose to serve animals that must also have a purpose to serve human beings.

My understanding is that an African ontology-based, and bio-centric environmental ethics is a form of environmental ethical thinking that is centred on respecting nature and according it moral status based on the respect for the hierarchy of existence as well as the aspect of possession of life. For example, because non human animals and plants are thought to be vital forces that also live a meaningful and purpose-oriented life, it must also follow that such life ought to be respected. As he critiques some traditional anthropocentric environmental ethical theories, Nnamani sees a bio-centric ethics, like the one that I advance here, as "an ethical theory that evaluates natural things from the fact of their having life" (Nnamani 2005: 398). Ethical priority is given to all objects that do possess life in order for them to continue living and to promote more life. According to Nnamani, bio-centric environmental ethics is centred on the conviction that "all living species of living organisms form parts of a system of interdependence. Life of any sort, whether sentient or vegetative, rational or irrational, is the criterion for moral standing..." (Nnamani 2005: 398). This vitalist understanding is supported by the teleological view of existence.

While I accept Nnamani's understanding of bio-centric environmental ethics for its emphasis on life as a basic premise for intrinsic value, I reject the attempt to consider all life forms as equal and being at par. This is why I accept Mary Anne Warren's 'weaker animal rights' version in place of Regan's 'strong animal rights' version as compatible with the sub-Saharan African view of animal rights. This is because, Warren, just like my understanding of African ontology-based environmentalism, does not believe that the moral status of non human animals could be similar to those of human beings (Warren 1987: 345). Despite the admission that non human animals and plants have moral status, I still contend that such moral status ought not to be comparable to that of human beings. Human beings occupy a higher ontological level than that of animals and plants because of their varying degrees of life force and purpose. The degree of vitality and potency also differs and determines the degree of moral status notwithstanding the fact that life ought to be seen as sacred. Metz summarises this argument as he notes that the African view accounts for the moral status of both human beings and non human animals despite human beings having greater moral status than non human animals because of their greater capacity to communicate and make informed moral choices (Metz 2012: 399–400). For this reason, human beings must have greater purpose for existence than non human living beings the same way an elephant ought to be taken as also having greater purpose for existence than a thorn tree.

The African bio-centric conception of environmental ethics which I advance here is compatible with the African hierarchy of existence. The African order of existence which I see as a hierarchy addresses the question of 'what degree of inherent value could be assigned to different life forms?' This question is obvious because life forms differ in terms of their degree of inherent value and purposive orientation and function. This makes it easy to appreciate why for example, the protection and preservation of elephants and rhinos could be viewed as nobler than protecting houseflies and cockroaches. From both non anthropocentric and anthropocentric teleological reasons, elephants and rhinos must have greater purpose for continued existence than houseflies and cockroaches. This is because in the hierarchy of existence, elephants and rhinos are more vital such that cockroaches and houseflies must be their lower forces. Also, despite aiming at the same fundamental purposes for existence such as survival, well-being and balance, elephants and rhinos must be ontologically and teleologically superior to houseflies and cockroaches because of their ability to also accommodate higher forces such as the ancestors.

African ontology-based and teleologically oriented environmentalism respects this variation in degree of moral status because ontological status is itself hierarchically. This is because the kind and amount of vital force, which are some of the key supports for the moral status and value of non human beings, differ and vary from one being to the other. The other reason is that existence is entirely connected to vital force which is inherent in all beings. According to Tempels, "it is because all being is force and exists only in that it is force, that the category 'force' includes of necessity all 'beings': God, men living and departed, animals, plants, minerals" (Tempels 1959: 52). Although he does not explicitly show the import of this understanding of force to environmentalism, I explore it further and argue that these various levels of existence are seen as forces in so far as they do possess potency and that they are capable of influencing each other's well-being. For example, God and the ancestors could influence human and environmental well-being. At the same time, human beings are also capable of either positively or negatively affecting the life, harmony, balance and well-being of the other lower forces such as animals, plants and animals. In this kind of a vitalist view of moral status which is not egalitarian, the teleological dimension of existence comes in because of the relations that ought to subsist between vitality and well-being. In my view, vital force must be intrinsic to all beings. Consequently, since all being is vital force and that all beings have potency, it follows that all vital forces are teleologically oriented towards well-being, survival and life, although the degree and level of such *telos* differs from one being to the other depending on the level which such a being occupies in the hierarchy of existence.

Non human living beings complement the teleological and spiritual relationship and the interconnectedness between all other beings such as God, ancestors and human beings. The African ontological hierarchy ranks beings from God, ancestors, human beings, down to the animate and non animate beings. As a result, this African ontological hierarchy of existence determines the differing degrees of purpose from one being to the other. Notwithstanding this difference in degree of vitality and moral standing, among human beings for example, they still have the same or equal moral status. This is because human beings occupy the same ontological level in the hierarchy of existence. To this end, Izibili offers a useful elastic argument for inherent value. For him, inherent value is "… a matter of degree rather than an all or nothing affair such that those beings that have inherent value might comprise a hierarchy of those with the most inherent value being at the top and those with less occupying the bottom" (Izibili 2005: 386). This is perhaps one of the reasons why African life-centred environmental ethics is sometimes judged as being anthropocentric.

African ontology-based environmental ethics also takes into consideration the interests and well-being of non human animals on the basis of relationships or relations that are thought to actually exist between human beings and non human living beings such as non human animals. According to this view, human beings and non human living beings such as animals and plants are thought to be linked by certain relations. This view is captured by Murove who proffers an understanding of relatedness or *ukama*, which is a relational (Murove 2004: 195–215). It is relational in so far as it takes into account the non-anthropocentric ethical relationships that ought to exist between human beings and components of nature such as the various animal species which constitute human totems (Murove 2004: 195–215). This understanding of relatedness is what I see as being capable of being the foundation for the conception of moral status because it is not exclusive to human beings alone.

Also, following the philosophy of *ubuntu* which I take as a useful African moral theory, existence is strongly informed by having good ethical relations, not only among human communities alone, but even with the natural environment consisting of non human living beings. According to this African moral theory, what it means to be is not only anchored on the extent to which one relates well with other human persons alone, but it also takes into account the way such an individual treats the environment, particularly non human living beings such as animals and plants. The understanding of being is not entirely focussed on the human beings alone. This is why the idea of the good person is not only judged by the person's relations with persons alone, but also the person's treatment of components of nature like animals and plants.

The moral status of non human living beings could also be reasonably based on the possession of sentience for non human animals apart from the ownership of life in the case of non animate things like plants. This view is also integrated in the teleological framework that I discussed in the previous section. Accordingly, one other reason to strongly suspect that human beings have direct duties towards non human animals is the aspect of sentience, which I understand as the ability to either endure suffering or promote well-being. From a Western philosophical standpoint, as Peter Singer would like it to be understood, "if a being suffers, the fact that it is not a member of our own species cannot be a moral reason for failing to take its suffering into account" (Singer 1985: 479).

Although Singer is not a bio-centrist so understood, according to the above sentience-based position, which I take as supporting my version of an African bio-centric view of environmental ethics which is teleologically oriented, non human living beings ought to be accorded ethical standing because of their ability to feel pain. The rational basis for such ethical standing that is based on sentience is that the well-being of non human living beings can be positively or negatively affected by human actions. This is because non human living beings also feel pain and pleasure, some of whom do just like what human beings do, and that pain does not further their purposes for existence as it actually prevents it. My argument here is that despite sentience being characteristic to both human beings and non human living beings; it remains influential in determining purposiveness among different animate beings. It would be reasonable to take this view as a function of teleological ontology because the aspect of sentience must remind human beings to treat with respect, other beings that also feel pain and pleasure. This is so because if happiness and pleasure enhance a pleasurable life in human beings and pain does not enhance it, then it must be the same for other non human living beings that also feel the same way human beings do. Implicit in this view is a claim about the purpose of both human and non human beings, which is to live a happy life as one teleological *end*.

Overall, human beings can either positively or negatively affect the well-being of other non human living beings such as animals and plants. This is despite the fact that these natural beings are not strictly speaking, 'moral agents' while human beings are. In spite of this view, I still maintain the argument that human beings ought to have ethical obligations towards nature, particularly non human living beings on the basis that they have moral standing.

3.4 The Moral Status of Non Living Beings

Besides non human animals and objects of life like plant species (which I have treated as non human living beings in the previous section), there are also certain aspects of nature that I suppose to possess moral standing such that human beings should be deemed to also have direct moral duties towards them. This view of moral consideration of non living beings is such that components such as rocks, soils, water and the air can be held to have direct ethical standing as well. Accordingly, these non living beings must be treated as having moral status, which is to say that human beings have some direct duties towards them. Although I have partly addressed this question when I examined the teleological connection between human beings and nature, I now intend to go beyond the aspect of teleology. I consider teleology in terms of how it could be the basis for moral status of non living beings.

One strong reason to suspect that non living beings such as rocks, water and the air have moral status is the aspect of vitality which I have already discussed with reference to non human living beings. Vitality in African ontology is not only restricted to non human living beings, but that it is also characteristic to non living beings as well. According to this view, non living objects like mountains, rivers, rocks, soils and the air are to some extent *alive*. They are thought to be alive because of the way in which these components actively participate towards the completeness of various life forms. For example, one way in which they do so is the way that they accommodate spiritual forces such as the ancestors. In this way, the vitalist understanding of beings which I emphasise here enables an interconnection of beings in African ontology such that environmental ethical thinking could be inculcated in such a view. Advocating for the same view, Shutte sees an interconnection and network between all beings in the universe (Shutte 2009: 89). For that reason, it would be plausible to argue that there ought to be direct duties and obligations that human beings have towards these life forces. This basis for this view is energy, potency and power that these beings are thought to possess (see also Tempels 1959: 50.).

The view that the physical environment is animate permeates in sub-Saharan African thinking. This view is largely informed by the understanding and acceptance that there is some ontological interconnection between beings (that is both animate and non-animate beings) (Taringa 2004: 201). Although it is not explicitly apparent, there seem to be some ontological interconnection between human beings and the physical environment that includes the rivers, soils, rocks, caves and mountains. To confirm this view of ontological interconnection between human beings and other animate and non animate reality such as the physical environment of non living beings, Behrens argues that:

> African thought extends moral considerability to include all things that are part of the inter-connected web of life, that is, all individual living things, groups of living things such as families, species and ecosystems, as well as inanimate natural objects such as rivers and mountains. (Behrens 2014: 66)

Although Behrens' view is almost similar to what I have in mind here, he does not think that these non living beings are alive and have vital force. My vitalist view is largely compatible with some attempts to personify the physical environment as what is the case with African ontology-based environmental ethics. Consequently I argue that the attempt to personify the physical environment is oriented towards sustaining good relations with the natural environment, which ultimately must have moral status. This is implicit in the way human beings revere certain hills, mountains, rocks and rivers among others (Taringa 2004: 201). In this way, it is thought that before human beings can explore any of these hills, mountains, rocks and rivers, they ought to "ritually ask its permission" (Taringa 2004: 201). I light of Taringa's view; I therefore put forth the argument that African ontology must be environmentally oriented, especially as it relates to the ontological and teleological interconnections between human beings and the natural world.

Like I have argued, in African ontology it is generally believed and acceptable that the physical environment is the habitat of God and the ancestors. Because of this belief and acceptance, this kind of thinking should largely inform environmental ethical thinking because the environment is given reverence on the basis that it is the habitat of the higher forces in the hierarchy of ontology. Although he is more focussed on the role of the territorial cults and their environmental ethical significance, Van Binsbergen confirms this view as he sees the physical environment as also the habitat of the higher forces as he argues that, "hills, pools, imposing trees, caves, streams, falls and rapids become associated with invisible entities and thus become objects of veneration" (Van Binsbergen 1978: 56). In addition to their contribution to life and purpose of other beings, this kind of veneration to these components of the physical environment is what I also see as the basis for a reasonably acceptable environmental ethics for traditional sub-Saharan African thought that stem from African theism and vitalism.

The other way in which non living beings such as rocks, rivers, the air and the soil might be taken as having purpose for being could be on the basis of their teleological role of sustaining both human and non human life in general. For example, it is in mountains that various animate and non animate beings are home to, while rivers sustain aquatic and non aquatic life as well. Similarly, soils and the air sustain almost all life forms. The roles that these non living beings perform could reasonably be taken as some of their purposes for being.

Notwithstanding the fact that they have vital force and purpose to sustain other beings which are some of the reasons to believe that they have moral status, I will treat all beings that do not possess life as 'non living' beings because they do not have a determinate and meaningful life comparable to that of human beings and other non human animals that have motion, feelings, hopes and desires. However, I contend that these non living beings still complement the teleological order of existence as they have an independent existence and purpose to that of human beings. This is also the basis for the moral status of non living beings, and the reason why human beings ought to have some direct moral duties towards non human beings. For example, non living beings such as the soil, rocks, mountains and rivers may seem not to morally matter to human beings such that human beings may not be thought to have direct moral duties towards them. However, the duties that human beings may claim towards these beings are also direct in so far as they are related to some other beings in various ways. For example, human beings themselves, other animals and various life forms relate with, and rely on, the soil, rocks, mountains and rivers for their survival. Although it could be a fairly anthropocentric view, this could be the basis for the possibility of direct duties towards these non living beings.

Except for having vital force and the purpose to sustain life forms, the basis for taking the environment as worth of moral consideration must have to do with the direct moral duties that human beings must have towards some aspects of the natural environment which I consider as non living. For example, while human beings may seem not to have direct moral duties towards non living things and non animate reality like rivers, rocks, water, and the air, I contend that they do have direct moral duties to safeguard the well-being of these aspects since their well-being and quality of existence also affects positively or negatively the life and purpose of other beings. It may sound absurd to consider either the rock, the soil, the air or mountains as having well-being and quality of existence. However, my conviction is that if these non living beings are destroyed, that will also have a bearing on their quality and the quality of other life forms as well. This explains why I contend that human beings have direct moral obligations to protect them.

Non living beings also possess their own aesthetic value and *telos* in life which are independent to those of human beings. While human beings and other animals may have moral value, non human beings like mountains and rivers have their own intrinsic aesthetic value and purposes. This aesthetic value is what I suspect could be the foundation for their moral status and the reason why they ought to be respected and safeguarded so that they continue to be what they are and achieve what they are made to achieve. Aesthetic value refers to the beauty of appreciation that a being or object has by virtue of its natural existence. It is intrinsic because it naturally inheres in each and every object of existence. This kind of beauty may vary from one being to the other and from person to person, such that we may not value the same object the same. A rock, mountain or the soil may be aesthetically appreciated differently and from different angles by different individuals. However, each non living object remains with its own intrinsic aesthetic value which is independent to other beings. Consequently, aesthetic value must impart moral value to a being because it is intrinsic to it. This is why non living beings must be left to exist without disturbing their aesthetic appreciation.

The vitalist understanding of the physical environment should be understood as central to, and being capable of shaping African ontology-based environmental ethics. This is the view where all beings, whether animate and inanimate, are thought to possess a certain force or energy that enables them to balance the teleological order of existence in the world (see also Tempels 1959: 46.). In the light of the vitalist view of existence, I argue that components of the physical environment that are without biological life such as rivers, rocks, hills, caves and mountains are important and possess vital force because they help towards shaping African environmental ethics in various ways. This suggests that these non living beings have a moral status since they have vital force as I have already argued in this section. Although he is not explicit about environmentalism, Tempels alluded to the interdependence of the vital forces in the universe as they influence one another (Tempels 1959: 60). This is the understanding of vitalism that I explore further in the context of environmentalism. For example, according to Taringa, "some of these aspects of the tangible world are believed to be imbued with the power of the great spirit (mwari), ancestral spirits (midzimu), both family and territorial and are therefore spiritually connected" (Taringa 2004: 201). Because these physical components of the environment are connected with vital forces, I take and consider that as the basis for an acceptable environmental ethics in African ontology.

To strengthen the argument developed here is the understanding in African ontology that all beings are part of the interconnected web of existence. This explains why the African hierarchy of existence includes almost everything from God, ancestors, human beings down to the non human beings, including non living beings. Behrens alluded to this view of interconnectedness of beings as he argues that "a belief that all natural things are interconnected and that all humans are part of, rather than set apart from, nature provides a sound foundation for treating other entities with respect, and for valuing other natural objects as morally considerable entities" (Behrens 2014: 70). The fact that human beings are interconnected with other natural beings such as the air, water and the soil could give them strong reasons to treat them in a respectable way because they have a moral status to some extent. They have moral status in so far as they also have independent existence to human beings and possessing their own purposes and aesthetic value as what has been argued here. African ontology recognises the complex web of existence in the various forms of beings. In addition, it takes into consideration the ontological and ethical link between the living human beings, the non-human animals, the spiritual forces and the natural environment at large. This is what prompts me to take as useful, Odera Oruka and Juma's African eco-philosophical approach that takes into consideration the "totality of (spatial, temporal, spiritual and other) interlinkages in nature" (Odera Oruka and Juma 1994: 114).

3.5   Conclusion

In this chapter, I discuss the question of whether the environment has any moral status in the light of African conceptions of existence. I address this question in the affirmative as I critically grapple with the problem of whether there could be any teleological connections between the human community and the environment such that there ought to be any ethical obligations and duties that human beings have towards the environment. In the end, I examine what I see as the direct moral duties that human beings must have towards nature. These duties could reasonably derive from the realisation of the moral status of non human living beings and that of non living beings respectively. The argument that I proffer is that these direct moral duties, together with other views such as force and teleology could be meaningfully taken as the bases for the ethical connection between human beings and nature. This is why I conclude that, on the basis of the moral status of non human living beings as well as the direct moral duties that human beings owe to the environment, there ought to be a strong ethical link between human beings and nature.

References

Aristotle. 2011. *Nicomachean Ethics: Book 1*. Translated by Robert C. Bartlett and Susan D. Collins as *Aristotle's Nicomachean Ethics*. Chicago: Chicago University Press 1094a–1095b.

Behrens, K.G. 2014. An African Relational Environmentalism. *Environmental Ethics* 36 (Spring): 63–82.

Bujo, B. 1998. *The Ethical Dimensions of Community*. Nairobi: Paulines Publications.

Chemhuru, M. 2016. The Import of African Ontology for African Environmental Ethics. D Litt et Phil (Philosophy) [Unpublished]. University of Johannesburg.

Izibili, M.A. 2005. Environmental Ethics: An Urgent Imperative. In *Kpim of Morality. Ethics: General, Special and Professional*, ed. P.O. Iroegbu and A.O. Echekwube, 383–390. Ibadan: Heinemann Educational Books.

Metz, T. 2012. An African Theory of Moral Status: A Relational Alternative to Individualism and Holism. *Springer Science* 15: 387–402.

Murove, M.F. 2004. An African Commitment to Ecological Conservation: The Shona Concept of *Ukama* and *Ubuntu*. *The Mankind Quarterly XLV* 2: 195–215.

Nnamani, A.G. 2005. Ethics of the Environment. In *Kpim of Morality. Ethics: General, Special and Professional*, ed. P.O. Iroegbu and A.O. Echekwube, 391–400. Ibadan: Heinemann Educational Books.

Ojomo, P.A. 2010. An African Understanding of Environmental Ethics. *Thought and Practice: A Journal of the Philosophical Association of Kenya (P.A.K)* 2 (2): 49–63.

Odera Oruka, H., and C. Juma. 1994. Ecophilosophy and Parental Earth Ethics (On the Complex Web of Being). In *Philosophy, Humanity and Ecology*, ed. H. Odera Oruka, 115–129. Nairobi: ACTS Press.

Shutte, A. 2009. Ubuntu as the African Ethical Vision. In *African Ethics: An Anthology of Comparative and Applied Ethics*, ed. M.F. Murove, 85–99. Pietermaritzburg: University of KwaZulu-Natal Press.

Singer, P. 1985. Not for Humans Only: The place of Nonhumans in Environmental Ethics. In *Ethics: Theory and Practice*, ed. M. Velasquez and C. Rostankowski, 476–490. New Jersey: Prentice-Hall.

Tangwa, G.B. 2006. Some African Reflections on Biomedical and Environmental Ethics. In *A Companion to African Philosophy*, ed. K. Wiredu, 387–395. Oxford: Blackwell Publishing.

Taringa, N.T. 2004. How Environmental is African Traditional Religion? *Exchange* 35 (2): 191–214 (BRILL Academic Publishers).

Taylor, P.W. 1986. *Respect for Nature: A Theory of Environmental Ethics*. Princeton and Oxford: Princeton University Press.

Tempels, P. 1959. *Bantu Philosophy*. (Trans. Rev. Colin King) Paris: Présence Africaine.

Van Binsbergen, W.M.J. 1978. Explorations in the History and Sociology of Territorial Cults in Zambia. In *Guardians of the Land*, ed. J.M. Schoffeleers, 47–88. Gweru: Mambo Press.

Varner, G. 2001. Sentientism. In *A Companion to Environmental Philosophy*, ed. Dale Jamieson, 192–203. Oxford: Blackwell Publishers.

Warren, M. A. 1987. Difficulties with the Strong Animal Rights Position. *Between the Species* 2 (4) (Fall.): 345–351.

Chapter 4
Environmental Ethics in the Context of African Traditional Thought: Beyond the Impasse

Patrick Giddy

Abstract I approach environmental ethics here through an appeal to the human capacity for appreciating value wherever it is found, contesting the supposed disunity of person and external world that is arguably at the root of the global disrespect for the natural environment. In the more dominant *non*-anthropocentric approach attention is drawn to the overarching eco-system equalizing the functional roles of both human and non-human. But this seems self-undermining, as appeal is necessarily made to that human moral and rational consciousness whose regulating role is at the same time being called into question. Drawing on an Aristotelian/Thomist metaphysics, congruent with the African traditional idea of "vital force" running through natural and social reality, I argue that organisms—human or otherwise—are *not* functional elements in the ecosystem but historically viable co-determinants thereof. The role of the human organism is that of co-determining through narrative and history. Human subjectivity is not, pace Nagel, confined to a species-perspective but there is a supra-biological patterning of experience intending understanding and true value. However, the development of these powers of agency, and sympathy, are stultified by a picture of self-determination as the most absolute independence from the "other". In contrast, the African traditional value of ubuntu posits a normative development of agency through others that can be unpacked to apply beyond simply social custom. The contribution this cultural tradition brings is enhanced if the metaphysics of "force" or "spirit" is interpreted non-dualistically and without appeal to a supernaturalism.

4.1 Introduction

It is the supposed disunity of person and external world that is at the root of the global disrespect for the natural environment. Non-anthropocentric approaches to environmental ethics draw attention to the overarching eco-system equalizing the functional roles of both human and non-human. But in appealing precisely to human

P. Giddy (✉)
University of KwaZulu-Natal, Durban, South Africa
e-mail: jpgiddy@gmail.com

© Springer Nature Switzerland AG 2019   47
M. Chemhuru (ed.), *African Environmental Ethics*, The International
Library of Environmental, Agricultural and Food Ethics 29,
https://doi.org/10.1007/978-3-030-18807-8_4

understanding and rational conscience this seems self-undermining. Drawing on
an Aristotelian/Thomist metaphysics, congruent with the African traditional idea
of "vital force" running through natural and social reality, I argue (Part One) that
organisms—human or otherwise—are *not* functional elements in the ecosystem but
historically viable co-determinants thereof. The role of the human organism is that
of co-determining through narrative and history. In Part Two I argue that human
subjectivity is not, pace Nagel, confined to a species-perspective but there is a supra-
biological patterning of experience intending understanding and true value. However,
the development of these powers of agency, and sympathy, are stultified by a picture
of self-determination as the most absolute independence from the "other". In contrast,
the African traditional value of ubuntu posits a normative development of agency
through others that can be unpacked to apply beyond simply social custom. In Part
Three this contribution of our cultural tradition is further specified by suggesting that
the metaphysics of "force" or "spirit" be interpreted non-dualistically and without
appeal to a supernaturalism.

4.2   The Raskolnikov Problem

A new mentality is required. In Dostoevsky's novel, *Crime and Punishment*, the
central character Raskolnikov cannot see the point of another human being, his land-
lady, whom he owes money and. he calculates, is of less utility than himself, and
he does away with her. His changed view, in prison for the murder, comes about
through the influence of another, kind, person. The question we are addressing is
whether the African traditional ethics of ubuntu, framed by a metaphysics of "vital
force" running through the social and natural world, can contribute to overcoming
the dominant and unhelpful picture of the person as likewise disengaged from and
indifferent to the natural world.[1] I think it can, avoiding the idea of "humans understood to be just discrete entities", as Brian Henning at Gonzaga University puts it in
his 2017 call for contributions to an anthology of non-anthropocentric approaches
to climate change. Can it at the same time "reconceive subjectivity and agency" (as
the call for contributions adds) so as to avoid the impasse pointed to in our opening paragraph above? I am going to put forward the interpretative framework of the
Aristotelian/Thomist understanding of living beings, non-human and human, as both
cognate with the African traditional picture and grounding just such a re-conception
of subjectivity and agency. The challenge is to reformulate the African traditional
ethic and metaphysics so as to facilitate its reception in a culture of science. Empathy
with other persons, central to the ubuntu interpretation of being human, allows for a
transformation of mentality that appreciates the value of our shared natural milieu.
At least this is what I shall argue.

---

[1] This is an indifference pointed to by Coetzee (1999: 35) when he refers to a general lack of empathy
with the suffering of animals in abattoirs, "we do not feel tainted. We can do anything, it seems,
and come away clean."

4.3   Part One. The Human Animal and the Eco-System: The Role of Sympathy

Seeing human persons not as separate but indeed as *part* of a larger encompassing reality (something like an eco-system) is a typical African traditional approach, as Murove (2009) points out, a reality of spirit or "force" or *seriti* (Sesotho), *isithunzi* (isiZulu) or the interdependence of *ukama* (Shona), and Bujo (2009: 114) refers to as "the moral order". But the appeal of any environmental ethic is precisely to human (superior?) reason. To resolve this impasse, we need then to show that placing living beings as functional elements in an eco-system misunderstands what it is to be a living organism. And in the Aristotelian tradition taken forward by contemporary Thomists,[2] the identity of an organism is not properly explained in terms of its roles or functions within a whole, since it is itself a viable whole, what is called the organism's "form". It is this approach that can, I will argue, answer to our problematic.[3]

Timothy McDermott, a contemporary Thomist, argues the organism is not simply an organ in a system but co-determines the "system" itself. The organism is an existing historically stable whole which cannot be fully explained in terms of mechanisms. The organism is favoured by nature not because of its *function*, even the function of reproducing itself, for one could ask, What is the function of that? The attempt to fix the defining function is faced with an ever-receding horizon. We may ask what an eye is for but it seems quirky to ask what a cow is for. Cows may be employed within a farm; of themselves however they are not parts of a production process but members of an ecosystem. They do of course play roles in that ecosystem, but, as McDermott adds, "they are not simply implementations of a function that the ecosystem demands of them. Rather they are historical facts that have just proved to be viable in that ecosystem, or rather in the ecosystem as itself changed by their viability." (McDermott 1989, Preface: xxviii).

The "historical fact" that McDermott talks of is a synthesis of evolutionary biology and human history. The key to an environmental ethics that does not pit "man" against "nature" lies in this synthesis. Appreciating the "historical fact" (some animals have been found to be domesticatable, others not) enables a responsible and creative further taking up of the planet's eco-system. The age of the Anthropocene is characterized by not only by evolving nature but historical narrative. We are inserted into nature.[4] The

---

[2]This way of unpacking the kind of human participation in the whole of reality posited in African traditional metaphysics, was something that African philosophy pioneer Placide Tempels (1959) was aware of through his Thomistic philosophical training, although he does not himself make reference to this (see Giddy 2012).

[3]J. M. Coetzee, in contrast, suggests the dichotomy reason/nature goes back through Descartes to Aquinas and Aristotle. He references (Coetzee 1999: 22) Aquinas' idea that cruelty to animals is of no moral concern except insofar as it may accustom us to being cruel to humans (see Aquinas 1964, *Summa Theologiae* IaIIae, Q.10 art. 6 and 8.). LeBlanc's (1999: 299) account of "eco-Thomism" is more sympathetic to Aquinas.

[4]Darwin's impact on environmental thinking has been crucial, and has been extended to take into account the noosphere, Teilhard de Chardin's term, the sphere of consciousness and mind. Wilhelm Wundt in the late 19th century sees human consciousness as constituting "a decisive point in

task is to self-consciously take up nature more and more into the human imagination and in this way overcome the knee-jerk reaction to the realisation that nature will after all literally deliver the death blow to each individual person. This work on the human psyche is part and parcel of any environmental ethics that will have real purchase on our moral imagination and hence on our actions.

The novelist J. M. Coetzee understands this very well, pointing to our indifference to the suffering of animals, "we can do anything, it seems, and come away clean" (1999: 35). As Midgley (1995: 259) puts it in a piece of analysis Coetzee (2003) later acknowledges as influential in his own approach, "criticism of the undeveloped heart is moral criticism." Environmental ethics calls for a maturing of our faculty of sympathy, and in particular a greater integration of our ideas, especially about values, and our habitual decisions, and both of these with our feelings. The impotence resulting from such conflict within ourselves is well illustrated by Prozesky (2009) in his phenomenology of our feelings about nature juxtaposed with feelings about those living on the margins of development whose struggle against poverty might further degrade the natural milieu. His examples are from rural Kwazulu-Natal, site of both nature reserves and of extreme poverty. What is crucial is, therefore, a process of growth towards a less conflictual set of choices. We will argue that this is achieved for any particular individual (as pointed to in African traditional ethics) only through the beneficial influence of other persons.

4.4   Part Two. Objection: Is Human Subjectivity Species-Specific?

We turn now to deal with a major objection to this way of approaching environmental ethics, namely the contention that the project of developing a more consequential set of feeling-reactions to the lives of animals and the natural world in general, is nothing more than an expression of human hubris. Human subjectivity is in fact enclosed within its species-perspective. This is the view of Nagel (1979a), who argues we cannot get to the value, to the "how it is experienced as a value", of another species, to what it is like to for them to be themselves—his example is that of a bat. We can get no further, beyond our subjectivity, in finding some "objective" description of the organism living its life.

> Facts about what it is like for the experiencing organism are accessible only from one point of view... It is unlikely that we will get closer to the real nature of the experience by leaving behind the particularity of its point of view and striving for a description in terms accessible to beings that could only imagine what it was like to be that organism. (Nagel 1979a: 172–174)

These beings are us. Humans. But is Nagel right? Can we not, in response, point to a broader understanding of subjectivity? While it is true that we do experience a

---

nature's course, a point at which the world becomes aware of itself" (in Menaud 2001: 269), an insight developed at length by Brian Swimme and Thomas Berry in *The Universe Story* (1994).

reality circumscribed by our sense-capacities unique to our species, still, it can be argued, this is just one *patterning* of experience among others. It cannot be *identified* with subjectivity since we can also have the subjective experience of coming to an objective understanding of things, for example when we affirm our understanding of something as probably true (we are not saying it is probably true to us, but really so). I can explain this kind of experienced reality further.

It is common to refer to intentional actions as "mental events", suggesting that they are simply there, as physical events are. This however is misleading in the case mentioned above, the experienced fact of sometimes actively "standing by" certain standards of reasonableness as apt for the purposes of considering rival claims to truth. In taking responsibility for one's own contribution to the common growth of knowledge and understanding, one is becoming more present to oneself as being under certain normative demands—basically, to make something of one's powers of intelligence. Nagel's example of subjectivity is therefore a special case of conscious experience, not at all definitive of it.

The notion of patterns of experience comes from Lonergan (1970; see Giddy 2009), and it enables us to account for the data brought forward by Nagel while avoiding the impression that this experience exists somehow "alongside" the objective physical reality. What Nagel describes as the ineluctably subjective character of experience Lonergan describes in terms of the idea of the biological patterning of experience which is characterized by knowing through sense and imagination, what he calls "extroversion" (1970: 181–184). Such experience is non-objective, but *other* patterning of our experience are possible, according to how we are intentionally oriented. Experience is not uniform, all of one kind, but always patterned. A flock of birds passing overhead signifies for me simply that, but my ornithologist hiking friend sees climate change. Same sensation, different perception. Lonergan points to the artificiality of speaking simply of pure sensation. Acts such as seeing, hearing, tasting never occur in isolation but always in some intentional framework.

> When I would see with my eyes, I open them, turn my head, approach, focus my gaze… [But] besides the systematic links between senses and sense organs, there is, immanent in experience, a factor variously named conation, interest, attention, purpose. (1970: 181)

We can compare animal living with that of plants. *Conscious* living is only *part* of the animal's total living: vital processes go on willy-nilly. Consciousness is called forth to deal with the drive to sustain life, to respond to opportunities and dangers. The biological pattern of experience is concerned with these externalities within the full pattern of living (Lonergan 1970: 183–184).

Lonergan distinguishes a range of patterns of experience, biological, aesthetic, religious, intellectual, dramatic (In the aesthetic pattern, for example, the biological drives are to some extent disregarded in favour of an interest in following a line which appeals primarily to one's imagination, evoking a wider range of emotions and desires.). And this helps us to understand the confusion in Nagel's Cartesian construction of the dichotomy of the external and the internal (or subjective) points of view (Nagel 1979b: especially 202). This dichotomy pertains specifically to the biological patterning of experience, whose intentional object is aptly referred to as "the already out there now real". This refers to an object to which we are oriented already before taking thought—the table in front of me as I traverse the room after a power failure to get to the matches. I don't have echolocation, so I bump into the table—my sense-organs are a limit, and the table has the immediate "reality" of a being "out there", external to me, of relevance to the biological success or failure of the organism (Lonergan 1970: 252).

But thinking of reality as what is external to me is not however of relevance to another patterning of experience, the intellectual, which aims at another kind of knowing, through experiencing, intelligent understanding and finally passing reflective judgment on the adequacy or otherwise of one's grasp of the object at hand. In the latter case, sensible, realistic concerns of the biological organism are put aside in favour of the exigencies of the enquiring mind. Objectivity now comes to mean the goal of dealing with (raising and answering) all the questions relevant to the question posed to the understanding. Thus, Thales trips into the well (failure in the operation of the biological organism) because he is contemplating the intelligible order in the movements of the planets.

The upshot is that our subjectivity is not something species-restricted, or not necessarily so. In giving my intelligence its scope, and my capacity for reasoned not rash judgment, I live more fully in the real world—of living things, for example. Nature is not something "out there" *on which* I act either only to serve human needs (anthropocentrism) or not only as this (non-anthropocentrism). No, nature is equally *ourselves* as subjects and agents. The lives of animals are shared by being taken up in our understanding and being made part of our world and our history; not only domesticated animals but fynbos and game parks become treasured elements in our world. Truly to do this is no easy task. There are problems with how detached one is about one's habitual horizon of *willingness* to follow through such inquiry. A transformation of one's feeling life, of one's psyche, is called for. The beast that is nature and that terrifies can be tamed by beasts in nature. Out of fear come projections of that fear, and in the ensuing hoarding of forces to fortify oneself against those enemies, it is the environment—sufficient for our needs but not our traumas—that suffers.

4.5   The Problem of Underdeveloped Human Agency

Our focus must therefore be on the problem of the underdevelopment of human agency. In an age of cultural relativism and consumer preference, agency is seen not in terms of how it is developed but simply in terms of free will or choice. The normative element comes in only as a procedural regulation: all agents have *equal* sovereignty over their lives. This is a major reason why animal and environmental ethics is often discussed in terms of the extension of this norm of equality. But African traditional ethics takes a different line, thinking of persons in terms of a norm of development, and positing duties to the more developed members to exert influence over the less developed, in particular children (Giddy 2002). What needs unpacking is how this is to be conceived of in a way that does not posit a metaphysical hierarchy in terms of which that norm of being human is thought of as above nature, an essence that has a super-natural quality, the "soul".

In the Aristotelian/Thomist picture we have a way through this dilemma: it lies in seeing non-human animal life in terms of voluntariness rather than mechanistically. The animal is not simply at our disposal, as we might think if we consider it as a tool, a machine, devoid of an inner life. The machine does not act purposively—the rear sensors of the SUV do not actually *see* the wall as we come too close to it, because the car does not "have a world" in which certain objects play significant roles, as the bird does in the life of a spaniel. The dog chases the bird precisely because it sees it; it acts voluntarily. Making this behaviour intelligible to us (hence, appreciating it as *of value*) takes an effort of mind and of will, and we make an effort to consent to a range of appropriate feelings, inhibiting ones that would discount such purposefulness. We have to appreciate the voluntariness of the animal, its acting for a purpose, and see how its network of meanings make sense: an example would be when we are taken up in the singular intent of the lioness' hunt for the impala. This is more difficult but not impossible in the case of a bat. McCabe (2005: 96) argues that cruelty to animals is not so much a failure of justice (as would be the case if animal ethics was founded on "rights") but of temperance, in other words of the virtue that responds to feelings of undue domination over or taking pleasure from the object.

The non-human animal reveals something undeniably true of the natural world: its directionality, its value, and this is revealed *in* the life of the animal. We do not have to take the implausible step to saying that animals have "rights": the non-human animal does not share the space of meanings in which claims on other members make sense. Rather the world of the cow is pre-defined by a set of meanings or responses that are biological in origin. McCabe argues that in the case of the human animal the world is, in contrast, self-defined, invented, through tradition and history, and part of that self-understanding is "rights" talk.

Has this however simply shifted the problem raised by Nagel, from our (limited) structures of *perception* to the (limited) perspectival structures of our particular *society* and *language*? Does the ubuntu idea—determination by virtue of our social participation—restrict us to an identity which is that of "the tribe", as Stephen Theron suggests (in Murove 2009: 328–329)? And in that case, wherein lies its supposed universal normative force? In response we can briefly point to a "non-tribal" under-standing of an ubuntu framing of human agency. In the act of choosing, it can be pointed out, it is not my social or biological determinants—or my ideas, for that matter—that act *on* me, as the heat acts on the molecules to cause the water to boil. Rather, it is I myself who acts on myself. The self that I choose and consent *to* (the more temperate rather than indulgent one, say), is *the same as* the self that does the choosing and consenting. It is not one part of me acting on another part, as was the case in the water being caused to boil. In other words, in reflective delibera-tion I am able to *take into consideration* possible biases due to my particular social influences, my particular "language" or "tribe". Being self-moving in this radical way—Shutte (1984) uses the term "self-enacting"—has traditionally been termed spirit, precisely to distinguish it from entities not thus constituted, without the power of self-reflexivity here at issue.

4.6 Human Spirituality but not a Dualism

This might seem to have re-introduced a dualism of spirit and matter, human and nature. This is not so. In the African approach, the self-enactment is achieved, as already argued, through relatedness to the other-than-self. The quality attaching to this acting on good reasons is something that is *developed*; its very coming into being in the neonate and child is arguably only possible through the intentions of the beneficial "mother" (See Shutte 1993, Chap. 7 and 2001, Chap. 4). And the development happens through the quality of its relatedness to other-than-self. Self-determination grows in direct proportion (and not in indirect proportion) to a certain kind of *other*-determination: so far are we from the idea that freedom is *independence* from the other. One thinks here of any person's dependence on the world around them, and in particular other persons. In finding and appreciating value in the other person one comes, through their influence, to a less conflictual self-affirmation. I affirm them affirming me as less conflictual (I respond to their initiative), and so overcome in this way my habitual self-image and orientation. My feelings are released to allow me to respond proportionately to nature (rather than disproportionately, for example to grizzly bears, as does the central character in Werner Herzog's 2005 docu-film *Grizzly Man*). Nature becomes, bit by bit, our common home, where we can be "at home". By showing how my self-enactment is achieved precisely through the other person, African traditional philosophical thought heads off any idea that the self is over and against the world "out there", and this undercuts the basis for environmental neglect.

4.7 Part Three. African Traditional Thought—Not a Supernaturalism

Finally, we need to say something specific about the core African idea of *ser-iti/isithunzi*, or *force vitale*, and secondly about ubuntu. The former idea should not be understood supernaturalistically. B. Bujo, for example, agrees there is a moral order over and above the social nexus. He argues African traditional ethics is not simply anthropocentric, but that there is another-worldly reality to which reference must be made. And he adds that God, as creator, "has to intervene in the moral order if the human person does not follow the laws set by him" (2009: 114), and, furthermore, punish crimes. Here we have one reason why sensible folk might be suspicious of the African traditional framework of thought: the God intervening—perforce breaking one of the four fundamental forces of the universe, say, gravitational—would undermine, first, the causality of human agency, sketched above; secondly, the integrity of the scientific enterprise (including the science of climate change); and finally the universe itself. Whereas a reference to a value-pervasive natural reality such as *seriti* lends itself to seeing the human person as becoming fully human through a dependence on the natural and social milieu, the supernaturalistic interpretation of this once again downgrades the natural world, *pace* Bujo the only world there is. African traditional thought has to come to terms with a shift away from a dual world-view, heaven and earth (which at any rate never was a reified dualism as it was in some European versions thereof), one that detracts from responsibility for the planet. The oversights of the European Enlightenment, which we have stressed, should not encourage us to discard its very liberating achievements in secularizing human consciousness.

4.8   Ubuntu—Not a Moralism

Secondly, the ubuntu idea. I am looking to this to ground the shift in mind-set that we have tasked ourselves with. I take ubuntu as an attitudinal ideal—not a metaphysical essence or nature. I am not advocating an environmental "moralism", something imposed which does not particularly resonate with people: to the claim that this or that is the human telos or essence or the moral status of animals, the reply could be, So what? Rather, I am doing "transformational philosophy", addressing the problem of a lack of development, and moving it along. In the face of our disengaged Raskolnikov character, we offer the idea of a growing self-enactment (more intensely engaged) as one moves from sensing (seeing the bat fly away in the dark) to making sense of how it does this (echolocation). Does one not value such understanding, or rather oneself as understanding? Of course one does. Again, one takes up, engages, one's personal powers in not rushing into a claim for the truth of one's interpretation, but reflects on and judges its possible inaccuracy. Oneself as being reasonable (rather than unreasonable), at least with respect to this object at hand, is something to celebrate. Similarly, with oneself consenting to a desire because it is all things considered worthwhile—it corresponds to the value of the animal living its life, say—and inhibiting other desires because they are shallower (the desire to kill the bat). Again, this human phenomenon, oneself as responsible, is, it goes without saying, of value. The awakening to these subject-enhancing moments as of value fashions the kind of mentality we are seeking, engaged rather than disengaged. Raskolnikov appreciates his new transformed self.

The engine of this self-development, in the ubuntu approach, is the other person. For in ethics we are concerned not simply with successful action (say, the effective culling of elephants), where the *means* taken might be irrelevant, but also with the *intention* behind the action. Is the chain around the dog's neck for its own protection or an instance of cruelty? This concern presupposes a "you" that "gets" the intention, among a range of possible intentions. If I am doing ethics in a cross-cultural context (such as the present one) I make my point carefully so as to bring clarity to my interlocutor in terms that can be seen by them as possible intentions. The interlocutor and I must necessarily share a common life, in which a range of intentions make sense. I correctly interpret the Bulgarian official at the gate to be indicating "yes" (because he is smiling) to my request to enter even though he is shaking his head rather than nodding, which would be the more common gesture for indicating assent. The only foundation possible for ethics is not something already determined ("nature") of which one must convince others ("moralism"), but rather the *reasonable attitude* of commitment to achieving some viable community with others rather than getting one's own way. To the extent that environmental *ethics* (rather than an environmental pressure group!) has actual purchase, it will be hand in hand with a commitment to the achievement of a community of engaged persons.

4.9   Conclusion

How far have we succeeded in responding to the Raskolnikov problematic? Peter Singer is not convinced of our approach. Responding to Coetzee's idea of sympathy, he argues that "we can't take our *feelings* as moral data, immune from rational criticism" (1999: 89, emphasis added). Any unit of life, he says, is basically equivalent in value to any other unit; there is no place for basing values on how we *feel* about any living being. Your feeling of loss at the killing of an animal (or the animal's own loss of certain lived experience) is simply *subjective* data, not of any significant account in a moral calculus. There is no moral harm if such killing is painless: another equally valuable life can furnish a replacement. This seems close to Raskolnikov before his change of heart. Singer's challenge reinforces the importance of overturning, as we have tried to do, this truncated and unhelpful view of "subjectivity".

I have argued, in response to the impasse of a non-anthropocentric conception of environmental ethics, that animals—human, non-human—are misrepresented as equal functional elements in an eco-system. Organisms co-define the system, and are historically viable facts. The human organism takes up the evolving cosmos into a self-conscious narrative, doing this either well or badly. Human subjectivity is not, pace Nagel, imprisoned in one perspective—this perspectival attitude corresponds only to the biological patterning of experience, pitting ourselves over and against the world "out there". But there is the problem of an underdeveloped human intelligence, integrity of will, and feeling. To the extent that human self-determination is thought of in terms of the most absolute *independence* from the "other," there will be a neglect of the need to address the conflicted and undeveloped core of personal agency.[5] The African traditional concept of agency as developmental and normative is a counter to this, and can be unpacked so as to avoid any notion of such a norm being restricted to social custom. The framing metaphysics of "force" or "spirit" needs, I have argued, to be developed so as to avoid any dualism of "man"/world, and also any supernaturalism. So far as distrust of the other leads to the kind of hoarding that

---

[5] A neglect well-articulated by M. Robinson in her 2011 critique of contemporary culture's "absence of mind".

has detrimental effects on the environment, the ubuntu idea is a useful weapon in dialogues on the ecology. And the current politics of the USA does indeed suggest a link between such distrust, finding expression in the unbridled competitiveness of the free market, and environmental disregard.

References

Aquinas, St. Thomas. 1964. *Summa Theologiae*, 60 Volumes. Trans. Dominican Fathers. London: Blackfriars.

Bujo, B. 2009. Is There a Specific African Ethics? In *African Ethics. An Anthology of Comparative and Applied Ethics*, ed. M.F. Murove, 113–128. Scottsville: University of Kwazulu-Natal Press.

Coetzee, J.M. 1999. *The Lives of Animals*. Princeton: Princeton University Press.

Coetzee, J.M. 2003. *Elizabeth Costello*. London: Secker and Warburg.

Giddy, P. 2002. African Traditional Thought and Growth in Personal Unity. *International Philosophical Quarterly* 42: 315–327.

Giddy, P. 2009. Objectivity and Subjectivity: Rethinking the Philosophy Syllabus. *South African Journal of Philosophy* 28: 359–376.

Giddy, P. 2012. The Ideal of African Scholarship and Its Implications for Introductory Philosophy: The Example of Placide Tempels. *South African Journal of Philosophy* 31: 504–516.

Henning, B. 2017. Call for Papers. Edited Anthology on Non-anthropocentric Climate Ethics. http://Connect.gonzaga.edu/henning/call-for-papers. Accessed 18 Sept 2017.

LeBlanc, J. 1999. Eco-Thomism. *Environmental Ethics* 21: 293–306.

Lonergan, B. 1970. *Insight. A Study of Human Understanding*, 3rd ed. New York: Philosophical Library.

McCabe, H. 2005. *The Good Life*. London: Continuum.

McDermott, T. 1989. "Preface". In *Aquinas, Summa Theologiae. A Concise Translation*, ed. T. McDermott. London: Methuen.

Menaud, L. 2001. *The Metaphysical Club*. New York: Farrar, Straus and Giroux.

Midgley, M. 1995. *Beast and Man*, Revised Edition. London: Routledge.

Murove, M.F. 2009. An African Environmental Ethic Based on the Concepts of Ukama and Ubuntu. In *African Ethics. An Anthology of Comparative and Applied Ethics*, ed. M.F. Murove, 315–332. Scottsville: University of Kwazulu-Natal Press.

Nagel, T. 1979a. What Is It Like to Be a Bat? In *Mortal Questions*, ed. T. Nagel, 165–180. Cambridge: Cambridge University Press.

Nagel, T. 1979b. Subjective and Objective. In *Mortal Questions*, ed. T. Nagel, 196–213. Cambridge: Cambridge University Press.

Prozesky, M. 2009. Well-Fed Animals and Starving Babies: Environmental and Developmental Challenges from Process and African Perspectives. In *African Ethics. An Anthology of Comparative and Applied Ethics*, ed. M. F. Murove, 298–307. Scottsville: University of Kwazulu-Natal Press.

Robinson, M. 2011. *Absence of Mind*. New Haven: Yale University Press.

Shutte, A. 1984. The Spirituality of Persons. *South African Journal of Philosophy* 3: 54–58.

Shutte, A. 1993. *Philosophy for Africa*. Cape Town: UCT Press.

Shutte, A. 2001. *Ubuntu. An Ethic for a New South Africa*. Pietermaritzburg: Cluster.

Singer, P. 1999. Reply to Costello. In *The Lives of Animals*, ed. J.M. Coetzee. Princeton: Princeton University Press.

Swimme, B., and T. Berry. 1994. *The Universe Story*. Harper Collins Paperback.

Tempels, P. 1959. *Bantu Philosophy*. Trans. C. King. Paris: Presence Africaine.

Chapter 5
The Criticism of Secular Humanism in African Philosophy

Motsamai Molefe

Abstract In this article, I motivate for the view that the best account of the foundations of morality in the African tradition should be grounded on some relevant spiritual property—a view that I call 'ethical supernaturalism'. In contrast to this position, the literature has been dominated by humanism as the best interpretation of African ethics, which typically is accompanied by a direct rejection of 'ethical supernaturalism' and a veiled rejection of non-naturalism (Gyekye 1995: 129–43; Metz 2007: 328; Wiredu 1992: 194–6). Here primarily, by appeal to methods of analytic philosophy, which privileges analysis and (moral) argumentation, I set out to challenge and repudiate humanism as the best interpretation of African ethics; I leave it for a future project to develop a fully-fledged African spiritual meta-ethical theory.

Keywords Ethical supernaturalism · Humanism · Meta-ethics · Moral status · Vitality

---

[1] I use the notion of 'humanism' to distinguish a meta-ethical position that is neither super-naturalist nor non-naturalist but one that grounds the source of morality on some fact(s) about human beings. As such, to refer to an African ethics as humanistic is tantamount to referring to it as secular, and to claim that the relevant secular moral property is to be found on some human property, or so I interpret those who defend this view.

A version of this article was first published in the Journal, *Theoria*, 2015, under the title: 'A Rejection of Humanism in the African Moral Tradition'.

M. Molefe (✉)
University of Fort Hare, Alice, South Africa
e-mail: motsaik@yahoo.com

© Springer Nature Switzerland AG 2019   59
M. Chemhuru (ed.), *African Environmental Ethics*, The International
Library of Environmental, Agricultural and Food Ethics 29,
https://doi.org/10.1007/978-3-030-18807-8_5

5.1 Introduction

The debate about whether African ethics is best interpreted as religious or secular is dominated by the latter position. A secular interpretation of foundations of
African morality is typically described in terms of 'humanism'[1]—the literature visi-
bly favours humanism as the best interpretation of African ethics,[2] and this position is
accompanied by a direct rejection of 'ethical supernaturalism'[3]—the view that morality is grounded on some spiritual property and a veiled rejection of non-naturalism.[4]
In this article, primarily, I reject the claim that a secular humanism best interprets
African ethics. Furthermore, I will content myself, in this instance, to merely motivate, note, not argue for, ethical supernaturalism—I leave it for a future project to
develop a fully-fledged African spiritual meta-ethical theory.[5]

I reject humanism as a basis for African ethics because it fails to capture some
of the prevalent thoughts and intuitions we Africans typically have about our duties
towards the natural environment—the idea that, in some sense, we are one substance
with nature (Murove 2007) and that some aspects of nature matter for their own
sakes to some degree. I observe that a truly African ethics must cohere with a holistic and supernaturalist tenor that often characterises African ontology, which in turn
demands that we accord moral status to some aspects of the environment, like animals, for their own sakes.[6] I show that humanistic moral theories in the sub-Saharan

---

[2]The following influential African philosophers defend humanism: Wiredu (1992: 194), Gyekye
(1995: 143), Metz (2011: 390). The following are not so influential but also advocate humanism:
Okeja (2013), Dzobo (1992: 224).

[3]Gyekye (1995: 129–43) and Wiredu (1992: 194–6) offer arguments in which they attempt to
demonstrate that ethical supernaturalism is implausible. Metz, on his part, does not give an argument
that rejects supernaturalism but endorses the interpretation by Gyekye and Wiredu (Metz 2007: 328)
and he also offers considerations that motivate for a secular approach to ethics (Metz 2010: 81–2).

[4]Metz (2007: 321) rejects ethical supernaturalism and further observes that if his ethical account is
true, it will be enough to reject some, if not all, kinds of non-naturalism. I also inform the reader,
so far as I am aware of the literature in African ethics, there is no systematic account that directly
advocates and defends an African version of non-naturalism.

[5]Space does not permit me to give both an argument against humanism and one defending ethical
supernaturalism. The reader could consider some of publications where I advocate ethical supernaturalism (Molefe 2014, 2017b, 2018).

[6]It is important to note that in the African tradition the *is/ought* distinction is not taken seriously;
in fact, my familiarity with the literature treats it as no problem at all. For example, Menkiti talking
about the biological fact that each person has their own body observes: 'That sort of given fact
is a brute biological fact. But it need not be read as conveying a message that each stands alone.
Normative standing is one thing, and superficial biological considerations quite another. I use the
word "superficial" advisedly because, on a deeper level, both norm and biology do tend to converge'
(2004: 324). The idea is that factual claims at a deeper level have a tendency to converge with moral
claims. Gyekye also observes that 'Moral questions … may … be said to be linked to, or engendered
by, meta-physical conceptions of the person' (1997: 36). This view I think can best be understood
when we stop insisting on treating African traditional morality within the dominant epistemological
canons of Western modern morality, which accepts the is/ought gap. African ethics can best be
understood, I insist, within a thought system wherein 'the ontological relationship and significance
of existence of being as such within the cosmic world of other beings that are in turn closely morally

tradition have much more difficulty ascribing fundamental moral consideration to nature for its own sake. This failure on the part of humanism, as defended by many scholars of African (moral) thought, warrants its rejection as it departs from the web of interconnectedness and interdependence that characterises African thought. This failure is interesting given that it appears that these scholars are also committed to granting some moral standing to some aspects of nature (Metz 2012: 387–402), but their human-centred ethical accounts renders them unable to do so (see, Molefe 2017a).

I first inform the reader about the method of enquiry I will use in this article. This is a philosophical enquiry, in that it seeks to go beyond merely rehearsing anthropological and historical claims about what Africans actually believed, important as these might be. I seek an account that is both African, namely one which draws from indigenous intellectual resources and one that is also philosophically plausible. I appeal to the techniques of analytic philosophy, which are characterised both by conceptual analysis and by evaluation of (moral) arguments. All things being equal, I favour an account that is both African and philosophically plausible. Whilst I grant that humans may reflect certain features of African cultures, as a matter of anthropological fact, I argue the position is nevertheless philosophically untenable.[7]

To demonstrate the implausibility of humanism within the African moral tradition, I structure this article as follows. In the first section, I define humanism and show how it typically reveals itself in the literature on African ethics by considering the theories of Kwame Gyekye, Kwasi Wiredu and Thaddeus Metz, respectively. In the second section, I show how humanistic accounts fail to accommodate a dominant conception of African metaphysics, which I understand to be tri-logical, in so far as spiritual, social and environmental aspects are held to constitute one reality. In the final section, I motivate, though I do not argue, for ethical supernaturalism as a viable and probably plausible alternative to a humanist account of African ethics, in so far as it best accommodates our duties to some aspects of the environment.

---

related. Hence, being or existence in general and morality are closely intertwined among ... most African communities' (Chemhuru 2013: 74). Alasdair MacIntyre's observation that 'it is only in the seventeenth century, when this distinguishing of the moral from the theological, the legal and the aesthetic has become a received doctrine that the project of an independent rational justification of morality becomes not merely the concern of individual thinkers, but central to Northern European culture' (1981: 39). The African moral tradition insists on rejecting this distinguishing of the moral and metaphysical (Imafidon 2013: 48, 49). The separation of these categories makes sense if one removes God as premise, an approach I reject. I leave a thorough enquiry into this issue for another project to justify why Africans should not take seriously the *is/ought* gap. In that project, I will give a thorough response to Metz (2013: 189–204).

[7] My comments and analysis only involve analysis of humanism as is dominant in African philosophy, they may apply to other related forms of humanism in other traditions that share similar features to the humanism rejected here.

5.2 Defining (Secular) Humanism

In teasing out humanism, I consider the works of three influential African scholars: Wiredu,[8] Gyekye[9] and Metz.[10] I consider these three scholars based on their influence and the quality of their work in the African tradition. Gyekye defines 'humanism' as the 'the doctrine that sees human needs, interests and dignity as fundamental, thus constitutes the foundation for Akan morality' (1995: 143). Thus, according to Gyekye, one cannot meaningfully and sufficiently talk about morality unless one has made essential reference to some human properties, specifically human needs, interests and dignity. We need not now resolve the question of which, among these three properties mentioned by Gyekye, is the foundational property. It suffices to observe that some human property is a foundation for morality.

Like Gyekye, Wiredu defines 'humanism' as the claim that 'it is a human being that has value' (Wiredu 1992: 194); or, as he puts it in another place, 'the first axiom of all Akan axiological thinking is that man or woman is the measure of all value' (Wiredu 1996: 65). According to Wiredu, the source and sit of all value, including moral value, is found in a human person. Metz, on his part, describes his view as 'ethical naturalism' (2007: 328), but never quite identifies his view as based on facts about human beings, although he implies humanism—as I will show below.

So, we aptly observe that humanism is a meta-ethical a claim—a view about the nature of moral properties—that the source of all moral value is essentially inherent in some human property or fact, hence natural/physical and secular. I note and emphasise that these authors deliberately sever God or any spiritual entity as responsible for the relevant moral property that inheres in human beings. In other words, in the absence of human beings there is no legitimate ground to talk about morality even if God were to be present in the world. All other aspects of reality,

---

[8]Kwasi Wiredu can truly be described as an elder of African philosophy, boasting more than forty years as a professional philosopher. He is a Professor Emeritus at the University of South Florida; he has held a number of visiting professorships internationally; he has served on a number of distinguished committees and his publications record speaks volumes about the quality of his work. It is for this reason that I decided to explore the ethical work of this seasoned African philosopher, who has been exploring various issues in the African tradition.

[9]Kwame Gyekye, in his own right, is an elder of African philosophy. He is a professor of philosophy at the University of Ghana. He has published books and articles in the area of African philosophy. He is famous for his intense debate with a Nigerian philosopher Ifeanyi Menkiti with whom he graduated from Harvard. I picked his account because his ethical and political view of 'moderate communitarianism' has had a great influence on African moral and political philosophy for the past twenty years or so.

[10]Thaddeus Metz is an American scholar who has relocated to South Africa, a Distinguished Research Professor of Philosophy at the University of Johannesburg. Metz's philosophical contribution to African philosophy or ubuntu is impressive both in quality and quantity; it is thus not surprising that he has been granted an A-rating research status by the National Research Funding (South Africa). I included him in this list firstly because of the quality of work he has done in the field of African ethics. In the space of about seven years or so, he has developed an ethical system that is influenced, among others, by Desmond Tutu, famous for chairing the South African Truth and Reconciliation Commission, and turned it into a philosophically robust view that has interesting implications for bioethics, environmental ethics and political philosophy.

the supernatural and the natural (environment) are morally neutral; morality is only possible when there are human beings.

I do not wish to give the reader a false impression that it is not possible to talk of a non-secular humanism in the African tradition, and other traditions. But, here, I am addressing myself to a dominant (view in the literature) but problematic secular humanism that interprets morality purely in terms of some human property. Thinkers like Bujo (2005), Magesa (1997), Shutte (2001) (and others) appear to be articulating a spiritual humanism. But, it is not a task of this article to consider this spiritual moral vision.

5.3   Three Humanistic Theories in the African Tradition

5.3.1   Gyekye's Humanistic Ethics

I think it is best to interpret Gyekye's moral theory as flowing from his onto-logical conception of human nature, which is dualistic: individuality (autonomy) and community (common good). This interpretation is best borne out in his defence of what he calls 'moderate communitarianism', a view he pro-pounds as a response to what he considers to be 'extreme communitarianism' (1995: 39). The latter view, according to Gyekye, has been advocated by African leaders after independence and finds philosophical expression in the works of a Nigerian philosopher Menkiti (2004: 324–8[11]). Gyekye identifies one major problem with 'extreme communitarianism': this view defines a person as entirely constituted by social relations and as a result tends to overlook the individual aspects of a person, which in turn implies that this theory has no place for (individual) human rights (1995: 39).

On his part, Gyekye favours a conception of communitarianism which at heart balances the individual and communal aspects of a human person, a view he believes to be consistent with basic human (individual) rights. In this regard he states:

> The restricted communitarianism offers a more appropriate and adequate account of the self…in that it addresses the dual features of the self: as a communal being and as … autonomous …. (Gyekye 1992: 113)

In his later statement of moderate communitarianism, he avers:

> The view seems to represent a clear attempt to come to terms with the natural sociality as well as the individuality of the human person. It requires the recognition of communality and individuality… I think the most satisfactory way to recognize the claims of both communality and individuality is to ascribe to them the *status of equal moral standing*. (Gyekye 1995: 41, emphasis mine)

---

[11] I here only reference Menkiti's (2004) piece since it is a more systematic and accurate expression of his position with regards to the personhood debate than the initial statement.

It is interesting to note that Gyekye believes that these supposed ontological properties that constitute a self are also a basis for determining moral value.[12] In other words, humanity itself, or some understanding of what it means to be human, is a function of morality: the human feature of *autonomy* grounds dignity, as a fundamental moral fact, and that of *community* grounds welfare as a basic moral fact.[13] If my interpretation of Gyekye is true, then his is truly a humanistic ethics.

5.3.2   Wiredu's Humanistic Ethics

To elucidate on his moral theory, Wiredu appeals to an Akan maxim—'it is a human being who has value' (1992: 194)—which when correctly construed amounts to two moral claims:

> Through the first meaning the message is imparted that all value derives from human interests and through the second that human fellowship is the most important of human needs. (ibid.)

From this quotation it is clear that value—in fact, as an ardent reader would have observed, Wiredu states that *all* value, and I may add, moral value—derives from human interests. Thus, moral value on Wiredu's ethics is derived on some facts, interests or welfare, about human beings—I observe that Wiredu in his writings uses the words 'interests' and 'welfare' interchangeably (Wiredu 1992: 194, 1996: 65, 2004: 18). The source or foundation of morality is some human property: welfare.

5.3.3   Metz's Humanistic Ethics

In terms of moral foundations, Metz favours a secular ethics, which he describes as 'ethical naturalism'. On face value, it is not clear what natural item in the furniture of the world will serve as a basis for his naturalistic ethical theory. His proclivity towards humanism is indicated by his endorsement of humanistic interpretations by Gyekye and Wiredu (Metz 2007: 328, special attention to footnote 25). Metz's clearest statement of humanism is found in his theory of moral status (2011: 387–402, see also Molefe 2017a, b). In this particular article, he defends a 'modal–relationist' interpretation of moral status. On this account, some entity has moral status in so far

---

[12]The *is/ought* distinction is generally ignored in the African tradition or does not appear to be considered to be a problem, as I noted earlier. Furthermore, I hope the reader has noted that I, unlike Gyekye, used the phrase 'moral value' rather than 'moral standing' since the latter is typically used in bioethical context to refer to moral status.

[13]Gyekye on his part argues that his ethic is only based on one fundamental fact of welfare. I argue (along with Metz) that if one takes into consideration Gyekye's moderate communitarian view, his ethics is best construed as dualistic: dignity and welfare (common good) as basic moral facts (Metz 2012: 61, 62). My argument for this interpretation of Gyekye is in my Ph.D. dissertation, which is currently being marked.

as it has the ability to commune with human beings in a particular way. The relevant relational property that qualifies some entity for a full moral status is essentially a human feature. Human beings thus serve a basis for determining the moral standing of other entities. Metz defends this conception of moral status thus:

> Below I contend that the most promising kind of relationalism is one according to which something has moral status insofar as it has a certain relation to human beings in particular .... (2011: 390)

I advise the reader to note that, according to Metz, the moral standing of non-human entities, say animals, is not a function of their possessing the relevant interactive moral property but a function of how they can commune with human beings who alone have this relevant moral property. We may ask here: why must a possession of moral status (on the part of animals for example) depend on relations with human beings? In the same article, Metz observes:

> The theory might appear to be anthropocentric in that it cashes out moral status in terms of certain human capacities. To be able to be an object of a communal relationship, on this view, is analysed in terms of a capacity to relate to normal human beings in a certain way. *And so there is an irreducible appeal to humanity in its conception of moral status.* (2011: 390, emphasis mine)

So, Metz explains moral status by appeal to some fact about a human being (human nature), specifically, the capacity for friendliness. Other entities have moral status in so far as they can be included in communal relations with human beings, but, other than that, they have no independent moral standing. On this account of moral status, if there were no human beings then there could be no talk of moral status at all since such a talk depends on some moral property which is essentially human. On this view, even if Martians may have the relevant capacity for friendliness towards other beings, like animals, they nevertheless cannot be objects or subjects of friendship with human beings, for whatever odd biological reason they have no moral status. To have moral status, for Metz is unequivocal, there is an irreducible appeal to humanity. I leave it for another project to show the implausibility of this conception of moral status insofar as it is not African and insofar as it fails to provide a satisfactory argument. It is sufficient, however, for the purposes of this article to note the humanistic moral grounds entailed by Metz's conception of moral status.

I now proceed to reject humanism as a meta-ethical theory in the African moral tradition.

5.4 Rejection of Humanism

I reject the claim that rightness and wrongness (or, morality) are definable only in terms of some human property(s), be it their interests, welfare or friendliness. My argument is predicated on certain fundamental intuitions that generally characterise African thought—that all reality is interconnected and interdependent. This argument will be successful only if one holds the view that some aspects of nature matter for their own sake, that is on facts independent of human beings.[14] I advance an argument that seeks to restore and protect the moral standing of some aspects of nature, since such an approach best coheres with an African metaphysics, which is typically represented as holistic and spiritual. By 'holism' I am referring to the claim that social (human), natural (environment) and spiritual (God, ancestors and spirits) communities are interdependent and interrelated (Bujo 2005: 424). This view is best captured thus: 'Everything – God, ancestors, humans, animals, plants and inanimate objects – is connected, interdependent and interrelated' (Verhoef and Michel 1997: 395). According to this dominant conception of African metaphysics, there is no place for separating these three categories of reality. The human is not seen as separate and above, but is considered to be an intrinsic part of this interconnected whole (Tangwa 2004: 389).

My major argument is that these humanistic accounts give an interpretation of African ethics that stands outside of this holistic metaphysical understanding. Metz, for his part, completely severs his moral theory from any supernatural considerations, though he believes his principle of right action can inform one about how to relate to these spiritual beings (2007: 328). Gyekye and Wiredu, interestingly, though they advocate a naturalist ethics, withdraw from this African metaphysics when it suits them[15] (for example, see in Deng 2004: 501). Thus, my challenge is to maintain consistency, in that, if Gyekye and Wiredu seek to articulate naturalist (humanist) moral theories, these theories must be consistent with the metaphysics that grounds it. I further challenge Metz seriously to reconsider the African status of the metaphysics that informs his ethical theory, whether it is African or non-African, if it is his quest to articulate a view that has an African pedigree (Metz 2007: 324). To facilitate my argument for rejecting humanism, I employ the following case.

5.4.1 Animal Torture and Humanism

I ask you to consider these two cases of animal torture. I imagine a Thabo who enjoys microwaving cats just for the fun of it. Or, I imagine Thabo taking pleasure in throwing chimpanzees or some animal from a tall building. These two cases in my opinion are clear instances of animal torture. It is my strongly held intuition, and of many others, that this act is not only morally wrong but also wrongs the animals in question. But, for this intuition to be acceptable, one must be committed to the claim that animals morally matter for their own sakes, that is, they have some moral status—I will define this phrase below.

---

[14] This is the view that informs much of environmental ethics: non-human components matter for their own sake (Brennan and Lo 2011).

[15] Gyekye (2010), more accurately, does not rule out completely the supernatural aspects in the domain of morality but merely assigns it the role of reinforcing it rather than grounding it. My problem with this account is that it trivialises the role of the supernatural in morality.

The heart of my argument is that secular humanism, as represented by these three influential theories, fail to give a plausible account of why Thabo's act of torturing these animals is wrong. If they do give a plausible account, they nonetheless give an unsatisfactory rationale. With regards to this case, I work on the assumption that a plausible moral account in African ethics ought to grant animals some moral status. This is why we who hold an African understanding of metaphysics find the above cases to be morally abhorrent. My position in this regard is grounded on my commitment to a certain understanding of African metaphysics.

'Moral status' is the idea that some aspects of nature, for example, in this case, cats or chimpanzees, are owed some (direct) moral duty on the basis of some moral consideration (Behrens 2011: 87). This talk of moral status serves as a normative parameter that defines what is permissible or impermissible with regards to our treatment of some aspects of nature (Toscano 2011: 14). Metz holds that talk of moral status is two-pronged: on the one hand, it is a claim about the *wrongness* of the act, that is breaking some moral code; and, on the other, it is about *wronging* the entity in question, that is making it worse off (Metz 2011: 389).

Thus, a theory of moral status must specify the relevant moral feature(s) in virtue of which some aspects of nature have moral status and others do not. Some accounts of moral status are *individualist* (they locate the relevant moral property on some internal feature of the entity in question, like memory, consciousness, rationality etc.); some are *holist* (they locate the relevant moral property on the group itself, like the ecosystem) and some accounts explain moral status by appeal to some *relational* property, like care, friendliness or love (Behrens 2011: 70).

The key issue for me with regards to humanism of whatever interpretation is: can it account for the moral status of animals, for example, without appeal to some facts or consequences for human beings? Thus, I am asking, or rather arguing that secular humanism fails to secure the idea that the act of torturing animals is wrong and wrongs the animal in question by appeal to some facts about the animal itself. Humanism, I hope to show, by its very nature does not have the *corpus* to grant animals an intrinsic moral status, that is animals cannot be good in and of themselves, insofar as humanism only grants animals moral standing that is predicated on some instrumental relationship with human beings or by derivation from some human fact. This kind of ethics, I argue, fails plausibly to capture the idea that animals matter for their own sakes in African ethics. Environmental ethics emerged as a rejection to such human-centred theories of value (Murove 2004: 196).

If all moral value is somehow essentially derived from human beings, it is not clear how and why we can say that Thabo is doing something wrong and is wronging the poor chimpanzees. It appears that common sense morality presses upon us to say something wrong is going on here. One famous line of defence for the animal is Immanuel Kant's claim to the effect that animals, for example, are valuable only indirectly (1996: 296). At the heart of this defence is the claim that torturing animals, on the part of a human being, will harden the heart and predispose one to be so cruel to human beings. One is enjoined not to harm animals as that would hurt her humanity. Thus, 'We disrespect our humanity when we act in inhumane ways towards non-persons, whatever their species' (Lori 2014).

This line of reason is interesting, but I doubt it will do the job. It fails to explain the wrong in question by appeal to some facts about the victim, the animal. The key question is: is the animal being wronged when it is tortured for fun? My intuition is that, yes it is being wronged. The indirect defence does not at all concern itself with the animal; it focuses entirely on the human person. Furthermore, we can suppose, for argument's sake, that Thabo will not develop a cruel disposition towards other human beings, his humanity will be intact. Does this mean the act of torturing animals is justified? The indirect defence, I observe, does not quite do the job of securing the moral status of animals.

I proceed to consider whether these three scholars can offer an account that shows the wrong in question with regards to animal torture, such that the animal matters for its own sake.

The challenge for Wiredu and Gyekye is almost similar, and so I consider them together initially—though I think the best reading of Wiredu is that he advocates what I dub 'humanistic-welfare' and Gyekye 'humanistic-dignity'. One possible response by Wiredu and Gyekye would be to include in their account, of that which has moral status, all aspects of nature that have a capacity for welfare. If they adopt this line of reason, then, what makes some entity morally valuable is its capacity for welfare; and, thus, dogs, human beings, cats morally matter because they all share a capacity for welfare. If they make this move, however, it immediately damages the humanist basis of their views. They must then also be willing to change their positions, to base moral values not on *human* interests/needs but on the interests or the needs of any entity which has the capacity for welfare. It appears that what does the work of accounting for moral status is not some human property per se but the relevant moral property, which can also be had by animals and also extra-terrestrial beings like Martians. Grounding moral status on some capacity for welfare itself is tantamount to rejection of humanism.

The virtue of basing moral status on some relevant moral property and not human beings per se is that it allows animals to have moral status for their own sake. It is wrong to torture a cat for fun because one would be making it worse off, that is wronging it or not respecting its capacity for welfare. But, Wiredu and Gyekye cannot comfortably take this line of reasoning, more so Wiredu, since it goes against the assertion that all moral value is derived from human beings.

The above argument, however, does more damage to Wiredu's 'humanistic-welfare' than it does to Gyekye's 'humanistic-dignity'. Wiredu's humanism only traces welfare, whereas Gyekye's traces two moral properties: welfare and dignity; thus, Gyekye's ethical account is dualist. The claim by Gyekye would thus be: animals morally matter for their own sakes since they are susceptible to welfare, they have partial moral status, but only human beings have full moral status since they also have dignity. This interpretation of Gyekye appears to save secular humanism. But, I argue that humanistic-dignity is attended by a unique problem: one of lack of *specificity* (is dignity best interpreted as based on a naturalist or supernaturalist property?) and of *identity* (to what extent does his appeal to dignity *qua* autonomy still make his account one that we can comfortably refer to as 'African' humanism).

I start with the *specificity* problem. Gyekye is committed to the notion of dignity as a central feature of a human person but he appears to be non-committal about the metaphysics that grounds this stance (Metz 2012: 63).In his first statement of his commitment to dignity and human rights, he mentions both the Christian conception of dignity *qua* the image of God and the naturalist conception of dignity *qua* autonomy as defended by Kant (Gyekye 1992: 114). If he appeals to a supernaturalist account of dignity then he is involved in a direct inconsistency (Gyekye 1992: 114) since he wants to defend a secular moral grounding; and, if he appeals to autonomy, a natural property, then he is stuck with the fact that he has no *African* metaphysical basis for this conception of dignity. I am not suggesting that it is wrong to borrow ideas from other cultures. My contention, however, is that this borrowing, on the part of Gyekye, results from a failure to articulate an ethics grounded on an African metaphysics. It is this failure that provokes the need to borrow alien concepts.

If Gyekye settles for autonomy as the basis for dignity, for the sake of consistency of seeking a natural interpretation of morality, as his writings do, in his elaboration of a self that is constituted by autonomy and communality, then one is tempted to accuse this account of being not *appropriately* African (1995: 54). Though his account, as characterised by dignity *qua* autonomy, is humanistic, I observe that it fails to bean *African* humanism. I am not claiming that for a view to be 'African' it must be devoid of foreign or alien elements—there is no such a thing as a pure culture. The essence of my argument is based on Gyekye's 'criteria of what would count as genuine African philosophy' (1995: 7). I observe he fails his own test.

Interestingly, Gyekye articulates a criterion of what is to count as a genuine African theory. His criterion stipulates two conditions. Firstly, African philosophy is to be generally derived from some 'African cultural and historical experience' (1995: 7). This implies that there must some historical or anthropological basis for grounding a position as African; it must be traceable to some facets of African culture (see also Metz 2007: 323–4). Secondly, foreign or alien elements may also be considered as part of African philosophy; but, this can be the case only if they meet certain conditions: they (foreign items) must in the unfolding of time be so infused in the stream of African culture that they will lose their alien status, that is future generations of African culture must lose sight of their alien status; and, lastly they must be accepted by the general population of the recipient culture rather than merely by its elite (Gyekye 1995: 8).

It is obvious to me that the notion of autonomy, which is a dominant Western moral concept, which grounds an influential moral and political system in its culture, is foreign to Africa (Kant 1996: 434–5). And, it is also empirically true that this notion of autonomy has not met the conditions specified by Gyekye himself before it can rightly qualify as 'African' so as to ground African humanism.[16] I hope with the unfolding of time, this notion of autonomy will take ground. But as things stand,

---

[16]I am not familiar with an African conception of what constitutes individual or even political freedom. Even the one article I am familiar with does not appeal to the common liberal stock of civil liberties or even the notion of autonomy (Siame 2005: 53–67).

it has not been infused in the mainstream of African culture and it is largely used by the elite philosophers.

Furthermore, my major concern is that Gyekye's approach is not consistent with the Akan metaphysics to which he typically appeals to ground much of his philosophical work (Gyekye 1995: 85–6). Moreover, it is even more disconcerting when local cultural resources have not been exhausted for one to conveniently select an idea that at heart clashes with his ontological conception of a self (Gyekye 1995: 85–102). Gyekye's appeal to a foreign concept would have been justified had he first demonstrated that the African cultural or historical resources cannot proffer a plausible ground for humanism or his quest for dignity and human rights—this exercise, however, is absent in his work. This is surprising given that Gyekye's conception of personhood, or his interpretation of the Akan's ontological conception of personhood, contains promising supernaturalistic categories that could be adduced to ground such an account. But such a task is abandoned and Gyekye hastily prefers 'alien' notions: the Christian idea of the image of God and/or Kant's idea of autonomy.

Thus, Gyekye's humanistic-dignity can explain what is wrong about torturing an animal—that, one is undermining the welfare of the animal in question. But, this account succeeds in being truly a humanistic theory, insofar as it is dualist, as it also appeals to dignity, but it fails to be an African humanistic theory as it flies opposite to a criteria advocated by Gyekye himself of what is to count as 'African'. We are thus stuck with a dualist account that is humanistic, but not African in the relevant sense, as it appeals to a foreign cultural item.

Metz on his part has developed a conception of moral status, which, as I have shown above is human-centred. I now criticise his human-centred theory of value. On this account, animals have moral status because they can be *objects* of friendly relationships (they can be positively affected by a friendly treatment by human beings and can be made worse off by unfriendly treatment), but they are not *subjects* of such relations—it appears only humans can be both subjects and objects of such relations, as such have full moral status, and animals have partial moral status since they can only be objects of friendly relations. This theory of moral status, as it stands, appears to have the *corpus* to tell us what is wrong with torturing animals for fun. Since animals can benefit, as objects of human friendliness, then unfriendliness makes them worse off, therefore it is wrong to torture animals for fun.

I insist however that this theory is implausible as it offers a weak rationale for protecting animals. Consider the case of a last human being on earth, who will be dying in the next few seconds. Imagine a world (W_2) with Martians who are like us in every way except that they do not have a capacity for friendship but, only, something like it, call it *friendship*. There are no animals on W_2, only Martians. It appears, upon some investigation, that Martians can have communion with animals on earth since they can be objects of *friendship*, but, for whatever reason—I stipulate—they cannot have a relationship with human beings either as objects or subjects.

On the basis of Metz's theory, Martians with their capacity for *friendship* do not have moral status since they cannot be included in community with human beings either as objects and/or subjects. Say human beings go extinct and Martians take over planet earth, on Metz's account, we have no basis to talk about moral status without an essential reference to human beings. The extinction of human beings is tantamount to the disappearance of moral status. Thus, in spite of the entities with a relevant (or close enough) capacity for moral status, since there are no human beings, there is still no moral status. If a Martian version of Thabo tortures an animal for fun, there would be no ground of even talking about the wrong or even wronging of the animal in question despite the fact that these animals can be made better or worse off by Martian *friendship* or lack thereof. The absence of human beings in the equation is decisive in Metz's conception of moral status—no human being, no moral status since Metz insists on an irreducible appeal to humanity. The animal is only protected if there are human beings, not by its own right.

The above objection, with regards to Metz's conception of moral status, is raised to motivate the case for a theory that locates moral status on some intrinsic relevant feature that does not depend on any relation to human beings. Metz's approach to moral status, wherein 'there is an irreducible appeal to humanity in its conception of moral status', makes his theory anthropocentric[17] in a problematic way for African ethics (Metz 2011: 400). This theory makes human beings a necessary feature of the world, a view that has been demonstrated to be false (Ramose 2009: 309–10). This view also commits us to speciesism, a position Metz himself wants to avoid (Metz 2011: 400).

Above, I considered whether the three accounts can account for what is wrong with the act of torturing animals. Wiredu's humanistic-welfare ultimately fails to secure animal's moral standing, if it does, it must forgo its humanism. Gyekye's dualist humanist-dignity account does secure the animal's standing at a cost of being unAfrican. And, Metz's theory does account for the wrongness of torturing animals for fun but not for their own sake, the moral standing of animals depends on the moral standing of human beings.

5.5   Failure as Grounds for the Rejection of Humanism

Why is humanism's failure to capture some aspects of the environment essential for its rejection? I argue that this failure is one that reflects the coherence test on the part of humanism. In this sense, the secular version of humanism fails to be 'African' in the relevant sense. It ease out this failure by appeal to a criterion for successful African meta-ethics, as adumbrated by Imafidon (2013: 48, 49) thus:

> an all-inclusive metaphysical notion of being permeates the notion of the good in the African traditions…Every valid norm would by all means promote and sustain equilibrium and stability in the all-inclusive structure of being united by the common essence, force. Norms that do not meet this condition cannot be justified as moral.

---

[17] More accurately, I understand Metz to be arguing for some kind of 'weak anthropocentrism', a claim that non-human components have moral status but it is less than that of human beings (Behrens 2011: 39; Metz 2011: 389). But, I think all interpretations of anthropocentrism fail correctly to capture an African ethics.

I take seriously the claim that 'the good' (all moral value) is a function of an all-inclusive metaphysical notion of being. The failure of these three accounts of humanism follows from their failure to present an understanding of 'the good' in a way that coheres with this all-inclusive structure of being, that is a holistic (spiritual) ontological system that characterises African thought.

Before I further analyse and expand on the criteria set out by Imafidon, I show the reader that this idea that morality flows from an all-inclusive structure of reality is a common one in the African tradition. Africans do not merely advocate what we described above as 'metaphysical holism', they further talk about 'moral holism'—the claim that things are interconnected, but these relations matter morally. For example, Munyaradzi Felix Murove, an African philosopher from Zimbabwe who studies the notions of 'ukama' and 'ubuntu', argues that 'African ethics arises from an understanding of the world as an interconnected whole whereby what it means to be ethical is inseparable from all spheres of existence... This relatedness blurs the distinction between humanity and nature, the living and the dead, the divine and the human' (Murove 2009: 29).

On the same note, Nel argues 'that the most common feature of this cosmology is the integration of three distinguishable aspects, namely environment, society, and the spiritual. All activities are informed by this holistic understanding ... An act is never separated from its environmental, societal and spiritual impact' (Nel 2008: 37–8). In this thinking, morality ought not to be reduced to one aspect of reality, it must encompass all aspects of reality—the environment, the social and spiritual—something that secular humanism fails to do must serve as a basis for morality.

To build my case further, I need to clarify what Imafidon means by an 'all-inclusive metaphysical notion of being'. I understand this phrase, as I indicated above, to represent a typical understanding of an African ontological system as holistic, both descriptively and normatively (see also Bujo 2005: 424; Imafidon 2013: 40–2; Menkiti 2004: 328–9; Shutte 2001: 22; Teffo and Roux 2003: 196–7). If 'the good' truly is to be a function of this holistic understanding of reality, it is problematic, it appears to me, to reduce the good to one aspect of this system—some human feature. A commitment to metaphysical/moral holism resists the kind of *reductionism* that characterises humanism, wherein one reduces all morality to one aspect of the whole, human beings. This reductive approach fails the criteria, as set out by Imafidon, that the good is a function of the interaction of three aspects of reality.

Moreover, this failure is best reflected by these accounts' inability to plausibly accommodate some aspects of nature in their moral system. This failure is a result, I observe, of working with only one fragment of reality as the basis for moral value.

I further observe that secular humanism exaggerates on its conception of a position occupied by human beings in the African ontology—human beings are generally considered to hold a *central* role (Shutte 2001: 14). These African scholars, I observe, take a leap from the view that human beings play a *central* role, to an untenable position that human beings play a *high (foundational)* role—the role of God. I use the words *central* and *high* informed by a dominant African conception of an African ontological system, which is sometimes represented spherically (Menkiti 2004: 327) and often hierarchically (Bujo 2005: 424; Shutte 2001: 13). In the latter representation, God is located at the apex ('high'), followed by ancestors and spirits and at the centre is human beings and then followed by lower forms of life like animals, plants and so on. It appears strange to me that a central being can be the source of morality rather than a being that is most sublime and transcendental, God. I am here not making an argument but merely expressing an intellectual concern that this way of interpreting the African system of reality does not strike the chord of my intuition at all, given the dominant conception of African ontology.

I hold the view that the central role played by human beings does not imply anthropocentrism. This view is best defended by these works (Behrens 2011: 2, 33, 49–56; LenkaBula 2008: 375–94). I also reject the view that interprets the central role played by humans to mean that 'in ethics, man proposes and God reinforces' (cited in Imafidon 2013: 51; see also Gyekye 2010). The idea that man *proposes ethics* does not necessarily imply humanism, it could just imply, 'ethical subjectivism'[18] or even 'cultural relativism',[19] the idea that man somehow invents morality, which is implied by the notion of *proposing* morality. A charitable reading, however, would imply humanism, where human interests objectively defined determine the right and God merely reinforces or upholds morality (Gyekye 2010).

A more moderate view—one which coheres with an African ontology—does not claim that man is the source of morality but, rather, man is the best entry to morality among the empirical beings. Since the social category stands at the centre of all reality, for the human being, she is the best interpreter of morality. The human community gives us some clues and cues on our quest for harmony among existing entities in the universe (Behrens 2011: 62). In this sense, morality depends on God insofar as he gave human beings a sense of morality or conscience (Gbadegesin 2005: 414–15) or, insofar as human beings have been endowed with some capacity that qualifies them to have a moral perspective that uniquely positions them to connect and respond to the *needs* of other human beings, the environment and the spiritual realm[20] (Cornell 2009: 47–8).

5.6 Motivation for Supernaturalism

I reconstruct a robust spiritualist African ethics. I observe that the notion of vitality offers a promising alternative to the humanist accounts I rejected here, both as a meta-ethical and as a normative theory. As a meta-ethical theory, it defines rightness as a function of some (positive) relation to this spiritual energy. On this view, the will of God is not expressed through His commands as found in the divine com-

---

[18]This is a meta-ethical value that claims that rightness is a function of a 'say so' of a subject or individual. Morality is here determined by the subject.

[19]This is a meta-ethical view that claims that morality is a function of a 'say so' of a culture. Morality here is determined by a culture.

[20]In my Ph.D. I defend this particular view, wherein I argue that human beings have a capacity for transcendental care, which serves as a ground-norm against which to distinguish right from wrong actions, a conception of moral status, human dignity and rights (Molefe 2014).

mands but, rather, the will of God is expressed by maintaining a balance among these 'spirit-filled' entities. This meta-ethical view promises at least three normative theories, which attempt to give some account of what counts as positive or negative relation to vitality: a perfectionist ethics—an act is right insofar as it perfects an individuals' spiritual nature; a vitalistic-utilitarian principle—an act is right insofar as it maximises the vital load of the society; and, lastly, a deontological principle of vitality—an act is right insofar as it honours a person's spiritual energy. This view also plausibly explains why it is wrong to torture a cat or chimpanzee for fun; by so doing, one would be failing to honour the vitality of the entity in question, since it possesses some.

5.7 Conclusion

I argued that humanism is not a plausible interpretation of the African moral tradition since it does not cohere with some dominant conception of African metaphysics, which is plainly religious. I demonstrated the implausibility of humanistic ethical theories through their failure to capture one vital aspect of African metaphysics, specifically the fact that some non-human components matter for their own sakes. Or, I argued to the effect that it is implausible to interpret the African moral theories to be anthropocentric, as do Gyekye, Wiredu and Metz, since this fails to cohere with the holistic picture of African metaphysics I described.

I also suggested a preferable theory of morality (the good) that best coheres with an all-inclusive African metaphysics, which is as much spiritual as it is material. The literature as it stands has not yet provided a systematic and rational account of ethical supernaturalism or even non-naturalism. I closed by motivating for a vitality based meta-ethics, that is a view that promises to give an interesting meta-ethical and normative theories, which, on the face of it, appear well poised to explain what is wrong with torturing animals for fun—one would not be respecting the vitality of the animal in question.

References

Behrens, K. 2011. *African Philosophy, Thought and Practice and Their Contribution to Environmental Ethics*. Johannesburg: University of Johannesburg.

Brennan, A., and Y. Lo. 2011. Environmental Ethics. In *The Stanford Encyclopaedia of Philosophy*, ed. E. Zalta. http://plato.stanford.edu/archives/fall2011/entries/ethics-environmental/. Accessed 16 Jan 2013.

Bujo, B. 2005. Differentiations in African Ethics. In *The Blackwell Companion to Religious Ethics*, ed. W. Schweiker, 419–434. Oxford: Blackwell Publishing.

Chemhuru, M. 2013. The Ethical Import in African Ethics: A Critical Discourse in Shona Environmental Ethics. In *Ontologized Ethics: New Essays in African Meta-Ethics*, ed. E. Imafidon and J. Bewaji, 73–89. New York: Lexington Books.

Cornell, D. 2009. Ubuntu, Pluralism and the Responsibility of Legal Academics to the New South Africa. *Law Critique* 20: 43–58.

Deng, F. 2004. Human Rights in the African Context. In *Companion to African Philosophy*, ed. K. Wiredu, 499–508. Oxford: Blackwell Publishing.

Dzobo, K. 1992. Values in a Changing Society: Man, Ancestors and God. In *Person and Community: Ghanaian Philosophical Studies*, vol. 1, ed. K. Gyekye and K. Wiredu, 223–242. Washington, DC: Council for Research in Values and Philosophy.

Gbadegesin, S. 2005. Origins of African Ethics. In *The Blackwell Companion to Religious Ethics*, ed. W. Schweiker, 413–423. Oxford: Blackwell Publishing.

Gyekye, K. 1992. Person and Community in Akan Thought. In *Ghanaian Philosophical Thought Studies*, vol. 1, ed. K. Gyekye and K. Wiredu, 101–122. Washington DC: Council for Research in Values and Philosophy.

Gyekye, K. 1995. *An Essay on African Philosophical Thought: The Akan Conceptual Scheme.* Philadelphia: Temple University Press.

Gyekye, K. 1997. *Tradition and Modernity.* New York: Oxford University Press.

Gyekye, K. 2010. African Ethics. In *The Stanford Encyclopedia of Philosophy*, ed. E.N. Zalta. http://plato.stanford.edu/archives/fall2011/entries/african-ethics. Accessed 16 Jan 2013.

Imafidon, E. 2013. On the Ontological Foundation of a Social Ethics in African Traditions. In *Ontologized Ethics: New Essays in African Meta-Ethics*, ed. E. Imafidon and J. Bewaji, 37–54. New York: Lexington Books.

Kant, E. 1996. *Groundwork of the Metaphysics of Morals.* Trans. M. Gregor. Cambridge: Cambridge University Press.

LenkaBula, P. 2008. Beyond Anthropocentricity-Botho/Ubuntu and the Quest for Economic and Ecological Justice. *Religion and Theology* 15: 375–394.

Lori, G. 2014. The Moral Status of Animals. In *The Stanford Encyclopedia of Philosophy*, ed. E. Zalta. http://plato.stanford.edu/archives/fall2014/entries/moral-animal/. Accessed 6 Feb 2014.

MacIntyre, A. 1981. *After Virtue.* Notre Dame: University of Notre Dame Press.

Magesa, L. 1997. *African Religion: The Moral Traditions of Abundant Life.* New York: Orbis Books.

Menkiti, I. 2004. On the Normative Conception of a Person. In *Companion to African Philosophy*, ed. K. Wiredu, 324–331. Oxford: Blackwell Publishing.

Metz, T. 2007. Toward an African Moral Theory. *The Journal of Political Philosophy* 15: 321–341.

Metz, T. 2010. Human Dignity, Capital Punishment and an African Moral Theory: Toward a New Philosophy of Human Rights. *Journal of Human Rights* 9: 81–99.

Metz, T. 2011. Ubuntu as a Moral Theory and Human Rights in South Africa. *African Human Rights Law Journal* 11: 532–559.

Metz, T. 2012. An African Theory of Moral Status: A Relational Alternative to Individualism and Holism. *Ethical Theory and Moral Practice: An International Forum* 14: 387–402.

Metz, T. 2013. Two Conceptions of African Ethics in the Work of D. A. Masolo. *Quest* 25: 7–15.

Molefe, M. 2014. *Explorations in African Meta-Ethical Thought: Can a Case be Made for a Supernaturalist Position.* Doctoral thesis. Johannesburg: University of Johannesburg.

Molefe, M. 2017a. A Critique of Thad Metz's African Theory of Moral Status. *South African Journal of Philosophy* 36: 195–205.

Molefe, M. 2017b. African Religious Ethics and the Euthyphro Problem. *Acta Academica* 49: 22–38.

Molefe, M. 2018. African Metaphysics and Religious Ethics. *Filosofia Theoretica* 7: 19–37.

Murove, F. 2004. An African Commitment to Ecological Conservation: The Shona Concepts of Ukama and Ubuntu. *Mankind Quarterly* 45: 195–225.

Murove, F. 2007. The Shona Ethic of Ukama with Reference to the Immortality of Values. *The Mankind Quarterly* 48: 179–189.

Murove, F. 2009. Beyond the Savage Evidence Ethic. In *African Ethics: An Anthology of Comparative and Applied Ethics*, ed. F. Murove, 14–32. Pietermaritzburg: University of KwaZulu-Natal Press.

Nel, P. 2008. Morality and Religion in African Thought. *Acta Theologica* 2: 33–44.

Okeja, U. 2013. *Normative Justification of a Global Ethic: A Perspective from African Philosophy*. New York: Lexington Books.

Ramose, M. 2009. Ecology through Ubuntu. In *African Ethics: An Anthology of Comparative and Applied Ethics*, ed. F. Murove, 308–314. Pietermaritzburg: University of KwaZulu-Natal Press.

Shutte, A. 2001. *Ubuntu: An Ethic for a New South Africa*. Pietermaritzburg: Cluster Publications.

Siame, N. 2005. Two Concepts of Liberty Through African Eyes. *The Journal of Political Philosophy* 8: 53–67.

Tangwa, G. 2004. Some African Reflections on Biomedical and Environmental Ethics. In *A Companion to African Philosophy*, ed. K. Wiredu, 387–395. Oxford: Blackwell Publishing.

Teffo, J., and A. Roux. 2003. Metaphysical Thinking in Africa. In *The African Philosophy Reader*, ed. P.H. Coetzee and A. Roux, 192–208. New York: Routledge.

Toscano, M. 2011. Human Dignity as High Moral Status. *The Ethics Forum* 6: 4–25.

Verhoef, H., and C. Michel. 1997. Studying Morality within the African Context: A Model of Moral Analysis and Construction. *Journal of Moral Education* 26: 389–407.

Wiredu, K. 1992. Moral Foundations of an African Culture. In *Person and Community: Ghanaian Philosophical Studies*, vol. 1, ed. K. Wiredu and K. Gyekye, 192–206. Washington DC: The Council for Research in Values and Philosophy.

Wiredu, K. 1996. *Cultural Universals and Particulars: An African Perspective*. Indianapolis: Indiana University Press.

Wiredu, K. 2004. Introduction: African Philosophy in Our Time. In *A Companion to African Philosophy*, ed. K. Wiredu, 1–27. Oxford: Blackwell Publishing.

Part II
Ubuntu and the Environment

Chapter 6
Ubuntu Environmental Ethics: Conceptions and Misconceptions

Ephraim Taurai Gwaravanda

Abstract Scholars of African Environmental Ethics have defended *Ubuntu* Environmental Ethics as an indigenous, attractive and relevant conception that is suitable for African culture and very little criticism has been offered to refine, revisit and problematise the concept. I argue that a generalised version of *Ubuntu* Environmental Ethics is problematic on several grounds. Firstly, the attempt to describe *Ubuntu* Environmental Ethics as shared in diverse African cultures commits the fallacy of hasty generalisation by trying to misrepresent diverse versions of environmental ethics into a single understanding. Secondly, considering various linguistic groups that share a common understanding of environmental thinking, it is hegemonic in tendency, to pick up a single linguistic version and come up with *Ubuntu* Environmental Ethics without showing other variants such as *unhu, bunhu, untu, vumunhu* and related versions. Thirdly, a generalized view of *Ubuntu* Environmental Ethics that is abstracted from specific cultural contexts such as Xhosa, Zulu, Ndebele, Shona, Ndau, Xitsonga, Venda, Tonga among others, results in ambiguity and vagueness rather than clarity and precision. Fourthly, a general view of *Ubuntu* Environmental Ethics gives a closed conception that fails to open up for debate and diversity in thinking about the environment in Southern African cultures. Fifthly, a geographical demarcation of *Ubuntu* Environmental Ethics that describes it as 'Sub-Saharan' is not only inadequatebut also arbitrary. The inadequacy of the demarcation is seen in the absence of the idea of *Ubuntu* Environmental Ethics in West Africa (Nigeria, Senegal, Ghana); East Africa (Uganda, Kenya Tanzania) and Central Africa (Gabon, Equatorial Guinea, Democratic Republic of Congo) yet all these regions are in Sub-Saharan Africa. The arbitrary nature of the demarcation is seen in failure to give a rational justification of the label resulting in a mismatch between the term and the region it attempts to refer. After examining these problems I shall give a proposal of how to re-conceptualise Environmental Ethics in Southern African cultures without falling into the said problems.

E. T. Gwaravanda (✉)
University of Johannesburg, Johannesburg, South Africa
e-mail: etgwaravanda@gmail.com

Great Zimbabwe University, Masvingo, Zimbabwe

© Springer Nature Switzerland AG 2019
M. Chemhuru (ed.), *African Environmental Ethics*, The International Library of Environmental, Agricultural and Food Ethics 29,
https://doi.org/10.1007/978-3-030-18807-8_6

6.1 Introduction

In this chapter, I critically examine the generalized view of environmental ethical thinking in sub-Saharan Africa. *Ubuntu* environmental ethics can be used to represent environmental thinking by way of drawing similarities from related cultures and come up with a general understanding of environmental ethics in a number of African countries such as South Africa, Zimbabwe, Mozambique, Zambia, Malawi, Namibia, Botswana, Lesotho and Swaziland among others. While the emphasis on shared characteristics or similarities may be noble, it is high time to examine the different approaches to environmental ethics that are culturally contextualized. The exclusion or silencing of other approaches produces a partial picture of environmental ethics. In this chapter, I defend the position that environmental ethics should be researched from specific cultural standpoints so as to avoid the fallacy of hasty generalisation and provide diversity and richness in the contributions to African environmental ethics. Several scholars have explored *Ubuntu* environmental ethics on the basis of similarities or shared characteristics that apply to either sub-Saharan Africa in general or southern Africa in particular.

According to Ramose (1999) in the context of *Ubuntu* environmental ethics, to care for one another implies caring for physical nature as well. Without such care, the interdependence between human beings and physical nature would be undermined. Moreover, human beings are indeed an intrinsic part of the physical nature although possibly a privileged part (Ramose 1999). Accordingly, caring for one another is the fulfillment of the natural duty to care for physical nature too. Murove (2004) examines the concept of *Ubuntu* in ecological conservation and demonstrates the importance of community and relationality in ecological thought. Behrens (2010) explores *Ubuntu* as an African holistic ethic that has relevance to the environment. Shumba (2011) argues that *Ubuntu* provides an ethical framework for sustainable resource utilization in Southern Africa and beyond. Mawere (2012) argues that *Ubuntu* can be used for environmental conservation by focusing on South-Eastern Zimbabwe. Le Grange (2012) connects *Ubuntu* to environmental *Ubuntu* and environmental ethics through education and argues that *Ubuntu* is a rich theory that is relevant to Southern African societies. Museka and Madondo (2012) maintain that *Ubuntu* provides insights for a relevant and sound environmental ethics pedagogy. Although these authors exploit the environmental educational implications of *Ubuntu*, they provide a foundation of elements of environmental ethics in *Ubuntu*. Mawere (2014) contends that *Ubuntu* is a robust ethical theory for environmental conservation in the face of pollution, global warming, droughts and degradation. All the above scholars have made significant contributions by exploiting the similarities of *Ubuntu* environmental ethics as drawn from several cultures in southern Africa. These scholars also hold that their findings can be generalized to Southern Africa and to Sub-Saharan Africa. With the aim of refining *Ubuntu* environmental ethics, this chapter attempts to examine the diversity of *Ubuntu* environmental ethics as represented by the multiple cultures and argue for further research into the cultural variants so as to enrich environmental ethics.

The work is divided into six main sections. In the first section I discuss the fallacy of hasty generalisation, its root causes and the misconceptions it gives to environmental ethics and possible remedies on how to avoid the fallacy. In the second section, I explore the role of linguistic hegemony in constructing a concept of environmental ethics that marginalizes and excludes languages from other cultures to give a misleading view of linguistic uniformity. In the third section, I argue that the generalized view of *ubuntu* environmental ethics, while it has roots in specific cultures, fails to apply meaningfully to cultures that may not use terms such as hunhu environmental ethics, vuntu environmental ethics and related notions. In the fourth section, my argument is that the generalised view of *ubuntu* closes instead of opening for debates, comparisons and analysis. In the fifth section, I argue that environmental ethics in sub-Saharan Africa is diverse because it is influenced by a variety of geographical factors such as climate, soils, vegetation, animals and water bodies among other factors. In the last section, I critically examine a number of approaches to environmental ethics and defend a cultural standpoint position to environmental ethics.

6.2   Generalisations About *Ubuntu* Environmental Ethics

An inductive generalisation is an argument that draws a conclusion about all members of a group from evidence that pertains to a selected sample. The fallacy of hasty generalisation occurs when there is a reasonable likelihood that the sample is not representative of the group. "Such a likelihood may arise if the sample is either too small or not randomly selected" (Hurley 2011:142). The most extreme forms of the fallacy involves proceeding from *one* individual to *all* members of a group. In the context of this study generalisations involve picking the concept of '*ubuntu*' from three Nguni cultures namely, "Zulu, Xhosa and Ndebele" (Van Nierkerk 2015: 3) and generalizing it to other cultures. The concept of *Ubuntu* is then tied to environmental ethics to give a generalised view of environmental ethics. The fallacy of hasty generalisation consists in a situation where the premises cite a few cases and the conclusion says something about the whole group. In this study, Zulu and Ndebele languages give the word *ubuntu* while Sesotho expresses it as Botho/Matho; isiXhosa gives umuntu; Shona gives hunhu; Bemba gives umuntu and Venda speaks of Vhuntu to name a few. The problematic aspect is in picking one linguistic word and generalizing it to other non-*ubuntu* indigenous languages. The generalisation may create the misconception that there is a homogenous environmental ethical thinking yet there are variations and diversities. Giving equivalent notions from cognitive languages gives a rich scenario where research can unearth specific notions of environmental ethical thought that are immune to generalisations. The use of equivalent ethical notions help to broaden *ubuntu* environmental thinking.

I shall identify and examine three levels of generalisations. First order—continental generalisations about environmental ethics attempt to extract elements that are applicable to the whole of Africa through some kind of inductive reasoning. This reasoning builds some degree of probability that is established when one builds from particular to the general. When one draws elements of environmental ethics from Akan, Zulu, Yoruba or Ndebele culture for instance, these elements are generalized to the entire continent. The advantage of this type of generalisation is that it makes it possible to examine issues in the context of "African environmental ethics." Second order or sub-regional generalisation allows scholars to pick elements from one or a few cultures and then apply them across the sub-region. The idea of *ubuntu* environmental ethics as advanced by a number of scholars takes this route. The advantage of this approach is that it yields a higher level of probability when one compares the content of the premises and the conclusion in the inductive argument. Third order generalisation occurs within a cultural grouping is more focused and it yields fruitful results since there is no room for a mismatch between the content of the premises and the content of the conclusion. The exactness obtained in the conclusion allows the researcher to generalize more accurately within the culture under investigation. *Ubuntu* environmental ethics, for example, fits very well for both Zulu and Ndebele cultures without any danger of going beyond the content of the finding.

However there is danger in that conclusions drawn from the inductive generalisations give rise to "lies, illusions and mystifications about Africa" (Ajei 2007: 227). Generalisations about environmental ethics in Africa tend to give a false impression of homogeneity in African environmental ethics. A closer analysis of African environmental thinking shows diversity based on environmental factors such as climate, physical features, water bodies and related aspects. Furthermore, Africa is treated differently from other parts of the third world, that is, South East Asia and Latin America. Africa is seen by the West as the most primitive and the most underdeveloped, the most miserable and the most incapable and the continent with the least culture (Palmberg 2001). Africa is a continent with 54 countries, nearly 2000 languages and more than 750 million people (Palmberg 2001) and this linguistic diversity makes generalisations almost impossible. If done, generalisations yield weakly probable conclusions whose cogency is doubtful. Cultural variety varies from the nomads in semi-arid lands to those permanently settled in the cities (Palmberg 2001). These cultural differences make it very difficult to defend generalised arguments about African environmental ethics based on ubuntu. Customs and habits vary from Tunusia in the north to the kwaZulu of south east South Africa (Palmberg 2001). These customs also influence diversity in environmental management, exploitation and conservation. Africa is talked about as if its parts are interchangeable and this problem is also seen in thinking about *ubuntu* environmental ethics. Although one must concede that generalisations sometimes have to be made, neither the standards of language nor the need to summarise and be brief can be used to defend the sweeping generalisations about Africa (Palmberg 2001). The need to bring about similarities in *ubuntu* environmental ethics, though acceptable, may not justify the extent of the generalisations made. Europeans saw sameness in Africa yet Africans saw it as all difference. If the concept of Africa is not dissolved into smaller parts, it will be difficult to encounter culture in Africa. Generalisations are to the extent that "one African is all Africans" (Palmberg 2001: 199). Such a sweeping generalisation not only logically untenable but it is also false. A picture of one Africa stands for all Africans with neither name nor place (Palmberg 2001: 199). Such a generalisation is sweeping and misleading.

"Unanimism," as coined by Hountondji (1996: 60) is "the illusion that all men and women in [African] societies speak with one voice and share the same opinion about all fundamental issues." The myth holds that African persons are fundamentally united in their views about the most important matters in life. This kind of thinking has been applied to *ubuntu* environmental ethics as well. This idea originated in colonial discourse about Africa, and Hountondji (1996: 60) argues that it is not enough simply to put a positive spin on the traits that define African identity. The very idea of a global African mentality or worldview distorts the richness and cultural diversity of African peoples. Hountondji (1996: 60) sees unanimism as a distinct liability, since it fails to take into account real differences among Africans in addressing the complex environmental problems that beset the continent.

The root causes of generalisations are firstly, the attempt to seek essential features. Generalisations are used in order to pick up essential features that are common in African environmental ethics. These essential features are used as the foundation and building blocks of a uniquely African environmental ethics. Secondly, the attempt to make a distinction with Western or Eurocentric approaches (Serequeberhan 1996) results in the tendency to contrast with 'Western environmental ethics' is one reason why generalisations are made in African environmental ethics. African environmental ethics is informed by the African epistemological paradigm as opposed to the Eurocentric epistemological paradigm (Gyekye 1997; Akena 2012). The third reason is colonial mentality as shown in Tempels (1969) who is the father of generalisations in African philosophy. Writing from the central Africa, Tempels generalized his philosophy across the continent without taking appropriate care. The same mistake was also followed by Mbiti (1999) when he claimed that Africans have no concept of 'future time.' Having discussed generalisation, the next section focuses on linguistic hegemony.

6.3 Linguistic Hegemony in Thinking About *Ubuntu* Environmental Ethics

Linguistic hegemony is a creation of colonialism where cognitive languages were grouped together for the sake of easy conceptualization of these languages by the coloniser. The hegemonic tendency involved the marginalisation of other languages and this creates a problem if environmental ethics follows the sidelining route. Environmental ethics should pick from the rich linguistic and cultural variations that have distinct environmental ethical thinking instead of lumping these together thereby giving the misconception that term *ubuntu* is easily understood outside the Nguni languages. Muchemwa and Mazuru (2016), for example, argue that Shona and Ndebele were used by the colonial Rhodesian government for language hegemony and imperialism. The term "Shona" does not capture any linguistic grouping. The linguistic groups that were originally found in Zimbabwe are Karanga, Ndau, Zezuru, Korekore and Manyika. Members of the mentioned linguistic groups preferred to call themselves by their totems and not by their languages. The term "Shona" was created by Doke who used Zezuru for standardising other dialects. Zezuru becomes the hegemonic dialect for writing of Shona because it sidelines other dialects. In most western parts of Zimbabwe, Ndebele language was used to sideline Tonga, Kalanga, Nambia, Venda, Sotho and Xhosa through systematic elimination of the sidelined languages. Such hegemonic tendencies can be seen in conceiving *ubuntu* environmental ethics.

The use of *ubuntu* in conceiving environmental ethics in sub-Saharan Africa fails to avoid colonial mentality that employed language hegemony and imperialism. Language hegemony consists of picking one language and it is used to represent other languages without a careful consideration of the linguistic variations. Language hegemony creates resistance rather than openness and dialogue in conceiving environmental issues in Southern African communities. It is surprising that researchers in Shona environmental ethics, for example, may use *ubuntu* instead of hunhu environmental ethics. This gives a discrepancy between the researchers' ideas and community ideas about environmental ethics. This points to the fact that *ubuntu* environmental ethics is more of an academic construction than reality which is found on the ground. Talk of *Vumuntu* environmental ethics in Venda gives a close link to the community in which the notion is found. If environmental ethics is tied down to linguistic variations, we may have as many environmental ethical thoughts as there are languages.

Variations ate found within specific languages and this gives the idea of dialects. In Shona, for example, the following dialects are found; Karanga, Ndau, Zezuru, Korekore, Manyika. While these dialects have the same notion of hunhu philosophy, their environmental ethics differ and it may be prudent to research into these. While common characteristics may be found, these should not be used to blind the diversity of these linguistic dialects. Samkange and Samkange (1980) use the term Hunhuism/*Ubuntuism* apparently to represent dominant languages in Zimbabwe which are Shona and Ndebele. The characterisations may have been following the official languages by then, but there is exclusion of other languages and this becomes an example of language hegemony. This hegemonic tendency was a creation of the colonisers and it gives problems when trying to impose this notion on other languages while excluding dialects. These dialects have proverbs, sayings, taboos and stories that can be used to inform environmental ethics. Hegemonic thinking may rather contradict the very idea of *ubuntu* as summarized by Metz (2017: 143) who writes, "the idea of *ubuntu* expresses entering into a communal relation with others, or seeking to live harmoniously with them." The idea of *ubuntu* may not in itself negate the harmonious relationship with other indigenous cultures within Southern Africa. I now turn to ambiguity and vagueness in the next section.

6.4 Ambiguity and Vagueness in *Ubuntu* Environmental Conceptions

A generalized view of *Ubuntu* Environmental Ethics that is abstracted from specific cultural contexts such as Xhosa, Zulu, Ndebele, Shona, Ndau, Xitsonga, Venda, Tonga among others, results in ambiguity and vagueness rather than clarity and precision. Warburton (1996: 13) asserts, "An ambiguous word or phrase is one with two or more meanings". For Warburton, three kinds of ambiguity can be identified, namely; lexical, referential and syntactical. A lexical ambiguity occurs when a word with two or more meanings is used so that the phrase or sentence in which it is used can be understood in more than one way. *Ubuntu* environmental ethics can be understood on the context of Nguni dialects or it can also mean environmental ethics of sub-Saharan Africa. Referential ambiguity occurs when a word is used so that it is taken to refer to two or more things. Such an ambiguity arises when using *ubuntu* environmental ethics is used both as a cultural and regional environmental ethics. In the use of environmental ethics, there are several senses that are possible. The first sense is the primary and legitimate sense where *ubuntu* environmental ethics is with reference to the cultures in which the term *ubuntu* originates. These cultures are Zulu, Xhosa and Ndebele. The second sense is when *ubuntu* refers to the secondary application where linguistic variants get a derived connotation which is extended from the Nguni languages. The third sense of talking about *ubuntu* environmental ethics involves its application to the sub-continent of southern Africa. The fourth sense, which is the most extended meaning refers to the application of *ubuntu* environmental ethics to the whole sub-Saharan Africa. Though scholars normally demarcate the sense in which they use terms, the concept of *ubuntu* environmental ethics has been taken for granted and scholars can mean any of these senses discussed resulting in ambiguity.

Vagueness is lack of precision and this is always relative to context (Martinich 1989). What is vague in one context may be clear in another. For instance, the phrase "*ubuntu* environmental ethics" is precise in the context of contrasting with Western approaches to environmental ethics that base on Kantian ethics or Utilitarianism. However, it may be vague when a scholar discusses *ubuntu* environmental ethics within the context of African ethics context because it may be unclear whether the context is South African, regional, sub-regional, Zulu, Tonga or Shangani. While vagueness cannot be multiplied in the sense of ambiguity, it can be intensified by continued use of vague terms. One way of fighting vagueness in thinking about *ubuntu* environmental ethics is by listing conditions under which an environmental ethic can be classified as *ubuntu*. This may involve picking necessary and sufficient conditions so as to limit vagueness. The occurrence of vagueness gives a scenario where the application of a term fails to give a definite truth value. Tonga environmental ethics, for example, may not be properly described as *ubuntu* and at the same time, it may not be seen as completely outside *ubuntu*. The chapter now focuses on closed and open conceptions of *ubuntu* environmental ethics.

6.5   Closed Versus Open Conceptions of *Ubuntu* Environmental Ethics

Ubuntu Environmental Ethics gives a closed conception that fails to open up for debate and diversity in thinking about the environment in Southern African cultures. For Tutu (1999: 35) *ubuntu* implies "I participate, I share and harmony, friendliness, community are great goods." *Ubuntu* ought to be a shared ethical theory beyond the original Nguni languages (Newenham-Kahindi 2009). It may be contradictory for *'ubuntu'* to give a closed conception of environmental ethics since the term itself implies the virtues of friendliness and community concern. In the spirit of such thinking, *ubuntu* environmental ethics should open up for multiple and diverse thinking rather than giving a misconception that there is unity without diversity in *ubuntu* environmental ethics. This calls for the participation of indigenous cultures in environmental ethics. This participation should involve the deconstruction of the sense of unity and encourage other cultures to open up and offer their environmental ethics. Venda, Zulu, Xhosa, Shona, Twana among others, should pick up significant elements that contribute meaningfully to environmental ethics and share the conceptions. Openness implies knowledge democratization and ecology of knowledge.

The openness of environmental ethics should give room for emerging shared meanings of knowledge democracy and ecology of knowledge. Knowledge democracy allows other conceptions of environmental ethics to be articulated so that there is diversity of views concerning environmental ethics. An ecology of knowledge is a way of holding diversity in knowledge that supports the growth and integrity of the whole (Whitehead et al. 2015). Basing on ecology of knowledge, environmental ethics on *ubuntu* benefits more by getting support from cognitive linguistic groups. The unified approach to environmental ethics should be revisited so that there are other ways of looking into environmental ethics without assuming unanimity. An ecology of knowledges gives us the opportunity to forge a new field of coherences in recognising the value of, but moving beyond, scientific materialist empiricism while grounding on relationality (Behrens 2010). As different knowledge systems interact, they can learn from these interplays. Instead of disintegration between competing reality claims, an ecology of knowledges leads to new possibilities of integration (Mignolo 2009). The different approaches to environmental ethics should enrich each other and promote an accurate representation of views.

6.6   Geographical Demarcation Problems in *Ubuntu* Environmental Ethics

The term "Africa" is philosophically problematic and it cannot be taken for granted because of inherent complexities and contradictions involved in the term. Palmberg (2001: 198) argues that the term "Africa" is an ideological construct born in Europe and is as old as European penetration and exploitation of Africa. An ideological construct, the term Africa fails to meet the self-understanding of Africans themselves. Ramose (2003: 114) traces the origin of the term "Africa" as follows: "In antiquity, the Greeks are said to have called the continent Libya and the Romans Africa, perhaps from the Latin *aprica* (sunny), or the Greek *aphrike* (without cold)." The origin of the term Africa depicts weather elements and it fails to be a self-category among Africans themselves. The name Africa, however, was chiefly applied to the northern coast of the continent, which was in effect regarded as a southern extension of Europe. Zeleza (2006: 14) sees African identities as "existential and epistemic" constructions. Zeleza's observation points to the fact that while there is an extent of reality contained in the term "Africa" as shown in the adjective 'existential' there are also knowledge based conceptions that are captured by the word 'epistemic'. The origins of the term "Africa" are foreign in derivation and the term is not derived from the self-understanding of the indigenous people themselves. Given the above problems, it may still be problematic to talk of sub-Saharan Africa today. A geographical demarcation of *Ubuntu* Environmental Ethics that describes it as 'Sub-Saharan' is not only inadequate but also arbitrary. The inadequacy of the demarcation is seen in the absence of the idea of *Ubuntu* Environmental Ethics in West Africa (Nigeria, Senegal, Ghana); East Africa (Uganda, Kenya Tanzania) and Central Africa (Gabon, Equatorial Guinea, Democratic Republic of Congo) yet all these regions are in Sub-Saharan Africa.[1] The arbitrary nature of the demarcation is seen in failure to give a rational justification of the label resulting in a mismatch between the term and the region it attempts to refer. After examining these problems I shall give a proposal of how to re-conceptualise Environmental Ethics in Southern African cultures without falling into the said problems.

To give an example, Shona environmental ethics shares similarities with the broad African environmental ethics, it can be argued that the content of Shona environmental ethics is shaped by Shona people's experiences on and reflections about their physical environment. The savanna climate that characterises most locations of Shona communities is marked by hot, wet summers and cool dry winters. The average annual rainfall of nearly 600 mm per year, interrupted by dry spells and droughts in some cases, influences vegetation growth, the type of wild animals that survive under these conditions and the seasonal flow of rivers. The type of environmental philosophy that arises out of Shona communities would be different from what can be obtained the equatorial regions for example, where water conservation may not be a critical issue.

Geography becomes an important factor that gives variations on the basis of (1) physical features such as mountains, valleys, rivers, oceans, sand dunes, soils (2) vegetation (3) climatic factors such as rainfall, temperature, sunshine, humidity etc. (4) water bodies such as lakes, rivers, wells, springs etc. (4) animals found within these regions. Given the above, a generalized *ubuntu* environmental ethics fails to

---

[1] While I acknowledge historical migratory patterns of people in Sub-Saharan Africa, these migrations give rise to similarities in language. However, the similarities do not necessarily constitute exactness in the languages concerned. As a result, it is ethical to respect language diversity without any form of linguistic hegemony.

take into account distinct features that provide the foundation of an environmental ethic. The Tonga who live along the Zambezi valley, for example, are characterized as the Basilwizi "People of the Great River" and their environmental thinking revolves around but not limited to water conservation, fish breeding, river bank cultivation and gulley reclamation efforts. These environmental concerns are sharpened by the type of environment their communities are found. Tonga environmental ethics may be lost when we talk of *Ubuntu* environmental ethics. The Manyika of Eastern Zimbabwe, whose environment is characterized by mountains and valleys, are conscious of the importance of terracing, soil conservation and wetland conservation, among other environmental ethical concerns. It may be appropriate therefore to talk of Manyika environmental ethics because it speaks to the immediate environment. The web of life has complex interactions including "rivers, mountains, forests, ocean currents, winds and even the atmosphere" (Behrens 2010: 466). These interactions cannot be uniform and they must be understood in their complexity.

6.7 Reconceptualising *Ubuntu* Environmental Ethics: Some Critical Proposals

Four possible strategies may be employed in addressing the challenges faced in thinking about *ubuntu* environmental ethics. These strategies involve either the use of '*ubuntu*' with some other variant or variants or dropping the use of '*ubuntu*' altogether in environmental ethics so that it becomes accommodative of other cultural groupings. I shall critically examine each of these strategies and defend the best way of representing environmental thinking.

The first strategy consists of accepting a dualistic way of presenting the idea of environmental ethics in southern Africa. The strategy involves acknowledgement of the source while at the same time offering a linguistic variation of a similar concept so as to express both linguistic diversity and the original concept. In expressing *Ubuntu*/Unhu environmental ethics, there is a linguistic parity. The strategy avoids brushing aside the linguistic variant of the environmental ethics under which the linguistic variant falls. This helps to avoid a sense of hegemony in conceptualising environmental ethics. Murove (2004) and Le Grange (2012) employ this strategy by expressing the concept of ukama (relatedness) side by side with *Ubuntu* in their contributions to African environmental ethics. The difference in their approaches lies on the fact that Murove begins with Ukama while Le Grange begins with *Ubuntu*. In Zimbabwe, this strategy of talking about environmental ethics recognizes Ndebele and Shona variants but it excludes Tonga, Venda. Shangani, Nambia and Kalanga among other cultural groupings. It also involves a hegemonic tendency that was created by colonial thinking. To avoid this hegemony, the linguistic group providing the environmental ethics should be written side by side with *Ubuntu* so that there is *Ubuntu*/Hunhu environmental ethics, *Ubuntu*/Environmental ethics, *Ubuntu*/Ntu environmental ethics, *Ubuntu*/Vumuntu environmental ethics. The dualistic way of representing environmental ethics may give the impression of equivalent notions of environmental thinking yet there may be differences that require to be researched upon.

Listing a limited group of three or four linguistic variants shows the richness of the concept while acknowledging linguistic diversity is the second strategy. The choice of the list should be based on the proximity of the language being used. The use of three or four linguistic variants to characterize environmental ethic may show evidence of diversity, avoid hegemonic thinking and acknowledge parity of linguistic variations in the characterization of southern African environmental ethics. The listing of three or four variants breaks the hegemony of *ubuntu* and attempts to show the richness of approaches to environmental ethics. Instead of showing that there is one ethic that may embrace others, the approach shows that the approaches are multiple and allow readers to be aware of the diversity without hiding them. The list may help to show the idea of parity or equivalence in thinking about the environment.

Problems may arise in deciding which language variant of *ubuntu* should be expressed first. It may be decided that the linguistic culture providing elements of environmental ethics should be written first but this may also make the presence of other variants redundant. The second problem is that expression of similarity is not the same as exactness, hence the translation problems may leave the matter indeterminate. The third problem is that the matter may remain misleading since the impression of cross cutting or common approach may still be implied.

Avoiding the linguistic terms and using a geographical demarcation for instance, Southern African environmental ethics may be the third possible strategy. The hope of such a strategy is that it is neutral about linguistic inclinations such as 'ubuntu', 'hunhu', 'untu' and 'vumuntu', among other variations though it shall feed from them. It becomes open for all other cultures to participate since there is no element of sidelining. The southern Africa approach captures the tropical and sub-tropical environments without the danger of assuming that there is uniformity in the geographical factors that influence environmental ethics. Finally, the adoption of a geographical location deconstructs colonialist mentality in thinking about environmental ethics within sub-Saharan Africa.

However, the use of a geographical approach may be faced with demarcation problems because it becomes very difficult to give a clear starting point and an end point to southern Africa. Secondly, the approach may still fail to overcome the problems of ambiguity and vagueness when making reference to Southern African environmental ethics. Thirdly, reference to geographic space in trying to capture environmental ethics dilutes the notion and fails to conceptualise the cultural ties to indigenous conceptions. These problems give rise to the last strategy in the section that follows.

The last strategy involves the use of a distinct linguistic variant under which the environmental ethic is found. This consists of naming the environmental ethic using the linguistic variant as a prefix, for example, Shona environmental ethics; Tonga environmental ethics; Venda environmental ethics etc. The strategy avoids the fallacy of unanimism and gives a specific environmental ethic that corresponds to the linguistic group under which an environmental ethic is found. At the same time, it avoids a linguistic hegemony that may hide diversity and distract efforts to enrich the varieties of environmental ethical thoughts in southern African societies. This strategy has been developed in West Africa where it is possible to examine Yoruba environmental ethics, Akan Environmental ethics and related notions. The approach promises to bring diversity in thinking about environmental philosophy in southern African countries. This approach is employed by a number of scholars including Chemhuru and Masaka (2010) who explore the use of taboos in Shona environmental ethics. Their understanding of Shona environmental ethics as a distinct ethic is significant because it gives a precise and straight forward environmental ethics that applies to Shona culture. Chemhuru (2014) argues for the ontological import of Shona environmental ethics where he defends the use of Shona environmental ethics to avoid the unanimist fallacy.

The approach can be defended because it locates environmental ethics in the culture in which it arises so that there is real correspondence between the content of environmental ethics and the community in which it arises. It is specific to a culture wherein environmental duties and responsibilities arise and it connects to the land, ecosystems, water bodies, vegetation and animals, among other factors. The use of a cultural standpoint environmental ethics avoids colonialist hegemony and the fallacy of generalisation.

6.8   Conclusion: Pluriversal Thinking About Environmental Ethics

In this chapter, I have argued that the general approach to *Ubuntu* environmental ethics should now be avoided and focus should now be on specific and related versions such as *hunhu/umuntu/vuntu*etc. The cultural rootedness of environmental ethics should be upheld to avoid the colonialist unanimist fallacy and promote diversity at the same time. The cultural rootedness of environmental ethics should help scholars to match environmental ethics with practical concerns of the communities involved. The linguistic hegemony that is used in describing environmental ethics should be replaced by other cultural equivalent notions with the aim of promoting diversity in thinking about environmental ethics. I have argued that the term "*ubuntu* environmental ethics" should be refined so that ambiguity and vagueness in the application of the term are replaced by clarity and precision respectively. I have shown that environmental ethics should be linked to the land, community and resources under which the ethics arises for diverse ideas to be contributed. Water bodies, vegetation, soils, animals and climatic factors, among others, tend to influence environmental ethics in different parts of southern Africa and sub-Saharan Africa to the extent that the richness and diversity of environmental ethics cannot be reduced to *ubuntu* environmental ethics. I therefore propose an environmental ethics that departs from the general view to a cultural standpoint such as Tonga environmental ethics, Zulu environmental ethics, Shona environmental ethics and related versions.

References

Ajei, M. 2007. *Africa's Development: The Imperatives of Indigenous Knowledge and Values*. PhD Thesis, Pretoria: UNISA unpublished.

Akena, F.A. 2012. Critical Analysis of the Production of Western Knowledge and Its Implications for Indigenous Knowledge and Decolonisation. *Journal of Black Studies* 43 (6): 336–400.

Behrens, K. 2010. Exploring African Holism with Respect to the Environment. *Environmental Values* 19 (4): 465–484.

Chemhuru, M., and D. Masaka. (2010). Taboos as Sources of Shona People's Environmental Ethics. *Journal of Sustainable Development in Africa* 121–133.

Chemhuru, M. 2014. The Ethical Import of African Metaphysics: A Critical Discourse in Shona Environmental Ethics. In *Ontologized Ethics: New Essays in African Meta-Ethics*, ed. E. Imafidon and J.A. Bewaji, 73–87. New York: Lexington Books.

Gyekye, K. 1997. *Tradition and Modernity*. Oxford: Oxford University Press.

Hountondji, P. 1996. *African Philosophy: Myth and Reality*. Bloomington: University of Indiana Press.

Hurley, J. 2011. *A Concise Introduction to Logic*. Belmont: Wadsworth.

Le Grange, L. 2012. *Ubuntu*, Ukama, Environment and Moral Education. *Journal of Moral Education* 41(3). 329–340.

Martinich, A. 1989. *Philosophical Writing*. London: Prentice-Hall.

Mawere, M. 2012. Buried and Forgotten But Not Dead': Reflections On '*Ubuntu*' In Environmental Conservation In Southeastern Zimbabwe. *Afro Asian Journal of Social Sciences* 3 (3.2 Quarter II): 1–20.

Mawere, M. 2014. *Environmental Conservation through Ubuntu and other Emerging Perspectives*. Bamenda: Langaa Publications.

Mbiti, J. 1999. *Africans Religions and Philosophy*, 2nd ed. London: Heinemann.

Metz, T. 2017. Managerialism as Anti-Social: Some Implications of *Ubuntu* for Knowledge Production. In *Knowledge and Change in African Universities*, ed. M.C. Ndofirepi, 139–154. Rotterdam: Sense Publication.

Mignolo, W. 2009. Epistemic Disobedience, Independent Thought and Decolonial Freedom. *Theory, Culture and Society* 159–181.

Muchemwa, K., and M. Mazuru. 2016. Language Imperialism in Zimbabwe. *Dzimbabwe Arts Festival*. Masvingo: Great Zimbabwe University.

Murove, F. 2004. An African Commitment to Ecological Conservation: The Shona Concepts of Ukama and *Ubuntu*. *Mankind Quarterly* 45 (2): 195–215.

Museka, G., and M.M. Madondo. 2012. The Quest for a Relevant Environmental Pedagogy in the African Context: Insights from *Ubuntu* Philosophy. *Journal of Ecology and Natural Environment* 258–265.

Newenham-Kahindi, A. 2009. The Transfer of *Ubuntu* Indaba Business Models Abroad: A Case of South African Multinational Banks and Telecommunication Services in Tanzania. *International Journal of Cross Cultural Management* 9 (1): 87–108.

Palmberg, M. 2001. A Continent without culture. In *Same and Other: Negotiating African Identity in Cultural Production*, ed. M.B. Palmberg, 197–209. Stochholm: Nordiska Afrikainstutet.

Ramose, M.B. 1999. *African Philosophy*. Harare: Mond Books.

Ramose, M. 2003. I Doubt, Therefore African Philosophy Exists. *South African Journal of Philosophy* 22 (2): 113–127.

Samkange, S., and T.M. Samkange. 1980. *Hunhuism/Ubuntuism: A Zimbabwean Indigenous Political Philosophy*. Harare: Graham Publishing.

Serequeberhan. 1996. The Critique of Eurocentrism and the Practice of African Philosophy. In *Postcolonial African Philosophy: A Reader*, ed. E.C. Eze, 141–161. Oxford: Blackwell.

Shumba, O. 2011. Commons Thinking Ecological intelligence and the Ethical and Moral Framework of *Ubuntu*: An Imperative for Sustainable Development. *Journal of Media and Communication Studies* 258–265.

Tempels, P. 1969. *Bantu Philosophy*. Paris: Presense Africaine.

Tutu, D. 1999. *No Future Without Forgiveness*. New York: Random House.

Van Nierkerk, J. 2015. *Ubuntu and Moral Value*. PhD Thesis, University of Johannesburg: Unpublished.

Warburton, N. 1996. *Thinking from A-Z*. London: Routledge.

Whitehead, J., J. Delong, and M. Huxtable. 2015. Participation and democratization of Knowledge: Living theory research for reconciliation. In *ARNA*, 1–20. New York: ARNA.

Zeleza, P. 2006. The Invention of African Identities and Languages: The Discursive and Developmental Implications. In *30th Annual Conference of African Linguistics*, 14–26. Somerville: Cascadilla Proceedings Project.

Chapter 7
Ubuntu and Environmental Ethics: The West Can Learn from Africa When Faced with Climate Change

Aïda C. Terblanché-Greeff

Abstract The human race is experiencing climate change and the catastrophic ripple effects, e.g. increased levels of droughts, flooding, food insecurity, etc. It is cardinal that humankind adopts post-haste collective behavior to mitigate climatic changes. Interestingly, although Africa contributes less greenhouse gas emissions (that lead to climate change) than more developed continents, it is one of the most vulnerable continents when faced with climate change. International stakeholders are motivated to implement climate change adaptation strategies, e.g. sustainable development and the introduction of genetically modified crops in Africa's agricultural sector, to lower the continent's vulnerability. However, when developing and implementing adaptation strategies, cognizance must be allocated to the unique cultural values of various stakeholders. This is often not the case as cultural value systems of communities are neglected in these processes, e.g. the African values system of Ubuntu (which focuses on relationality). It is imperative to investigate and compare individualistic-capitalistic Western values (with its focus on sustainable development and economic growth) and the values of Ubuntu as it pertains to environmental ethics. Both value systems attribute different significance to relationality between humans, non-humans, and the natural environment. From this, I argue that the individualistic-capitalistic West has much to learn from Africa's Ubuntu and the ensuing potential for climate change adaptation. Subsequently, a call for a universal paradigm shift will be made, away from the economic and development foci of individualistic-capitalistic values, towards Ubuntu degrowth which prioritizes communitarianism, and the principle of sufficiency. I suggest that relevant and diverse stakeholders meet around the "global roundtable" to consider and discuss different perspectives and cultural values when developing climate change adaptation strategies on a global level.

A. C. Terblanché-Greeff (✉)
University of Johannesburg, Auckland Park, Johannesburg, South Africa
e-mail: actgreeff@gmail.com

© Springer Nature Switzerland AG 2019
M. Chemhuru (ed.), *African Environmental Ethics*, The International
Library of Environmental, Agricultural and Food Ethics 29,
https://doi.org/10.1007/978-3-030-18807-8_7

7.1 Introduction

Climate change is a significant challenge faced by all of humanity. However, Africa is one of the most vulnerable and impacted continents, as it experiences increased levels of droughts, flooding, food insecurity, etc., and it is imperative to implement various climate change adaptation strategies to lower communities' vulnerability.[1] It is noteworthy that developed countries' adaptation strategies to address climate change are often based on the sustainable development paradigm, which is a characteristically Western socio-economic-environmental approach.[2]

In this chapter, I will present a brief discussion on climate change as it affects Africa and the resulting push from the globalized individualistic-capitalistic West to introduce genetically modified (GM) crops as a sustainable development strategy to address the adverse effects of climate change. Often cultural values of communities (which may differ from contemporary Western values) are not taken into consideration when decisions are made regarding the development and implementation of climate change adaptation strategies.[3] Supportively, the Intergovernmental Panel on Climate Change (IPCC 2012: 758) states:

> Indigenous, local, and traditional forms of knowledge are a major resource for adapting to climate change… Natural resource dependent communities, including indigenous peoples, have a long history of adapting to highly variable and changing social and ecological conditions… Such forms of knowledge are often neglected in policy and research, and their mutual recognition and integration with scientific knowledge will increase the effectiveness of adaptation.

An example of such a cultural value system is Ubuntu, and it is worth recognizing that Africans have vast cultural knowledge systems regarding their relationality to humans, non-humans, and nature.[4] For this reason, the African cultural values of Ubuntu will be presented in detail and then compared to differing values of the West to indicate that the sustainable development paradigm (focused on economics and growth), and the subsequent proposal to extensively introduce GM crops in Africa, cannot be considered the ideal solution to address the continent's vulnerability when faced with climate change. Degrowth, more specifically Ubuntu as degrowth, will be presented as an alternative *to* development—an unconventional approach to contemporary climate change adaptation strategies.

---

[1] "Africa contains seven out of 10 of the countries that are considered the most threatened by climate change globally: Sierra Leone, South Sudan, Nigeria, Chad, Ethiopia, the Central African Republic, and Eritrea" (Bishop 2017: 88).

[2] The Brundtland Report defines *sustainable development* as: "Development that meets the needs of the present without compromising the ability of future generations to meet their own needs" (WCED 1987: 43).

[3] In this chapter, the term "West" refers to developed countries that are individualistic-capitalistic orientated, e.g. North America.

[4] Ubuntu is a cultural value system that "stresses the importance of community, solidarity, caring and sharing. This worldview advocates a profound sense of interdependence and emphasizes that our true human potential can only be realized in partnership with others" (Ngcoya 2009: 1).

The focus on Ubuntu as a solution to various environmental issues (e.g. climate change) is not a novel notion and the issues for which Ubuntu present as a solution are context-specific or focused on specific research areas. In a context-specific manner, Kelbessa (2014, 2015) argues that environmental policies in Africa can benefit from African environmental ethics by applying the principles of Ubuntu when faced with climate change and other environmental issues. Concurrently, Le Grange (2015: 301, 307) states that Ubuntu as an ecological philosophy can serve as the "framework for all policies and practices aimed at responding to the pressing environmental problems facing the southern African region". Following an approach that is more focused on a specific research area, Pavel (2015: 97) promotes the use of Ubuntu on metropolitan regional levels (inclusive of "urban centers, surrounding suburbs and rural cities and towns") as local communities thereby might identify with such strategy more intimately.

These examples of Ubuntu as environmental ethics are just the tip of the iceberg and multitudinous proposals exist for Ubuntu as context-specific or focused climate change solutions. Nonetheless, I want to propose the unprecedented—an overall environmental ethic based on Ubuntu as degrowth.[5] I aim to develop an intricate relational approach that can be utilized in the global climate change context as an alternative *to* the sustainable development paradigm, which focuses on expansive economics. I will not suggest the implementation of a greener or better model of development. Instead, I call for a break from the *status quo*, and a global paradigm shift towards Ubuntu degrowth ethics by indicating what the West can learn from Ubuntu, as an environmental ethics theory, when faced with climate change.

To facilitate this universal paradigm shift, I propose that all relevant stakeholders convene around the global roundtable when discussing alternative climate change adaptation strategies that are to be sustainable. It is imperative that cognizance is allocated to the values of communities when developing climate change adaptation strategies, as communities might have inherent strengths that can be utilized and combined with other existing strategies.

7.2   Climate Change and Sustainable Development

Beyond reasonable doubt, the Intergovernmental Panel on Climate Change (IPCC) asserts that Earth's climate is warming at an exceptional rate from the mid-20th century (CDKN 2014: 4). The IPCC (2012: 557) defines climate change as:

A change in the state of the climate that can be identified (e.g. by using statistical tests) by changes in the mean and/or the variability of its properties and that persists for an extended period, typically decades or longer. Climate change may be due to natural internal pro-

---

[5]Ubuntu as an extension of degrowth is mentioned by multiple scholars in passing (D'Alisa et al. 2014: 117; Kothari et al. 2014; Martines-Alier et al. 2014: 43; Kallis 2015: 3; Maynard 2016: 71; Perrot 2015: 27; Zozuľakova 2016: 190; Cosme et al. 2017: 331; Gupta and Pouw 2017: 87; Paulson 2017: 430). In this chapter, Ubuntu as degrowth will be presented in detail.

cesses or external forces, or to persistent anthropogenic changes in the composition of the atmosphere or in land use.

Due to current anthropogenic behavior that subsequently leads to increased greenhouse gas emissions into the atmosphere, climatic fluctuations are escalating exponentially, and in effect, the biosphere cannot adapt to the post-haste climate change currently experienced.[6]

Although Africa emits fewer greenhouse gasses into the atmosphere than more developed and industrialized continents, it is exceedingly affected by climate change. Supportively, the IPCC's *Fifth Assessment Report* provides evidence that surface temperatures in Africa have increased by 0.5–2 °C over the past decade, and during the 21st century, the continent's temperatures (specifically arid regions) will rise more rapidly than on other continents (CDKN 2014: 4). Consequently, access to water; food security; and a decrease in wealth and health are some of the ways in which societies can be disrupted by climatic change, and these will especially be experienced in Africa (CDKN 2014: 4).

It comes as no surprise that the sustainable development paradigm and the ensuing push from developed countries in the West to introduce and commercialize GM crops in Africa's agricultural sphere are a proposed solution to address Africa's vulnerability due to climatic change. The purpose of sustainable development is to provide structure whereby "economic growth, social welfare and environmental protection" can be harmonized (Asara et al. 2015: 375) to facilitate specific "development that meets the needs of the present [generations] without compromising the ability of future generations to meet their own needs" (WCED 1987: 43).

As a sustainable development strategy, it is argued that the use of GM crops in Africa can alleviate the continent's hunger and poverty levels which are worsening due to climate change. Philanthropic foundations (e.g. Bill and Melinda Gates; Rockefeller) and development agencies (e.g. USAID) are supportive of introducing GM crops in Africa. According to these international stakeholders, there is an immense need for the allocation of focus to "technologies such as hybrid seeds, fertilizers, pesticides and genetic modification… to improve yields and livelihoods throughout the [African] continent" (Schnurr 2015: 202).

On face value it might seem that GM crops are the answer to Africa's climate change challenges, as there are many advantages of its implementations, such as "increased crop yields, reduced costs for pesticides, less fungal contamination, and reduced labor" (Huesing and English 2004: 92). Nonetheless, it will be useful to investigate differing cultural values of the contemporary West and Africa to indicate that this sustainable development strategy might not be an ideal solution, even though it has been successfully implemented in various other continents and countries.

---

[6]The concept *Greenhouse gasses* is defined as "any of the gases whose absorption of solar radiation is responsible for the greenhouse effect, including carbon dioxide, methane, ozone, and the fluorocarbons" (Anon s.a.1).

7.3   Cultural Values

As it cannot be assumed that all humans share the same socio-economic-environmental values, it is necessary to focus on deeply ingrained cultural, moral, and religious values when investigating means to address climate change on local and global levels. The investigation of differing values are significant for climate change adaptation as these will indicate varying priorities allocated to the perceived risk and need for adaptation. A contemporary cultural value (found in some world-views of the West) is self-enhancement, and in a contrasting manner, conservation is associated with more traditional values (as found in Ubuntu) (O'Brien 2009: 168). Such traditional worldviews and following values can be described as a need "for belongingness and group identity, that recognise local knowledge, and that support traditional sectors and livelihoods" by preserving cultural identities (e.g. relationality to nature) (O'Brien 2009: 170).

Regardless of a variety of climate change adaptation aid from the West to Africa (e.g. GM crops as a sustainable development strategy), the unique African cultural spheres of communities have often been neglected (e.g. the cultural environmental ethics of Ubuntu). This oversight should be addressed as various values can serve as motivation for behavior which is imperative for the sustainability of climate change adaptation strategies. Subsequently, Ubuntu will be discussed in detail to highlight some of its key aspects.

7.3.1   Ubuntu: *"A Person Is a Person Through Others"*

Ubuntu is a cultural concept originating from sub-Saharan Africa and is often expressed by the pervasive maxim "A person is a person through other persons".[7] This linguistically loaded concept extends normatively into the embodiment of human relations and prescribes moral obligation towards other humans, non-humans, and nature.

The popular maxim "A person is a person through other persons" can be rewritten as "A person is a Person through others" to provide clarity. Here the word "person" (small letter p) refers to individual humans, whereas "Person" (capital letter P) refers to the personhood, self-hood, and humaness a person should strive for by interacting with "others" (humans, non-humans, and nature) to *become* fully human.[8] According to Metz (2011: 537), "one can be more or less of a person, self or human being, where

---

[7]Although multiple definitions of Ubuntu are present in literature, conceptual traits as applicable to environmental ethics and climate change adaptation will be presented.

[8]The concept *humaness* should not be confused with the concept *humaneness*. *Humaness* refers to a the development of "one's (moral) personhood, [which is] a prescription to acquire *Ubuntu*" (Metz 2011: 537); whereas *humaneness* is descriptive of "characterized by tenderness, compassion, and sympathy for people and animals, especially for the suffering or distressed" (Anon s.a.2). Noteworthy, *humaneness* does not by definition extend to the natural environment.

the more one is, the better". As such, the ultimate goal in life should be to *become* a Person. That is "a (complete) person, a (true) self or a (genuine) human being" (Metz 2011: 537). This can be achieved by moral interactions with others to attain Ubuntu.

7.3.2   Communitarianism in Ubuntu: "I" in "We"

As stated, *becoming* a Person cannot happen in isolation as Ubuntu is attained through the interaction with others. Therefore, it is useful to investigate communitarianism as a trait of Ubuntu where the individual does not exist in isolation but is instead seen as an inherently communal being as focus is allocated to social relations and interdependency.

Communion is the "conceiving of communal relationships as an objectively-desirable kind of interaction that should instead guide what majorities want and which norms become dominant" (Metz 2011: 38). In reality, the person does not lose individual identity; instead, it is exemplified by communion. Through the interaction with unique others, a person can subjectively grow and attain Ubuntu—to *become* truly human (Person). This communitarianism has a moral dimension as it motivates the social virtue of practical altruism through sharing and communion with others (Wiredu 1996: 22).

"Identity" and "solidarity" are interlinked themes when investigating communitarianism in Ubuntu. In group context the members will identify themselves as "I" in "We", and this will motivate the coordination of behavior to achieve shared goals by engaging in communal projects (Metz 2011: 538). This attainment of shared ends is expressed through solidarity whereby members engage in mutual aid and exhibit positive attitudes through sympathy and altruism (Metz 2011: 538).

7.3.3   Ubuntu and Ukama

The idea of community in Ubuntu also prescribes communion between humans and nature, which is often expressed through identity, respect, and solidarity. Supportively, "no person is complete in him/herself; s/he is fully human in as far as s/he remains a part of the web of life, including creation and the earth" (LenkaBula 2008: 378). This is conveyed by the concept of *Ukama*, which is an extension of Ubuntu. This concept refers to relatedness, more specifically, relatedness as found in the cosmos.

Human relations in a community is seen as a microcosm of relationality in the cosmos. When investigating the relationships between humans, as well as humans and nature, Ubuntu (humaneness) is the tangible form of Ukama (relatedness) (Murove 2009: 316). The relationship between humans and nature plays an integral role in a person *becoming* a Person, as the principle that all relationships must be based on respect, dignity, collaboration, identity, and solidarity creates the foundation of Ubuntu environmental ethics.

Ubuntu as a concrete form of Ukama does not only prescribe moral behavior towards the present generations. Instead, Ukama represents a bond between past, present, and future generations based on relatedness (Le Grange 2015: 306). The question arises: "*How does inter-generational relatedness influence attitudes toward nature?*" Responsibility towards others is founded on Ukama, and this dual moral responsibility that extends to past and future generations is based on respect and gratitude.

In many traditional African beliefs, ancestors (predecessors) are still included in the community.[9] This is supported by Ukama where everything is related in the cosmos. That being so, the current generation has moral responsibilities toward past generations due to respect and gratitude owed to predecessors as they were responsible for looking after nature as prescribed by Ubuntu. This respect towards nature as exhibited by predecessors facilitated responsible stewardship, which in turn created the beneficial natural environment inherited by the current generation (Wiredu 1996: 46). Gratitude towards the past generations motivates the continuous guardianship of nature, and by treating nature with respect and dignity, the current generation can ensure that future generations inherit a natural environment that will satisfy their basic needs.[10]

This dual responsibility can also be explained by the Ubuntu characteristics of identity and solidarity. The identity of a person in terms of "I" in "We" (as part of a group) includes both past and future generations. The current generation acknowledges that predecessors lived in solidarity which extended to intergenerational relatedness, and thus the current generation must act altruistically towards future generations.

From the above discussion, it is apparent that a person wanting to attain Ubuntu should strive to *become* a Person through relationships with others—humans (past, present, and future generations), nonhumans, and the natural environment. Ubuntu prescribes the principle of sufficiency whereby the present and future generations are provided with resources to meet their basic needs through acts of altruism and the achievement of shared goals.[11]

It is worth noting that the principle of sufficiency is not equated to the sustainable development paradigm, which focuses heavily on development as a means for the current generation to meet their basic and false needs while also ensuring that future generations will be able to meet their needs.[12] As can be deduced, the Western *status quo* of the individualistic value of non-relational autonomy and capitalism differs

---

[9]It is useful to refer to predecessors instead of ancestors (which is culture-specific) to facilitate a more secular conceptualisation of Ubuntu.

[10]Basic needs are essential for physical survival.

[11]The *principle of sufficiency* refers to sustainable livelihoods whereby natural resources are used and distributed to meet basic needs for human survival.

[12]In contrast to basic needs which are essential for physical survival, false needs refer to economic and material "wants" that are not considered essential for survival.

from the described traits of Ubuntu. It is imperative to compare these values to indicate the noticeable differences between the modern ideology of the West and the more traditional cultural values of Ubuntu.

7.3.4 The Individualistic "I" in "Me"

Prevalent in contemporary Western culture is the important individualistic value of non-relational autonomy, which can be described as "I" in "Me". Each individual has an obligation to develop an autonomous identity to differentiate the person from others; individualistic values and personal freedom are pursued and the individual's human rights take precedence over the rights of others; the needs of the individual are higher priority than that of a group; the individual can exist outside a community without loss of identity; and independency, self-sufficiency, and self-reliance are highly praised as the individual is responsible for the achievement of personal goals through competition with others.

These individualistic values stand in contrast to communitarianism in Ubuntu. According to Murove (2014: 37), colonial scholars view Ubuntu as a phenomenon of human primitivity and a "manifestation of an infliction of dependency complex syndrome" which should be conquered by individualistic values. Theron (1995: 35) similarly asserts that Ubuntu "side-steps the slow Western development of the idea of personal responsibility… Without this consciousness the fruits of technology cannot be enjoyed. …[it] teaches Africans to evade responsibility, rather, to hide behind the collective decision of the [group]."

This judgement of Ubuntu is faulty as the identity of the person is not lost because s/he is part of a group. On the contrary, individual plurality is significant in Ubuntu. A person can *become* a Person, a genuine human, through the interaction with unique others. Furthermore, responsibility towards others is based on consideration of the interests and concerns of others *in relation* to the individual's. For that reason, Ubuntu challenges the doctrine of individualistic values such as "I" in "Me", as Ubuntu "… is derivative from [the] relationship with other persons, … it is not an incorrigible property of the individual but something that is shared with others and finds nourishment and flourishing in relationships with others" (Murove 2014: 42).

7.3.5 Homo œconomicus

Individualistic values and the pursuit of self-interest in the capitalistic-orientated West motivate behaviour. *Homo œconomicus*—economic human—pursues false needs in the name of economic growth and development with limited attention being allocated to the differentiation between basic and false needs. In individualistic-capitalistic societies, the person's identity is often defined by the accumulation of wealth through the fulfillment of self-interest. Capitalism is based on the commodification of resources to facilitate economic growth, and the person is often defined as a consumer. Success and happiness are determined by materialistic gratification, which is ironic as false needs can never truly be satisfied and thus the individual is trapped in an ongoing cycle where behavior is motivated by self-interest and greed. Through individualistic values and the pursuit of self-interest in the capitalistic society, human beings are alienated from each other following "I" in "Me".

In the pursuit to attain Ubuntu, identity is ascribed in terms of "I" in "We" instead of "I" in "Me". Ubuntu rejects the model of *Homo œconomicus*. Instead, focus is allocated to meaningful relationships with others which should be based on empathy, caring, harmony, and altruism as opposed to competition. Based on the traits of identity and solidarity, Ubuntu can be described as "anti-egoistic as it discourages people from seeking their own good without regard for, or to the detriment of, others and the community" (Munyaka and Motlhabi 2009: 71–72). Hence, it is argued that Ubuntu stands in opposition to "market-oriented economic logic of maximalisation [sic]" (Van Binsbergen 2001: 58).

7.3.6 Nature

Homo œconomicus focuses on mass-consumption, economic growth, technological innovation, and material accumulation. In individualistic-capitalistic Western societies, humans have authority and control over nature as it should be dominated and utilized to meet basic and false needs. From humankind's god-like stance towards nature, technological and scientific approaches focusing on concepts like growth, progress, and development are often implemented to augment nature (e.g. through genetic engineering) so that the environment can meet the needs of *Homo œconomicus.*

Nature is seen as something that should be commodified, and it is routinely interpreted through economic terminology—where resources are measured in monetary values as described by the concept "natural capital". This attitude towards nature is prevalent in the sustainable development paradigm where economics dominate both society and the natural environment as illustrated by the fact that gross domestic product (GDP) growth is regularly used to measure sustainable development (Giddings et al. 2002: 190).[13]

Dominance over nature and the commodification of natural resources stand in sharp contrast to the prescribed relational attitude towards others in Ubuntu (as the concrete form of Ukama—relatedness). In *becoming* a Person through others (humans, non-humans, and nature), it will be counter-productive to commodify and misuse natural resources to satisfy self-interest that will support the accumulation of personal wealth. Instead, Ubuntu prescribes the principle of sufficiency as humans should live in such a way that others' needs are met in relation to one's own needs

---

[13]Gross domestic product (GDP) can be defined as "[the] total market value of the goods and services produced by a country's economy during a specified period of time... It is used throughout the world as the main measure of output and economic activity" (Bondarenko 2017).

(Murove 2014: 40). By striving for a lifestyle based on sufficiency, the person and the community only utilize resources in nature to satisfy their basic needs. Nature is not commodified and used in competition that will satisfy self-interest (cf. Box 7.1).

Box 7.1: Interview with Sense Mokoti (E.A.G.E.R.: Voices of Southern Africa—Documentary)
Examples of how rural communities in Africa live according to the Ubuntu value of communitarianism and the principle of sufficiency are prevalent in an interview held with Sense Mokoti, a woman living in rural Botswana (Chobe flood plains, Kachikau).

She explains how the community's livelihood is based on the principle of sufficiency when she describes how natural resources are used when building a homestead: "Like this is a tree branch [points to the frame of the house front door]. This is just soil [points to the walls of the house]. This is grass [points to the roof of the house]. We can just pick a pole from a tree; we dig mud from the ground; then we cut grass. Then it's a home. We don't have to have money to have a home." (NWU-ACDS 2018). She goes on by saying: "The community here in the rural areas, they are self-reliant. They keep their cattle; they keep goats; they keep chickens. They make their food, they plow... and they are very generous. We have our food, we have everything, and we help each other. That's how we live." (NWU-ACDS 2018).

She mentions natural phenomena and how the rural community experiences it. "I heard that there was drought last year. But I did not experience it because my neighbors here ... they plowed their fields and I went to help them to harvest; so I got a lot of maize and pumpkins...". Also, "when it's flooding there [points to the flood plains], there's fish, there's waterlilies, and we have plenty of food even if it floods." (NWU-ACDS 2018).

This interview is indicative of communitarianism and how the community members identify as "I" in "We". Through communal activities, goodwill is exhibited to meet shared goals. Here nature is not commodified and used in competition with others. The community practices the principle of sufficiency as they live in close proximity to nature.

When considering Ubuntu and the contrasting traits of the individualistic-capitalistic West, it will be useful to indicate why the sustainable development strategy of utilizing GM crops in Africa, might not be an ideal climate change adaptation strategy. Alternatively, Ubuntu will be presented as an alternative *to* development.

7.4 Sustainable Development and GM Crops

Philanthropic foundations (e.g. Bill and Malinda Gates; Rockefeller) and bilateral international organizations (e.g. USAID) are moving to implement practices and programs in Africa to lower the continent's vulnerability when faced with climate change. From a sustainable development stance, it might seem that the West has genuine, selfless concerns for Africa and the effects of climate change on vulnerable communities, as they are pushing the utilization of GM crops in Africa's agriculture to address poverty and food insecurity. Sustainable development, in its attempts to modernize ecology, subsequently "renders environmental problems [as] technical, promising win-win solutions and the (impossible) goal of perpetuating development without harming the environment" (D'Alisa et al. 2014: 9).

It is noteworthy that foreign economic interest in Africa is often presented under the guise of sustainable development, and nature is frequently described as "natural capital" which is an indication of the monetary value allocated to the environment. Supportively, the billionaire Bill Gates asserts that "the great thing about agriculture is that… once you get the right [GM] seeds and information—a lot of it can be left to the marketplace" (as cited by Thompson 2013).

As the focus is placed on increasing income and international market-related competition, the incorporation of GM crops in Africa undermines the Ubuntu principle of sufficiency. Here cultural traditions are ignored, and socio-cultural power is taken away from the local community members by "forcing" transition towards modern technologies. This process of commercialization (based on economics) promotes the over use and often abuse of nature, and disregards the relatedness of humans and nature as stipulated by Ukama. Commercialization also stands in contrast with the prescribed behavior that current generations should sufficiently utilize the environment based on gratitude towards past generations. Interestingly, Ubuntu and the prescribed principle of sufficiency are similar to the concept of degrowth, and this will be discussed in the following section.

7.5 Degrowth and Ubuntu

The paradigm of sustainable development has been reformulated to fit capitalistic ideals, and it is argued that growth takes center stage when implementing sustainable development strategies (Asara et al. 2015: 380). This paradigm prescribes that the needs of the present generation should be met through development as prescribed by capitalism, without compromising the future generations' ability to satisfy their needs. Supportively, Swyngedouw (2014: 9) states that the "the public management of things and people is hegemonically [sic] articulated around a naturalization of the need of economic growth and capitalism as the only reasonable and possible form of organization of socio-natural metabolism". It is based on these capitalistic traits of sustainable development, and the socio-economic-environmental crisis currently experienced by humankind, that degrowth is presented as an alternative *to* sustainable development and growth (Zozuľakova 2016: 187).

So what is degrowth? The Degrowth Declaration of the Paris 2008 conference (Research & Degrowth 2010: 524) defined degrowth as "a voluntary transition towards a just, participatory, and ecologically sustainable society... The objectives of degrowth are to meet basic human needs and ensure a high quality of life, while reducing the ecological impact of the global economy to a sustainable level, equitably distributed between nations". It might seem that degrowth is partially in agreement with sustainable development; however, this is not the case. Degrowth does not focus on "alternative, better, or greener development" as proposed by sustainable development (D'Alisa et al. 2014: 9). It calls for a break from the modern state of affairs and its capitalistic-orientated sustainable development by imagining an entirely different global society where consumption is lessened. D'Alisa et al. (2014: 4) elaborates that:

> [E]mphasis here is on *different,* not only *less.* Degrowth signifies a society with a smaller metabolism... a society with a metabolism which has a different structure and serves new functions. Degrowth does not call for doing less of the same... In a degrowth society everything will be different: different activities, different forms and uses of energy, different relations, different gender roles, different allocations of time between paid and non-paid work, different relations with the non-human world.

To facilitate the imagining of a new and unique global society, degrowth can set the stage for the implementation of different cultural practices, such as Ubuntu. Various authors (D'Alisa et al. 2014: 117; Kothari et al. 2014; Martines-Alier et al. 2014: 43; Kallis 2015: 3; Maynard 2016: 71; Perrot 2015: 27; Zozuľakova 2016: 190; Cosme et al. 2017: 331; Gupta and Pouw 2017: 87; Paulson 2017: 430) identify Ubuntu as an extension or ally of degrowth, as Ubuntu represents a different type of development model when compared with modernization and its focus on growth. However, these authors only mention Ubuntu in passing, and a detailed discussion of Ubuntu as degrowth will be presented.

Based on the preceding discussion of Ubuntu the link with degrowth is clear. This is particularly prevalent when Ubuntu as degrowth prescribes alternative activities and relations to others (human, non-human, and nature). To elaborate, Ubuntu advocates respect, dignity, collaboration, identity, and solidarity in a person's relations to others and the principle of sufficiency is prominent. Based on communitarianism, "I" in "We" should coordinate behavior to reach shared goals through joint projects by means of mutual aid and altruism instead of chasing self-interests. Similarly, degrowth prescribes this same principle which is based on sharing, simplicity, care, and commons (D'Alisa et al. 2014: 3).

If a person is orientated towards communitarian well-being, the commodification and misuse of non-humans and natural resources will be counterproductive in the attainment of Ubuntu. Similarly, Watadza (2016: 82) asserts that Ubuntu "encourage[s] the development of a non-exploitative attitude towards the environment, an attitude that if cultivated by all will leave the world more sustainable [than] it currently is". Therefore, Ubuntu as degrowth is proposed as a viable alternative *to* modernized development.

7.6   The Call for Change: What the West Can Learn from Ubuntu

Anthropocentric behavior is one of the leading causes of climate change. The *Homo œconomicus'* drive to satisfy self-interest through material wealth accumulation is contributing to our planet's death. The idea that capitalism and sustainable development will save us from extinction is a theory that must be set aside as it is precisely this notion that has set us on this apocalyptic path. A key reason why the modern individual is not taking climate change seriously enough to motivate the needed collective post-haste behavior is that such actions directly challenge the Western individualistic-capitalistic paradigm where humankind is seen as autonomous and separated from nature (cf. Klein 2014).

The Earth, and all its life forms, are at war with the global economic system (which favors the individualistic-capitalistic paradigm) and Klein (2014: 19) supportively states the "what the climate needs to avoid collapse is a contraction in humanity's use of resources; what our economic model demands to avoid collapse is unfettered expansion. Only one of these sets of rules can be changed, and it's not the laws of nature".

Subsequently, I call for a change; not only a change in human economic behaviour but also a call for a universal paradigm shift. This paradigm shift should be from the "I" in "Me" ideology which is rooted in individualistic values, capitalism, and authority over nature, towards the "I" in "We" paradigm as found in Ubuntu degrowth, which encompasses communitarianism, respect for nature and future generations through the principle of sufficiency.

This paradigm shift calls for the birth of a "global village" whereby individuals from across the world identify as a group—the human race, "I" in "We". Furthermore, the maxim "It takes a village to raise a child" should rather be read as "It takes a global village to raise present and future generations". All people should be seen as partners, who in solidarity should work together on communal projects, such as climate change adaptation strategies. It is imperative that self-interest and greed be set aside so that the global community can come together and help each other, especially the most vulnerable people when faced with changes in climate that will determine not just our future on this planet, but also the existence and quality of life of future generations.

This call for change should not be interpreted as a move to socialism or communism under the guise of Ubuntu as degrowth. The paradigm shift that is needed should move away from the focus allocated to economic terms, and the *Homo œconomicus* (economic human) must evolve into the *Homo Empathicus* (empathetic human) that recognizes relatedness to nature and others as in Ukama.

7.7   The Global Roundtable

When discussing climate change and which strategies to employ for adaptation, it is crucial to recognize that conflicting values can have a dire effect on the implementation of such strategies. For Le Grange (2015: 307) it is mandatory that the cultural, moral, and religious values be considered and that these values "should be aligned to common principles defined in the interest of the environment".

It is therefore essential to recognize that the values of the individualistic-capitalistic West differ when compared to the values of Africa's Ubuntu. Noteworthy, the aim of this chapter is not to demonize the West and to consequently state that vulnerable communities cannot benefit from sustainable development and GM crops for food production when faced with climate change. However, Asara et al. (2015: 382) wisely states that "[u]ncovering the ideology and practice of economic growth (connected to capitalism) as the ultimate driver of unsustainability [sic] may help sustainability science to further flourish and be more influential in re-defining the Earth's sustainable future".

From this, it is suggested that when formulating climate change adaptation strategies, all relevant stakeholders should be included in the conversation around the "global roundtable". It is imperative to acknowledge various cultural views that might differ from the West and that value systems, such as Ubuntu (where alternative values are allocated to others in the community, nature, and future generations), can provide unique perspectives when identifying climate change adaptation strategies.

The West has much to learn from others who are not driven by individualistic values and economics, but by the need for survival. These communities, e.g. indigenous Africans, live in close proximity to nature and have "strong reciprocal relationships with nature, drawing on local ecosystems on a small scale while caring for and regenerating the land so [that] it continues to provide for them and their descendants" (Klein 2014: 192). Humans should no longer be seen as separated from each other, non-humans, and nature. Rather, human existence is relationally rooted in ecological life (Le Grange 2015: 306) and Ukama (as an extension of Ubuntu) "provides the ethical anchorage for human social, spiritual and ecological togetherness" (Murove 2009: 317). The individual's focus should be on *becoming* a Person through others, and it is through relationality that humans can attain ensuing socio-ecological well-being.

Conclusively, Ubuntu should be "harnessed and combined with other values to support common principles aimed at addressing a deepening global socio-ecological crisis" (Le Grange 2015: 307). Ubuntu cannot be equated to the loss of identity, as it praises pluralism and diversity, and this makes it possible for shared principles to be defined even though various groups with different values are sitting at the "global roundtable" when discussing much-needed climate change adaptation strategies.

7.8   Conclusion

Climate change is a challenge faced by all of humanity and Africa is one of the continents that will be exponentially impacted. It is imperative that humankind, in a post-haste collective manner, implements appropriate climate change adaptation strategies to mitigate the effects of extreme temperatures and natural phenomena that can have dire consequences for human existence and the planet.

A popular adaptive strategy proposed by individualistic-capitalistic Western societies, based on the sustainable development paradigm and its focus on growth, is the commercialization of GM crops to address hunger and poverty in Africa which are amplified by climatic changes. Unfortunately, "[International and] national policies can inadvertently disregard or undermine cultural, traditional and context-specific practices that support local adaptation to climate change" (CDKN 2014: 28). Thus, cultural values in Africa, e.g. Ubuntu, are often ignored in the formulation and implementation of adaptive strategies.

As it cannot be assumed that values regarding relations toward humans, non-humans, and the natural environment are the same across all cultures, the individualistic-capitalistic values were compared to Ubuntu values. Ngcoya (2009: 1) asserts that "Ubuntu stresses the importance of community, solidarity, caring and sharing. This worldview advocates a profound sense of interdependence and emphasizes that our true human potential [*becoming* a Person] can only be realized in partnership with others". Ubuntu's "I" in "We" is the antithesis of "I" in "Me" (based on individualistic values) and should be implemented in response to the individualistic-capitalistic Western values where it is acceptable to misuse and abuse natural resources in the name of capitalism, progress, growth, and development.

It is argued that Africa has inherent strengths that can be utilized for climate change adaptation, such as sustainable and sufficient livelihoods (Skidelsky and Skidelsky 2012: 6). Ubuntu is extensively similar to the degrowth paradigm which proposes an alternative approach *to* development. From this, a call for a universal paradigm shift is made—away from an individualistic-capitalistic orientation; towards the environmental ethics of Ubuntu degrowth.

Humankind can rethink and restructure the way they perceive their relation to humans, non-humans, as well as nature and it is suggested that various stakeholders, with diverse perspectives, converse around the "global roundtable" when developing climate change adaptation strategies.

References

Anon. s.a.1. Greenhouse gasses. *Dictionary.com Unabridged*. Random House, Inc. http://www.dictionary.com/browse/greenhouse-gas. Date of access 4 Sept 2017.

Anon. s.a.2. "Humane". *Collins English Dictionary—Complete & Unabridged 10th Edition*. HarperCollins Publishers. http://www.dictionary.com/browse/humaneness. Date of access 4 Sept 2017.

Asara, V., I. Otero, F. Demaria, and E. Corbera. 2015. Socially Sustainable Degrowth as a Social–Ecological Transformation: Repoliticizing Sustainability. *Socially Sustainable Degrowth as a Social-Ecological Transformation* 10: 375–384.

Bishop, R. 2017. Confronting Climate Change Africa's Leadership on an Increasingly Urgent Issue. In *Foresight Africa: Top Priorities for the Continent in 2017*, ed. S. Amadou, 76–91. Brookings Institution. https://www.brookings.edu/multi-chapter-report/foresight-africa/. Date of access 4 Sept 2017.

Bondarenko, P. 2017. Gross domestic product (GDP). *Encyclopædia Britannica*. Encyclopædia Britannica, Inc. https://www.britannica.com/topic/gross-domestic-product. Date of access 4 Sept 2017.

Climate and Development Knowledge Network [CDKN]. 2014. *The IPCC's Fifth Assessment Report: What's in it for Africa?* London, UK: Overseas Development Institute/Climate and Development Knowledge Network.

Cosme, I., R. Santos, and D.W. O'Neill. 2017. Assessing the Degrowth Discourse: A Review and Analysis of Academic Degrowth Policy Proposals. *Journal of Cleaner Production* 149: 321–334.

D'Alisa, G., F. Demaria, and G. Kallis. 2014. *Degrowth: A Vocabulary for a New Era*. New York: Routledge, Taylor and Francis.

Giddings, B., B. Hopwood, and G. O'Brien. 2002. Environment, Economy and Society: Fitting Them Together into Sustainable Development. *Sustainable Development* 10: 187–196.

Gupta, J., and N. Pouw. 2017. Towards a Trans-Disciplinary Conceptualization of Inclusive Development. *Current Opinion in Environmental Sustainability* 24: 96–103.

Huesing, J., and L. English 2004. The Impact of Bt Crops on the Developing World. *AgBioForum* 7 (1–2): 84–95.

Intergovernmental Panel on Climate Change [IPCC]. 2012. Glossary of Terms. In *Managing the Risks of Extreme Events and Disasters to Advance Climate Change. A Special Report of Working Groups I and II of the Intergovernmental Panel on Climate Change (IPCC)*, ed. M. Tignor, and P.M. Midgley, 555–564. Cambridge, United Kingdom and New York, NY, USA, Cambridge University Press.

Kallis, G. 2015. The Degrowth Alternative. *Great Transition Initiative*. Tellus Institute. http://www.greattransition.org/publication/the-degrowth-alternative. Date of access 4 Sept 2017.

Kelbessa, W. 2014. Can an African environmental ethics contribute to environmental policy in Africa? *Environmental Ethics* 36 (1): 31–61.

Kelbessa, W. 2015. Climate Ethics and Policy in Africa. *Thought and Practice: A Journal of the Philosophical Association of Kenya* 7: 41–84.

Klein, N. 2014. *This changes everything: Capitalism vs. the climate*. New York: Simon and Schuster.

Kothari, A., F. Demaria, and A. Acosta. 2014. BuenVivir, Degrowth and Ecological Swaraj: Alternatives to Sustainable Development and the Green Economy. *Development* 57 (3–4): 362–375.

Le Grange, L. 2015. Ubuntu/Botho as Ecophilosophy and Ecosophy. *Journal of Human Ecology* 49 (3): 301–308.

LenkaBula, P. 2008. Beyond Anthropocentricity—Botho/Ubuntu and the Quest for Economic and Ecological Justice in Africa. *Religion and Theology* 15: 375–394.

Maynard, M. 2016. *The Green Economy Within an Emerging New Cosmology Perspective: Rethinking Sustainability*, M.Phil diss. Faculty of Economic and Management Sciences, Stellenbosch University.

Martinez-Alier, J., I. Anguelovski, P. Bond, D. Del Bene, F. Demaria, J.F. Gerber, L. Greyl, W. Haas, H. Healy, V. Marín-Burgos, G. Ojo, M. Porto, L. Rijnhout, B. Rodríguez-Labajos, J. Spangenberg, L. Temper, R. Warlenius, and I. Yánez. 2014. Between Activism and Science: Grassroots Concepts for Sustainability Coined by Environmental Justice Organizations. *Journal of Political Ecology* 21: 19–60.

Metz, T. 2011. Ubuntu as a Moral Theory and Human Rights in South Africa. *African Human Rights Law Journal* 11 (2): 532–559.

Murove, M.F. 2009. An African Environmental Ethic Based on the Concepts of Ukama and Ubuntu. In *African Ethics: An Anthology of Comparative and Applied Ethics*, ed. M.F. Murove, 315–331. Pietermaritzburg: University of Kwazulu-Natal Press.

Murove, M.F. 2014. Ubuntu. *Diogenes* 59 (3–4): 36–47.

Munyaka, M, and M. Motlhabi. 2009. Ubuntu and Its Socio-Moral Significance. In *African Ethics: An Anthology of Comparative and Applied Ethics*, ed. F.M. Murove 69: 71–72.

Ngcoya, M. 2009. *Ubuntu: Globalization, Accommodation, and Contestation in South Africa*, Ph.D. Thesis. Faculty of the School of International Service, Amsterdam University.

North-West University—African Centre for Disaster Studies [NWU—ACDS]. 2018. *EAGER Profile—I am Sense Mokoti*. [Video]. https://www.youtube.com/watch?v=kkEdZbq3qgg&list=PL2vxcQcthAk2NkpaLZiuTW0Xr_-YqC7y3&index=6&t=400s. Date of Access 6 Mar 2019.

O'Brien, K. 2009. Values and the Limits to Adaptation. In *Adapting to Climate Change: Thresholds, Values, Governance*, ed. W.N. Adger, I. Lorenzoni and K.L. O'Brien. Cambridge University Press.

Paulson, S. 2017. Degrowth, Culture and Power. *Journal of Political Ecology* 24: 425–666.

Pavel, M.O. 2015. A Climate Justice Compass for Transforming Self and World. *World Futures* 71(3–4): 96–113.

Perrot, R. 2015. The Trojan Horses of Global Environmental and Social Politics. In *Earth, Wind and Fire: Unpacking the Political, Economic and Security Implications of Discourse on the Green Economy*, ed. L. Mytelka, V. Msimang, and R. Perrot. Johannesburg: Real African Publishers.

Research & Degrowth. 2010. Degrowth Declaration of the Paris 2008 Conference. *Journal of Cleaner Production* 18 (6): 523–524.

Schnurr, M.A. 2015. GMO 2.0: Genetically Modified Crops and the Push for Africa's Green Revolution. *Canadian Food Studies/La Revue canadienne des études sur l'alimentation* 2 (2): 201–208.

Skidelsky, R., and E. Skidelsky. 2012. *How Much is Enough?*. New York: Other Press.

Swyngedouw, E. 2014. Depoliticization ('The Political'). In *Degrowth: A Vocabulary for a New Era*, ed. G. D'Alisa, F. Demaria, and G. Kallis. London: Routledge.

Theron, S. 1995. *Africa, Philosophy and the Western Tradition: An Essay in Self-Understanding*. Frankfurt: Peter Lang.

Thompson, B. 2013. Agricultural Productivity is Key to Reducing World Poverty. *AG Web, Farm Journal*. FarmJournal, Inc. https://www.agweb.com/article/bill_gates_agricultural_productivity_is_key_to_reducing_world_poverty/. Date of access 4 Sept 2017.

Van Binsbergen, W. 2001. Ubuntu and the Globalization of Southern African Thought and Society. *Quest* 15 (1–2): 53–89.

Watadza, M. 2016. *A Critical Assessment of African Communitarianism for Environmental Well-being*, M.A. diss. Philosophy, University of South Africa.

Wiredu, K. 1996. *Cultural Universals and Particulars: An African Perspective*. Indianapolis: Indiana Press.

World Commission on Environment and Development [WCED]. 1987. *Our Common Future*. Oxford: Oxford University Press.

Zozuľakova, V. 2016. Degrowth—A Way of Social Transformation. *ZeszytyNaukowe. OrganizacjaiZarządzanie/PolitechnikaŚląska* 94: 185–195.

Chapter 8
African Environmental Ethics as Southern Environmental Ethics

Nompumelelo Zinhle Manzini

Abstract This chapter argues that African Environmental ethics or African beliefs regarding the environment (which includes plants, animals and the immaterial objects) is not as anthropocentric as Kai Horsthemke (US-China Educ Rev 6(10):22–31, 2009) has argued for it to be. Instead African Environmental ethics proves itself to be biocentric in nature. In this chapter, I first argue against the views supported by anthropocentrism. My aims are to show how Tempels 'force thesis' allows us to see how African beliefs/views regarding the environment are not anthropocentric. Having said that, the chapter questions whether biocentric views like Father Placide Tempels force thesis are uniquely African?. I gesture towards the view that such arguments are not uniquely African. That is, we cannot talk about a unique African thinking/approach about the environment. Instead, I argue for a "Southern Environmental Ethics". Here South refers both to the geographic South and the South within the North. The argument for "Southern Environmental Ethics" refers to individuals who are located on the marginal side of the Abyssal line as theorised by Boaventura de Sousa Santos (2016).

8.1 Introduction

Debates regarding African ecological perspectives have received much attention in the 20th century both from the West and within Africa. The motivations behind this interest differ depending on who is doing the enquiry. Africans themselves have engaged in these debates by way of indicating that there is something particularly unique about an African ethic versus a Western ethic. The West, on the other hand, have exhausted their knowledge base, with the desire to learn from 'alternative epistemologies', with the recognition that they have been the contributors to the environmental issues that we are facing today. Whilst Africans have asserted that there is a distinct African worldview that can aid the West in developing better and greener

N. Z. Manzini (✉)
University of the Witwatersrand, Johannesburg, South Africa
e-mail: hlemanzini@gmail.com

© Springer Nature Switzerland AG 2019
M. Chemhuru (ed.), *African Environmental Ethics*, The International
Library of Environmental, Agricultural and Food Ethics 29,
https://doi.org/10.1007/978-3-030-18807-8_8

Climate goals; much disagreement has been had on whether African ecological ethics are anthropocentric, biocentric or ecocentric. Equally, there have been other cultural worldviews that have been leaned on such as Hinduism, Confucianism and so forth that equally purport that they have a unique ecological ethic.

In light of these considerations, I have two aims for this chapter. The first is to discern the views that African ecological perspective(s) show themselves to be anthropocentric. I contend that they are biocentric.

Now if it is the case that particular African ecological ethics are biocentric, what makes these views distinctly African? I am of the view that these views are not distinctly African, by way of analysis I consider other cultural groups of subjugated[1] people, which includes the Hawaiian or Indian ethic. These are cultural groups that fall within the realm of Southern epistemologies as conceptualised by Boaventura De Sousa Santos (2016). The stronger claims of this chapter lie within this section. Whilst the links between African ecological perspectives and the cultural groups identified here are not new, the chapter argues for a stronger transcultural perspective than the one offered in existing literature. I hereby argue for a clustering of the transcultural epistemological framework to be termed as: Southern Environmentalism.

8.2   African Environmentalism as Biocentric

So, let me begin.

I am an African.

I owe my being to the hills and the valleys, the mountains and the glades, the rivers, the deserts, the trees, the flowers, the seas and the ever-changing seasons that define the face of our native land (Mbeki 1996)

African Environmentalism is a subject area of African Philosophy. Arguably, when Father Placide Temples wrote *Bantu Philosophy* (1959), he sought to challenge the racist assumptions that underpin Western discourse—which takes the African[2] person as being non-human. Tempels force thesis came out of his exploration of the "Baluba's ontological system" (Matolino 2014: 10). By way of explaining the ontology of the Bantu.

Tempels theorisation of the Bantu has received much criticism from various scholars within African Philosophy, in particular Hountondji (1983) and Cesaire (1972).

---

[1]The term subjugated knowledge is derived from Michael Foucault Discipline and Punish: The Birth of the Prison (1977 cited in Collins 1990: 251). Foucault defines subjugated as the "local, discontinuous, disqualified, illegitimate knowledges' that are considered to be "beneath the required level of cognition or scientificity". African philosophy can be regarded as subjugated knowledge because it comes out of "music, literature, daily conversations, and everyday behavior", including proverbs (ibid.).

[2]The use of the term 'African', does not treat Africans as a monolithic group. Rather, it refers to a people of a set geographical location who hold the cultural values spoken about in this paper. Since African's are not a homogenous group, there is the awareness that the force thesis may only apply to a few.

Hountondji questions if Tempels was successful in his attempt to challenge how Western discourse has theorized about the African person. He additionally questions the authenticity, rigour and method applied by Tempels. I am in agreement with Hountondji's critique that Temples' work was not "addressed to Africans but to Europeans" (1983: 34), that is Africans are aware of their ontological status, it is the West that needs to be educated about African ontology and not the other way round.

Having said that, Tempels force thesis has been one of the most engaged texts within African Philosophy. One of the merits being its explanation of African environmental ethics. In what follows I outline Tempels force thesis,[3] the objectives here are two fold: (1) To argue that Kai Horsthemke is misguided when he argues that African ethics is anthropocentric. (2) To show that the African's approach to the environment shows itself to be biocentric.

A reasonable task to understanding the debate between anthropocentrism and biocentrism, would be to define the environment in which I have been lightly referring to. One could define the environment first as the ecosphere therefore referring to nature, referring to plants, animals, air, human beings and so forth. Or one could speak of the environment in reference to certain conditions that make a space inhabitable or workable. For example, one would say that the environment at home, makes it hard for one to complete their work. For the purposes of this chapter the concern is with the former, that being the ecosphere.

In *Bantu Philosophy* (1959), Tempels outlines the hierarchy of being which is anchored by the force thesis (see Diagram A). According to Tempels, "all beings in the universe possess vital force of their own: human, animal, vegetable, or inanimate" (ibid.: 31). Tempels expresses this as "being is that which has force" (ibid.). As stated by Tempels force is characterised by a hierarchy which is primogeniture: where God is at the top of this hierarchy. Following God are the first fathers to man whom God first communicated her vital force to, they are the "archipatriarchs" and they have the power of "exercising their influences on all posterity" (ibid.: 42). Although the first fathers may be dead, they are regarded as the spiritualised beings that have *influence and participate*[4] in the divine force. Tempels adds that those who are living belong to this hierarchy (below the archipatriarchs).

Accordingly, force is not something that is exclusive to human beings, rather all beings have force: "human, animal, vegetable, or inanimate" (ibid.). Whilst all beings may have force, what differentiates Muntu from the inferior forces is that Muntu has *intelligence and will.* It is important to note that because all beings have force, this is what makes the force thesis communitarian. In so far as all beings that stay in this community are endowed with force from God; they share a common element/bond that binds them; that is force (the communitarian nature of the force thesis and its implications are explored later). Furthermore, not only does this force bind them

---

[3] The original outline appears in my master's Dissertation (entitled "African Conceptions of Person as Gendered, Ableist and Anti-queer" (see Manzini 2017). Here I critique certain African conceptions of personhood as being gendered, anti-queer and ableist. One of those studied conceptions include Tempels force thesis.

[4] Own emphasis.

together but their force interacts in various ways. According to Tempels, there is an "interaction of being with being" that transcends the "mechanical, chemical and psychological interactions" that marks the interaction of forces as an ontological relationship (ibid.: 40).

God: The source of force for every creature. She possesses force in herself.

↓

Archipatriarchs/Spirits beings: whom God communicated her vital force with; they constitute the most important chain binding the muntu to God.

↓

Muntu: a reflexive self-aware force endowed with intelligence and will. Muntu can directly influence inferior beings.

↓

Inferior forces: animal, plant, mineral: they exist to increase the vital force of uMuntu i.e. they are created for the disposal use of man. They do not exercise influence over themselves.

Force: The integrity of being. All things in the universe possess this vital force on their own.

Diagram A

All these forces are said to have something in common, that being their origin, growth, change, destruction, "or the achievement of the beings, passive and active causality, and particularly the nature of the being as such supporting those universal phenomena" (ibid.: 34). Tempels further adds that whilst each force may be different, there is unity between the forces. That is individuality, ought to be understood as "individuality of forces" (ibid.: 36). By this I understand Tempels to be stating that each force has intrinsic value. It may seem as though the inferior forces have instrumental value when looking at the diagram above. However, this is not the case, so long as they have force, they possess intrinsic value. As stated by Tempels: "force is being, being is force" (ibid.: 35). Meaning that there is an ontological unity that entails some connectedness and harmony, that is based "on the organic solidarity and complementarity" (Mazama 2002: 220) of all forces. Paul W. Taylor argues that an entity has intrinsic value in so far as it is a member of "the Earth's community of life" (1981: 201). Simply put, this would be a reinforcement of Tempels argument that all being is force.

Tempels argues that at the top of this hierarchy is God. One can infer from this that the relationship of man to inferior forces (the environment or animals) is not anthropocentric. One can understand why Horsthemke (2009) and those who support this view infer that African Environmentalism is anthropocentric. Rightly one would assume that since Muntu, can gain her force from inferior forces then the hierarchy of being is centred on her; therefore making the hierarchy anthropocentric (as indicated in Diagram A). Kwasi Wiredu acknowledges this and states that any environmental approach whether it be anthropocentric, biocentric or ecocentric will to a certain degree be controlled by the demands of human survival, "and beyond that, of any reasonable form of human flourishing" (1994: 45). Yet, a closer reading of the force thesis suggests that it is biocentric. Meaning that it places the biosphere at the centre.

A biocentric environmental approach is grounded on four tenants as defined by Taylor (1981: 206):

(1) Humans are thought of as members of the Earths community of life, holding that membership on the same terms as applied to all the nonhuman members.
(2) The Earth's natural ecosystems as a totality are seen as a complex web of interconnected elements, with the sound biological functioning of others […]
(3) Each individual organism is conceived of as a teleological centre of life, pursuing its own good in its own way.

Tempels force thesis is not at odds with the biocentric outlook as defined by Taylor. In the remainder of this section, the three tenets will be considered contra force thesis. Yet, in order to give a successful account, some inconsistencies in Tempels theory need to be resolved.

Tempels states that each force interacts with one another as they share a bond, their relationship is ontological (ibid.). According to Tempels (ibid.: 41),

> nothing moves in this universe of forces without influencing other forces by its movement. The world of forces is held like a spider's web of which no single thread can be caused to vibrate without shaking the whole network.

When Tempels states that being is force and force is being, such a statement indicates the manner in which all forces are dependent on each other for survival. At the same time, Tempels states that inferior forces exist to increase the vital force of uMuntu i.e. they are created for the disposal use of man. They do not exercise influence over themselves. If it is the case that inferior forces cannot influence themselves or other forces, then Tempels 'spider web' becomes impossible. Its impossibility would prove true that the force thesis is humanistic insofar as it is only the 'Muntu' who can exercise influence over other forces. However, this does not necessarily make the force thesis anthropocentric.

As highlighted earlier, what makes the Muntu a superior force to immaterial forces is that Muntu has rationality. Rationality would be an entity that a plant or lion would lack, yet this does not justify the superiority of Muntu. Rationality is the intrinsic value that Muntu does not share with other forces. Equally, there are other intrinsic values that Muntu does not share with say a cheetah. A cheetah has the speed that Muntu does not poses. Defenders of animal rights could argue that cheetahs and plants to a certain extent also poses a certain amount of rationality, a different kind of rationality. Having said that, the argument that humans are endowed with force that allows them to interact with the other forces still stands. Taylor highlights that this train of thinking only begs the question, insofar as, rationality is a characteristic that is valued by humans and so from a human viewpoint it is regarded as desirable. Yet, if one was to consider the capacities of material objects, we note that these would be in contrast to human standards (Taylor 1981: 211–212).

Such inconsistencies prove true to Hountondji's commentary that Tempels work lacked "severe rigour" (Hountondji 1983: 38). But, is this inconsistency reconcilable? I think so, but such a task falls outside of the objectives of this chapter. The task at hand, however, is to dispel the views of anthropocentrism. While Muntu may have influence over the inferior forces, this does not mean that inferior forces do not have intrinsic value since they have inherent force. The only reason that Muntu has influence over the inferior forces is because Muntu has rationality (will and intelligence) as stated by Tempels. A view that shows itself to be ableist.[5] According to Taylor, this kind of thinking presents us with a logical flaw that assumes that "humans are *morally* superior beings because of what they possess, while others lack, the capacities of a moral agent" (1981: 213) such as rationality or free will. Having said that, even though Muntu may have the ability to influence other forces, force is an element that is not centred around Muntu. That is, force is an element that is centred around God who is the source of force.

Another way to dispel the views of anthropocentrism is to assess the primary premises of the force thesis versus the primary thesis of anthropocentrism:

> **The anthropocentric thesis**: Anthropocentric views are the kind that places humankind at the centre of its theorisation.
>
> **The force thesis**: Being is force and force is being. Where God is the creature of all force.

Looking at these two statements, we note that the force thesis cannot be anthropocentric since God is at the centre or is the most important element. Even though a human being can use inferior forces at her disposal (see Diagram A), she is still not the important element. Rather force or God is the important element. Therefore, the force thesis cannot be anthropocentric. When looking at the force thesis we note that humans are not at the centre of nature, instead they form part of it as 'beings with force' to borrow Tempels language. An anthropocentric view, on the other hand, would be the kind that privileges the human being at the centre of its orientation; arguing that everything that exists around the environment is placed for its existence. Rather the force thesis shares characteristics with biocentrism as defined by Taylor.

Additionally, anthropocentrism treats nature as instrumental. As explained by Richard T. De George, anthropocentrism is a Western praxis that treats nature as an object, which is there for humans to "interrogate, subdue, dominate and manipulate" (1994: 16). An example of an anthropocentric would be the kind that argues that oil spills in the sea are bad, because of what they do to human beings. Or that they are bad for fish because human beings are the ones who eat the fish. A biocentric view, on the other hand, is that kind that recognises the intrinsic value of each living organism in the ecosystem. The communitarian nature of the force thesis reinforces this spider-web of relations. That is the relationship between the various forces are anchored by this relation that binds the forces together. The community in this regard does not refer to the community as the "aggregated sum of individuals" (Menkiti 1984: 179). Rather as Menkiti defines it, it refers to the community in a "collectivist sense"—which is

---

[5] See Manzini (2017), I indicate that Tempels view show's itself to be ableist towards people living with severe cognitive disabilities.

anchored by an organic dimension that holds a relationship between the community and the individuals living there (ibid.: 180).

Therefore, talk around the community is not anthropocentric, as the community in the African sense refers to those living and dead, animals, plants, ancestors. In a conversation with Gogo Dineo Ndlanzi,[6] Gogo Ndlanzi echoes that the relational relationship that Africans have with the environment can be seen during *ukophaahla*.[7] During the ceremony a healer asks permission to work with and in the water. According to Gogo Ndlanzi every living organism in African cultures is regarded as having intrinsic value. As echoed in the quoted lines of Thabo Mbeki's "I am an Africa" speech/poem. Mbeki starts off his speech/poem by acknowledging the natural environment, which he 'owes his being to'. Without this natural environment, Mbeki argues that he would not exist. Therefore, the community includes the "extra-human beings of various grades of power and intelligence, ranging from the super-human to the sub-human" (Wiredu 1994: 45). The point is that it would not make sense to speak of African communities as being human-centred communities. It is important to note here that the relationship that humans have with nature, is the kind that respects nature—that echoes that human beings are not superior rather they exist in relation to other forces.

The argument presented above rejects views that regard *Ubuntu* as anthropocentric (see Bujo 1998, 2009; Gyekye 1997 for further reading). Whilst the interests of this paper are not *Ubuntu* per say, a minor exploration of the debate seems worthwhile, so as to dispel the views that it is an anthropocentric ethic. The conceptual equivalent of the ethic in English would be "I am because we are, because we are therefore, I am", a more accurate translation would be "A human being is human because of other human beings". Preferably, in order to ensure that the meaning of the idiom is not lost in translation, the preference is to ground the explanation in its vernacular language: 'uMuntu umuntu ngaBantu'. Simply because an English translation does not capture the depth of the idiom. 'ngaBantu' is not limited only to the living human beings, but also to the living dead, those who are yet to come, and the ancestors as explained by Okot p'Bitek's article "The Sociality of Self" (1985).

When scholars like Horsthemke limit their translation, and focus on 'human', it is no surprise that they would think that the ethic is anthropocentric. It is a result of poor translation and a misunderstanding of the ethic. The 'we' is not limited to the "membership of human species" (Horsthemke 2009: 25), as articulated by the author. Rather 'we', is inclusive of all species that occupy the environment. Reducing an African ethic as anthropocentric, would be to deny the ethic of its complexity and richness. GogoNdlanzi (2017) rightly echoes that such views expressed by the likes of

---

[6]Gogo Ndlanzi is a spiritual healer. Referencing her is an explicit political move, one that ensures that our African healers voices are included in academic work. Partially because I think they have greater insight/lived experience about the topic at hand than any academic philosopher would. Moreover, to ensure that our healers are engaged with as subjects and not objects of academic enquiry.

[7]This is an acknowledgement ceremony, sometimes refereed to libation. The ceremony acknowledges the spirit that is alive in all living things.

Bujo, Gyekye and so forth interpret African spirituality or African environmentalism through a Western lens.

8.3   African Environmental Ethics as Southern Environmental Ethics

The preceding paragraphs have successfully argued against the view that certain African ecological ethics are anthropocentric. One is then inclined to ask if this thinking is uniquely African, and if so, what makes it unique? At first sight, one could argue that any eco-philosophical viewpoint regarding the environment that is grounded in an African ethic (whatever this may be) will be termed as 'African Environmentalism'. This question highlights an unresolved tension that the first section of this paper failed to define. That is, the first section of this paper accepted that Tempels force thesis is an 'African' exploration of African environmentalism. Tempels force thesis has been rightly defined as ethno-philosophy by Hountondji (Bodunrin 1981: 161). Following this logic, one could argue that arguments that present eco-philosophical vies from a certain geographical location, in this case, Africa—those views can be referred to as African. There is the awareness that such a question leaves one vulnerable to many criticisms and questions. Having noted that, let us assume that views like Tempels or *Ubuntu* as a moral ethic are African because they are grounded in a "thought system of a particular African community" (ibid.). One then is inclined to ask if these thought systems are really unique to Africa or any geography for that matter.

One could accept that eco-philosophical theories like Tempels, are uniquely African because of their geographical location. As Thaddeus Metz explains, geographical labels highlight "features that are *salient* in a locale" (2015: 1176). By way of example, Metz states that "baseball is American [...] insofar as it is salient there" (ibid.). Therefore, calling something African does not imply that it is "unique to the continent of Africa" (Metz 2011: 396), rather geographical labels facilitate dialogue and debate. If it is the case that we can ascribe certain practices to locales because they are most salient there, I am of the view that we cannot really speak about African eco-philosophical views as being distinct to Africa. The views expressed in Tempels thesis, as salient as they may be to Africa as a locale, are also salient in locales like the Amazon. As far as eco-philosophy is concerned, I caution against the rigid use of geographical labels that most eco-philosophical debates have depended on. Rather, the correct term that should be used is Southern Environmental ethics.[8]

---

[8]The rationale here is not to deny African people of their distinct methodological approaches about the environment or their knowledge systems. That is, my motives should not be regarded as an epistemicide, rather this is a genuine enquiry that is intercultural and cross cultural in its nature. The approach does not deny the difference across cultures, nor does it assume a narrowed theoretical thinking about the environmental approaches across cultures.

African thinking about the environment follows a similar logic as other subjugated cultural groups from the South. The South hereby refers to the South both as a geographical location and an epistemic South. Such a conceptualisation of African environmentalism is synonymous to post-colonial ecocriticism; defined as the attempt to "historicise nature (while putting nature back into history) in order to disrupt the naturalization of geographical identities and conditions that have been shaped by them" (Caminero-Santangeo 2014: 10). That is, it is the move away from colonial boundaries, and having an assumed universal or transcultural thinking about the environment. And so, the South would refer to, but not limited to Hinduism, Buddhism, Shintoism, Confucianism and Taoism. As rightly noted by Kwasi Wiredu, this refers to cultures that respectively have a moral concern for nature, where human beings are seen as "fellow participants with animals, plants, non-living things in a system of organically interrelated existence pervaded in their essences by one and the same principle of ultimate reality" (Wiredu 1994: 31). Edwin Etieyibo better defines this kind of thinking as *ecumenical environmentalism/ecumenical environmental ethic*, which is defined as an environmental approach the "emerges from some cultural and religious tradition[9]" (2011: 48).

By conceptualising African environmentalism as Southern[10] environmentalism, I am arguing for a particular environmental ecophilosophical[11] approach. It goes without saying that the links between say African environmentalism, Hinduism or Confucianism is one that is not new or controversial. Below a stronger link, than the subtle ones that have been alluded to by Wiredu (1994) or Oruka (1994) is articulated. As a point of departure, it would suffice to look at these cultures.[12]

Similar to the force thesis, the Indian ethic is not centred around humans. Rather it is centred around *dharma*. That is, it views all lives as being equal. The ethic states

---

[9]Notably, Judaeo-Christianity would be one of the *ecumenical environmental ethics* that would not be regarded as being part of the South, for known reasons. Conceptually one could categorize a Judaeo- Christian ethic as being Western and arguably anthropocentric in so far as it does view the individual as being the center of all life or the environment (see Etieyibo 2011 for further reading).

[10]The conceptualization of 'South' in this manner gains inspiration from the works of Santos and his conception of the "epistemologies of the South" (2016). This is a term that I first engaged with at the epistemologies of the South Summer School 2017, in Portugal. Santos defines this epistemological thinking as "a crucial epistemological transformation [that attempts] to reinvent social emancipation on a global scale" (2016: 18). In Santo's words, South is then a metaphor for "the human suffering caused by capitalism and colonialism on the global level, as well as for the resistance to overcoming or minimizing such suffering" (ibid.).

[11]Oruka defines ecophilosophy as "the totality of the philosophy of nature" (1994:119). In defining ecophilsophy he argues that it is different from environmental ethics, because environmental studies are limited to studying the earth and atmosphere. Equally, he argues that ecophilosophy is different from environmental ethic, since the latter has not gone extended "ethics from human beings to the non-human creatures on earth" (ibid.). I think that when Africans speaks about environmental ethics, the ethic is extended to the immaterial objects, including the understanding of the earth and the atmosphere. And so, whilst Oruka may argue for such a distinction to be made between ecophilosophy, environmental studies and environmental ethics. I take it that the term Southern environmentalism is inclusive of the three terms that Oruka takes to be distinct.

[12]I will not consider African cultures as the first part of this chapter has defined African environmentalism.

that human life, animal life and all immaterial life such as plants, trees, rivers and so forth is all of equal value. According to Okura, Indian philosophy treats human life as being in nature and not against nature (Okura 1994: 121). Hawaiian ontology is similar to that of the force thesis and the Indian ethic. That is, Hawaiian families believe that their social relationships are pan-Polynesian. Their concept of family (*ohana*) is comprised of a "matrix genealogical kinship that extends to include all elements of creation" (ibid.: 122). More specific examples of movements that are anchored in a cultural environmental ethic include the Himalayas of Uttarakhand in India, where the women and men of the "Chipko Andolan movement surrounded and hugged trees to protect local forests from state-approved logging companies" (Whyte and Cuomo 2016: 1 cited in Lui 2017) or the Anishinaabe community that walked the Great Lakes to raise awareness of the pollution and misuse of water. A more recent and radical example is the Whanganui River. Located in the north of New Zealand, the Whanganui River was accorded the legal status of a person in 2017. One of the indigenous people of the Whanganui Iwi, Adtian Rurawhe stated that from his cultural viewpoint the "wellbeing of the river is directly linked to the well-being of the people [...] and so it is really important that's recognised as its own identity" (ibid.)

The identified cultural groups share the characteristics of a biocentric environmental approach; one that is regarded as 'indigenous knowledge'. Importantly, one cannot speak about indigenous knowledge systems without the awareness of the politics of power and knowledge that underpin them (Green 2008: 146). Politically, what the above-mentioned groups have in common with African cultures is the colonisation that they suffered at the hands of the West,[13] including but not limited to the United States of America, New Zealand or United Kingdom of England. These are cultures that not only share the same political history but similar cultural ethics regarding the environment. Cultural beliefs that colonialism sought to destruct; thus, leading to the epistemicide of the cultural groups "ancestral links and their manner of relating to others and to nature" (Santos 2016: 18). It is because of this shared political history and cultural ethic that I argue that we ought to think about African environmental ethics as Southern environmental ethics because they all fall in the same bracket of what we would conceive of as the South. To borrow from Santos, such an approach is *teoriapvera*, meaning it is "a rear guard theory based on the experiences of large, marginalised minorities and majorities that struggle against unjustly imposed marginality and inferiority, with the purpose of strengthening their resistance" (Santos 2014: ix). According to Santos these cultural groups fall on the other side of the abyssal line where there is no real knowledge (see Santos 2007; Santos et al. (2007) for further reading).

---

[13] For the purposes of this paper, West refers to Eurocentric positivist epistemology. Whilst most of this thinking lands itself in the geographic West, we note that some of the cultural groups referred to as 'South' would also fall under the 'West'. Such as the Himalayas of Uttarakhand in India, and so when thinking about the West, here I refer to an epistemological framework that adopts a Cartesian paradigm towards nature. This is such a paradigm that I have argued is anthropocentric insofar as it views nature as "a *res extensa* and, as such, an unlimited resource unconditionally available to human beings" (Santos 2014: 23).

If the African approach towards the environment and all those that can be regarded as Southern approaches can be merged together, we stand a better chance at not only understanding the environment but also dealing with the issues regarding the environment and globalisation, issues of animal rights and so forth. This kind of thinking requires a post abyssal thinking. Santos (2014: 133) defines post abyssal thinking as a

> recognition that social exclusion in its broadest sense takes very different forms according to whether it is determined by an abyssal or a nonabyssal line, as well as that, as long as abyssally defined exclusion persists, no really progressive postcapitalist alternative is possible.

It entails that we learn "from the South through an epistemology of the South" (ibid.: 134).

It goes without saying that there will be some problems with clustering these cultural groups together and locating them in the South when we know for instance that some of these cultural groups may not identify with the geographical South. There are also some weaker arguments that one could advance against the suggested clustering, for instance, one could argue that these cultural groups thinking can be traced back to Africa, and so we ought to think about all these cultural groups as essentially having an African environmental ethic. This argument is weak because it would still lead to the same conclusions as I reach. Moreover, the quest for thinking about Southern Environmentalism is not about making the South another hegemony. Calling it African Environmentalism (following the logic of the weaker argument), runs the risk of making African epistemology hegemonic.

It should be noted that this approach does not deny any Afrocentric approach about the environment, rather it's a call for a transcultural approach that links cultures that have a similar history and culture. The aim here is not to collate them into one ontological or epistemological framework. Instead, it is the recognition that if common cultures come together, we stand a better chance at dealing with the effects that capitalism has had on the environment from a global point.

Another argument that could be advanced is that "Africa is the most vulnerable to climate change" (Horsthemke 2009: 23). As we are told by Horsthemke, South Africa as it stands "has the third highest level of biodiversity in the world" (ibid.). Consequently, it would make sense for environmentalists to adopt an Afrocentric approach to curbing the issues that we have. Be that as it may, I contend that a transcultural approach remains favourable. Especially because Africans are not a homogeneous group.

8.4 Concluding Remarks

> This soil belongs to Kenyan people. Nobody has the right to sell or buy it. It is our mother and we her children (Ngugi 1986: 98).

> The Environment Crisis facing humanity is due in part to the philosophy of possessive individualism... (Oruka 1994: 115).

A conclusion would be a premature act, as I think that the work explored here only sketches further philosophical consideration regarding a transcultural environmental ethic. What this will look like, whether it will work, are thoughts that need to be fleshed out. I think that the underlying issue here regards justice. Justice both for the environment and justice for cultures that suffer the consequences of possessive individualism that has no regard for nature in itself. A transcultural thinking conceived as Southern Environmental ethics offers nature a better chance at surviving or curbing environmental degradation.

References

Bodunrin, P. 1981. The Question of African Philosophy. *Philosophy* 56 (216): 161–179.

Bujo, B. 1998. *The Ethical Dimension of Community*. Nairobi: Paulines Publications.

Bujo, B. 2009. Is There a Specific African Ethic? Towards a Discussion with Western Thought. In *African Ethics: An Anthology of Comparative and Applied Ethics*, ed. F.M. Murove, 113–128. Scottsville: University of KwaZulu-Natal Press.

Caminero-Santangeo, B. 2014. *Different Shades of Green: African Literature, Environmental Justice, and Political Ecology*. London: University of Virginia Press.

Cesaire, A. 1972. *Discourses on Colonialism*. Trans. J. Pinkham. Monthly Review Press: New York.

Collins, P.H. 1990. Black Feminist Thought: Knowledge, Consciousness, and the Politics of Empowerment. Unwin Hyman: Boston. (Selected Chapter: "Black feminist epistemology", 251–270).

De George, R.T. 1994. Modern Science, Environmental Ethics and the Anthropocentric Predicament. In *Philosophy, Humankind and Ecology*, ed. O.H. Oruka, 15–29. Kenya: African Centre for Technology Studies Press.

Etieyibo, E. 2011. An Outline of an Ecumenical Environmental Ethic. *The Trumpeter* 29 (3): 48–59.

Foucault, M. 1977. *Discipline and Punish: The Birth of the Prison*. France: Pantheon Books.

Green, L.J.F. 2008. Indigenous 'Knowledge' and 'Science': Reframing the Debate on Knowledge and Diversity. *Archaeologies: Journal of the World Archaeological Congress* 4 (1): 144–163.

Gyekye, K. 1997. *Tradition and Modernity: Philosophical Reflections on the African Experience*. Oxford: Oxford University Press.

Horsthemke, K. 2009. Learning for the Natural Environment: The Case Against anthropocentrism. *US-China Education Review* 6 (10): 22–31.

Hountondji, P.J. 1983. *African Philosophy, Myth and Reality*. London: Hutchinson.

Lui, K. 2017. New Zealand's Whanganui River Has Been Granted the Same Legal Rights as a Person Time. http://time.com/4703251/new-zealand-whanganui-river-wanganui-rights/. Accessed 19 Sept 2017.

Matolino, B. 2014. *Personhood in African Philosophy*. South Africa: Cluster Publications.

Manzini, N.Z. 2017. African Conceptions of Person as Gendered, Ableist and Anti-queer. Unpublished Dissertation. http://wiredspace.wits.ac.za/bitstream/handle/10539/24215/Nompumelelo%20Zinhle%20Manzini%20MA%20Research%20Revisions%20After%20Examination%20%20283%29Final.pdf?sequence=2&isAllowed=y.

Mazama, M.A. 2002. Afrocentricity and African Spirituality. *Journal of Black Studies* 33 (2): 218–234.

Mbeki, T. 1996. *I Am An African*. http://www.soweto.co.za/html/i_iamafrican.htm. Accessed: 24 Sept 2017.

Menkiti, I.A. 1984. Person and Community in African Traditional Thought. In *African Philosophy: An Introduction*, ed. R. Wright, 171–181. Lanham: University Press of America.

Metz, T. 2011. An African Theory of Moral Status: A Relational Alternative to Individualism and Holism. *Ethical Theory and Moral Practice* 15 (3): 387–402.

Metz, T. 2015. How the West was One: The Western as Individualist, the African as Communitarian. *Educational Philosophy and Theory* 47 (11): 1175–1184.

Ndlanzi, D. 2017. Untitled Online Clip. https://www.facebook.com/getshanidineo.ndlanzi?hc_ref=ARTgsH0QvxLVlhzVeG8D8WiHZpQSs9ARG0GQRl33TCqkM75oSfnabIaPF9LK03srftY&pnref=story. Accessed 10 Aug 2017.

Ngugi, W.T. 1986. *A Grain of Wheat*. London: Heinemann.

Oruka, H.O. 1994. Ecophilosophy and Parental Earth Ethics (On the Complex Web of Being). In *Philosophy, Humankind and Ecology*, 115–129. Kenya: African Centre for Technology Studies Press.

p'Bitek, O. 1985. *The Artist as Ruler*. East African Educational Publishers Ltd.

Santos, B.D.S. 2007. *Another Knowledge is Possible: Beyond Northern Epistemologies*. London: Verso.

Santos, B.D.S. 2014. *Epistemologies of the South: Justice Against Epistemicide*. London: Paradigm Publishers.

Santos, B.D.S. 2016. Epistemologies of the South and the future. *From the European South* 1: 17–29.

Santos, B.D.S., M.P. Meneses, and J.A. Nunes. 2007. Opening Up the Canon of Knowledge and Recognition of Difference. In *Another Knowledge is Possible: Beyond Northern Epistemologies*, ed. B.D.S. Santos, xvix–lxii. London: Verso.

Taylor, P.W. 1981. The Ethics of Respect for Nature. *Environmental Ethics* 3: 197–218.

Tempels, P. 1959. Bantu Philosophy. Paris: Presence Africaine.

Wiredu, K. 1994. Philosophy, Humankind, and the Environment. In *Philosophy, Humankind and Ecology*, ed. O.H. Oruka, 30–48. Kenya: African Centre for Technology Studies Press.

Part III
African Ecocentric Environmental Ethics

Chapter 9
A (South) African Land Ethic? The Viability of an Ecocentric Approach to Environmental Ethics and Philosophy

Ernst M. Conradie

Abstract In the Southern African context, any reference to land in the context of ethical discourse is immediately related to matters of conquest, ownership, restitution and redistribution. This is obviously situated within the context of the destructive legacy of imperial conquest, colonial rule, segregation (as a British policy), apartheid and "separate development". To discuss land use, the proper stewardship of land and the extraction of natural resources assumes access to such land and hence reflects the position of land*lords* rather than the landless. From this perspective there seems to be no point of entry for an appropriation of the notion of a "land ethic" as proposed by Aldo Leopold, followed by J. Baird Callicot and further developed by Holmes Rolston in the North American context. Leopold's holism may even conjure up associations with his contemporary Jan Smuts, the former South African prime minister, who is often quoted in this regard. Nevertheless, an ecocentric approach such as the land ethic is not too far removed from the ecological wisdom embedded in more traditional rural villages across the African continent. Numerous scholars of African traditional religion and its interplay express this notion of belonging to the land with Christianity, including Gabriel Setiloane, Harvey Sindima and LaurentiMagesa. It is also expressed in the so-called Machakos statement entitled "The Earth belongs to God". In fact, such an ecocentric approach may serve as source of inspiration for resistance against colonial conquest and a settler view of land. It is another question whether such an approach remains viable within the context of an urbanised Africa, shaped by taxis, spaza shops, cell phones and soccer. Such questions will be explored in this contribution.

E. M. Conradie (✉)
University of the Western Cape, Cape Town, South Africa
e-mail: econradie@uwc.ac.za

© Springer Nature Switzerland AG 2019
M. Chemhuru (ed.), *African Environmental Ethics*, The International
Library of Environmental, Agricultural and Food Ethics 29,
https://doi.org/10.1007/978-3-030-18807-8_9

127

9.1 Introduction

What could a (South) African "land ethic" look like? This philosophical question is necessarily raised in highly contested terrain given the historical impact of imperial conquest, colonialism and apartheid, in South Africa best symbolised by the Natives Land Act of 1913. It conjures up contemporary debates on the failures of land restitution, Zimbabwean debates on land reform, the need for land redistribution, and economic debates on the feasibility of small-scale farming in terms of management skills, infrastructure, equipment and finances. Moreover, there are endless debates on the impact of nature conservation on indigenous peoples, land use rights, mineral rights, informal settlements, and so forth. There is little hope in finding clarity on a (South) African "land ethic" if such debates would need to be resolved.

A related question would be what a (South) African "land ethos" may look like, i.e. a characteristic way of inhabiting the land, of dwelling in a particular place. Ethos is best understood here as a descriptive term that articulates the visions, values, virtues, beliefs and convictions of a particular group of people as these are embodied and practised in forms of indwelling. This is again contested terrain given the ways in which issues of race and space interact, especially in the South African context.[1] Consider the symbols of the "Groot Trek", bantustans, Group Areas, townships, "informal settlements", xenophobic attacks, etc. An interesting angle to explore such patterns of indwelling may be related to access to water and sanitation (see Conradie 2014). A full exposition of such a "land ethos" would require nothing short of a comprehensive (South) African sociology. Suffice it to say that the dominant ethos (as practiced by the dominant groups) will need to be understood with reference to the impact of neo-liberal capitalism, while one will probably find a range of other, more marginal ways of inhabiting the land, including more traditional views that embody some reverence for the land, conservationist and preservationist approaches and the movements of the landless, seasonal workers, refugees, etc.

It is obvious that these questions cannot be explored here. To even consider such questions would also miss the implicit terminological reference to the notion of a "land ethic" as proposed by Aldo Leopold (1887–1848) and his followers in the North American context. However, this raises another set of thorny issues. Why would one need to import North American views on land or a land ethic in the (South) African context? Does this not sidestep current debates on the postcolonial and the decolonial? Moreover, is a hermeneutics of suspicion not required regarding Leopold and his followers, given the colonial conquest of land in the Americas, the genocide of indigenous peoples there, the impact of the slave trade and underlying notions of white supremacy? With cognisance of Leopold's emphasis on holism one may wonder whether his construction of "the whole" (the biotic community) is all that innocent. And this may remind one of the notion of holism developed by his

---

[1] The Theological Society of South Africa hosted a conference on "Race, Grace and Space: Towards a Theology of Place" in June 2008 to explore such questions. See Conradie (2009) for one contribution in this regard.

contemporary, i.e. the South African and British commonwealth statesman Jan Smuts (1870–1950)—that cannot be separated from his imperial assumptions either.

Such a hermeneutics of suspicion is entirely appropriate but would still underestimate the influence of an ecocentric approach to environmental ethics that remains a live option also in African and South African debates. Such an ecocentric approach may draw on indigenous ecological wisdom found in more traditional rural villages across Africa where a sense of belonging to the land—rather than an anthropocentric sense of land ownership—prevails. It may be found in different expressions amongst environmentalists. It is another question whether such an ecocentric approach is viable within the context of an urbanised Africa, shaped by taxis, spaza shops, shebeens, cell phones and soccer. It should nevertheless be considered a live option in current debates but then in critical dialogue with biocentric approaches, deep ecology, social ecology and various forms of ecofeminism.[2] Each of these more radical approaches to environmental ethics remains prominent in South African discourse. In each case there are foreign influences, blended with indigenous knowledge, traditional religion and culture, Western philosophies (whether deontological, teleological or utilitarian), and forms of Christianity and Islam, amidst ongoing fermentation, debates on sustainability and many challenges around ecological degradation, if not destruction.

Is a (South) African "land ethic" a viable option, then? The answer to this question is far from clear and it is equally unclear how such a question could be approached. In this contribution I will follow one particular avenue, namely to consider the revision of Leopold's land ethic offered by Holmes Rolston III. I will describe aspects of his position in the next section and then set that in juxtaposition with a collection of African theologians with specific reference to the so-called Machakos statement entitled "The Earth belongs to God". On this basis I will invite a critical conversation, keeping contemporary demographic shifts in mind.

9.2 An Ecocentric Approach: From Aldo Leopold to Holmes Rolston

Aldo Leopold is typically described as a forester, environmentalist, ecologist, public intellectual and author. His famous maxim was that "A thing is right when it tends to preserve the integrity, stability and beauty of the biotic community. It is wrong when it tends otherwise" (Leopold 1949: 262). The notion of a "biotic community" suggests that moral concern should be expanded to include air, water, soil, plants and animals, or collectively the "land". This emphasis on the biotic community shows some affinities with indigenous American ecological wisdom where reciprocal moral

---

[2]A module on environmental ethics taught at the University of the Western Cape focuses on this variety of classic and more radical approaches to moral discourse on the environment. The textbook used is the one by Desjardins (2013)—which speaks primarily to North American students and is therefore in need of recontextualisation in the light of debates on decoloniality.

responsibilities are stressed among humans, other living beings (animals, plants), and interconnected collectives (forests, the land) (see Whyte 2015: 1).[3] However, one may also argue that Leopold's ethics assumes a settler narrative, "the plot of which goes in the opposite direction of the narratives many Indigenous peoples would provide of their ethics" (Whyte 2015: 2).[4]

For Leopold, the biotic community is structured in the form of a biotic pyramid with abiotic and biotic elements (with multiple predator and prey relations) through which (solar) energy flows. The pyramid assumes that the prey should always be more bountiful than the predators. He pictured this as a series of "trophic" levels, with each higher level decreasing in size and where higher levels are predatory on the layer below. Predators obviously depend on their prey within food chains, but the predators also ensure genetic fitness amongst their prey by eating the weak. Leopold's land ethic therefore assumes a sense of holism and stressed stability, harmony and interdependent relationships.

This land ethic acknowledges our instincts to compete for a place in the biotic community, but at the same time requires us to cooperate with others within ecosystems. It recognises that individual members of a biotic community may be treated as resources (food) by other members of that community as long as the vitality of community itself is maintained. Any action which threatens the very existence of an ecosystem should obviously be avoided, if only on purely pragmatic grounds.[5] Leopold added that the "integrity, stability and beauty" of the biotic community should guide moral action. This offers a fairly comprehensive perspective to assess the well-being of ecosystems. It calls for respect for ecosystems as being in a sense alive and as undergoing changes during the course of history. Ecosystems may therefore be assessed as either healthy or sick and dying, stable or unstable and disintegrating.

This emphasis on the biotic community as a whole is admittedly vulnerable to the critique that no one (but God, presumably) is able to command an assessment of the well-being of the whole. This is not merely a theological comment but indeed expresses the standard criticism of a utilitarian calculus. The whole of reality will always elude our grasp. It would be impossible to understand or foresee the impact of decisions on a whole ecosystem, not only because of the incredibly complex nature of an ecosystem, but also because human beings form part of such a whole and cannot obtain a total perspective on that whole. Moreover, the whole of reality is not only

---

[3]It is interesting to note the absence of references to Leopold or the land ethic in work on environmental justice from a Native American perspective, e.g. in the representative volume entitled *Defending Mother Earth* edited by Weaver (1996).

[4]In a telling comment Whyte (2015: 11) adds: "there is not a strong social and environmental justice component throughout Leopold or a critique of the U.S. settler state as an oppressive force against Indigenous peoples, despite some instances where he may have addressed some of the problems of his time or shown strong emotional responses to the unethical treatment of animals and the land and problematic forms of settlement."

[5]Hattingh (1999: 77) notes that such an ecosystem ethics is often criticised for lacking a strong social theory and critique. Because the emphasis is placed on the ecosystem, the human origin of ecological problems may be neglected. The thought patterns embedded in the global economic system which threaten numerous ecosystems have to be addressed.

hidden, but is itself not yet there, since the whole of history remains incomplete. Our sense of the whole will therefore necessarily be a *construction* of the whole from a particular and limited perspective in proleptic anticipation of the completion of (human) history.[6] We cannot observe the whole, and can describe the whole only piece by piece. The limitations of the much-used rhetoric of "holism" therefore have to be recognised and such rhetoric may perhaps be replaced by one that calls for a sense of integration. The question remains: How is the story of what happened to the land to be told and how will the story end?[7] It also illustrates the complexity of deriving any moral (including a land ethic) from that story.

It may be noted that such an acknowledgement of the difficulty of knowing what would be in the interest of the whole also characterises Leopold's work. He repeatedly admits that, given the complexity of ecosystems, the ecologist does not know exactly what would benefit the integrity and stability of the biotic community. The functioning of such systems is so complex that it may never be possible to grasp such complexity. This requires more than a set of moral guidelines that can be applied to specific environmental problems. It requires an acknowledgment of human limitations, an attitude of respect for the fragility of ecosystems and an appreciation for beauty. In short, he may be regarded as an exponent of a form of virtue ethics despite the otherwise utilitarian flavour of his position (see Desjardins 2013: 177–202).

Another criticism that can be raised against such an ecocentric approach is that constructions of the whole may well be romanticised or totalitarian or, in the case of fascism, both. A sense of totality is indeed all too often based on the erasure of difference and a unification which has to be enforced. At the same time we need to recognise that such constructions of the whole cannot be avoided either. Perhaps the adequacy of any one construction of the whole is less important than an ability to pick up systemic distortions, that is, signals that the health of the whole is threatened and to identify the root causes of such systemic distortions. If we cannot avoid such constructions of the whole, we do need to search for relatively less totalitarian constructions of the whole.

It should be noted that ecosystems cannot always be preserved since they are subject to evolutionary and geological changes over longer periods of time. Although ecosystems tend to maintain a certain equilibrium, the ability of an ecosystem to adapt

---

[6] In Christian theology Wolfhart Pannenberg has made this point throughout his voluminous writings. He sees the (testimonies to the) resurrection of Christ as the heuristic key to understand the direction of history. This suggests an ethics based on the proleptic anticipation of the "end of history". Capitalist readings of the (rather premature) "end of history" by Francis Fukuyama and others suggest a rather different ethic. For one discussion (amidst too many references to include here), see Peters (2000), who also recognises an African notion of narrative time.

[7] In biblical theology there are interesting examples of such a story told from the perspective of the degradation of the land through injustices (internally) and imperial oppression (externally). Land is not given to the people of Israel to own, use and control. People are given to the land to care for it. If they subsequently mess it up, people are removed from the land so that it can lie fallow and replenish itself. This suggests an ongoing dialectic between landedness and landlessness. See especially the pioneering work of Brueggemann (1977) and texts such as 2 Chronicles 36:21 and Ezekiel 36.

to fluctuations and to ongoing changes is even more important for its well-being. This is where Rolston addresses some shortcomings in Leopold's position.

Holmes Rolston (1932-) studied, science, mathematics, philosophy of science and theology, started his career as a Presbyterian minister, and became professor of philosophy at Colorado State University (see the biographical overview by Preston 2009). He is best known as an environmental philosopher but also worked on the interface between religion and science with his almost encyclopaedic interests in the natural sciences, humanities, philosophy and theology. He lectured on all seven continents (including South Africa in 1990), including the Gifford lectures in 1997/1998 (see 1999), is the author of rather many books and won the prestigious Templeton prize in science and religion in 2003, alongside many other honours.

Instead of seeking to offer a full description of his environmental philosophy (see especially 1988, 1989, 1994, 2012; Light and Rolston 2003), I will only highlight a few features that I find attractive and that may arguably be engaged with from within the South African context. These exclude other features of his environmental ethics such as wilderness preservation (see 1989, 1994, 2012: 173–190) that may also be relevant but would require more circumspection given contextual differences.

Firstly, Rolston consistently argues that the naturalistic fallacy is overstated. Facts and values remain closely related. Nature is indeed valuable in many respects, to humans and in itself. Indeed, one cannot derive an "ought" from an "is"—as attempts to derive an ethos from biological evolution suggests. However, a disconnection of values from the natural systems in which they emerged (remembering that humans form part of nature) is equally disastrous. For ecosystems one does need to hold "is" questions and "ought" questions together (see 2012: 159–168).

Secondly, he employs the category of values "carried" by nature and identifies numerous aspects of such value: life-support value, economic value, recreational value, scientific value, aesthetic value, genetic diversity value, historical value, symbolic value, character building value, stability and spontaneity value, dialectical value, life value and religious value (see Rolston 1988: 3–27). He argues that as moral agents we humans can recognise such value and have a moral obligation to protect such value. He admits that human interests do not constitute the only measure of things (which would be anthropocentric) but insists that humans are indeed the only moral measurers of things (2012: 40–44).

Thirdly, Rolston distinguishes between *intrinsic* value (value richness), *instrumental* value and *systemic* value (see also 2012: 167). A hierarchy of value richness may be considered in which endangered species are more valuable than others while chimps have more value richness compared to mice. Amongst humans such a value richness may be more controversial given the deontological emphasis on equal human dignity—although remuneration in a company of course correlates with the value that an employee adds to the company. Value richness may be inversely proportioned with instrumental value. A blind person's guide dog has instrumental value to the blind person more than the person has for the dog. Grass and bacteria may not have much value richness but they have more systemic value than mammals in order to maintain the stability and adaptability of an ecosystem. Plants can do without us as humans but we cannot do without them. To emphasise value richness is therefore not inversely proportioned to the integrity of nature, although finding criteria for value richness would pose many difficulties.

Fourthly, Rolston moves away from an essentialist understanding of ecosystems that still characterises Leopold famous maxim. Rolston introduces the notion of the "projective thrust" of an ecosystem, i.e. its ability to adapt to changing circumstances in order to continue flourishing. While individual specimens are subjected to struggle, violence and death, the system as such allows for interdependence and ever-continuing life on condition that its projective thrust is maintained (see Rolston 1988: 225).

Finally, Rolston's ethics has a much broader scope than Leopold's land ethic, although it stays true to its (holistic?) emphasis on comprehensive well-being. For Leopold, one needs to "think like a mountain" in order to take a long-term perspective (see Flader 1974). For Rolston, this requires an evolutionary perspective that can take into account all three "big bangs" (see 2010), i.e. cosmic evolution, biological evolution and human emergence. His is no longer a land ethics but a biosphere ethics that is concerned about a sustainable biosphere for the sake of ultimate survival in the Anthropocene (2012: 217–220). In *A New Environmental Ethics* he recognises the need to confront the capitalist roots of climate change and the related issues of overconsumption, overpopulation and economic inequality (2012:194–222). Rolston's earlier, rather narrow focus on wilderness preservation is thus considerably broadened to address concerns raised in social ecology.

9.3 "The Earth Belongs to God"

In this section I will juxtapose such a land ethic to an African understanding of "belonging to the land", with specific reference to an African Regional Consultation on Environment and Sustainability was held at Machakos, Kenya, from 6 to 10 May 2002, in preparation for the World Summit on Sustainable Development (WSSD) held in Johannesburg later that year. This consultation produced a statement[8] that maintains an ecocentric orientation, blending African traditional sensibilities with Christian convictions for the sake of discourse on sustainability. It also reframes such an ecocentric approach in the context of prophetic critique against forms of neo-colonialism. As a participant in this consultation and member of the quite lively drafting committee of this statement, I opt here to quote the text in full (excluding a number of footnotes) and then offer some reflections on it.

> "The Earth is the Lord's and all that is in it, the world and those who live in it; for he has founded it on the seas and established it on the rivers. Who shall ascend the hill of the Lord? And who shall stand in his holy place? Those who have clean hands and pure hearts, who

---

[8]This statement was released electronically through ecumenical channels, was published in the *Bulletin for Contextual Theology in Africa* (2002) and reprinted in South African Council of Churches, Climate Change Committee (2009), 74–76, without some footnotes that were included in the original.

do not lift up their souls to what is false, and do not swear deceitfully. They will receive blessing from the Lord, and vindication from the God of their salvation. (Psalm 24: 1–5)

In the household of God (oikos) the management of the house (economy) has to be based on the logic of the house (ecology).

1. *In Africa today, it does not appear as if the earth belongs to God. Instead, it belongs to:*

   - Governors who control the earth's resources often for their own benefit;
   - Business and industry, Trans-National Corporations (TNC's), the World Bank, the International Monetary Fund (IMF) and the World Trade Organization (WTO), the forces of globalization that control the global economy in their own interest;
   - Developers whose development projects do not benefit local communities;
   - The affluent 20% of the world's population who own 80% of the world's resources;
   - Industrialists whose factories pollute the environment at the expense of the poor;
   - Men;
   - Foreign investors who are more interested in profits on their investments than in poverty eradication and in the impact of debt on poor countries;
   - The affluent and not the meek who will inherit the earth (Mt. 5:3-5).

2. *God has entrusted the land and all its natural resources to all people to care for, keep and use it within communities. This requires a vision of sustainable communities in which there will be:*

   - A just sharing of the earth's resources;
   - A working together in community;
   - Participation of all in decision-making processes;
   - The right to contribute to and sustain the common good;
   - Cherishing of indigenous knowledge systems that are inclusive, participatory and consultative;
   - A recognition and utilization of people's indigenous knowledge and skills;
   - Putting in place structures and mechanisms that will ensure the provision of a community's daily needs;
   - Responsible leadership and self-reliant citizenry;
   - Public institutions that address people's legitimate needs;
   - Engendering a harmonious co-existence between all stakeholders;
   - Respect for all forms of life.

3. *The land given to us by God does not only belong to the present community.*

   - It also belongs to our ancestors on whose contributions we build and whose memories we keep;
   - It also belongs to the coming generations for whom we hold the land in trust and whose needs we should not compromise;

4. *The land does not belong to us as people. Instead, we belong to the land.*

   - We came from the earth and to the earth we will return.
   - We are not living on the earth; we are part of the earth's biosphere.
   - We form part of the land and we live from the earth for the flourishing of the earth.
   - The well-being of the earth transcends all of us because it is something bigger than our own interests.

5. *The land does not belong to itself. Ultimately, it belongs to its Creator, the One who sustains the Earth, and who will finally restore it. In the light of these considerations we are challenged to respond in the following ways:*

   - We CONFESS that we as human beings have not always allowed the earth and its creatures to flourish. We have all too often abused and brought death to the land. We confess that we, especially as churches, have often been indifferent to environmental degradation and that, as a result, we have participated in the destruction of the environment. In many ways, we are doing to the land what AIDS is doing to our bodies. Now the land itself is infected with AIDS.
   - We ACKNOWLEDGE our responsibility, especially as churches, to keep the land and to care for it as the land cares for us.
   - We COMMIT ourselves, especially as churches, to promote relationships that enhance and do not undermine sustainable communities. Therefore, we commit ourselves:
     - To promote the harvesting of water, especially in small community projects in arid or semi-arid areas;
     - To help ensure food security for all, especially through indigenous means of food production, and to avoid dependence on external means of agricultural production;
     - To promote practices that enhance the fertility of the soil;
     - To resist all forms of deforestation and to promote tree-planting;
     - To speak out against industrial pollution caused elsewhere in the light of its impact on geographical areas such as the African continent and the Island States that are particularly vulnerable to climate change;
     - To seek appropriate forms of waste management and to resist the disposal of toxic and other forms of waste in impoverished countries;
     - To promote the use of new and renewable sources of energy;
     - To promote technologies that add to natural resources and that do not only extract from nature. Where technologies do extract from nature, ways of replenishing such resources must be sought;
     - To promote participatory and inclusive forms of governance;
     - To promote gender justice in the light of the crucial role of women in ensuring sustainability;
     - To attend to the re-education and re-orientation of local communities.
   - We CALL upon leaders of Christian churches, of other faith communities and various levels of government, in African countries and elsewhere in the world:

- To promote the well-being of the land and all its creatures.
- To resist the greed and self-interest of affluent and powerful minorities.
- We PRAY for the healing of the land.

God, help us not to destroy the land and to stop fighting over resources that ultimately belong to you. God graciously hear us. AMEN."

This statement may clearly be regarded as an expression of some form of a land ethic, albeit without reference to Leopold and his followers. Each of the main statements is undermined by the next. Nevertheless, it is clear that we as human beings belong to the land more than that the land belongs to us. In the fourth statement it explicitly adopts a non-anthropocentric position, i.e. "the view that human beings form the centre of the created order and that everything in nature is there to serve human needs only" (footnote 8 in the original).

The statement does invite a theocentric position in insisting that the land does not belong to itself either but to "its Creator, the One who sustains the Earth, and who will finally restore it". This theological position is not clarified even though there are references to the Christian tradition and to churches. There are allusions to the Supreme Being of indigenous African religion (but not to Islam) so that any sense of exclusivism is undermined. I will not explore such a theocentric approach here, partly since I have discussed that at length elsewhere (see e.g. Conradie 2011, 2015). Instead, I suggest that this statement draws on sentiments expressed in African philosophy and African theology where such a belonging to the land is articulated.

A few examples and quotations may suffice here: Emmanuel Asante (Ghana) uses the concept of "panvitalism", Harvey Sindima (Malawi) speaks of the bondedness, sacredness and fecundity of the "community of life" that goes beyond an anthropocentric emphasis on ubuntu, Eugene Wangiri (Kenya) calls for an *urumwe* spirituality which sees God's presence in creation and stresses social and ecological harmony and oneness, while Gabriel Setiloane (South Africa) celebrates an African biocentric theology and ethos:

> Reality is inseparable. The African is kin to all creatures – gods, spirits and nature… The whole of nature must be understood as sacred because it derives its being from the Supreme Being who is the Creator-Animator of the universe. (Asante 1985: 290, 292)

> The African idea of community refers to bondedness; the act of sharing and living in the one common symbol – life – which enables people to live in communion and communication with each other and nature. Living in communication allows stories or life experiences of others to become one's own. (Sindima 1989: 537)

> Harmony is therefore life. Oneness and harmony thus make up *urumwe* which is a harmonious existence of entities whose being is being-together-with-others. (Wangiri 1999: 72)

> We Africans sincerely believe that by taking into its fabric these African interpretations and views about the universe, creation and nature, the Christian understanding is enriched rather than impoverished and the image of God becomes more worthy, inspiring greater wonder, love and praise. (Setiloane 1995: 52).

Similar expressions can probably be multiplied. However, these rather more traditional sentiments, mostly derived from rural villages, are reframed in the Machakos statement to address urban Africa amidst the many challenges associated with neo-colonialism and neo-liberal globalisation. This is evident from its critique of industrial pollution and its recognition of the need for appropriate technologies.

9.4   Conclusion: On a Storied Sense of Place

If Rolston's biosphere ethic is rooted in but expands the scope of Leopold's land ethic, how could an African version of the land ethic, based on an indigenous understanding of the sacred "community of life" (Sindima), be transformed into a contribution to global discourse that can address global environmental challenges? Such challenges obviously include the detrimental if not devastating impact of climate disruptions in Africa, in different forms in different places.[9] In the Machakos statement a first step in this direction is the emphasis on sustainable communities[10], including urban communities, in the face of global economic distortions. Others have called for sustainable livelihoods (see e.g. De Gruchy 2015), again emphasising the needs of the marginalised on the periphery of the global economy. In climate change speak this is about adaptation but not mitigation. For that, prophetic critique is typically adopted, i.e. to blame the problem on industrialised capitalism and imperialism. Such critique draws from the same wells, namely the disruption of the community of life.

Does such a critique also offer a constructive contribution? Here one may, following an aside from Rolston (2012: 218), consider the available earth-images that may be employed to address a problem that is biospheric in scope. These images include the photographs of the blue Earth from space (taken from an alienating distance, requiring a very high degree of technology!), the global village, Gaia and God's creation. This may help to counter other "warped" images, namely the romantic, liberal dream of unspoilt nature, the neo-Darwinian notion of a fierce struggle for survival, the capitalist exploitation of "natural resources" and the New Age illusion of Earth as something to be worshipped (see Snyder 2011: 42–45; Conradie 2015). None of

---

[9]See the volume of articles entitled "Praying for Rain? African Perspectives on Religion and Climate Change", published in *The Ecumenical Review* (Chitando and Conradie 2017). The opening statement of the editorial notes that, "There is ample evidence that various regions of the African continent will be adversely and disproportionally affected by climate change. Many scholars have contributed to ongoing reflection on climate change in Africa, but relatively few voices have addressed the interface between religion and climate from within the African context." The volume contributes to such debates with reference to one of the most urgent challenges, namely droughts and floods.

[10]There is a significant corpus of ecumenical literature on the notion of a sustainable society following the call for a "Just, Participatory and Sustainable Society" already expressed at the 1975 Assembly of the World Council of Church in Nairobi. This is complimented by an emphasis on the need for sustainable communities picked up in the Machakos statement. In two footnotes caveats on the notions of sustainability and of community are recognised: "The notion of sustainability implies an emphasis on the provision of basic sustenance that can be sustained over time. In the African context, the provision of such sustenance is often challenged by the more immediate need for livelihood and survival" (footnote 6); and "In the emphasis on local community life, the dangers of traditionalism, authoritarianism, conformity, and the oppression of women and children that characterized many traditional societies have to be taken into account" (footnote 7). For an exploration of the literature on the notion of "sustainable community", see Conradie (2000).

these images are rooted deeply in the African psyche. The problem though, as illustrated by the quotations from Asante, Setiloane, Sindima and Wangiri above, is that authentically African images of the world are all too often romanticised, assuming the need to return to some pre-colonial dispensation. Moreover, traditional African cosmologies are hard to reconcile with an understanding of evolutionary change over longer time frames.

It is not for me to offer such a constructive (South) African version of a "land ethic", if such a name for an ecocentric approach is to be retained. However, if I may suggest a sense of direction, it would be that of a storied sense of place. Ellen Kuzwayo once said that Africa is a place of storytelling:

> If you cannot understand my story, you do not accept me as your neighbour. I am an African woman. I try to share my soul, my way of seeing things, the way I understand life. I hope you understand. … Africa is a place of storytelling. We need more stories, never mind how painful the exercise might be. This is how we will learn to love one another. Stories help us to understand, to forgive and to see things through someone else's eyes. (quoted in Villa-Vicencio 1995: 115)

A (South) African land ethic would need to be one where the story of the land would need to be told—from the perspective of the land. It would need to tell the story of what went wrong in the world (see Conradie 2017). This would need to address the imperialist conquest and environmental destruction of the past few centuries. It could make ample use of creation myths, myths of the "fall" of humanity, woven together with African fables (recognising the place of fauna and flora), scientific insights, ancestral stories and biblical stories. This should now be a story that also includes the likes of *Homo Naledi*, living together from the land with the ancestors of the Khoi and the San. The land itself is not stable but subject to geological and evolutionary changes. After all, Africa as a continent emerged only from around 120 million years ago and will become more fragmented along the Great Rift Valley. An African notion of time is not necessarily cyclical but narrative in structure. Such a story would typically be about the distant, mythical past but, when retold in the present, is always narrated with a view to the future. Indeed, as the Machakos statement holds, the land belongs to the ancestors and to the future generations for whom we hold the land in trust.

References

Asante, E. 1985. Ecology: Untapped Resource of Panvitalism in Africa. *AFER: African Ecclesial Review* 27: 289–293.

Brueggemann, W. 1977. *The Land: Place as Gift, Promise and Challenge in Biblical Faith*. Philadelphia: Fortress Press.

Chitando, E., and E.M. Conradie (eds.). 2017. Praying for Rain? African Perspectives on Religion and Climate Change. *The Ecumenical Review* 69 (3): 311–435.

Conradie, E.M. 2000. A Few Notes on the Heuristic Key of "Sustainable Community". *Scriptura* 75: 345–357.

Conradie, E.M. 2009. Towards a Theology of Place in the South African Context: Some Reflections from the Perspective of Ecotheology. *Religion & Theology: A Journal of Contemporary Religious Discourse* 16 (1&2): 3–18.

Conradie, E.M. 2011. *Christianity and Earthkeeping: In Search of an Inspiring Vision.* Stellenbosch: SUN Media.

Conradie, E.M. 2014. From Land Reform to Poo Protesting: Some Theological Reflections on the Ecological Repercussions of Economic Inequality. *Scriptura* 113: 1–16.

Conradie, E.M. 2015. *The Earth in God's Economy: Creation, Salvation and Consummation in Ecological Perspective. Studies in Religion and the Environment,* vol. 10. Berlin: LIT Verlag.

Conradie, E.M. 2017. *Redeeming Sin? Social Diagnostics amid Ecological Destruction.* Lanham: Lexington Books.

De Gruchy, S.M. 2015. *Keeping Body and Soul Together: Reflections by Steve de Gruchy on Theology and Development.* Pietermaritzburg: Cluster Publications.

Desjardins, J.R. 2013. *Environmental Ethics: An Introduction to Environmental Philosophy,* 5th ed. Belmont: Thompson Wadsworth.

Flader, S.L. 1974. *Thinking Like a Mountain: Aldo Leopold and the Evolution of an Ecological Attitude Toward Deer, Wolves and Forests.* Madison: University of Wisconsin Press.

Hattingh, J.P. 1999. Finding Creativity in the Diversity of Environmental Ethics. *Southern African Journal of Environmental Education* 19: 68–84.

Leopold, A. 1949. *A Sand County Almanac.* New York: Ballantine.

Light, A., and H. Rolston III. 2003. *Environmental Ethics: An Anthology.* Oxford: Blackwell.

Peters, T.F. 2000. *God—The World's Future: Systematic Theology for a New Era.* Minneapolis: Fortress Press.

Preston, C.J. 2009. *Saving Creation: Nature and Faith in the Life of Holmes Rolston III.* San Antonio: Trinity University Press.

Rolston, H. III. 1988. *Environmental Ethics: Duties to and Values in the Natural World.* Philadelphia: Temple University Press.

Rolston, H. III. 1989. *Philosophy Gone Wild.* Buffalo: Prometheus Books.

Rolston, H. III. 1994. *Conserving Natural Value.* New York: Columbia University Press.

Rolston, H. III. 1999. *Genes, Genesis and God.* London: Cambridge University Press.

Rolston, H. III. 2010. *Three Big Bangs: Matter-Energy, Life, Mind.* New York: Columbia University Press.

Rolston, H. III. 2012. *A New Environmental Ethics: The Next Millennium fir Life on Earth.* New York & London: Routledge.

Setiloane, G. 1995. Towards a Biocentric Theology and Ethic—Via Africa. *Journal of Black Theology in South Africa* 9 (1): 53–66.

Sindima, H. 1989. Community of Life. *The Ecumenical Review* 41 (4): 537–551.

Snyder, H. A. 2011. *Salvation Means Creation Healed: The Ecology of Sin and Grace.* Eugene: Cascade Books.

South African Council of Churches, Climate Change Committee. 2009. *Climate Change—A Challenge to the Churches in South Africa.* Marshalltown: SACC.

The Earth Belongs to God. 2002. *Bulletin for Contextual Theology in Africa* 8 (2&3): 112–113.

Villa-Vicencio, C. 1995. Telling One Another Stories: Towards a Theology of Reconciliation. In *Many Cultures, One Nation,* ed. C. Villa-Vicencio and C. Niehaus, 105–111. Cape Town: Human & Rousseau.

Wangiri, E. 1999. Urumwe Spirituality and the Environment. In *Theology of Reconstruction: Exploratory Essays,* ed. M.N. Getui and E.A. Obeng, 71–89. Nairobi: Acton Publishers.

Weaver, J. (ed.). 1996. *Defending Mother Earth: Native American Perspectives on Environmental Justice.* Maryknoll: Orbis Books.

Whyte, K. 2015. How Similar Are Indigenous North American and Leopoldian Environmental Ethics? SSRN: https://ssrn.com/abstract=2022038, 1–15. Accessed 17 Nov 2017.

Chapter 10
African Environmental Ethics: Lessons from the Rain-Maker's Moral and Cosmological Perspectives

Garikai Madavo

Abstract Can African Environmental Ethics learn anything from folk ecology? Simultaneously, I wonder if the rain-making ceremony and African Ecological accounts from the Rain-makers, are still relevant to prevailing philosophical debates about human relations with the environment. This paper is a retrospective attempt to engage African Environmental Ethics in a conversation with traditional wisdom from 'folk' ecology. In a similar manner with the quest to decolonize African Philosophy in general, I argue that African Environmental Ethics is fundamentally inseparable from the Rain-maker's understanding of reality and the moral status of the environment. In this chapter, I will put the rainmaker's worldview into conversation with African Philosophy's search for a normative Environmental ethics. I hold the argument that the nature of such an ethic ought to be trans-anthropocentric and I make use of the Rain-maker's perspectives to show the intrinsic moral value of non-human forms of life in African Philosophy. The important point to note is that Rain-makers in their time, had an eco-political authority which enabled them to prescribe on various moral and environmental issues in a way which can be argued to depict an African Environmental Ethics. This 'primitive' epistemological epoch cannot thus be sidelined in contemporary discourses about African Environmental Ethics.

10.1 Introduction

Can African environmental ethics learn anything from traditional folk ecology; in particular, the rainmaker's account of proper human relations with the environment? In this chapter, I will argue for the position that the philosophical quest for a purely African environmental ethics has a lot to learn from the narratives and various literature resources from rainmakers and the rain making rituals they practiced. This chapter is thus an attempt to expose the invaluable worth of the rainmaker's worldview to contemporary environmental ethics. I will use the narratives of the rainmakers

G. Madavo (✉)
University of Johannesburg, Johannesburg, South Africa
e-mail: gmadavo@yahoo.com

© Springer Nature Switzerland AG 2019
M. Chemhuru (ed.), *African Environmental Ethics*, The International
Library of Environmental, Agricultural and Food Ethics 29,
https://doi.org/10.1007/978-3-030-18807-8_10

to respond to the question on whether African environmental ethics recognizes the intrinsic moral value of the environment beyond its instrumental gains to human beings. This is an ongoing debate among many scholars who inquire on the nature of African thought (Callicott 1994; Bujo 1999). Their enquiry is mainly on whether African environmental ethics can be classified as anthropocentric, eco-centric, eco-bio centric, theocentric and so on. This paper does not claim to resolve the debate, except to reconcile some varying points of view by arguing for a trans-anthropocentric dimension of African environmental ethics. The rainmaker's narratives will be used to support the argument that; African environmental ethics is 'trans-anthropocentric,' implying that it goes beyond an anthropocentric concern, towards a broader and complex concern for the environment in itself. The environment in African thought, is regarded as a reality which qualifies for a moral status on its own, for reasons which are more than anthropocentric gains.

This chapter in defense of a trans-anthropocentric dimension of African philosophy will begin by a short account which depicts a profile of shared characteristics among rainmakers. This profile serves to introduce the reader to the realm of rainmakers, making it possible for one to understand their relevance to the philosophical issues in this paper. The next section will contextualize the debate on the nature of African environmental ethics. This comprises of a definitive overview of anthropocentrism in general, telling it apart from other standpoints like eco-centrism, eco-bio centrism; as well as highlighting its implications on the nature of African environmental ethics. Following from this overview, I will then situate and respond to the question on whether African Philosophy recognizes the intrinsic moral value of nature beyond instrumental gains to human beings. This latter part of the chapter continues to expose and defend a trans-anthropocentric dimension of the African worldview with reference to the rain maker's worldview and the rain making ceremony in general.

10.2 A Profile of Rainmakers Which Shows Common Characteristics Among Them

The Rain makers in traditional African societies were highly regarded as individuals who lived harmoniously with nature and in a way they role modelled the way in which all the members of the community were supposed to live. One might say that their lifestyle displayed some form of African Environmental Ethics given their moral and political authority to advice the Chiefs and Kings of the time on environmental issues; particularly agriculture. This authority is more explicit in David Lan's work *Guns and Rain* (1985) also cited in Matsuhira (2013: 166). Accordingly, he argues that traditional leaders and spirit mediums had some form of political power upon the community. They held wisdom and a certain kind of moral ethic for the entire clan. Mawere and Ken (1995) argues in the same line of thought making the observation that cults mobilized communities to uphold the laws of the land. The 'Mwari' cult, cited in Machoko (2013) is said to have,

> operated a system of ecological religion which it used to control the environment, determine which areas should be cultivated and which not, which water was for the people to drink and use for cooking, and which water was for animals and washing; which trees were to be cut down, and which were not to be cut down. Machoko (2013: 289)

The general idea which I seek to bring out is that shrine guardians such as the Rain makers displayed and promoted a certain kind of environmental ethic which can be argued to be African in its essence.

It is plausible to make the claim that; the roles and responsibilities of Environmental Management Authorities in prevailing civilizations can retrospectively be paralleled to some of the Rain-maker's fundamental duties in the diverse socio-political civilizations of traditional African societies. The rainmaker prescribed on human relations with the environment, just as any environmental management authority ought to do in recent times. In most cases, rainmakers had an eco-political authority, and in fact they had a jurisdiction on human relations with sacred lands, wildlife, trees, water reserves... (Fauna and Flora in a nutshell).

Rain-makers were believed to possess more than just a meteorological ability to forecast on weather and to make rains fall. This gave them the authority to prescribe on agricultural activities as well as other human relations with the environment such as access to water reserves. The rainmaker would for instance reserve some sacred water springs and in turn locate the right place where the community could dig a well, to sustain domestic livelihoods. This is similar to the manner in which Environmental Management authorities to date, regulate the drilling of boreholes and construction of dams while preserving some historically significant water reserves.

Other than the priestly role of interceding for rains, Krige and Krige (1943) and Feddema (1966) both sources cited in Chidester (1997) contend that "the rainmaking ritual had a political character that linked agricultural fertility with the well-being of the polity." (Chidester 1997: 280). The point which is worth noting is that, Rain-makers prescribed to the community on various moral and environmental issues in a way which can be argued to depict an African Environmental Ethics.

It is a regrettable fact that the wisdom of rain-makers has suffered the same epistemological challenges as any other African Philosophy. They have not been spared from the suppression and neglect of traditional African worldviews. The undermining of the Rainmaker's eco-political authority and the suppression of their perspectives could have been propelled by the mystification of the Rain-maker's accounts on nature and the massification of Western paradigms of environmental management, as well as the dominance of empirico-rationalist explanations of the world. Various socio-political factors are at play in this suppression of thought, keeping in mind the inseparable impacts of colonization on African epistemologies.

In recent times, the philosophy of the Rain-maker is regarded as primitive folk wisdom and it is often difficult to retrieve the exact philosophical depth of their invaluable environmental worldview since very little has been documented about this purely African Philosophy. I acknowledge that a handful of Anthropologists and Theologians have given scholarly attention to the Rain-makers, despite the fact that most of their researches have a particular focus on the history of African Traditional Religion (Chidester 1997; Beach 1980; Maravanyika 2012; Ngara 2014). These scholarly works have very little to say on Environmental Ethics in rigorous and plausible philosophical ways. Traces of the Rain-maker's accounts can also be found in-part from other philosophical works such as Oruka (1990, 1993) and Mbiti (1970).

The common characteristics among rainmakers served to introduce the reader to the status of rainmakers in traditional African societies; as well as to show their relevance to African philosophy's quest for a normative environmental ethics. The next part of this chapter will contextualize the debate among philosophers on the nature of African Environmental Ethics.

10.3   Various Perspectives on the Nature of African Environmental Ethics

The claim that African Philosophy is anthropocentric and thus cannot have a direct moral duty towards non-human realities raised a lot of attention among various philosophical platforms. Such a claim implies that human beings only have a direct moral duty to their species; anything other than human beings can only be treated with an indirect respect, not entirely for its sake. Various forms of environmental ethics which are derived from Ubuntu face this same critique. This echoes Mbiti (1969: 92) who views African ontology as basically understanding the world and every other thing which exists in an anthropocentric perspective, where all realities are ordered towards human beings. In this same volume, (ibid, 1969: 92) God is perceived as central to the origins and sustenance of human lives; it is as if God exists for the sake of man and thus one can say that every other thing is ordered towards human beings. This metaphysical worldview puts human beings at the center of all that exist and as such it only commands a direct moral duty to humans. The philosophical challenge of this ontology by Mbiti (1969) is that, it cannot directly justify an authentic direct duty for the environment, and neither can it show the moral status of the environment in itself. Given that the place of non-human beings in the cosmos is only significant in so far as they are valuable to humanity, there is no basis upon which one can show their moral status apart from their instrumental value to humanity.

Horsthemke (2015) dedicates an entire chapter of his book to expound on the same claim on anthropocentrism. He debates with the claim that Ubuntu 'focuses exclusively on human beings' and therefore it is in strict terms an anthropocentric philosophy which does not have a direct duty towards non-human species. Following from his argument, Ubuntu at its best can be given an 'indirect-duty view.' Human beings in this view; endorse moral worth to other beings which co-exist with them. The author suggests that perhaps an African interest towards the Environment can be deduced from a concept of *"Ukama"* which indirectly extends to human relations with any other living beings. Africans could have had an indirect concern for the environment in so far as they could foresee some benefit from it to humanity. The notion of an indirect-duty entails that the African's moral commitments towards other species was not necessarily for their sake as ends or beings in themselves; it could only have been an instrumental duty in so far as the environment, or animals for instance could assist in human endeavors such as transportation, farming and food in general.

The aforementioned claim that African metaphysics does not recognize the intrinsic moral value of non-human forms of existence has the implication that it limits the possibility of a direct moral concern for the environment in African Environmental Ethics. If non-human forms of life do not have an intrinsic moral status, Africans were justified in treating them entirely as means rather than ends in themselves. It would also mean that one cannot authentically make a direct moral judgement on environmental realities entirely from an African perspective. These implications cannot be said to be true for African thought as I will show from the rainmakers' perspectives in the last section of this paper.

These implications are some of the reasons why the classification of African environmental ethics as an anthropocentric philosophy has been critiqued by some scholars as 'an undermining of the true attitudes and relations which Africans embraced towards their environment.' (Sindima 1995; Ramose 2009; Murove 2009; Le Grange 2013). These selected scholars argue in a way which echoes Ubuntu as an interconnectedness and interdependence with the totality of all beings in existence regardless of the species demarcation. Sindima (1995: 126) particularly observes that nature and human beings are interwoven into one fabric of life. This entails that in the African mind, existence is inseparable from other co-existing beings whether spiritual or non-human. This background sets an important foundation to my line of argument which claims that the rain making ceremony necessarily calls for a more broader understanding of African thought, some understanding which can best be called 'trans-anthropocentric' in nature.

10.4   The Rainmaker's Trans-anthropocentric Environmental Ethics

In this part of the paper, I seek to refute the anthropocentric claim on African philosophy by posing challenging evidence from rainmaker's accounts which point to an African sensitivity and understanding of the intrinsic moral value of non-human forms of life. From a philosophical analysis of particular rituals such as the rain-making ceremony and the Rain maker's cosmology, I will argue that Africans acknowledge the intrinsic moral worth of the environment, regardless of its resourcefulness or momentary gains to human beings. I will introduce the reader to four key concepts which I extracted from various accounts about rainmakers and the rainmaking ceremony. From these four cases, I seek to support the argument that; rainmakers in traditional African societies embraced a trans-anthropocentric environmental ethics. This argument thus leads to the view that African environmental ethics ought to be trans-anthropocentric in its original nature.

10.4.1 Case 1: The Rain-Maker's Conception of Evil and Its Implications on Environmental Ethics

The African conception of 'evil in the land' which was a guideline to the observances necessary for the rainmaking ceremony; goes beyond inter-human encounters. Unlike the Judeo-Christian conception of evil as purely depicting inter-human relations, the African rainmaker's account of evil can be thought of as going beyond human interactions. This entails that the notion of moral status, as well as wrong doing in African thought, encompasses human relations with other forms of life, non-human beings interacting among themselves, as well as human and non-human encounters with sacred inanimate beings such as mountains, sacred shrines and forests. Haruna (1997: 227) explains this holistic account of evil in the African conception by imposing rain as an empirical indicator of harmonious relations among everything that exists; human and non-human forms of life. He notes how Africans thought of rain as a product of harmonious relations with the totality of 'Being.' This claim comes from the observation that if there was evil in the land, if sacred forests were tempered with or sacred animals were killed, the earth would be angry "*pasiratsamwa*" and there would be no rains in the land (ibid: 233). In this same account, he extends the realm of sacred beings to include sacred lakes which were an abode to sacred animals as well as the spirits of the people's ancestors who were thought of as depended on these sacred lakes for drinking water. Evil or immoral actions could thus be drawn from human interactions with these epochs of non-human beings as well as animals. Given that the ancestors were for instance said to drink water from the same lakes, the implications were that humans among other species had to safeguard the sanctity of these epochs of nature. Even non-human forms of life could defile a sacred place, and this is in reference to the way in which animals such as dogs, goats and cows were prohibited from drinking water from the sacred pools. A similar standard would apply to grazing lands, where animals in particular livestock was prohibited from grazing in the sacred forests and mountains.

This particular case could be interpreted as a traditional way of preserving nature and securing the existence of all species of life beyond human concerns. One wonders how such a broad conception of evil can fit within the claims of scholars who argue that African worldviews were entirely anthropocentric. From this conception of evil which goes beyond human interactions amongst themselves, and rather extends to relations among all beings, (human and non-human) it follows that a better way to conceive of African environmental ethics, is to think of it as trans-anthropocentric, implying that it goes beyond human interest. This particular case of the rainmaker's understanding of evil in a broader sense, points towards an African philosophy which also understands the unity of existence as going beyond the concerns of human species.

10.4.2   Case 2: The Rain-Maker's Understanding of the Ecosystem

Other than the trans-anthropocentric understanding of evil, the African understanding of the ecosystem also shows a trans-anthropocentric dimension of existence. In contrast to the contemporary and westernized understanding of the ecosystem, the African mind understood seasonal changes as well as ecological realities such as air, water and the sun in a unique way. I do not seek to debate on the scientific strengths of these accounts except to state that the African way of understanding the ecosystem as relative to existential activities of human beings among other forms of life has a similar sense to the modernistic causes of global warming and other ecological challenges. In particular, rains were understood to be part of the hallmark of existence given that all species and forms of life need water to survive. The idea that rain is determined by the moral status of all living beings is still prevalent in African thought. This is similar to the Judeo-Christian accounts of how God could bless people with rain, or punish them with a drought, although it is important to note that in the African conception of seasonal changes, even non-human forms of life could defile the land and affect the ecosystem. In general, although the scientific explanations of the ecosystem are more plausible, one cannot deny that this kind of knowledge had a functional role of preserving correct relationships with the environment in a non-anthropocentric way. There was an element of a direct duty towards the environment in itself as a reality which deserved moral recognition. People would not just do as they wish with the environment given the belief system which bounded them to environmental justice, lest there will be no rains. An ecological understanding which goes beyond human relations with the environment gave a broader ecological worldview which is consistent with the ethos of environmental conversation in a trans-anthropocentric manner.

10.4.3   Case 3: The Rain-Maker's Understanding of Industrialization and Its Impact on the Environment

The African understanding of industrialization and development is also worth of philosophical scrutiny in exposing the trans-anthropocentric dimension of African ethics. Due to the traditional worldview, aforementioned in preceding paragraphs, one can understand why Africans would not just welcome industrial development irrespective of how it affects other species in existence. This sensitivity to the environment is misrepresented and often associated with extreme cases where various mythological mentalities could have restrained technological developments. A popular account mocks the mentality of some African chiefs among the Bantu people in Southern Africa who were said to be primitive. Bernard and Kumalo (2004) cited in Machoko (2013) documents a scenario where,

> … the people of Umnga municipal area in the Eastern cape objected to the construction of a hydropower plant in their area, arguing that the hydropower would disturb the tranquility of mermaids at the local waterfalls, the electricity generated would drive mermaids away from the pools, lead to droughts, electrical storms, and floods. Bernard and Kumalo (2004). Cited in Machoko (2013: 292)

Although the truth value of this account is debatable in contemporary thought, I still argue that it reflects the way in which the African understanding of the ecosystem went beyond anthropocentric gains.

Despite this extreme case, there are many other undocumented cases where dams were constructed, trapping water for human welfare in a way which was insensitive to other wild animals which then had to travel long distances to access water. African conceptions of technological development as well industrialization were for the most part more eco-friendly models although probably less efficient for macro-production. Despite the inaccuracy of the ecological model in explaining environmental realities as well as its lack of effectiveness in terms of production, one cannot deny that such human interactions with nature depict a trans-anthropocentric philosophy which had the totality of nature in mind.

10.4.4   Case 4: The Rain-Makers Concerns on Contemporary Agricultural Practices

Agriculture is the highest manifestation of human relations with the environment. Traditional African societies lived 'in and with' their environment. The Khoisan people among other 'hunting and gathering' societies, blended so well with nature to the metaphoric extend of being regarded as 'animals.' Images of Africa as a jungle, the vast plains of nature, fauna and flora in Africa reflect this reality that Africans blended with their environment. The shift from 'hunting and gathering' as a source of livelihood to the domestication of plants and animals for the same cause, marked the dawn of Agriculture. Etymologically, the word Agriculture comes from the Latin words *Ager* 'field' and *cultura* 'cultivation.' Human beings are the only species of animals which practice agriculture and in a way, this practice depicts a certain way of relating with the environment for purely anthropocentric ends. Defined in general, Agriculture is the growing of crops and rearing of animals for livelihood. It is marked by the domestication of non-human forms of life to serve human ends. Such as domestication includes animals, land, plants as well as water in scenarios where dams are constructed and boreholes are sunk for irrigation purposes.

It is important to note that the rain maker's concerns on Agriculture go beyond folk stories of the construction of dams in areas which were believed to be habitats for mermaids and spiritual forces. Haruna (1997) notes that "Through modern education and values, many of the traditional beliefs of the people are distorted, changed or partially abandoned, but they are by no means extinct." Haruna (1997: 237). The misrepresentation of Rainmakers and the over emphasis on their mystical paradigms overshadows the fact that rainmakers have effectively held advisory positions pertaining to African attitudes towards food production. Such arguments can still speak to contemporary challenges. They for instance critic the culture of wasting or throwing away food which in a way shows their relevance to contemporary agricultural production. Another argument could be their concern over the unbridled expansion of farm lands into forests which were reserved for other forms of life.

The emergence of commercial farming in Africa, characterized by a market driven obsession to maximize on economic gains with less or little concern for other forms of life which co-exist and inhabit the earth with human beings is an issue of philosophical concern. The central question asks if it is justified for human beings to cut-down any tree, construct dams anywhere, and to farm on any piece of land in so far as it is arable. In a way, there is no doubt that Agriculture is an anthropocentric activity and it is expected of it to be in contradiction to the principles of trans-anthropocentric ethics. This dichotomy however can be minimized by employing an Agricultural ethics which recognizes the intrinsic moral value of other species of life. My paper argues that the anthropocentric nature of prevailing Agricultural practice is a problem which can be solved by looking back at history and rigorously considering the rain-maker's worldviews.

The analysis of the rain making ceremony referred to in previous sections points to the way in which the practice of throwing away food was considered an evil in traditional African thought. The moral worth of food was imperative probably because of anthropocentric factors, including the thoughts on other poor members of the community who could have made use of the same food. In traditional African societies, the rate at which food was produced was relative to reasonable demand which did not allow the culture of wasting. Although there could be a surplus in production, historical studies show that the size of the farmland could only allow for a reasonable surplus.

Agriculture was dominantly at a subsistence level and very little environmental degradation was occurring. The culture of wasting and throwing away food was thus restricted in many ways. It seems as if this taboo is still prevailing in a subtle way particularly owing to the emergence of commercial farming. People continue to produce food without an idea of how much food is enough. One can consider the way in which cereals are refined and processed in such a manner that much of what was essentially contained in the grain goes to waste. This echoes the Rain maker's concern on throwing away food as an insult to the gods who provide food. Despite the spiritual association of this claim, one can still decipher that an African environmental ethic must uphold this particular issue in liaison with the views which were held by the people in its jurisdiction. There is no justification for throwing away food given that its production affects other species of life.

The rain maker's eco-political authority might not be restored to its original state, yet I argue that these individuals and their worldviews can still be integrated into contemporary practice. Machoko (2013) argued in this line of thought from the premise that the root problem in environmental degradation was more than a technological error but rather the loss of an environmental ethic which is imperative to the people. He suggests that "the solution to sustainable natural environmental conservation in Zimbabwe lay in the belief systems and spiritual links between the people and their natural resources." Machoko (2013: 293). In a way he was advocating for the integration of a spiritual ecology into existing empirico-based and mechanistic ethics. He argues along with Bernard and Kumalo (2004) who in their definition of Spiritual ecology emphasize "on how the concepts of the supernatural and the spiritual world influenced a group's management and use of an ecological resource." Bernard and Kumalo (2004) cited in Machoko (2013: 293). The invaluable characteristic of spiritual ecology is not in its logical explanation of reality, but rather in its imperative approaches which many African minds find plausible and consistent with their overall worldviews.

I recommend that an enculturation of contemporary agricultural practice with traditional environmental ethics is a practicable and plausible solution to environment management challenges. Such a thesis is endorsed by a recent initiative to practice Community-Based Natural Resource Management (CBNRM). Breen (2013) documents on this activity as a communal approach to ecological challenges. Community Based Natural Resource Management as a methodology acknowledges the crucial role of every member of the community in environmental conservation. This in a way resembles the African understanding of communal responsibility over the environment, which exposes a trans-anthropocentric dimension of African thought and practice in harmony. The human selfishness which is exhibited in an ever increasing expansion of commercial farming land continues to be a concern for a purely African ethic. Despite the benefits of Agriculture to humanity, it is necessary that land tenure systems recognize that not all of the land on earth belongs to human beings. Some epochs of land have to be reserved for non-human species and this observation was safeguarded by an element of sacredness in traditional African societies. This enabled individuals to respect and reserve the forests although this was done in pursuit of a mythological ethos.

The ongoing quest for sustainable natural environmental conservation methodologies has a lot to learn from traditional African environmental ethics. In as much as one cannot restore the mythological narratives of environmental conversation which Africans held, it is still possible to learn lessons from them and to integrate them with modern practice. Such a methodology echoes the insistence on organic farming which is already ongoing in Africa. The ethic behind all these eco-friendly farming methodologies can be paralleled and supported with an indigenous understanding of the moral value of the environment.

10.5   Conclusion

African Environmental Ethics necessarily has to be informed by the invaluable accounts of the Rain-maker's worldview. I hope that this account will probably raise further issues on the nature of African Environmental Ethics in general. The central question to its nature would ask if African ethics ought to be purely rationalistic and informed solely by empirical causations. This is not an entirely new question to African ethics and I acknowledge that there are on-going investigations into the nature of African scientific enquiry. I argued that the essence of African Environmental Ethics cannot be separated entirely from the Theo-centric worldview of the indigenous people's metaphysics. The rain maker's account of cosmology, although it lacks empirical and or scientific evidence, it is instrumentally valuable in instilling preservation and conservation attitudes. In a way, my paper does not seek to claim that the superstitious and mythical dimension of African thought ought to be the bedrock of African Environmental Ethics. Rather, this inseparable aspect requires that Philosophers as well other scientific disciplines with a similar interest ought to carry out more researches and investigations into the analysis of the truths behind these mythological worldviews. More inter-disciplinary research has to be done on the philosophy of the rain-maker and prevailing knowledge systems in Africa have to be enriched by enculturation. One might call such an academic endeavor with a similar title of decolonizing African Environmental management systems. The two accounts on nature can be intertwined, intrinsically gaining from the strengths of each other in a way which complements their weakness. This is similar to the way in which Greek mythology as well as Judeo-Christian beliefs influenced Western Philosophical thought. Ethics as such; is one field of scientific enquiry which can accommodate religious or non-empirical realities in its deepened relationship with metaphysics. I hold that African Environmental Ethics and Environmental management in general ought to accommodate the people's conceptions of reality.

References

Beach, D.N. 1980. *The Shona and Zimbabwe 900–1850: An Outline of Shona History*. Gweru: Mambo Press.

Bernard, P., and Khumalo, Z. 2004. Indigenous knowledge and the cultural importance of woodland and forest species in southern Africa: The case of ubulawu. In *Indigenous Forest and Woodlands in South Africa: Policy, People and Practice*, ed. M. Lawes, H. Eeley, C. Shackleton, and B. S. Geach, 498–504. Pietermaritzburg: University of KwaZulu-Natal Press. ISBN 1-86914-050-8.

Breen, C. 2013. *Community-Based Natural Resource Management in Southern Africa*. Centre for African Studies at the University of Florida.

Bujo, B. 2009. Ecology and Ethical Responsibility from an African Perspective. In *African Ethics: An Anthology of Comparative Applied Ethics*, ed. M.F. Murove, 281–297. Pietermaritzburg: University of KwaZulu-Natal Press.

Callicott, Baird J. 1994. *Earth's Insights: A survey of Ecological Ethics from the Mediterranean Basin to the Australian Outback*. Berkeley: University of California Press.

Chidester, D. 1997. *African Traditional Religion in South Africa: An Annotated Bibliography*. London: Greenwood Press.

Feddema, J.P. 1966. Tswana ritual concerning rain. *African Studies* 25: 181–195.

Haruna, A. 1997. *Rituals and Ceremonies Accompanying Rainmaking among the Guruntum and Bubbure People*. University of Maiduguri.

Horsthemke, K. 2015. *Animals and African Ethics*. South Africa: University of the Witwatersrand.

Le Grange, L. 2013. Ubuntu, ukama and the healing of nature, self and society. *Educational Philosophy and Theory* 44(sup2): 56–67.http://doi.org/10.1111/j.1469-5812.2011.00795.x.

Machoko, G.C. 2013. *Water Spirits and the Conservation of the Natural Environment: A Case Study from Zimbabwe*. Canada: Huntington University.

Maravanyika, S. 2012. Local responses to colonial evictions, conservation and commodity policies among Shangwe communities in Gokwe, North-western Zimbabwe, 1963–1980. *African Nebula* 5: 1–20.

Matsuhira, Y. 2013. Rain Making Ceremony in the Nyandoro Region, Zimbabwe. *African Religious Dynamics* 1: 165–182. (Nagoya University, Japan).

Mawere, A., and Ken, W. 1995. Socio-religious movements, the state and community change: Some reflections on the ambuya juliana cult of Southern Zimbabwe. *Journal of Religion in Africa* 25(3): 252–287.

Mbiti, J.S. 1970. *Concepts of God in Africa*. London: SPCK.

Murove, M.F. 2009. An African Environmental Ethics Based on the Concepts of Ukama and Ubuntu. In *African Ethics: An Anthology of Comparative and Applied Ethics*, ed. M.F. Murove, 315–331. Pietermaritzburg: University of KwaZulu Natal Press.

Ngara, R. 2014. Shangwe Indigenous Knowledge Systems: An Ethnometrological And Ethnomusicological Explication. *International Journal of Asian Social Science* 4(1): 81–88.

Oruka, H.O. 1990. *Trends in Contemporary African Philosophy*. Nairobi: Shirikon Publishers.

Oruka, H.A 1993. *Sage Philosophy: Indigenous Thinkers and Modern Debate on African Philosophy*. Nairobi: ACTS Press.

Ramose, M.B. 2009. Ecology through Ubuntu. In *African Ethics: An Anthology of Comparative and Applied Ethics*, ed. M.F. Murove, 308–314. Pietermaritzburg: University of Natal Press.

Sindima, J.H. 1995. *Africa's Agenda: The Legacy of Liberalism and Colonialism in the Crisis of African Values*. Greenwood Press.

Chapter 11
New Waves: African Environmental Ethics and Ocean Ecosystems

Michelle Louise Clarke

Abstract The persistent image of the vast, open ocean has led to the underlying idea of the ocean as placeless, devoid of social interactions. The image of ocean as passive and placeless has a direct effect on environmental law and stewardship within maritime space. Further, this conception has led to the persistent belief that the sheer scale of the ocean makes it impervious to human harm. The ocean is expected to take our waste and pollution without repercussions. African Environmental Ethics is a largely 'landlocked field' and the chapter will examine Africa's position in the global ecology. Although marine ecosystems themselves are fluid, cross boundaries and pay no attention to governed borders (Merrie in Global ocean futures: governance of marine fisheries in the Anthropocene. Stockholm, 2016), marine protection requires an understanding of human activities in a placeful environment. Maritime stewardship must be imagined across global and local levels from an organic interconnected and post-local standpoint. Considerations will be made as how African Environmental Ethics can understand and advance environmental marine practices and be used as a site of resistance to new structures of 'hydro-colonisation'. The chapter will examine practices of marine conservation from the standpoint of African Relational Environmentalism (Behrens in Ontologized ethics: new essays in African meta-ethics. Lexington Books, Lanham, pp. 55–72, 2014; Ojomo in J. Pan Afr. Stud. 4(3):101–113, 2011; Tangwa in A companion to African philosophy. Blackwell Publisher, Oxford, pp. 387–395, 2004) and Janz's concept of 'travelling ethics' (New visions of nature. Springer, Dordrecht, pp. 181–195, 2009) as well as exploring ethics from interdisciplinary perspectives drawn from cultural theory and natural sciences. A renegotiation of the ocean space and new ways of imagining global-local ecosystems would seek to overcome the ocean as placeless and understand the interdependence of 'natural, human and ancestral worlds' (Wardi in Water and African American memory: an ecocritical perspective. University Press of Florida, Florida, 2011). The purpose of the chapter is to make suggestions for moving African Environmental Ethics into engaging with new discourses, whilst also applying the field to a 'blue' ethics of the ocean which has so far been overlooked.

M. L. Clarke (✉)
SOAS, University of London, London, UK
e-mail: Mc105@soas.ac.uk

© Springer Nature Switzerland AG 2019   153
M. Chemhuru (ed.), *African Environmental Ethics*, The International
Library of Environmental, Agricultural and Food Ethics 29,
https://doi.org/10.1007/978-3-030-18807-8_11

11.1 Introduction: Renegotiating the Alien

The opening chapter of Nnedi Okorafor's science fiction novel *Lagoon* (2014) is written from the viewpoint of a swordfish, which becomes transformed to monstrous proportions and attacks an oil pipeline. The monstrous swordfish wishes for a clean ocean and teams up with other creatures of the deep to attack the oil rigs off the polluted coast of Nigeria.

Interestingly, whilst this imagery may seem fantastical, Okorafor was drawn to write this chapter by a headline she saw online (Reuters 2010). *Lagoon* imagines the response of the city of Lagos as aliens make contact with Earth. As the aliens land in the ocean, just off the coast of the city, they merge and change the life that they find there, creating super powerful and huge sea creatures, which subsequently take revenge on humans for the pollution of their aquatic homes. The ocean life here becomes the alien, the vengeful and the terrifying, renegotiating the relationship of the human and non-human. The aliens in the meantime, are "cataclysms for change" (Lagoon 2014: 160). They have arrived on earth to make their home, and envisage a new future for Nigeria and its place in the world.

This may seem like a strange and far-fetched beginning for a chapter on African Environmental Ethics. However, what the novel does create, and what we should envisage for the school of thought that is African Environmental Ethics, is a space where Africa becomes a site for imagining new environmental futures, no longer at the periphery of geopolitics, but at a critical point for enacting change and contributing to real dialogue around environmental justice.

Maritime conservation and stewardship is also often on the periphery of environmental discourse, a landlocked field, with attention paid to green spaces, but the 'blue' ocean is overlooked as part of global ecosystems. Time and again, the image of the ocean as alien, as vast, open and hence placeless has had consequences for maritime conservation. The passive space of the ocean ignores the interconnectedness of the complex ecosystems which exists not only along shorelines, but in the deep realms beneath the waves. Pollution, overfishing and the degradation of biodiversity in marine habitats effects food stocks, livelihoods and climate regulation. Climate change and the acidification of seawater reduces the capacity of the oceans to absorb carbon and therefore regulate global temperatures and local weather patterns. The ocean is not only the origin of all life on earth, but is the engine that continues to sustain it. Earle (1995: 15) reminds us that, "Our origins are … reflected in the briny solution [of the ocean] coursing through our veins and in the underlying chemistry that links us to all other life".

Within Okorafor's *Lagoon*, the placeless-ness of the ocean is 're-placed' as a site of exchange and learning for better ecological futures. Although the ocean is literally transformed into something alien, this only enhances our awareness of our interconnectedness with the non-human. *Lagoon* then, allows for a renegotiation "between terrestrial human habitats and distant benthic and pelagic realms, between the aesthetic estrangement of sea creatures and the recognition of evolutionary kinship, between mediated, situated, and emergent knowledges…." (Alaimo 2012b: 490) of the ocean space, and new ways of imagining global ecosystems. This chapter will argue for an African Environmental Ethic which does just this, the ocean is not other, or alien, but an intrinsic part of global ecosystems.

It is also the idea of 'placeless' becoming 'placeful' I wish to attend to in my arguments for bringing of African Environmental Ethics into dialogue with global environmental issues. This is paramount to the future of African Environmental Ethics. I will particularly explore Bruce Janz's writing around 'placeful' ethics (2001, 2009, 2014a, b) and African Relational Environmentalism (Behrens 2014) in order to emphasize shared connections within both ethics and global ecosystem management. The aim is to understand how the ethos of an African Ethic could challenge thinking surrounding maritime conservation.

The first section of this chapter will address current discourse surrounding ocean space and maritime conservation. Secondly, the chapter will address how this discourse affects the current issues Marine Protected Areas face in terms of their management. Next, I will address how an African Ethics 'in place' could address issues of a placeless ocean. Finally, I will demonstrate how Janz's (2009) concept of 'travelling ethics' could be applied to the 'tragedy of the global commons' and be used as a site of resistance to new structures of 'hydro-colonisation'. The purpose of the chapter is to make suggestions for moving African Environmental Ethics into engaging with new discourses, whilst also applying the field to a 'blue' ethics of the ocean which has so far been overlooked.

11.2   The Tragedy of the Global Commons

The open ocean is seen as far removed from the shoreline ecosystems, as a distant alien space. The ideology of the ocean as a removed 'other' has long influenced maritime law and environmental marine policy. The ocean as alien "… implies that ocean life is conjured by science fiction fantasies. It also suggests that even if the creatures of the deep do exist, they dwell in a place so distant, so foreign, that they are radically disconnected from terrestrial environments, processes and flows" (Alaimo 2012b: 184). The mysterious deep scattering layer (DSL), migrations of a vast variety of organisms each day, several thousand feet below the ocean's surface, was discovered in the 1940s by marine scientists. Pollution causing depletion of the DSL leads to effects further up the food chain and yet is still seen a 'alien-like' mass of species. The species that make up the DSL even look alien, with their bulbous eyes and light-emitting organs. The DSL "demonstrates how deep sea environments are enmeshed with the marine regions with which humans are concerned … for the ocean, any loss of productivity in the deep scattering layer would be the biggest cataclysm of all impoverishing the surface waters, depleting the coasts, cascading across the boundaries between ocean and land to denude both natural and human economies" (Whitty 2010).

Maritime laws of the High Seas are based on the original doctrine of *mare liberum* (free seas for everyone), and the idea of an oceanic commons dates as far back as Roman history. However, it was the 1958 first United Nations Law of the Sea Conference where most states solidified a 3-mile limit to territorial seas. This was superseded in 1982 where Exclusive Economic zones were recognized, extending 200 nautical miles. In the EEZ, nations have the sovereign rights to natural resources within this maritime space. The 'global commons' then, are areas outside of political domains or nation states, whereby access to resources are shared. Legally speaking, the High Seas is one of these arenas (UNEP 2017; Buck 1998).

The open ocean remains therefore, largely an unregulated area, as it is viewed as 'common space', and this results in diminished responsibility of stewarding marine environment. Hardin (1968) describes this as the 'tragedy of the commons'. The ocean is expected to take our waste and pollution without repercussions—toxic chemicals, radioactive waste, and sewage. During the BP Petroleum deep sea drilling disaster of 2010, the representative of BP, Tony Hayward, was quoted as having said, "The Gulf of Mexico is a very big ocean. The amount of oil and dispersant we are putting into it is tiny in relation to the total water volume" (The Guardian 2017). Alaimo (2012a) argues that this particularly exemplifies the discourse of the ocean as both "lacking in substance and devoid of consequence" (Alaimo 2012a: 182). Often, with environmental disasters more attention is paid to short term damages of fishing and tourist industries than long term ecological considerations.

The persistent image of the vast, open ocean has led to the underlying idea of the ocean as placeless, devoid of social interactions. The sea is merely a point of crossing, within economic and political contexts. It is vessels and the goods they contain which are sites of exchange, the body of water below exempt from these interactions. This conception has led to the persistent belief that the sheer scale of the ocean makes it impervious to human harm. The image of ocean as passive and place-less has a direct effect on environmental law and stewardship within maritime space. As Germond et al. explains, "This representation has served the post-modern capitalism's interests by reducing the seas to an empty void through which capital and goods shall transit quickly and freely" (Germond and Germond-Duret 2016: 125).

Although the vision of the ocean as a connector is a motif often taken up by cultural and spatial studies as a way of promoting a transnational and intercultural perspectives and exchange, this can also lead to the ocean space becoming one single passive unit of analysis. For example, Gilroy's *Black Atlantic* privileges hybridity and movement (Gilroy 1993). The Deleuzian ocean is smooth and unobstructed: "the Ocean, the Unlimited, first plays the role of an encompassing element, and tends to become a horizon: the earth is thus surrounded, globalized, 'grounded' by this element, which holds it in immobile equilibrium and makes Form possible" (Deleuze and Guattari 1987: 495). The ocean hence becomes as a space between—a scene of liberation, transcendence, hybridity and fluidity. However, this hegemonic categorization does not allow for an understanding of the complex relationships of these ecosystems, which "barely register on anthropocentric horizons as living places" (Alaimo 2012a: 190).

Globalisation has changed and is continuing to shape how the world's oceans are negotiated as political sites. Developments in communication systems and technology result in marine environments becoming more accessible. New markets for trade are expanding all the time, from extraction of gas hydrates to blue biotechnology (Mackelworth 2016; Westwood et al. 2002). The lack of clarity regarding legalities of maritime boundaries therefore becomes increasingly a cause for concern. With distance from the coast, these boundaries become ever more contested, as they move further from national zones into the commons arena (Mackelworth 2016).

Water then, is not a passive space, but 'manifests as history' (Wardi 2011). Indeed, Mackelworth argues, "In many parts of the world, especially those influenced by colonial powers, borders were drawn with little regard for the many species and habitats that permeate these boundaries, and the local communities that are reliant upon them" (2016: 3). It has been argued that the European Union's Maritime Policy is a "surmounting of the maritime tradition of modernity entrenched in European geographical expansion, the building of colonial empires, and the development of modern science and maritime economy on the basis of the development of trade and the industrial exploitation of natural resources" (de Vivero 2007: 409). Europe's maritime policy then, is an extension of empire mentality and ocean governance is a social and political action (de Vivero 2007). Often, ocean policy suits more powerful global actors, and conservation becomes a guise, as concern for the welfare of ocean ecosystems is used for solidifying security and international boundaries (de Vivero 2007; Leenhardt et al. 2013; Germond and Germond-Duret 2016).

A further issue then, concerning the management of maritime ecosystems is the difference of conceptual languages, as often the political legalities of the zones may differ from ecological needs. Scientists and politicians will have divergent agendas, whereas local communities will have differing conceptualizations of ecosystems (Scovazzi and Tani 2016). Rogerson (2015) cites epistemological policing as a major concern. This is the process whereby only one kind of knowledge is recognized or acknowledged. Obviously, scientific knowledge and western centric thinking is the dominant dialogue, ignoring unique opportunities for conservation inspired by local actors and knowledges (Agardy 2005; Rogerson 2015). Epistemological policing means neoliberal strategies are often favored as these are deemed efficient and cost-effective, and scientific knowledge is held up as the source of objective knowledge about nature, whereas all other knowledges are deemed subjective and so less 'true' (Rogerson 2015). Attention to ecosystems is centred on how they function as 'markets resources' and emphasis is placed heavily upon economic value of ecosystem services. Note the use of the word 'services' here—nature is seen as a support for man, rather than as part of an interdependent whole.

Conservation policies instead of being carefully constructed to counter global issues of climate change and complex issues surrounding pollution, are foremost promoted as either a solution to problems with fisheries or as a creating a new market for tourism and trade (Mackelworth 2016). Approaches to maritime regulations are based in western-centric discourse, ignoring 'multiple rationalities' and alternative knowledges of the ocean. The placeless-ness of the ocean must be 're-placed' and renegotiated as a site of exchange and learning for better ecological futures, with interdependence of the natural and human at the forefront of this understanding.

11.3   Marine Protected Areas—A Problem of Scale

The term Marine Protected Area (MPA) refers to a geographic area where human activities are regulated in order to conserve ecosystem services and cultural values. IUCN's (International Union for Conservation of Nature) definition of a Marine Protected Area is: "Any area of intertidal or sub-tidal terrain, together with its over-lying water and associated flora, fauna, historical and cultural features, which has been reserved by law or other effective means to protect part or all of the enclosed environment" (Kelleher and Kenchington 1992: 7). RAMPAO (Réseau Régionald' Aires Marines Protégées en Afrique de L'Ouest) is the West African Network of MPAs, an ecoregion spanning 2.8 million hectares and encompassing 28 MPAs. RAMPAO's mission is to "ensure, within the West African marine ecoregion that encompasses Cape Verde, the Gambia, Guinea Bissau, Guinea, Mauritania, Senegal and Sierra Leone, the maintaining of a coherent set of critical habitats necessary for the dynamic functioning of the ecological processes essential to the regeneration of the natural resources and the conservation of biodiversity for the benefit of societies." (Rampao.org 2017). The network was established in 2007 by conservation actors and formally recognized by the 7 states in 2010.

RAMPAO has been deemed relatively successful. As well as establishing the net-work of MPAs to tackle degradation in marine and coastal areas, real changes and improvements have been made in the sustainable management of regional fisheries. The network was able to negotiate international and regional maritime laws in order to advantage and represent the needs of local communities. An overhaul in policy was established by the Sub-Regional Fisheries Commission (SRFC), an intergovernmen-tal organization for cooperation in the fisheries sector covering the same geographic area as the RAMPAO (Duval-Diop 2016).

Overall, the RAMPAO network built upon "the capacity of local actors and finance(d) their participation in regional and international dialogue, it facilitates direct access that influences national policy implementation and alter(ed) the balance of power" within the ecoregion (Duval-Diop 2016: 194). By bringing local actors into a regional dialogue, RAMPAO was able to influence national and regional policies that were situated within two international frameworks: The Convention on Biolog-ical Diversity and the Fish Stocks Agreement (Duval-Diop 2016). This is a prime example of how maritime Africa has had to renegotiate with policy that was unsuited to its local domains. Current policies and practices such as the policies mentioned were formed with Euro-centric laws and values in mind.

RAMPAO is an example of the transboundary management of MPAs. These are MPAs which cross one or more national territories. There is no official regime to monitor or regulate economic zones or continental shelves. It is up to individual states to reach agreements and to manage MPA formation and agreements (Scovazzi and Tani 2016). This means it is extremely difficult to find cooperative solutions to boundary implementation and to reach the establishment of polices which suits all states economically, politically and socially. The aim of MPAs is twofold, to protect the biodiversity of ecosystems, whilst allowing for development of local economies.

In many cases MPAs face management issues due to conflicting stakeholders. Effective governance of MPAs is a much debated issue. Scovazzi and Tani (2016: 15) write, "To be effective, MPAs need to have a number of characteristics, including: clearly delineated boundaries; a strong causal link between the harm being addressed and management measures, which should be flexible and adaptive; implementation, compliance and enforcement measures consistent with international law."

However, this means Marine Protected Areas are often drawn into static sectors and adhere to rigid policy (Rogerson 2015; Agardy et al. 2011). Oceans do not always fit neatly into these zones, nor do they always follow patterns or models (Rogerson 2015). Small, static zones will not help in any way to preserve global ecosystems. Larger regional areas of MPAs should be established and transboundary management should seek to be understand how ecosystems will be affected by many stakeholders and coastal land use practices (Duval-Diop 2016: 182), as well as taking into account local issues of governance, and social and cultural differences (Agardy 2005). International maritime laws try to account for differences in locality. However, this is usually insufficient as specific social, political and cultural settings are not understood (Agardy 2005). Often this is due to polices being too generalized, or even conflicting with local priorities (Agardy 2005).

There is then, a 'mis-match' in scale within conceptualizing ecosystems, and marine policy and conservation often falls foul of this. Geier (2016: 58) writes that, "Ecosystems, may fit local scales, but then those scales fall apart when considered against global pollution indexes or rises in temperature". Environmentalists have long argued for the campaign 'Think Globally, Act Locally', yet this may actually lead to a disconnection between the global and local, and so lead to inefficiency in international polices. There is a tendency within environmental discourse to assume that geographic categories of scale work in binaries of power: the global north versus global south, the global/local, the national/transnational and so on. A further assumption is that resistance to these power relations is obtained through transgression of boundaries. However, this infers the 'hegemony of space', ignoring the "multiple ways they are interrelated across different conditions and histories" (Crowley 2015: 18).

When we talk of the ocean, it is even more obvious that these binaries just do not stack up. Ecological systems span political boundaries. Indeed, Cetaceans and migratory birds do not follow national boundaries, but migrate across huge distances. Although marine ecosystems themselves are fluid, cross boundaries and pay no attention to governed borders (Merrie 2016), marine protection requires an understanding of human activities in a placeful environment.

Lombardi's imagery of the post-local wave allows a reimagining of the ocean space, in which organic interconnectedness can be envisaged rather than passive fluidity. He writes, "… the breaking wave is a provocative, material emblem of the give-and-take between global influence and local places…. The oceanic swell in contact with all points at once, is given form by variously particular shore breaks, even as its constant battering reshapes local coastlines, bringing to mind a fluid, physical nature and a globally networked culture that redefine the meaning of locale" (Lombardi 2015: 41). For Lombardi, the wave characterizes his concept of the 'post-local' where, "… the experience of immediate, immanent placement … is nevertheless globally connected" (Lombardi 2015: 41). Lombardi (2015) urges the need to explore the "organic interconnectedness of worldwide ecological systems" (Lombardi 2015: 41), going beyond binaries and 'mis-matches' of scale. Alaimo (2016: 9) further portends that, "The very liquidity of pelagic habitats … may dislodge us from our entrenched way of approaching the world". Maritime stewardship must be imagined on a global and local levels from an organic interconnected and post-local standpoint.

11.4 Placeful Ethics in a Placeless Ocean

The discourse of the placeless ocean and the consequences of this for maritime ecosystems and their conservation is a useful way of conceptualising how African Environmental Ethics could be understood in a 'placeful' way and so and its capacity to provide new and dynamic ways of engaging with environmental thinking as a whole.

Generally, philosophy is seen as having 'no place' and philosophical concepts are abstract without being rooted in place. However, Janz (2014a) asks us to consider where concepts are derived from in order to foster new dynamic philosophies through lived experiences. This idea of rooting philosophy 'in place' is essential for understanding how African Philosophy can be applied to the concept of Environmental Ethics. Instead of being placeless then, African Environmental Ethics should adhere to place, enabling the renegotiation of the vast and alien ecosystems of the ocean in doing so.

The debate of exacting 'What is an African Philosophy?' centres on questions of authenticity, methodology and historicity, which are constantly examined and re-examined within the field. African Philosophy is often thought of as location—a space to be carved out on the map of global philosophy, a territory distinct and apart from Western thought. This mapping has left African philosophy at the "edge of Western thought, defining its territory by that already claimed" (Janz 2001: 392).

Janz (2014b) argues for a phenomenological approach to African Philosophy, whereby instead of attending to 'philosophy of place', we construct a 'philosophy in place'. He argues we should attend no longer to "a philosophy *of* place, but philosophy *in* place, as well as philosophy which, for the first time, sees place as a condition of thought." (22).

African Philosophy and Ethics can be defined as 'radical critique' (Rettová 2016). It defies the "the self-image of philosophy as a prejudice-free, ahistorical form of knowledge" (Rettová 2016: 128). African Philosophy is then, usefully disruptive and can create new concepts with which to envisage environmental thinking. It is clear that African Philosophy "is seen as a philosophy containing and overcoming European philosophy" (Rettová 2016: 128). However, attention must be paid to the dynamism of African thought, with a focus upon 'exteriority' rather than 'interiority' (Janz 2001). Mosima (2016) argues against a 'grand narrative' of African Philosophy but instead argues the concern of African Philosophy should be to move philosophy 'beyond boundaries'. Instead of asking 'What is African' and adopting an 'essentialising' identity of philosophy from the continent of Africa, how can concepts and approaches that originate in African traditions deconstruct the hegemony of Euro-American centric philosophies?

In his book, *Animals and African Ethics* (2015), Horsthemke postulates that by looking at spiritualism, totemism and taboos within African societies, we can encounter worldviews that can have implications for more sustainable ecological practices. Mangena (2013) agrees that by looking at other forms of 'non-rational' (as western criteria would define) ways of understanding our relationship with nature, and alternate ways of determining moral status, ethical concerns of communities would not be excluded.

However, Makang (1997) calls for a 'demystification' of this outlook on African Philosophy and Ethics, arguing that there is a reduction of "African traditions to a fixed past and to a nostalgia for an original state, (and) the ethnological discourse strips African people of their historicity" (327). This reinstates colonial discourse upon Africa through its realignment with ahistorical and homogenizing narratives. Caminero-Santangelo and Myers (2011: 8) explains, "In the Western imagination, Africa has been and still is framed as a singularity constituted by absence—of time, civilization, or humanity—and this image has served to legitimate the exploitation of places and peoples in Africa".

Makang (1997) uses the term 'living tradition' to envisage a way forward for African Ethics which is both sensitive to different cultural practices, whilst allowing a shared ethic through a shared humanity. He argues that through learning from practices of the past, but realizing that tradition is not static but dynamic, tradition hence becomes a form of mobilization, not an entity which that encourages homogenization. "By appealing to the praxis and wisdom of our African foreparents, we do not mean to repeat them, but we mean to make use of this praxis and wisdom as interpretative tools to enlighten present generations of Africans" (336). Smythe (2015) conceptualizes the past as a way to reimagine creative possibilities for the future, not as a 'return to some preindustrial past' but "Instead older societies and those of different cultural backgrounds are crucial to understanding what kinds of behavior, institutions and values are truly sustainable... Insofar as the past departs from our modern paradigm, it offers us alternative ones. It can also provide creative and imaginative ideas and possibilities, freeing us from the structures and limitations that bind us both in terms of our own cultural traditions and experiences" (3).

African Philosophy on its own terms is dynamic and creative, although its constant aim to define itself through a static place of origin does not allow for new philosophical tools and concepts to be formed. Janz (2001: 400) notes, "African Philosophy becomes moribund if it does not create concepts". Tradition should not be restricting, but allow for reflection and reframing of key philosophical questions. By re-asking questions from African experience, new paths for Environmental Ethics can be explored. This will create new knowledges from liminal spaces, and so inform new ways of seeing (Janz 2014a)

Mosima (2016) writes, "Place and belonging become what we make of them through constructs of meaning and through the construction of community." In an ever more interconnected world, philosophy must move beyond 'fixed' geographies of space, and beyond its demarcated continent. This "enables us to go beyond the particularism of the ethno-philosophers and the universalism of the professional philosophers [...] and helps us deconstruct the hegemonic imposition of the North Atlantic model." (25) Overall, Mosima argues the need to work for an African 'sagacity' which goes beyond borders, taking into "consideration the oneness and interconnectedness of our humanity" (196).

Mosima, then, aims to break down a number of 'boundaries'. Firstly, the boundaries African Philosophy has set for itself as bound to a 'demarcated space' (see also Janz 2001). Secondly, the boundaries of the Western notion that philosophy consists of rational, abstract thought and should be practiced only by the professional thinker and philosopher. This means then that African Philosophy should encourage a move beyond the 'usual' philosophical genres—lived experiences and practices can also be containers for philosophy (I must also refer here to Rettová's 2007 work on Afrophone Philosophy and genre).

However, there is one further addition I would recommend to Mosima's, in regards to African Environmental Ethics and by way of deconstructing boundaries. If Mosima wishes to address "common problems across borders" (2016: 96), we must also redefine what we mean by the "interconnectedness of our humanity". I would again reiterate the idea within this discussion of our 'organic interconnectedness', and a reconsideration of our relationships with the non-human. The aim overall therefore is for radical, dynamic, decolonizing, deconstructive and interconnected philosophies for real impacts and change, within the field of Environmental Ethics.

This isn't to say then, that the role of African Ethics should be to purely apply traditional ethics to new issues. Nor is doing 'philosophy in place' about trying to find the universal within the local. Instead we should be aware that knowledge is constantly being generated by place, and this can produce new 'emplaced' concepts for environmental issues (Janz 2014a). We must understand place in relation with ecology and to examine "questions about place of man in nature by investigating how that relationship is played out through and shaped by the geospatial forces of those places" (Crowley 2015: 158). This calls for, "New ways of knowing the planet and news ways of organizing human responses to it..." (Trexler 2015: 196).

Janz (2009) argues that the natural, at a platial level, is not just known, but knowing. Nature embodies knowledge. Ethics, "does not rise above the *bios*, but exists within it" (Janz 2009: 185). The natural environment is shaped by the interaction of many different individual actors and entities, both human and nonhuman. Crowley (2015: 157) writes that "Human and nonhumans interact in relationally dynamic and mutually (if not always symmetrically) influencing ways", producing a social and ecological construction of place.

Complex ecological communities interact spatially with the "inhomogeneous and temporally changing" environment (Banavar and Amos Maritan 2009). This creates mutual interactions and a constant feedback loop within this community. In other words, there is a continuous negative or positive response through which nature creates its rhythms. Ecosystems build resilience by governing how populations respond to events, creating a form of palatial knowledge. "Natural places engage in both positive and negative feedback, they have memory (in the sense of temporal encoding and feedback within place), and they act on that memory" (Janz 2009: 185).

Earlier, the DSL (deep scattering layer) was exemplified as a perceived alien feature of the ocean's ecosystem. The movement of the DSL is caused through what is termed the Diel Vertical Migration. This is the movement of organisms from the deep ocean to closer to the surface of the ocean at night. Although extensive research has been carried out, scientists still have not worked out all the complexities surrounding the migration. General consensus is that a complex myriad of interactions explains patterns of movement of the DSL, including light and predator-prey relationships within the ocean space (Dumont and Purcell 2001). It is by further understanding these interrelations, that the alien will become the familiar. The DSL allows for an insight into how bodies and places extend into global flows (Alaimo 2012a). Marine conservation requires knowledge of these unknown realms. Or as Janz (2001, 2009, 2014a, b) would contend, knowledge being drawn *from* these unknown realms is paramount to an ethical understanding of place. As Alaimio (2012a) discusses, the DSL, "calls us to realize that what is, or was, invisible to human technologies of perception and knowledge should not be cast as simply alien or immaterial" (189).

11.5 Ethics and Place as Traveling Concepts: Local Ethos and Global Ocean Ecosystems

When we talk of philosophy and ethics 'in place', then, we are not talking of constructing a territorial boundary in which to implement these interventions. The concept of a place sensitive ethics means that knowledge can move beyond the static, and its mapped territories. It can become relevant for the local and global ecosystems alike. Places should not be considered 'fixed' but rather that their cultures are better understood as dynamic systems of flow and disjuncture between local and global, that borders and boundaries are socially produced and reproduced. Furthermore, every "local activity is in some sense both global and local as well" (Lombardi 2015: 41), just as no ecosystem is a disconnected entity. Although we should recognize knowledge as from place, its usefulness lies in the interdisciplinary, and discussion through regimes of knowledges (this includes the rational and 'non-rational').

Janz's (2009) idea of travelling concepts, (inspired by Mieke Bal) is useful here. By travelling between forms of knowledge, and questioning the construction, and the place that knowledge comes from is what forces us to encounter new rationalities. Janz (2009) writes "Concepts travel, and in doing so enable new forms of knowledge, and open new worlds. In our example here, we have multiple travels: that of place, ethics, and knowledge. In each case, the use of a term in a new context is jarring, but in each case, the violence inherent in travel forces a re-examination of the questions that produced the concept in the original discipline" (186) This violence, argues Janz, is not a reason for not engaging with different knowledges, but instead the 'instrumentalism' of modern reason and knowledge must be consciously interrogated. In this way, ethics will not be reduced to 'abstract universal principles' but it is possible for knowledge on the periphery to be presented as potential for change (Janz 2009).

Often, knowledge systems on the periphery are obscured by a universalist approach to ethics. Complexities and nuances are oversimplified and abstracted in order to fit universalist principles or methodologies. This leaves no space for new questions to be ask of knowledge (Janz 2009) It is interesting to compare here, the work of Cruikshank and her thought-provoking book *Do Glaciers listen?* (2005). In her research Cruikshank portrays narratives from indigenous peoples of Yukon and Alaska and their knowledge systems surrounding glaciers. Here, Glaciers are 'sentient beings', actors, animate, and make moral judgments and punish those who stray from moral codes. Oral histories from these areas hold a wealth of knowledge that could inform scientist's understanding of climate change and environmental history. Further the moral interactions of glaciers and people, where glaciers are seen as conscious entities, responsive to humans is a dynamic concept to consider in terms of an interconnected ecosystems.

However, Cruikshank (2005) warns that local knowledge often codified as TEK (Traditional Ecological Knowledge) by scientists and anthropologists, 'shifts in shape' and is overwhelmed, and subverted by its so-called inclusion into scientific space. "Sentient and social spaces are thus transformed into measurable commodities called 'lands' and 'resources'. Indigenous peoples then face double exclusion, initially by colonial processes that expropriate land, then by neo-colonial discourse that appropriate and reformulate their ideas" (Cruikshank 2005: 259). Once knowledge is taken out of place then, it can become lost in translation, as the richness of the morality and understanding of the ecosystem is reduced and simplified into a different rationality or language (in this case scientific language). Cruikshank (2005: 259) reminds us that these narratives, "provide rich alternatives to normalized values that now conventionally frame nature as a redeemable object to be 'saved'". Ingold (2000) further argues that the 'dwelling perspective' of communities, that is; narratives and knowledges, accumulated though the long passage of time within traditions and peoples, produces a unique understanding of how humans and nature are profoundly interconnected in their shared environment. Cruikshank's (2005) work is in agreement with this as she writes that narratives are "occurring within a deeply moral universe where natural-cultural-histories are always entangled" (4).

This inter-relational outlook between human and non-human morality is not dissimilar to current discussions in African Environmental Ethics. As Behrens (2014: 65) discusses: "We might as well regard the river itself as morally considerable because of the important systemic role it plays in the well-being of so many other morally considerable entities". Behrens (2014) argues for an African Relational Environmentalism, where an African understanding of nature is bound up with 'moral considerability', including towards the inanimate. There are many African philosophers and ethicists who agree that an African way of seeing the world is one that stresses the interconnectedness of all living things, with a tendency towards conceptions of harmony and respect for nature (Behrens 2014; Ojomo 2011; Tangwa 2004).

Ojomo (2011) argues that within the traditional African metaphysical worldview, the dichotomy between "plants, animals, and inanimate things between the sacred and the profane, matter and spirit, the communal and the individual, is a slim and flexible one". This metaphysical approach to nature bestows value upon the non-human. Behrens (2014) discusses what makes an African conception of the natural world different from western holism is that instead of an individual entity possessing life, instead life is shared. An African Environmental Ethics then recognizes the moral considerability of anything that is the 'complex web of life'. "This notion of life as a single texture, a web, or fabric of interdependence, interrelated entities provide an attractive construct for understanding moral considerability. It is not just each individual living organism that count morally, it is the web of life itself, with all of its complex interactions" (Behrens 2014: 66). Communities and ecosystems are therefore morally considerable, the same as an ocean or a rock would be.

Behrens (2014: 64) argues that this moral considerability extends to the intergenerational, "Just as humans recognize their own interests in perpetuating the family line, so they should recognize the interests of other species in perpetuating their own".

Behrens is not alone in this standpoint towards an African Environmental Ethics. Based within the notions of ancestorhood, African environmentalists have asserted that there is an intergenerational moral obligation based on the moral ideal of a "solidarity between past, present and future" (Murove 2004: 184). On this premise then, "The environment is an inheritance that is shared across generations, and should therefore be preserved as far as possible, and second, that we ought to honor the memory of those who left us an environment capable of preserving our lives by ensuring we do the same for our descendants" (Behrens 2014: 68). Ugwuanyi (2011) adds to the metaphysical outlook by arguing that land in African society is often seen as not having economic value but "social, metaphysical and ancestral worth", and thus allows a sustainable environmental ethic as the society is held accountable to future generations.

These concepts of the moral considerability of all living things, in the present, past and the future, is paramount to understanding how global ecosystems could be renegotiated in place. We can understand that a fisherman, a swordfish, and an organism of the DSL, are all interconnected as part of ever changing and entangled ecosystems. They are individual and part of a whole, both morally considerable as individual entities and morally intertwined. However, the swordfish does not have the same role as the organism or fisherman within an ecosystem. Environmental thinking must take into account the role of each individual in ecosystems, as well as its connections with other entities within the ecosystem. By understanding these relationships are wholly and individually relational across a multiplicity of scales, environmental discourse can renegotiate the vast expanse of the ocean space. I would like here to reemphasize Lombardi's image of the wave 'in contact with all points at once' to argue for an organic interconnectedness of worldwide ecological systems through a post-local lens, as way for envisaging African Ethics to move beyond its current liminal spaces.

If we refer back to Janz (2009) and his premise that, "It is the construction of places and the uncovering of ethos that gives us successive models for living as place matters" (184), we can see that by constructing a placeful ocean, in terms of navigating away from the ocean as vast and empty, and towards a Relational Environmentalism, inspired by African Environmental Ethics, we can then draw from this African experience of place and sail forward into new ways of envisaging global ocean ecosystems. No longer is the scale overwhelming, but an awareness of global and local interrelations existing across a multiplicity of scales, new concepts, inspiring a 'traveling ethics', one which spans boundaries and yet is fully aware of its origins and how it should be applied to maritime places.

11.6   Deconstructing Boundaries: Hydro-Colonialism and Resistance

Thirty-eight of Africa's fifty-four countries are coastal. Mauritius has territorial waters the size of South Africa. Yet, even within environmental scholarship that focuses on African Ethics there is still a 'green' focus, with little attention paid to its coastlines. Sub-Saharan Africa has rich marine ecosystems, coral reefs, mangroves, estuaries, wetlands, and coastal forests and dunes which provide for local communities and national economies. This makes these regions especially vulnerable to climate change, severe weather and sea level rise. For example, Senegal's fisheries sector provides employment for 17% of the countries population and across Sub-Saharan Africa the fisheries sector provides an estimated 10 million people with work (World Bank Group 2008).

The further trouble with ignoring or omitting African oceans and coastlines from conversations, is that it only adds to the trope of the continent being in a 'vacuum'—not connected or relevant to the rest of the world. This then, ignores Africa's location in the world ecology, which has actually been positioned by its access through the oceans surrounding it. What makes the continent today is the historicity of its oceans, not just in terms of both terrestrial and hydro-colonization, but also through its pre-colonial empires built on trade routes from the Swahili coast to the West African kingdoms. To ensure a 'placeful' ethics of our oceans, tracing saltwater connections and imperial legacies of maritime trade, and hence understanding current ecological catastrophes faced in present day as directly caused by such events is of paramount importance when attempting to deconstruct how to face environmental challenges and changes.

With The African Union's Agenda 2063 declaring the Blue Economy to be "Africa's Future," that is everything from fisheries to deep sea mining, aquaculture, desalination, tourism, marine biotechnology and bioprospecting, it is clear that the way in which oceans are managed will directly affect the future of the continent (African Union Commission 2015). Indeed, number 15 of 63 aspirations that the Agenda 2063 states that, "A prosperous Africa based on inclusive growth and sustainable development" will develop "Africa's Blue/ocean economy, which is three times the size of its landmass, shall be a major contributor to continental transformation and growth, through knowledge on marine and aquatic biotechnology, the growth of an Africa-wide shipping industry, the development of sea, river and lake transport and fishing; and exploitation and beneficiation of deep sea mineral and other resources" (African Unions Commission 2015: 3). On one hand this is an opportunity for socioeconomic transformation, investment however questions remain regarding sustainability and ethical practices. With the depletion of onshore resources, large corporations are looking to move on elsewhere. For example, as mining sites in South Africa become ghost towns, companies have moved on to Namibia as a site of offshore deep sea mining industry, vacuuming diamonds from the ocean floor (The Washington Post 2017). These types of industries create new tensions, problems and potential for new forms of neo-colonialism as yet again capital could end up moving into cores rather than the peripheries of global economies. The scramble for Africa's oceans is here.

We are currently witnessing a new 'sea grab' or 'scramble for the oceans' as new capital frontiers are opening up (Deloughrey 2015), and this continues to raise concerns about new forms of 'hydro-colonisation'. The ocean becomes a new site for neo-colonialism, as the commodification of marine life and ocean resources could be the next 'blue revolution', similar to that of the 'green revolution' (Cram et al. 2010: 153), whereby patented agricultural seeds and the introduction of GM crops caused further inequalities in countries such as India, Mexico, Brazil, and many African states. Furthermore, indigenous peoples have also accused nations and corporations of 'biopiracy' as resources become increasingly exploited and unsuitable within marine regions (Deloughrey 2015).

Fajardo (2005) states that "Oceans and seas are important sites for differently situated people. Indigenous Peoples, fisher people, seafarers, sailors, tourists, workers and athletes. Oceans and seas are sites of inequality and exploitation—resource extraction, pollution, militarization, atomic testing and genocide. At the same time, oceans and seas are sites of beauty and pleasure—solitude, sensuality, desire and resistance. Oceanic and maritime realms are also spaces of transnational and diasporic communities, heterogeneous trajectories of globalizations and other racial, gender, class and sexual formations." Amongst the ocean currents, connections and routes are subtle formations of power, and as I have hoped to demonstrate in this article, resistance. One way in which African Environmental Ethics can turn towards including a blue ethics of the ocean is to use the lens of 'hydro-colonialism' (Bystrom and Hofmeyr 2017). Bystrom and Hofmeyr (2017: 3) outline the definitions as: "(1) colonization by means of water (various forms of maritime imperialism); (2) colonization of water (occupation of land with water resources, the declaration of territorial waters, the militarization and geopoliticization of oceans); and (3) a colony on water (the ship as a miniature colony or a penal island)". This definition would also include, "hydro-imperialism,", whereby oceans are akin to maritime empires. By understanding oceans through this lens, we can renegotiate, reimagine or resist a narrative of the ocean which has the tendency to align our understanding of the ocean as passive space to be exploited. We then not only pay attention to 'entrenched colonial mapping' of oceans, but new forms of 'Wet Globalisation' (Mentz 2015). Envisaging the sea, not an empty space for free movement, but through a postcolonial lens which understands the ocean as subject to imperial legacies or maritime exploration. To challenge these geographical hierarchies of empires, old and new, allows for marine environments to become sites of resistance for new engagements and entanglements with our oceans, to allow for more sustainable ecological futures.

This is a critical time to be discussing ethics through a blue lens, as new outlooks and imaginings are essential to moving away from current frontier narratives of marine spaces. It is evident that the current mythologies of an abundant ocean space for exploration and trade is no longer viable, even for those who wish to envisage the ocean through a purely economic and political standpoint, as current crises in the Anthropocene demonstrate the finitude of the oceans resources and the need to reengage with how we interact with nature. A blue turn not only readdresses this but also contributes to destabilizing entrenched ways of thinking. Haraway (2016) is particularly pertinent here, as she argues, "it matters to destabilize worlds of thinking with other worlds of thinking, it matters to be less parochial. If ever there was a time to need to be worldly, it is surely now". Surely, then it is the worlds we cannot see, in the submarine regions beneath are waves that are best placed to approach, deconstruct and resist our terrestrial ontologies. The ocean is a unique space therefore for discussing new ways for the field of African Environmental Ethics can contribute to not only marine ethics, but also 'decolonization' projects of knowledge in general. In turn, African Environmental Ethics can create new and radical waves and be used site of resistance to new forms of neo-colonialism.

11.7   Conclusion: The Moral Considerability of a Swordfish

The 'ocean commons' is a space beyond geographical boundaries. Local versus global dichotomies sustain its empty expanse, ignoring dynamics of intertwined connections, histories and ecologies. Throughout this chapter I have argued that both the liminal spaces of the deep ocean realms, and the peripheral knowledge's of African concepts have exciting new potential for environmental theory. It has been noted that, "the scale, lack of boundary definition, connectivity and alien nature of the marine environment make its management complex" (Mackelworth 2016: 7). However, by renegotiating the alien space of the ocean by a placeful ethics, there can be the creation of dialogue over regimes of knowledge. These 'emplaced' knowledges offer new insights into maritime conservation as new understandings of interconnected ecosystems emerge, allowing the alien to become the familiar, and the vast to become part of postlocal.

The chapter has made us aware that in lacking deconstruction, knowledge patterns will uphold power structures, preserving Africa's place on the periphery of the world ecology. In terms of maritime policy, a need to move away from western-centric informed approached and strategies of conservation will be beneficial to managing ecosystems. In this way, both communities and seascapes will become sustainable through their shared knowledges of their environments. As Janz (2009) argues, we must examine our knowledge by 'knowledge of the place'. African Environmental Ethics may take inspiration from tradition but also renegotiate possible environmental futures and perceptions of nature, moving beyond just a pure critical tool answering back to western environmentalism. African Philosophy and Ethics can allow for a unique insight into how place and the historicity of ocean space interrelates with ecology. Further an African Environmental Ethics is very much aware of the interrelatedness of ethos and human to non-human relations.

I would like to end with a quote from Janz (2009: 194) which has very much informed this chapter as a whole,

> As we come to see that our moral universe is made richer when we interrogate, and are interrogated by, place-knowledge, we will also be able to create new concepts, new forms and ways of life. Our concepts will travel between forms of knowledge, and become newly integrated, enabling a richer vocabulary of both place and ethics, a new appreciation of ethos and peripherality, and a richer life. We will, in short, develop an ethics of place.

This in sum, and by envisaging an African Environmental Ethics 'in place' will allow us start to tackle issues of pollution, overfishing and the degradation of biodiversity in marine habitats, that often seem so vast and beyond our capabilities as communities. Instead the individual, and the community, can understand their moral considerability, even in relation to, let us say, a swordfish.

Acknowledgements   I would like to thank the editor Munamato Chemhuru and all the contributors and attendees of the 'African Environmental Ethics' conference at Johannesburg University in September 2017 for their wonderful feedback and discussions throughout. I would also like to express much gratitude to Alena Rettová for her support and advice in regards to this publication and throughout my Ph.D. I dedicate this chapter in loving memory of Peter Clarke.

References

African Union Commission. 2015. *Agenda 2063*. Available at: www.un.org/en/africa/osaa/pdf/au/agenda2063.pdf.

Agardy, T. 2005. Global Marine Conservation Policy Versus Site-Level Implementation: The Mismatch of Scale and Its Implications. *Marine Ecology Progress Series* (300): 242–248.

Agardy, T., G.N. di Sciara, and P. Christie. 2011. Mind the Gap: Addressing the Shortcomings of Marine Protected Areas Through Large Scale Marine Spatial Planning. *Marine Policy* 35: 226–232.

Alaimo, S. 2012a. Dispersing Disaster: The Deepwater Horizon, Ocean Conservation, and the Immateriality of Aliens. In *American Environments: Climate—Cultures—Catastrophe,* ed. C. Mauch and S. Mayer. Heidelberg: Universitätsverlag Winter.

Alaimo, S. 2012b. States of Suspension: Trans-corporeality at Sea. *ISLE* 19 (3): 476–493.

Alaimo, S. 2016. *Exposed: Environmental Politics and Pleasures in Posthuman Times*. Minneapolis: University of Minnesota Press.

Banavar, J.R., and A. Amos Maritan. 2009. Towards a Theory of Biodiversity. *Nature* 460: 334–335.

Behrens, K. 2014. Toward an African Relational Environmentalism. In *Ontologized Ethics: New Essays in African Meta-Ethics*, ed. E. Imafidon and J. Bewaji, 55–72. Lanham: Lexington Books p.

Buck, S.J. 1998. *The Global Commons: An Introduction*. Washington D.C.: Island Press.

Bystrom, K., and I. Hofmeyr. 2017. Oceanic Routes: (Post-It) Notes on Hydro-Colonialism. *Comparative Literature* 69 (1): 1–6.

Caminero-Santangelo, B., and G. Myers (eds.). 2011. *Environment at the Margins: Literary and Environmental Studies in Africa Athens*. Ohio: Ohio University Press.

Cram, F., T.A. Prendergast, K. Taupo, H. Phillips, and M. Parsons. 2010. Traditional Knowledge and Decision-Making: Maori Involvement in Aquaculture and Biotechnology. In *Proceedings of the Traditional Knowledge Conference (2008) Te Tatau Pounamu: The Greenstone Door Auckland: Te Pae o te Maramatanga*, ed. J.S. Te Rito, and S.M. Healy, 147–157.

Crowley, D. 2015. *Africa's Narrative Geographies: Charting the Intersections of Geocriticism and Postcolonial Studies*. London: Palgrave Macmillan.

Cruikshank, J. 2005. *Do Glaciers Listen?: Local Knowledge, Colonial Encounters, And Social Imagination*. Vancouver: UBC Press.

de Vivero, J.L.S. 2007. The European Vision for Oceans and Seas—Social and Political Dimensions of the Green Paper on Maritime Policy for the EU. *Marine Policy* 31 (4): 409–414.

Deleuze, G., and F. Guattari. 1987. *A Thousand Plateaus: Capitalism and Schizophrenia*. Minneapolis: University of Minnesota Press.

DeLoughrey, E. 2015. Ordinary Futures: Interspecies Worldings in the Anthropocene. In *Global Ecologies and the Environmental Humanities Postcolonial Approaches*, ed. E. DeLoughrey, J. Didur, and A. Carrigan, 352–372. New York: Routledge.

Dumont, H., and J. Purcell. 2001. Jellyfish Blooms: Ecological and Societal Importance. In *Proceedings of the International Conference on Jellyfish Blooms, Held in Gulf Shores, Alabama*, 12–14 January 2000. Netherlands: Springer.

Duval-Diop, D. 2016. The West African Regional Network of Marine Protected Areas. In *Marine Transboundary Conservation and Protected Areas*, ed. P. Mackelworth, 180–194. Routledge: Oxfordshire.

Earle, S. 1995. *Sea Change: A Message of the Oceans*. New York: Fawcett Columbine.

Fajardo, K. 2005. *Filipino Cross Currents: Histories of Filipino Seafaring-Asia and The Americas*. Presentation.

Geier, T. 2016. Noncommittal Commitment: Alien Spaces of Ecocosmopolitics in Recent World Literature. In *Ecocriticism and Geocriticism: Overlapping Territories in Environmental and Spatial Literary Studies*, ed. R.T. Tally Jr. and C.M. Battista, 55–73. London: Palgrave Macmillan p.

Germond, B., and C. Germond-Duret. 2016. Ocean Governance and Maritime Security in a Placeful Environment: The case of the European Union. *Marine Policy* (66): 124–131.

Gilroy, P. 1993. *The Black Atlantic: Modernity and Double Consciousness*. London: Verso.

Haraway, D. 2016. Anthropocene, Capitalocene, Chthulucene: Staying with the Trouble. In *Anthropocene Conference, University of California, Santa Cruz*, 9 April 2016. https://vimeo.com/97663518.

Hardin, G. 1968. The Tragedy of The Commons. *Science* (162): 1243–8.

Horsthemke, K. 2015. *Animal and African Ethic Basingstoke*. UK: Palgrave Macmillan.

Ingold, T. 2000. *The Perception of the Environment*. London: Routledge.

Janz, B. 2001. The Territory Is Not the Map: Deleuze and Guattari's Relevance to the Concept of Place in African Philosophy. *Philosophy Today* 45 (4): 388–400.

Janz, B. 2009. Thinking Like a Mountain: Ethics and Place as Travelling Concepts. In *New Visions of Nature*, ed. M. Drenthen, F. Keulartz, and J. Proctor, 181–195. Dordrecht: Springer.

Janz, B. 2014a. The Location(s) of Philosophy: Generating and Questioning New Concepts in African Philosophy. *Philosophia Africana* 16 (1): 11–24.

Janz, B. 2014b. Place, Philosophy, and Non-Philosophy. *Environmental and Architectural Phenomenology* 25 (3): 20–22.

Kelleher, G., and R. Kenchington. 1992. *Guidelines for Establishing Marine Protected Areas*. A Marine Conservation and Development Report IUCN: Gland, Switzerland.

Leenhardt, P., B. Cazalet, B. Salvat, J. Claudet, and F. Feral. 2013. The Rise of Large-Scale Marine Protected Areas: Conservation or Geopolitics? *Ocean & Coastal Management* 1–7.

Lombardi, W.V. 2015. Global Subcultural Bohemianism: The Prospect of Postlocal Ecocriticism in Tim Winton's Breath. In: *New International Voices in Ecocriticism*, ed. S. Oppermann, 41–54. London: Lexington Books.

Mackelworth, P. 2016. Introduction. In *Marine Transboundary Conservation and Protected Areas*, ed. P. Mackelworth, *1–11*. Routledge: Oxfordshire.

Makang, J.M. 1997. *Of the Good use of Tradition: Keeping the Critical Perspective in African Philosophy*. In *Postcolonial African Philosophy*, ed. E.C. Eze. London: Wiley.

Mangena, F. 2013. Discerning Moral Status in the African Environment. *Phronimon* 14 (2): 25–44.

Mentz, S. 2015. *Shipwreck Modernity: Ecologies of Globalisation 1550–1719 Minneapolis*. Minnesota: University of Minnesota Press.

Merrie, A. 2016. Global Ocean Futures: Governance of Marine Fisheries in the Anthropocene, Ph.D. diss. Stockholm. Available at: http://urn.kb.se/resolve?urn=urn:nbn:se:su:diva-127618.

Mosima, P.M. 2016. *Philosophic Sagacity and Intercultural Philosophy: Beyond Henry OderaOruka*. Tilburg: Tilburg University.

Murove, M.F. 2004. An African Commitment to Ecological Conservation: The Shona Concepts of Ukama and Ubuntu. *Mankind Quarterly* 45 (2): 195–196.

Ojomo, P.A. 2011. Environmental Ethics: An African Understanding. *The Journal of Pan African Studies* 4 (3): 101–113.

Okorafor, N. 2014. *Lagoon*. Hodder & Stoughton Ltd.

Rampao.org. 2017. Réseau Régionald Aires Marines Protégées en Afrique de l'Ouest. Available at: http://www.rampao.org/. Accessed 10 August 2017.

Rettová, Alena. 2007. *Afrophone Philosophies: Reality and Challenge*. Středokluky: Zdenek sSusa.

Rettová, A. 2016. African Philosophy as a Radical Critique. *Journal of African Cultural Studies* (28): 127–131.

Reuters. 2010. Swordfish Attack Angolan Oil Pipeline. Available at: https://af.reuters.com/article/oddlyEnoughNews/idAFTRE6113BU20100202. Accessed 1 June 2017.

Rogerson, J.M.J. 2015. Being Heard: Thinking Through Different Versions of Rationality, Epistemological Policing and Dissonances in Marine Conservation. *Marine Policy* 60: 325–330.

Scovazzi, T., and I. Tani. 2016. Problems Posed by Marine Protected Areas Having a Transboundary Character. In *Marine Transboundary Conservation and Protected Areas*, P. Mackelworth, 15–32. Routledge: Oxfordshire.

Smythe, K. 2015. *Africa's Past, Our Future*. Bloomington, Indiana: Indiana University Press.

Tangwa, G. 2004. Some African Reflections on Biomedical and Environmental Ethics. In *A Companion to African philosophy*, ed. KwasiWiredu, 387–395. Oxford: Blackwell publishers.

Trexler, A. 2015. *Anthropocene Fictions: The Novel in a Time of Climate Change Virginia*. U.S: University of Virginia Press.

The Guardian. 2017. BP Boss Admits Job on the Line Over Gulf Oil Spill. Available at: https://www.theguardian.com/business/2010/may/13/bp-boss-admits-mistakes-gulf-oil-spill. Accessed 1 June 2017.

The Washington Post. 2017. A New Frontier for Diamond Mining: The Ocean. Available at: https://www.washingtonpost.com/world/africa/a-new-frontier-for-diamond-mining-the-ocean/2017/07/01/a04d5fbe-0e40–4508-894d-b3456a28f24c_story.html?noredirect=on&utm_term=.34aa26847de0.

Ugwuanyi, L.O. 2011. Advancing an Environmental Ethics Through the African World-View. In *1st International Technology, Education and Environment Conference* Omoku, Nigeria Human Resource Management Academic Research Society (HRMARS) and African Society for Scientific Research (ASSR), 1–10. http://hrmars.com/index.php/pages/detail/Proceeding2.

UNEP. 2017. *The Global Commons*. Available at: http://staging.unep.org/delc/GlobalCommons/tabid/54404/Default.aspx Accessed 29.11.17.

Wardi, J.A. 2011. *Water and African American Memory: An Ecocritical Perspective*. Florida: University Press of Florida.

Westwood, J., B. Parsons, and W. Rowley (2002) *Global Ocean Markets*. Canterbury, UK: Douglas-Westwood Associates. Available at: www.dw-1.com.

Whitty, J. 2010. *The BP Cover Up. Mother Jones*, [online] (SEPTEMBER/OCTOBER 2010 ISSUE). Available at: http://www.motherjones.com/environment/2010/08/bp-ocean-cover-up/. Accessed 3 June 2017.

World Bank Group. 2007–8. The Importance of Africa's Coastal and Marine Ecosystems. *Environment Matters Annual Review*, July 2007–June 2008. Available at: http://siteresources.worldbank.org/INTENVMAT/Resources/3011340-1238620444756/5980735-1238620476358/11AFR.pdf.

Part IV
Environmental Justice in African Philosophy

Chapter 12
Environmental Justice: Towards an African Perspective

Margaret Ssebunya, Stephen Nkansah Morgan and Beatrice D. Okyere-Manu

Abstract The main argument of this paper is that current debates and discussions on environmental justice seem to focus more on the West. In a typical African communitarian society, the idea of environmental justice has not been adequately conceptualised. Key scholars in African environmental ethics such as Godfrey Tangwa, Segun Ogungbemi and Murove Munyaradzi have mainly focused their attention on the preservation of nature for both current and future generations, thereby giving less attention to the equitable distribution of environmental resources and environmental burdens in Africa. As such, issues of environmental justice seem to be conspicuously absent from African environmental ethics discourse. The contribution of this chapter is to explore an African understanding of environmental justice by showing the major characteristics of how an African environmental justice ought to look like. The study proposes *the eco-collective responsibility theory*—an environmental justice model that is specific to the African communitarian society characterised by mutual dependence, cooperation, harmony, relationality and communion in order to promote the common good of the people as well as the good of the environment for both current and future generations.

12.1 Introduction

The concept of environmental justice is one of the key issues in environmental debates that has gained recognition among environmentalists in recent times, especially in such a time of climate change, global warming and severe environmental degradation. It majorly centres on the "disproportionate sharing of environmental benefits and

M. Ssebunya (✉) · S. N. Morgan · B. D. Okyere-Manu
University of KwaZulu Natal, Pietermaritzburg, South Africa
e-mail: smaggie2012@gmail.com

S. N. Morgan
e-mail: greatmorgan2003@gmail.com

B. D. Okyere-Manu
e-mail: okyere-manv@ukzn.ac.za

© Springer Nature Switzerland AG 2019
M. Chemhuru (ed.), *African Environmental Ethics*, The International
Library of Environmental, Agricultural and Food Ethics 29,
https://doi.org/10.1007/978-3-030-18807-8_12

burdens between different categories of persons" (Kameri-Mbote and Cullet 1996:
1). The Environmental Protection Agency (EPA) of the United States of America
defines environmental justice as "the fair treatment[1] and meaningful involvement[2]
of all people regardless of race, colour, national origin, or income, with respect to the
development, implementation, and enforcement of environmental laws, regulations,
and policies". The EPA definition illustrates that environmental justice is demarcated
by fairness in the environmental decision-making processes. Describing the concept
further, the South African Environmental Justice Networking Forum (EJNF) argues
that:

> Environmental justice is about social transformation directed towards meeting basic human
> needs and enhancing our quality of life—economic quality, health care, housing, human
> rights, environmental protection, and democracy. In linking environmental and social justice
> issues, the environmental justice approach seeks to challenge the abuse of power, which
> results in poor people having to suffer the effects of environmental damage caused by the
> greed of others. This includes workers and communities exposed to dangerous chemical
> pollution, and rural communities without firewood, grazing and water (EJNF 1997).

This description of environmental justice does not only aim at encouraging fair
distribution of environmental resources and burdens but also interrogates social issues
to do with the abuse of power which renders the vulnerable to environmental destruction. It challenges the social, political and economic inequalities that make people
of a particular class (usually the lower class) suffer the negative impacts of environmental degradation caused by the avaricious-driven behaviours and attitudes of
others (usually the wealthy). With this in mind, environmental justice places a moral
responsibility for the wellbeing of all people.

While the concept of environmental justice came under the spotlight in the West
around the mid-20th Century (Bullard 1999), it has not been clearly theorized in a
typical African communitarian society. The works of key scholars in African environmental ethics such as Godfrey Tangwa, Segun Ogungbemi and Murove Munyaradzi
have focused on the preservation of nature for both current and future generations,
thereby giving less attention to the equitable distribution of environmental resources
and environmental burdens in Africa. Equally, the misuse of power that makes the
poor susceptible to environmental damages has not been hypothesized. As a result,
major issues of environmental justice such as harmful practices to the environment,
atmospheric and water pollution, deforestation, overgrazing, health care, and sanitation seems to be conspicuously absent from the African environmental ethics
discourse. It is against this background that the chapter asks: Is there such a thing
as environmental justice in the African narrative and if so, how does it look like?

---

[1]Fair treatment means that no group of people should bear a disproportionate share of the negative
environmental consequences resulting from industrial, governmental and commercial operations or
policies.

[2]Meaningful involvement means that: (1) people have an opportunity to participate in decisions
about activities that may affect their environment and/or health; (2) the public can contribute to
regulatory agency's decision-making; (3) their concerns will be considered in the decision-making
process; and (4) the decision makers seek out and facilitate the involvement of those potentially
affected.

Through the exposition of the works of the African environmentalists mentioned above, the study answers this question by proposing an environmental justice model that is specific to the African communitarian societies. In particular, it calls for a model characterized by mutual dependence, cooperation, harmony, relationality and communion in order to promote the common good of the people in addition to the good of the environment for both current and future generations.

The chapter is divided into five sections: first, it explores the background of environmental justice, emphasizing on the need that necessitated the environmental justice movement. Second, it examines the notion of environmental justice from the Western perspective, arguing that the concept originated from the West with much of its theories born out of Western thoughts and experiences. Third, it explores the works of key African environmental ethicists with the aim of extending their viewpoints on African environmental ethics towards the creating of an African environmental justice theory. Fourth, it proposes the *eco-collective responsibility theory* as an example of how an environmental justice theory that is specific to the African experience should look like. This is followed by a conclusion.

12.2 Origin and History of Environmental Justice

Bullard (1999) notes that the concept of environmental justice traces its origin to the Environmental Justice Movements (EJM) and their intricate links with the Civil Rights Movements of the 1950s and 1960s in the United States. The environmental justice movements developed from local struggles against environmental discrimination and environmental racism. Environmental justice was initially known as environmental racism due to the fact that the race factor was crucial and important (Pojman and Pojman 2012). Poor and non-white people especially African Americans not only had the least access to environmental resources but they also suffered most from environmental pollution. This led to public demonstrations against such injustices in different parts of the United States. For instance, in 1982 in Warren County, North Carolina, a polychlorinated biphenyl (PCB) landfill ignited protests and over 500 arrests (Bullard 2001: 5).

Following the protest, the United States General Accounting Office on four hazardous landfills in three South-eastern States conducted a study on "Siting of Hazardous Waste Landfills and Their Correlation with Racial and Economic Status of Surrounding Communities" in 1983. The study showed that three out of four commercial hazardous waste landfills were situated in primarily African-American communities. The report further revealed that 26% of the population in all the four communities had income below the poverty level and most of the population was black (1983: 1). The protests also led to the United Church of Christ Commission for Racial Justice to publish a study in 1987 observing the pattern of distribution of waste sites in the United States. The Commission published their findings in what was to become a classic article titled "Toxic Waste and Race in the United States." In this article, the Commission reported, among others, that three out of every five African-Americans and

Hispanic-Americans, and over half of all Asian Pacific islanders and American Indians live in communities with one or more uncontrolled toxic waste sites (UCC 1987; Warren 1999: 152). In effect, the conclusion of the Commission was that race was in no doubt a major factor in the location of hazardous waste sites in the United States.

Although environmental justice originated from the United States as people of colour struggled against and reacted to the disproportionate and racially prejudiced disparities and inequalities involving dumping of toxic waste, the term has since advanced beyond these historical, conceptual and physical boundaries to other regions around the globe. Environmental justice has over time extended to Latin America, Asia and Africa. Symbolic examples include the mobilization in Istanbul in defense of Gezi park, the toppling of the government in Madagascar over land-grabbing, and the aboriginal 'Idle No More' movement in Canada, where indigenous opposition to fracking led to a violent stand-off between the Royal Canadian Mounted Police and Native communities in New Brunswick (Temper et al. 2015: 256).

In Nigeria, environmental justice came to the fore when the Movement for the Survival of the Ogoni People (MOSO) issued the "Ogoni Bill of Right" to the Federal Government of Nigeria in 1990 following disputes between the Ogoni people, Shell and the Nigerian government. The people demanded local autonomy of the resources entrenched in Ogoni land (Saro-wiwa 1990). In South Africa, race was more socially and politically important in environmental justice discussions than it was in the United States. Elaborating on the concept of environmental justice in South Africa, Martinez-Alier notes that environmental justice in South Africa has been a movement in defense of majority population rather than a defense of a minority population as it rather pertains in the United States. He further asserts that there have been some attempts made in South Africa to do away with the old ways of preserving nature where indigenous people were removed from their lands to involving the local people in managing nature reserves (2009: 252).

Altogether, the environmental justice movements across the globe have advanced environmental wellbeing and sustainability through public participation in the environmental decision-making processes. Such public participation does not only ensure a sense of communal belonging but it is also fundamental in the realization of justice for all. As Amartya Sen observes in *The Idea of Justice*, "Open-minded engagement in public reasoning is quite central to the pursuit of justice" (2009: 390).

12.3 Environmental Justice from the Western Perspective

Much of the Western literature on environmental justice places emphasis on finding the best social and distributive model that will ensure equity and fair redistribution of environmental burdens and resources across generations. Peter S. Wenz suggests one of such model. In a bid to solve the inequalities in the distribution of environmental burdens, Wenz proposes what he thinks to be the basic principle governing distributive justice. He calls it 'the principle of commensurate burdens and benefits'. This principle assumes that, "other things being equal, those who derive benefits should sustain commensurate burdens." Explicitly, individuals and corporates who are benefiting or stand to benefit from the use of any of the environmental resources should be held liable for the burdens they produce. In applying this principle to the issue of environmental justice, Wenz argues that "in the absence of countervailing considerations, the burdens of ill health associated with toxic hazards should be related to benefits derived from processes and products that create these hazards" (Wenz 2012: 531–532). Wenz later applies this principle to what he calls the allocation of LULU (Locally Undesirable Land Uses) points to all communities, a tactic he believes will help reduce environmental injustices and make wealthy communities more responsible towards the environment.

Others have resorted to the use of John Rawls' model of distributive justice in their proposal of an environmental justice theory. Derek Bell, for example, is of the view that going by a Rawlsian approach to environmental justice would firmly locate environmental issues within a broader theory of social justice. This he thinks, will provide a clear rationale for environmental justice and a framework for assessing the relative importance of particular environmental issues in the context of competition for public spending (2004: 287). Rawls, coming from a deontology moral tradition, interprets justice as fairness. According to him, a just society is one in which everyone receives a fair share of the available benefits and resources. In his *Theories of Justice* (1999), Rawls develops two principles of justice that he believes should be chosen by self-interested rational beings behind a veil of ignorance. The veil of ignorance is supposed to be an imaginary prehistoric place (original position) where individuals who are going to form society know nothing of their position in the society to be created: they know nothing of their sex, race, nationality, individual tastes or the social status they would occupy.

Rawls holds that these individuals under the veil of ignorance would eventually come up with principles of justice that are fair and beneficial to all. These individuals, according to Rawls, will ultimately come up with two principles of justice, namely the principle of equal liberty and the difference principle. The principle of equal liberty states that each person has an equal right to the most extensive liberties compatible with similar liberties for all. The difference principle however demands that social and economic inequalities should be arranged such that they are both to the greatest benefit of the least advantaged persons, and attached to offices and positions open to all under conditions of equality of opportunity (Rawls 2001: 122–24). Putting the two principles together, gives the sense that Rawls advocates for basic equality of liberty or resources and permits inequality only when it serves to benefit those who may not have similar access. This implies that the basic structure of any society ought to be arranged in such a way that no social group advances at the cost of another. From this position, Keller believes that a Rawlsian model of environmental justice will be one where "a social group bears a disproportionate burden of the costs on industrialization in comparison to a wider population, and that group would be better off without industrialization" (2011: 302). Bell, on his part, asserts that a Rawlsian environmental justice "is committed to the idea of guaranteed minimum environmental standards as part of the social minimum for the least advantaged group" (2004: 303).

12.4 Charting an African Perspective of Environmental Justice

It is evident that discussions on environmental justice in the West have mainly concentrated on cases that are unique to their experiences and contexts. Attempts at theorizing solutions to environmental injustices have also relied mostly on the use of Western theories of social and distributive justice based on principles of libertarianism, utilitarianism, free-market approach and right-based approach. Even though the principles underpinning environmental justice may be universal, they cannot be discussed without taking into consideration the unique cases of the people involved. When dealing with environmental injustice on the African continent there is a need to factor the drivers behind the various instances of environmental injustice in Africa and propose tailor-made solutions to them, solutions embedded in our Africanness.

Ecofeminist, Warren (1999), rightly acknowledges that the framing of issues of environmental justice entirely or primarily in terms of distribution is seriously problematic. As a result, she relies on both ecofeminist understandings concerning what she termed as the inextricable interconnections between institutions of human oppression and the unjustified domination of the natural environment as well as on feminist understandings concerning non-distributive justice given by Iris Young. She later proposes for a more inclusive notion of justice by arguing for an additional non-distributive model of justice which would supplement, complement, and, in some cases, pre-empt a distributive model. It is this search for non-distributive conceptions of justice that we propose a conception of environmental justice born out of the African communitarian ethics and the African conception of a good life.

As earlier indicated, some African environmental ethicists including Godfrey Tangwa, Segun Ogungbemi and Munyaradzi Murove have proposed theories of African environmental ethics focussing on the ethics of human-nature relationship. The centrality of their works essentially is to draw away from the Western approaches of environmental ethics, which in their view, were more anthropocentric in nature and reflected the Western ideal of individualism.

Godfrey Tangwa in his eco-bio-communitarian ethic recognizes the interdependency and peaceful coexistence between humans and the natural environment—plants, animals and the earth. He argues that in a communitarian African society, people are cosmically humble, cautious in their approach to nature, reverentially respect nature and fellow human beings, and are more mindful of both animate and inanimate beings including the various invincible forces around them. From a metaphysical position, Tangwa notes that there is a minute difference between the animate and inanimate, between spirit and matter, between the individual and the communal as well as between the sacred and the profane (2004: 389). He maintains that "since a human can conceivably transform or be transformed (with or without knowledge and consent) into any of the other ontological entities, in this life or in the life after death, no human being can confidently claim to know that he/she is not the 'brother/sister' of any other things in existence" (Tangwa 2001: 170). Such traditional African worldview ensured that people do not harm the environment, for in so doing they would be harming their relatives or even themselves, he claims.

Segun Ogungbemi on his part, notes that the traditional African relationship with nature was that of not taking more than what one needed from nature. He refers to this relationship as an "ethics of care." He writes that:

> In our traditional relationship with nature, men and women recognize the importance of water, land and air management. To our traditional communities the ethics of not taking more than you need from nature is a moral code. Perhaps this explains why earth, forests, rivers, wind, and other natural objects are traditionally believed to be both natural and divine. The philosophy behind this belief may not necessarily be religious, but a natural means by which the human environment can be preserved. The ethics of care is essential to traditional understanding of environmental protection and conservation (1997: 266).

To make this ethics of care relevant or appropriate to present day African situations, Ogungbemi refines it to what he terms "ethics of nature-relatedness." To Ogungbemi, this ethics of nature-relatedness allows for humans to "co-exist peacefully with nature and treat it with some reasonable concern for its worth, survival and sustainability" (1997: 270). In similarity to Tangwa's eco-bio-communitarianism, ethics of nature-relatedness promotes an appreciation for and understanding of our interconnectedness with the natural environment.

Finally, Murove also explores the Shona (from Zimbabwe) concept of *Ukama*, and the southern African concept of *Ubuntu/Botho* to argue for an African environmental ethics of care and virtue of interrelatedness and relationality between humans and the environment.[3] According to him:

> When these two concepts [*Ukama* and *Ubuntu*] are compounded, together they provide an ethical outlook that suggests that human well-being is indispensable from our dependence on, and interdependence with, all that exists and particularly with the immediate environment on which all humanity depends (2009: 315).

Murove further explains that from *Ukama* and *Ubuntu* we understand that we exist because of others and because we are members of a community. He adds that "because of the fact that our humanness has been contributed to by the community as well as those who existed in the past, the individual's interest should be linked to the interests of others so that s/he will contribute positively to those who will exist in the future" (2005: 211).

Tangwa, Ogungbemi and Murove's works draw attention to an African centred environmental ethics, which they consider to have a non-anthropocentric feature. Their works and other works that argue along similar lines fail to extend the implications of their theories to the issue of environmental justice in Africa. However, while the above works do not necessarily argue for an African environmental justice, this paper is of the view that key insights should be drawn from them to propose how an African environmental justice ought to look. Tangwa's eco-bio-communitarianism,

---

[3]Other writers including Prozesky (2009) and Ramose (2009) also have employed similar use of either Ukama or Ubuntu or both and arrived at similar ethic of human interrelatedness with the natural environment. Likewise, Buju (2009) and Behrens (2010, 2014) did arrive at a similar conclusion that identifies human relational connection with the natural environment.

Ogungbemi's nature-relatedness and Murove's ethics of interrelatedness all point to a non-anthropocentric ethic that lays emphasis on human-nature relatedness. This, compounded with features of an African communal life that promote solidarity and mutuality between humans, can inform us on how any theory of environmental justice in Africa should look like. The paragraphs that follow look at how this feature of solidarity existed in the African communitarian setting and how this can factor in the framing of an appropriate Afrocentric environmental justice theory.

Since an individual in the African communitarian setting belonged to the community, care for others within the community was paramount. This formed the basis for the use of environmental resources such as rivers, lakes, streams, forests, grasslands and vegetation. Resultantly, individuals were mindful of deliberately polluting the environment because this would be contrary to the African communitarian society's values. Such negative actions towards the environment would show a lack of care and concern for others. The African communitarian society, as argued by Murove and others, was characterized by *Ubuntu*. The *Ubuntu* philosophy expressed in the aphorism: *UmuntuNgumuntuNgabantu*, which is translated as "a person is a person because of or through others" (Shutte 1993: 46) expresses values of compassion, reciprocity, dignity, humanity, cooperation, harmony, relationality and communion in the interests of building and maintaining communities with justice and mutual care (Khoza 1994: 6). These *Ubuntu* principles were incorporated into all aspects of life, andpoint to group solidarity, which was an important element to survival of communities in Africa. An individual did not exist in isolation but in communion with others. In view of this solidarity, all community members evenly shared resources. Resources were held in common "with everybody having the same rights to the same thing and belonged to nobody" (Bennett 2004: 374).

The community members made collective decisions with regard to the use of resources. There existed a social order where people related to each other. According to Okoth-Ogenda, this social order created reciprocal rights and obligations that bound the community together and vested power in the community members (2008: 100). It also ensured inclusiveness and imparted a duty to everyone to protect the community's resources. Even though resources were held in common, offenders were charged and fined heavily to deter others from repeating the offence.

Communalism, collectivism and working with others as a team were and continue to be essential components of the African communitarian society through which Africans ensured proper management of the environmental resources. For instance, it was every community member's responsibility to ensure that water sources, roads and other public facilities are kept clean and unpolluted. In pre-colonial Rwanda, *umuganda* was a traditional practice and cultural value of working together to solve social and economic problems for mutual benefit (Mukarubuga 2006: 7). Through the practice of *umuganda*, "every national, irrespective of race, religion or social status is supposed to participate in communal through *umuganda* the community de-silting drainages, sweeps streets and village paths, makes composts, clears bush lands and builds houses for the elderly and ultra-poor" (Luberenga 2010: 20–21).

In Buganda region of Uganda, there is a practice of *bulungibwansi* literally translated as "for the good of the country". This is a community-based initiative of collective responsibility in which all people living in a particular community come together to clean the environment including roads, water sources, farming, food harvesting and its storage, hunting down wild animals and destroying vermin that were a potential danger to both human security and food crops (Bakuluki and Mubiru 2014: 34). In the same way, Kenya has a similar practice known as *Harambee.* Harambee stands for a practice, which involves community members undertaking communal work as a contribution towards individual and communal causes. Literally translated as "pooling efforts together", it embodies ideals of cooperation, mutual assistance, joint effort, mutual social responsibility and self-reliance (Okyanda 2014: 72).

Among the Akans in Ghana, this practice of communal labour is commonly known to the people as *Omanadwuma.* According to Nick Fobih, *Omanadwuma* literally means "working in the interest of the community/nation-state." During *Oman adwuma*, members of the community come together under the leadership of the village chief, elders or anyone who volunteers to lead or organize the people for communal work (2001: 213). Thus, everyone in the community commits their time and strength to work towards protecting their community of environmental harm irrespective of who the individual is. Offenders were severely dealt with and in most cases through the payment of fines to the chiefs and the elders of the community. This corrective practice served as a deterrent to the individuals in the community. As a result, people were mindful of what they did to cause harm to the environment.

The principles underlining *Umuganda, harambee, bulungibwansi, Oman adwuma* and many other related practices within the African context were seen as a form of collective action of participation and belonging. Such collective actions were paramount in ensuring social and environmental justice. These principles stand in disparity to the widespread selfishness, capitalism, oblivious competitiveness, and the prevailing large scale private ownership of property that have greatly contributed to environmental injustices today.

Poovan, Du Toit and Engelbrecht have noted that through the practice of *Ubuntu,* "the capacity of an African culture in which individuals expressed compassion, reciprocity, dignity, humanity and mutuality in the interests of building and maintaining communities with justice and communalities was unlocked" (2006: 23–25). As such, respect for others played an important role in the African communitarian society. This respect entailed a common humanity and responsibility of individuals towards each other. One could argue that because of this respect for others, self-serving activities that led to the pollution of the environment from which others drew their livelihoods were minimal if not non-existent. In a typical communitarian society, the community interest was more important than that of the individual. Desmond Tutu notes that "Africans are social beings that are in constant communion with one another in an environment where a human being is regarded as a human being only through his or her relationships to other human beings" (Battle 1997: 39–43). This implies that the continued existence of an individual depends on the existence of others. Maintaining such communion implies looking out for other community members.

12.5   Towards an Afrocentric Environmental Justice

From the discussion of the Western perspectives on environmental justice, it is evident that environmental justice theories appear to mainly concentrate on humans (that is, attaining fair distribution of environmental burdens and resources for both the rich and the poor, majority and minority groups as well as the advantaged and the disadvantaged) with little or nothing said with regards to the wellbeing and sustainability of the natural environment. Thus, one is forced to ask: How does the environmental benefit from environmental justice if humans are the only beneficiaries? This is a genuine question that renders the usually anthropocentric Western theories of environmental justice inadequate. There has also been the absence of an environmental justice theory that takes into consideration the cultural and traditional principles of the African people.

What then should be the features of an African environmental justice theory? From what has been discussed so far about the features of African communitarian societies and about the principles underpinning the various African environmental ethics, it should be unmistakable that any African theory of environmental justice cannot be whole or complete without incorporating features of solidarity and interconnectedness of humans with one another and also with the environment. Thus, an Afrocentric environmental justice theory ought to take into account the principles which stress the importance of human interconnectedness with one another and with the natural environment. Such a theory should integrate the important principles of solidarity, shared values, and mutual responsibilities that permeate the communitarian lives of the African people. As a result, an Afrocentric environmental justice theory should not be anthropocentric in approach such that only the needs of humans for a fair distribution of the environmental resources and burdens are tabled for consideration but should also consider a more sustainable use of flora and fauna in the process. Thus, an environmental justice discussed in the context of Africa should look out for the interest of the natural environment as well as that of humans.

This suggestion is informed by the ethics of nature-relatedness by Ogungbemi, Tangwa's Eco-bio-communitarianism and Murove's ethics of interrelatedness. This Afrocentric environmental justice theory we are envisaging should also underscore the African communitarian character of shared responsibilities and the projection of the community's good above that of anyone else rather than suggesting that only individuals who are benefitting from the environmental resources should be held equally liable as argued by Peter Wenz. It is a theory that underscores the importance of the shared bond with ourselves and with the natural environment. It does call upon each one of us to join in the solving and management of environmental burdens and in the sharing of environmental benefits together as a group in such a manner that secures the sustainability of the natural environment for ourselves and for the future generation. Thus, this theory, which we are calling *eco-collective responsibility theory,* can be viewed as a theory that fulfils our intra-generational and intergenerational obligations in an environmentally friendly way. For there is no justice served for the environmental if the theory of environmental justice only goes as far as to benefit humans without considering the preservation and sustainability of the environment itself. What we are suggesting is therefore a more holistic approach to environmental justice that should expand the definition of environmental justice to include nature sustainability as well.

The eco-collective responsibility theory argues that the environment is a public good whose resources should be enjoyed by everyone in the community regardless of their gender, race, economic status or even political affiliation. However, the consumption of these environmental resources should come with a collective duty of care for these resources by everyone. All community members are required to use as well as contribute to environmental conservation efforts in order to achieve environmental justice. Collective responsibility towards the environment should be analysed from a community point of view to avoid the free rider problem where some individuals may only want to consume the environment resources than to take care of them. For Eco-collective responsibility to be realized, the community members ought to have common interests in preserving the environment. Individuals working collectively to care for the environmental resources will promote optimal interest for all. We assume a community where all people are equal and where no one has more rights than others. A community where all people receive the same utility from the use of environmental resources, a community where everybody will be better-off if everyone cooperated in caring for the environment.

In order to ensure that all people engage in collective action, there must be certain practical conditions instituted. First, there ought to be an acknowledgment by the local communities that environmental justice is fundamental for community development and that it is within their ability to address environmental injustices together as a unit. Second, willingness to cooperate by all members is also important. For, if there is lack of willingness from all members then some may only want to use the environmental resources for their selfish interests without concern for the rest of the community including the future generation and the sustainability and protection of the natural resources. If some members are of the opinion that others are taking advantage of them and exploiting nature for their own betterment, they may also abstain from taking any further collective action towards the environment and this may adversely affect the entire community. Third, there should be indigenous institutions in place that can help ensure compliance from all the community members. Indigenous methods for engaging communities in collective responsibility, as have been demonstrated, have long existed in all African communities, and these are traditional cultural institutions that people have strong attachments to. People tend to pay allegiance to indigenous institutions such as kingdoms and chiefdoms. Through their systems of rule and addressing community problems, they can be important support structures for ensuring that all members communally engage in collective action towards environmental conservation and ensure environmental justice. Since these institutions have Councils of Elders who offer advice and guidance to the Chief/King from time to time, we believe that self-centeredness from the Kings/Chiefs will be minimised as the Council of Elders deliberates in favour of the community. Such institutions should also have discipline systems in place for those members who fail in their duty of engaging in collective action of environmental conservation. Also, in order for the broader citizenry not to be mere spectators and leave decision making only in the hands of Kings/Chiefs and their Elders, they can form civil and advocacy groups that could send petitions and act as checks on the traditional council.

The indigenous institutions would serve as gatekeepers and at the same time insist on good environmental practices from industries and factories located in their communities. They should be made privy to the modus operandi of industries and factories in their communities and commit their owners to a signed bond to ensure that their operations will do no harm to the health of the community dwellers and to the environmental resources. Where there is likely to be some harm, the industries may have to stipulate clearly how they are going to engage the community to alleviate the harm or ameliorate the situation causing harm. Where the operations of the industry would involve the use of exhaustible environmental resources, there have to be in writing a clear method of sustaining these resources. In so doing the community become participators and serve as checks against wanton abuse by any selfish individuals.

The eco-collective responsibility theory provides a degree of mutual insurance against the occurrence of environmental pollution that could put pressure on the minority groups in the community and on the natural environment. It is a clarion call for communities to stand in solidarity with one another and with nature, thereby acknowledging our interconnectivity with each other and with nature. Standing in solidarity is then dependent on individual's willingness to act as they would wish others to act. It involves the community making a collective decision to conserve the environment as well as the commitment to abide by such decisions. Solidarity involves suffering environmental burdens together and sharing environmental benefits together. Solidarity then puts special obligations between members of a community to support each other and ensure the wellbeing of each other. This promotes fairness in the use and distribution of environmental resources and burdens.

The eco-collective responsibility theory has the potential to deal with environmental injustices meted to Africa by the first world countries by exposing current patterns of human activity and fostering a shift in how to relate to others and to nature. This will then bring about conscious and intentional civic behaviour motivated by a desire to create transformative environmental change. Such civic action may involve protesting and petitioning firms whose activities are endangering the environment and the masses.

12.6   Conclusion

The chapter sought to propose an environmental justice theory born out of principles embedded in African traditions, beliefs and practices. A look at the literature on environmental justice revealed the general lack of an environmental justice that is specifically drawn out of the African cultural and traditional experiences. As a result, the chapter has attempted to frame such a theory of environmental justice that may not necessarily be unique to Africans but nevertheless emerges from the beliefs, traditions and practices of the African people. The motivation behind this attempt, among other things, is the conviction that an environmental justice theory embedded in the African people's own experiences can better address the environmental injustices prevailing on the African continent due to the fact that the people can easily relate with its recommendations and dictates.

The chapter first briefly reconnoitred the history that merited the environmental justice movement beginning first in the United States of America almost thirty-five years ago. It further examined the nature of environmental justice theories in the West, arguing that not only do they depend on Western contexts and history, but they also employ the use of Western theories and principles in formulating recommendations and solutions. Thus, formulating an environmental justice theory specific to African's own experiences and traditions is important if we are to effectively tackle current occurrence of environmental injustices such as pollution, deforestation and sanitation, including the challenges posed by capitalism and free-market ideologies that have characterised our contemporary society.

The Chapter showed that because of the communal nature of African societies, issues of environmental injustice in Africa were not predominant. The community came together to address issues that served as threats to the environment. Offenders were publicly punished and this served as a deterrent to other community members. These communitarian features in addition to the principles of concatenation, human-nature relatedness and the principle of live-and-let-live, among others, underpinning the various theories of African environmental ethics proposed by Tangwa, Murove and Ogungbemi, informed the study to propose an environmental justice theory of eco-collective responsibility as an appropriate theory to respond to issues of environmental injustice on the African society. The principal features of our proposed theory are firstly, the inclusion of the sustainability and preservation of the natural environment in the bid to seek fair and just distribution of environmental burdens and benefits and secondly, the call to seek both intra-generational and intergenerational justice. Finally the chapter concludes with the suggestion of some practical ways to make the attainment of this eco-collective responsibility theory a reality.

References

Bakuluki, P., and J.B. Mubiru. 2014. *The Status of Social Security Systems in Uganda: Challenges and Opportunities*. Kampala: Konrad-Adenauer-Stiftung.

Battle, M. 1997. *Reconciliation: The Ubuntu Theology of Desmond Tutu*. New York: Pilgrim Press.

Behrens, K.G. 2010. Exploring African Holist with Respect to the Environment. *Environmental Ethics* 19(4): 464–484.

Behrens, K.G. 2014. African Relational Environmentalism and Moral Considerability. *Environmental Ethics* 36(1): 63–82

Bell, D. 2004. Environmental Justice and Rawls' Difference Principle. *Environmental Ethics* 6 (3): 287–306.

Bennett, T.W. 2004. *Customary Law in South Africa*. Durban: Juta Publishers.

Buju, B. 2009. Ecological and Ethical Responsibility from an African Perspective. In *African Ethics: An Anthology of Comparative and Applied Ethics*, ed. F.M. Murove, 281–297. Pietermaritzburg: University of KwaZulu-Natal Press.

Bullard, R. 1999. Dismantling Environmental Justice in the USA. *Local Environment* 4 (1): 5–20.

Bullard, R. 2001. *Confronting Environmental Racism in the 21st Century*. Paper prepared for the United Nations Research Institute for Social Development (UNRISD) Conference on Racism and Public Policy, September 2001, Durban, South Africa.

EJNF (Environmental Justice Networking Forum). 1997. *Environmental Justice Networker*, Autumn.

Fobih, N. 2001. In Search of an Alternative Model of Development in Africa: The Role of the State, Donor Agencies, International Non-Governmental Organizations and Community-Based Organizations in Ghana's Development. Master of Arts Thesis, St. Mary's University, Canada.

Kameri-Mbote, P. and Cullet, P. 1996. *Environmental Justice and Sustainable Development: Integrating Local Communities in Environmental Management*. International Environmental Law Research Centre (IELRC) Working Paper 1996—1.

Keller, D. 2011. Environmental Justice. In *Encyclopedia of Global Justice*, ed. D. Chatterjee, 298–302. Berlin Heidelberg: Springer-Verlag.

Khoza, R.J. 1994. *Managing the Ubuntu way*. Enterprise Magazine, October 4–9.

Luberenga, P.M. 2010. *Traditional African Collective Actions for Community Development: A search into the Internal and External Factors that Arouse Collective Synergies for Sustainable Grassroots Development in Kalungu District*. Uganda Martyrs University Nkozi.

Martinez-Alier, J. 2009. Environmental Justice in the United States and South Africa. In *The Environmental Responsibility Reader*, ed. M. Reynolds, C. Blackmore, and M.J. Smith, 247–255. London: Zed Books.

Mukarubuga, C. 2006. *The Experience of Social Forums Against Poverty: The Case of Rwanda*, 1–36. Agency for Co-operation and Research in Development (AC0RD).

Murove, F.M. 2005. The Theory of Self-Interest in Modern Economic Discourse: A Critical Study in the Light of African Humanism and Process Philosophical Anthropology. Ph.D. diss., University of South Africa.

Murove, M.F. 2009. An African Environmental Ethic Based on the Concepts of *Ukama* and *Ubuntu*. In *African Ethics: An Anthology of Comparative and Applied Ethics*, ed. F.M. Murove, 315–331. Scottsville: University of KwaZulu-Natal Press.

Ogungbemi, S. 1997. An African Perspective on the Environmental Crisis. In *Environmental Ethics: Readings in Theory and Application*, 2nd ed, ed. L. Pojman, 265–271. Belmont, CA: Wadsworth Publishing Company.

Okoth-Ogendo, H.W.O. 2008. The Nature of Land Rights Under Indigenous Land Law in Africa. In *Land, Power and Custom: Controversies generated by South African Communal Land Act*, ed. A. Claassens and B. Cousins, 95–108. Cape Town: UCT Press.

Okyanda, M.R. 2014. *The Local Development Dynamics of the Third Sector in Kenya: The Empowerment Dimension*. Italy: University of Trento.

Pojman, L.P., and P. Pojman. 2012. Race, Class, Gender: Environmental Justice, Ecofeminism and Indigenous Rights. In *Environmental Ethics: Readings in Theory and Application*, 6th ed, ed. L.P. Pojman and P. Pojman, 512–513. California: Wadsworth.

Poovan, N., M.K. Du Toit, and A.S. Engelbrecht. 2006. The Effect of the Social Value of Ubuntu on Team Effectiveness. *South African Journal of Business Management.* 37 (3): 17–27.

Prozesky, M.H. 2009. Well-fed Animals and Starving Babies: Environmental and Development Challenges from Process and African Perspectives. In *African Ethics: An Anthology of Comparative and Applied Ethics*, ed. F.M. Murove, 298–307. Scottsville: University of KwaZulu-Natal Press.

Ramose, M.B. 2009. Ecology through Ubuntu. In *African Ethics: An Anthology of Comparative and Applied Ethics*, ed. F.M. Murove, 308–314. Pietermaritzburg: University of Kwazulu Natal Press.

Rawls, J. 1999. *A Theory of Justice*. Cambridge: Harvard University Press.

Rawls, J. 2001. *Justice as Fairness: A Restatement*. Cambridge, MA: Harvard University Press.

Saro-Wiwa, K. 1990. *Ogoni Bill of Rights*. Available at http://www.mosop.org/OgoniBillofRights1990.pdf. Accessed on 15th September 2017.

Sen, A. 2009. *The Idea of Justice*. Cambridge, MA: Belknap Press.

Shutte, A. 1993. *Philosophy for Africa*. Cape Town: University of Cape Town Press.

Tangwa, B.G. 2001. The Tradition African Conception of a Family: Some Implications for Bioethics. In *Personhood and Healthcare*, ed. D.C. Thomasma, D.N. Weistubb, and C. Herve, 165–172. The Netherlands: Kluwer Academic Publishers.

Tangwa, B.G. 2004. Some African Reflections on Biomedical and Environmental Ethics. In *A Companion to African Philosophy*, ed. K. Wiredu, 387–395. Oxford: Blackwell publishers.

Temper, L., D. Del Bene, and J. Martinez-Alier. 2015. Marking Frontiers and Frontlines of Global Environmental Justice: Environmental Justice Atlas. *Journal of Political Ecology* 22: 255–278.

UCC. 1987. *Toxic Waste and Race in the United States: A National Report on the Racial and Socio-Economic Characteristics of Communities with Hazardous Waste Sites*. New York: UCC Commission for Racial Justice.

United States General Accounting Office. 1983. *Sitting of Hazardous Waste Landfills and Their Correlation with Racial and Economic Status of Surrounding Communities*. GAO/RCED-83-168 Washington, DC.

Warren, K.J. 1999. Environmental Justice: Some Ecofeminist Worries about a Distributive Model. *Environmental Ethics* 21: 151–161.

Wenz, P.S. 2012. Just Garbage: The Problem of Environmental Racism. In *Environmental Ethics: Readings in Theory and Application*, 6th ed, ed. L.P. Pojman and P. Pojman, 530–547. California: Wadsworth.

Chapter 13
The African Emphasis on Harmonious Relations: Implications for Environmental Ethics and Justice

John Mweshi

Abstract To appreciate what an African perspective can contribute to environmental ethics, we should be careful, all things considered, not to get entangled in the dualisms that have characterized the central debates in Western environmental ethics. Dualisms such as anthropocentrism versus non anthropocentrism; or individualism versus holism may have been useful in informing particular positions on certain issues, however, they have often led to seemingly irreconcilable differences. Moreover, the positions taken by choosing either side of the dualisms are individually inadequate to capture what goes on in real life given the multifaceted human interactions with the natural world. Understanding justice within the framework of the African emphasis on harmonious relationships has a lot to contribute to an African conception of environmental ethics. Furthermore, some of the fundamental concerns about justice have the potential to stand up to the tide of Western influences which may not be the case with mere nostalgic references to African beliefs and attitudes toward the natural environment.

13.1 Introduction

In dealing with an African perspective on environmental ethics, we need to appreciate the African emphasis on harmonious relations characterised by a worldview that is "accommodative, conciliatory and cooperative" (Ibanga 2016: 19). From this perspective, we should be careful, all things considered, not to get entangled in the dualisms that have characterised Western philosophy in general and environmental ethics in particular. Dualisms such as anthropocentrism versus non anthropocentrism; or individualism versus holism (not to mention biocentrism and ecocentrism), on which debates draw on for inspirational or comparative purposes, have often led to seemingly irreconcilable differences. Moreover, the positions taken by choosing

J. Mweshi (✉)
University of Zambia, Lusaka, Zambia
e-mail: j_Mweshi@yahoo.com

© Springer Nature Switzerland AG 2019
M. Chemhuru (ed.), *African Environmental Ethics*, The International
Library of Environmental, Agricultural and Food Ethics 29,
https://doi.org/10.1007/978-3-030-18807-8_13

either side of the dualisms are individually inadequate to capture what goes on in real life given the multifaceted human interactions with the natural world. Against this background, the African emphasis on harmonious relations offers a plausible way out of the theoretical quagmire that characterises Western environmental ethics. Further, understanding justice within the framework of the African view of harmonious relations allows us to broaden the concept of environmental justice and has a lot to contribute to an African perspective on environmental ethics. The fundamental concerns about justice have the potential to stand up to the tide of Western influences which may not be the case with mere nostalgic references to African beliefs and attitudes toward the natural environment. However, as Polycarp Ikuenobe notes:

> A fundamental problem with environmentalism in Africa [today] is that many Africans are beginning to understand that the underpinnings of the contemporary environmentalist views and movements represent traditional beliefs, ways of life, and moral views that have been rejected by Europeans; these are views or beliefs which Africans have been taught to accept as bad and uncivilized (Ikuenobe 2014: 20).

Be that as it may, there are also Western influences that Africans have adopted willingly or otherwise, such as the desire to accumulate wealth, or the treatment of land as mere property for instance. Taming the tide of these influences requires a stronger appeal to justice which I believe can also help a great deal in preserving the African environment and cultural heritage.

This discussion is divided into four sections. Drawing on existing literature the first section presents an overview of an African perspective on morality. This is for the purpose of contrasting such a view against Western perspectives. It is not intended to give the impression that all African views about morality are homogenous, but only to show that an emphasis on harmonious relations is one of the common features of African morality. Section two examines the dualistic thinking that has characterised Western environmental ethics in order to show that this approach is incompatible with the African emphasis on harmonious relations as a basis for an African conception of environmental ethics. In section three, I briefly explore how Western conceptions of justice fair in an African context and how the connections between ethics and justice can be utilised to reinforce an African conception of environmental ethics. The last section explains why the relationship between ethics and justice has posed some challenges for Western environmental ethics as characterised by the disagreements between deep ecology and social ecology. In concluding this discussion, I argue for a broadening of the current conception of environmental justice in order to provide a firm foundation for environmental ethics in Africa.

13.2 An African Perspective on Morality

In an African context morality is generally associated with character[1] (Gyeke 2011), and one of the fundamental measures of a person's character is the audacity to tell and defend the truth. In this case, the concept of truth is also essential to an African view of morality and is based on a person's testimony whereas in Western philosophy dealing with truth has been predominantly viewed as an epistemological question as compared to it being a moral issue. Alternatively, one can argue that Western philosophers seem to have been more concerned with the truth value of moral claims (or propositions) than with the value of truth for morality.

Another important aspect of African morality is the emphasis placed on harmonious relations. Putting emphasis on harmony as Thaddeus Metz notes, "does not mean that African values forbid individuality, creativity or nonconformity, but it does mean that some weight in moral thinking is given to whether behaviour upsets communal norms" (Metz 2007: 327). Now character and truth, as indicated above, may not guarantee harmony. Hence, justice is also seen as a fundamental link between truth and harmony. In fact, there cannot be real justice without the truth. Overall, highlighting character, truth, justice, and harmonious relations provides the context within which the actions of individuals can be judged.

For an African perspective on environmental ethics, the question then is how do we explain the African view of morality to include nonhumans and the natural environment? Again we have to look at the African view of the world and life in general. Explaining an African view of ontology in terms of cosmology Ikuenobe writes:

> Reality is seen as a composite, unity of harmony of natural forces… a holistic community of mutually reinforcing natural life forces consisting of human communities…, spirits, gods, deities, stones, sand, mountains, rivers, plants, and animals. Everything in reality has a vital force or energy such that the harmonious interactions among them strengthen reality. (Ikuenobe 2014: 2)

This stance also rests on the interconnections and mutual interdependences of all living things. "All these indicate that no specie in nature, whether human or nonhuman, no matter how developed the intellect, can survive on its own without the contribution of other species to its wellbeing and sustainability" (Ibanga 2016: 12). From this perspective, there is a strong basis to argue that the African worldview does not favour the dualistic thinking that has characterised Western philosophy where, for instance, there is clear separation between matter and spirit. In particular, the African view of reality does not seem to separate human beings from the rest of nature or to view humans as though they are independent from or above nature.

There is, of course, an awareness of how human beings differ from other creatures. However, this is not used as a basis to set humanity apart from nature. This position is based on the understanding that our humanity can only be appreciated in

---

[1]In this sense, an African view of morality is something akin to virtue ethics although it is based on different motivations and ontology as opposed to the mere questions about politics and the good life.

relation to other creatures. Our uniqueness as human beings is overlaid by the inter-connectedness and interdependencies that characterise the whole of reality. Hence there is a strong realization that in spite of our uniqueness, our fate and wellbeing is tied to the rest of nature. Against this background, the predominant Western view in environmental ethics that Africans are essentially anthropocentric can be misleading, especially if it is not understood in the larger context outlined above.

If the above is true, why would some think that "African environmental ethics" is essentially anthropocentric? (I will discuss the term anthropocentrism and other related concepts in the next section). Apart from the recognition that it is possi-ble that appreciation of interconnectedness and interdependencies can be used to serve utilitarian ends, there are some African writers who claim to have taken the anthropocentric position. However, this observation can be misleading if we do not care to distinguish between authors writing within the context of "African traditional ethics (or religion)" such as John Mbiti from those working within the framework of "African environmental ethics"[2] like Segun Ogungbemi.

Secondly, from the perspective of Western environmental ethics, Africa has no environmental ethics because of the absence of a perspective that can be seen to be explicitly non anthropocentric. Cognisant of the dominance of non anthropocentric perspectives in Western environmental ethics Amelia Peterson writes:

> Anthropocentrism is a kind of baseline against which Western environmental thinkers dis-tinguish and measure the various theories. Each environmental ethic deviates from anthro-pocentrism to varying degrees on the respective flaw it identifies... In short, societies want to be viewed as superior, having evolved beyond anthropocentrism. In the world of envi-ronmental philosophy, to be anthropocentric is equal to being primitive... (Peterson 2013: 101–102)

Consequently, the perception that African thought is essentially anthropocentric also entails an absence of an environmental ethic by Western standards.[3] In an attempt to rise to the above challenge we can understand why some African writers, such as Tangwa (2004)[4] or Ekwilo (2012) have devoted some attention to developing non anthropocentric perspectives in an African context. However, an exploration of some of the dualistic debates in Western environmental ethics will help to show how such perspectives are incompatible with the African emphasis on harmonious relations as a basis for an African conception of environmental ethics. I attend to this discussion in the next section. I will first examine the debate between anthropocentrism and non anthropocentrism and then look at the contention between individualism and holism.

---

[2]On the same basis, concepts such as Ubuntu can also be a source of confusion if not properly contextualised.

[3]It is from this perspective that Callicott would seem to claim that "…mention of African culture evokes no thoughts of indigenous environmental ethics" (Callicott 1994: 156).

[4]Tangwa, for instance, proposes what he refers to as "eco-bio-communitarianism".

13.3   An Overview of the Dualistic Debates in Western Environmental Ethics

We can consider the term 'non anthropocentric' simply as the opposite of 'anthropocentrism'. Anthropocentrism involves a claim that all value (intrinsic and instrumental) is grounded in value for humans (Holbrook 2009: 53). Something has value if and only if human beings stand to benefit from it. Anthropocentrism then confines the scope of concern, e.g., moral concern, "to human interests, and regards nothing but human wellbeing" (Attfield 2003: 188) or human consciousness (Norton 2003: 170) as being intrinsically valuable. In short, anthropocentric concerns are human-centred. In contrast, a non anthropocentric view would involve a claim that various elements are instrumentally valuable to other beings and entities in the environment apart from or in tandem with the interests of human beings. As Eugene Hargrove observes:

> In environmental matters non anthropocentric instrumental values – concerning the instrumental relationships of benefit and harm between nonhuman plants and animals – are quite common and completely uncontroversial ... One thing in nature either instrumentally benefits other things or it does not, regardless of what humans think about it and whether or not humans think about it and whether or not humans even know that these instrumental relationships exist.... (Hargrove 2003: 177)

The debate between anthropocentrism and non anthropocentrism is informed by the distinction between instrumental and intrinsic value. Often, the term 'intrinsic value' is used "to indicate merely one part of the twofold classification of values as being either intrinsic or instrumental", which means "that objects of value are, respectively, either valued for their own sake or valued for the sake of the contribution that they make to some other objective" (Beckerman and Pasek 2010: 83). In this sense, some have suggested that a more appropriate distinction would be between intrinsic value and extrinsic value (Korsgaard 1983: 170). Extrinsic value is defined as the value something has for the purpose of something else or for some entity apart from itself (Martell 2009: 28). Nonetheless, it is common in the literature to distinguish intrinsic value from instrumental value perhaps because instrumental value is understood as a typical example of extrinsic value.

In Western environmental ethics, as Hargrove observes, the distinction between anthropocentrism and non anthropocentrism is associated, or taken to be synonymous, with the distinction between instrumental and intrinsic value (Hargrove 2003: 175–177). Non anthropocentric claims are "simply assumed to be the opposite of instrumental value, making *anthropocentric* for all practical purposes a synonym for the word instrumental" (ibid. 175). However, attending to instrumental values need not necessarily entail that such considerations are restricted to 'anthropocentric' concerns, as it is commonly assumed, because certain things can be instrumentally valuable to things other than human beings. For example, we can understand why a river or an old growth forest can be said to be instrumentally valuable to entities or organisms that depend on these things for their continued existence. In fact, many conservation groups or individuals will find this to be a reasonable basis for objecting to any undue intrusions into certain areas of the environment by human beings. However, to infer that A is of instrumental value to B is one thing and to argue that B is therefore intrinsically valuable is a different matter.

From the perspective of this discussion the question may not be whether or not nonhuman beings have intrinsic value. Rather, it is more about the sense in which they can reasonably be said to have such value. There is a challenge in terms of accommodating the different senses of intrinsic value in some philosophical discussions. This is also part of the reason why this notion is a source of controversy and problems in Western environmental ethics debates. Some still think that it is important, while others argue that it is somewhat trivial or irrelevant to the most pertinent environmental concerns and challenges despite being one of the most important concepts in Western moral philosophy.

Intrinsic value is often defined as value that something has "in itself", or "for its own sake" (Zimmerman 2010: 1). These two senses of intrinsic value are much more basic, notwithstanding the fact that some discussions have offered as much as four different senses of the concept (see for example O'Neill 2003; Jamieson 2008), and this distinction will suffice here given that the aim is to appreciate the context of the debate as opposed to its philosophical intricacies. It also makes it easier to appreciate discussions about what may or not have intrinsic value in either of these two senses or both.

Some of the important considerations in discussions about intrinsic value involve distinctions between living and non-living things, as well as between conscious beings and living things which lack consciousness or the potential for consciousness. For example, it is difficult to see how something which lacks consciousness can be valued for its own sake. In contrast, it is reasonable to argue that a living thing which lacks consciousness can be of intrinsic value in the sense of having value-in-itself. In some discussions, however, there is more emphasis on intrinsic value that is based on consciousness (sentience/experience) which leads to the view that things which lack consciousness cannot be said to have intrinsic value. For example, as Luke Martell claims:

> It is hard to see a value in just being, living or growing. Value is the experience of these. Plants and rocks do not have the capacity to experience being or growing or gain wellbeing from them. But experience or wellbeing, which *are* of intrinsic value, can be felt by sentient beings – humans and animals – and it is in them that intrinsic value lies. (Martell 2009: 30)

It is however surprising that those who follow this line of thinking are willing to distinguish between beings that can have experiences and those that cannot, but are willing to ignore the distinction between living and non-living things. Nevertheless, some non anthropocentric perspectives may argue that non sentient living things can have intrinsic value in sense of value-in-itself. Trees or plants, for instance can arguably be said to have intrinsic value in this sense.

Attributing intrinsic value to nonhuman beings or the rest of nature has been at the centre of non anthropocentric attempts to extend the "moral community." Nevertheless, and besides what other critiques have said, the idea that whatever has intrinsic value is thereby morally considerable can be mistaken (O'Neill 2003: 126).

As one major proponent of arguments against attributing intrinsic value to nonhuman beings (Bryan Norton) points out, we can choose for rational or religious reasons "to live according to an ideal of maximum harmony with nature" without attributing intrinsic value to natural objects or nonhuman beings (Norton 2003: 165). Such an ideal can then provide a basis for condemning human actions that are detrimental to the environment and other species. We may not agree with his motivations,[5] but there is a point in Norton's suggestion. It also makes it possible for practical purposes to distinguish between things to which we may have moral obligations and those to which we may have rational obligations. I may for example not value a tree for "moral reasons". Rather I can value it as having value-in-itself. The rational constraint then is that I cannot cut down a tree without a reason that might make it necessary for me to cut it down. This need not necessarily entail that I have certain moral obligations to the tree. Making a distinction between moral and rational considerations does not entail a denial of the interconnections between moral and rational concerns. Nonetheless, it still makes it possible for us to distinguish between things to which we may have moral obligations and those to which we may have other rational obligations.

Whether African environmental thought lacks non anthropocentric perspectives or such perspectives have been ignored by Western scholars is not of major interest to this discussion. The understanding here is that the dualistic thinking that characterises Western environmental ethics is simply not reflected in the African ontology and worldview. The emphasis placed on harmonious relations in the African context does not seem to require a strong emphasis on dualistic thinking of anthropocentrism versus non anthropocentrism.

Given that the concept of intrinsic value can be understood in different senses, it is rather difficult to demonstrate completely that nonhuman beings cannot plausibly have intrinsic value in any of the two senses I have alluded to in this section. Arguments against attributing intrinsic value to nonhuman beings do not seem to sufficiently indicate that doing so is irrational. If that is the case, then the question is not whether or not nonhuman beings can be said to have intrinsic value at all. Rather it is more about the *sense* in which such beings can reasonably be said to have intrinsic value. In what follows I turn to the debate between individualism and holism.

The contention between individualism and holism is another debate connected to discussions about intrinsic value. Again, the two different senses of intrinsic value, namely, value-in-itself and value for its own sake seem to create an ambiguity which entrenches disagreements. For individualists, like Martell for instance, only individuals can be said to have intrinsic value. He writes:

> Giving value to systems has dangerous implications. It means we can value systems over individuals and individuals can be sacrificed for the sake of an impersonal structure. Making the ecosystem of intrinsic value creates a conflict between its interests and the interests of the individuals who make it up. Yet it is the latter who matter and the former which should

---

[5]As he claims, we need not recognise the intrinsic value of nonhuman objects; instead we can recognise the intrinsic value of our fellow humans and their preferences that nonhuman objects not be harmed.

serve them. If the system gains value in itself over and above individuals this can be very dangerous for them. (Martell 2009: 35)

Martell may be correct in claiming that systems, such as ecosystems, cannot have intrinsic value because the value they have is for individuals who make up the system. However, what Martell's position seems to imply is that only individuals can be valued for their own sake. I do not see why an ecosystem cannot be said to have intrinsic value in the sense of value-in-itself. The value of the ecosystem may be determined by the objective properties of the system as Martell admits, but it is value for individuals and not for the system. Hence, we cannot value an ecosystem for *its own sake.*

However, a shift from considering the value of individuals to considerations of collective entities such as species and ecosystems is a key feature of environmental thinking. From this perspective the focus is on defending *habitats*, 'which is a collective name including both instrumentally necessary inorganic features of the species' environment and other intrinsically and instrumentally valuable organisms' (Ferré 2010: 159). Species or ecosystems may not have intrinsic value in the sense that individual organisms can be said to have it. Nonetheless, concerns about species or ecosystems are inextricably linked to concerns about individual organisms and their environments. It is also in this sense that the emphasis on harmonious relations in the African context gets around the individualism versus holism debate. As Kevin Behrens argues:

An African environmental ethic, which is essentially relational, grounded in interdependencies and that prize harmonious relationships with nature, is most appealing because it is able to embrace the salient features of both holist and individualist theories. (Behrens 2011: 48)[6]

This approach does not prioritise systems over individuals nor does it prioritise individuals over systems. Dualisms, such as anthropocentrism versus non anthropocentrism; or individualism versus holism that have characterised Western environmental ethics, may have been useful in informing particular positions, however, they have often led to seemingly irreconcilable differences. Moreover, the positions taken by choosing either side of the dualisms are individually inadequate to capture what goes on in real life given the multifaceted human interactions with the natural world.

The next section will briefly explore Western conceptions of justice and examine how such conceptions fair in an African context. This comparison is intended to explore ways of broadening the current conception of environmental justice and to highlight the connection between ethics and justice.

---

[6]Behrens refers to his theory (or perspective) as "African Relational Environmentalism".

13.4   Western Conceptions of Justice and the African Context

The most influential conception of justice in the modern classical or contemporary sense is John Rawls' *Theory of Justice*. Central to Rawls' explanation of justice is the thesis that "all social primary goods—liberty and opportunity, income and wealth, and the basis of self-respect—are to be distributed equally unless an unequal distribution of any or all of these goods is to the advantage of the least favoured" (Rawls 1972: 303). This conception of justice is understood primarily as social justice because of the almost exclusive focus on the distribution of social goods and human liberties. However, some critiques, such as Iris Young, have also argued that besides the question of distribution, it is also important to pay attention to social structures and processes that determine social relations and patterns of distribution (Young 1990). There is also emphasis on the issue of participation, be it in decision-making or other political processes, in order to protect communities or individuals in their relationships with institutions. Further, some, for example Honneth (1995), have argued that there is an important link between participation and human dignity.

Of the three aspects of social justice noted above, concerns about distribution and participation have been the most dominant in the conception of environmental justice as it focuses primarily on the distribution of benefits and burdens from environmental activities. Overall, the basis for the current conception of environmental justice "relies on the idea that all human beings are equal and should be treated as such, so the discussion over environmental justice is a discussion about social justice as well, its meaning and its implication" (Finger and Zorzi 2013: 225). Hence, while a distinction is often made between social justice and environmental justice, some would argue that you cannot have environmental justice without social justice (and vice versa). However, considering the pride of place accorded to non anthropocentric perspectives in Western environmental ethics it is understandable why a conception of environmental justice that is seen to be predominantly anthropocentric will be a target of criticism. Be that as it may, one may still object to the claim that environmental justice so conceived "necessarily encompasses the widest possible definition of what is considered *environmental*" (McDonald 2002: 3). One may even wonder why a conception of justice which is primarily preoccupied with human beings should be referred to as environmental justice as the term social justice would still be adequate for such an understanding.

In view of the above concerns, the main challenge of how to broaden the concept of environmental justice still remains. However, broadening the notion of environmental justice in the context of Western environmental ethics runs up against the dualistic thinking discussed in the previous section, such as anthropocentrism versus non anthropocentrism. As I will argue below, this does not seem to be the case with the African context.

Given the emphasis placed on harmonious relations, justice in an African context can be viewed predominantly in terms of restorative justice focused on balance and harmony. The emphasis placed on balance and harmony is not restricted to human relations, but also extends to other living things. For example, as Kelbessa claims, "the Oromo[7] do not simply consider justice, integrity and respect as human virtues applicable to human beings but they extend them to nonhuman species and mother Earth" (Kelbessa 2005: 24). Over and above, in an African context, the relationship between human and nonhumans is couched in non-scientific terms of spiritual forces. The conception of a spiritual force "… asserts that any aggressive or non-harmonious behaviour within the spiritual chain would result in undesirable consequences for the whole system until the abnormality is corrected or the injured party assuaged" (Ibanga 2016: 11). Bearing in mind the colonial and post-colonial influences, one may ask about the extent to which African views such as this may have been ravaged, an issue which I believe is subject to debate.

For our purposes here, we can see from the foregoing why an African conception of environmental ethics needs to adequately capture the close ties between ethics and justice which does not seem to be the case with Western environmental ethics. As compared to ethical concerns, the issue of justice has not received as much attention in Western environmental ethics (Dobson 1998). Part of the reason for this trend could be the view that the notion of justice cannot be extended to nonhuman beings or nature. Even those who think that ethical concerns can be extended to nature have maintained that this is not the case with justice. However, there are some who hold a moderate view:

> When humans deal with plants, endangered species, ecosystems, wilderness, mountains, rivers, or wildlife, justice is not the most useful category. If one presses the etymology of the term far enough, justice is doing what is right, and so the term could be insisted upon. Nevertheless, justice in current use is so entwined with courts of law, with issues of fair distribution of benefits and burdens among humans …that one is better advised to employ the more comprehensive term, ethics, to speak of protecting values and goods, of appropriate respect and behaviour. (Rolston III 1988: 149)

In short, Rolston is concerned about stretching "the concept of justice into regions where it ceases to be the best category" (ibid. 149). In contrast, this discussion is of the view that the issue of justice is equally significant in dealing with our interactions with both humans and nonhuman beings. Overall, there is a basis for one to maintain that both ethics and justice are applicable or can be extended to nonhuman beings as the African perspectives on ontology and justice have shown.

In appreciating the distinction between ethics and justice, I do not wish to delve too much into the theoretical questions of which of the two is broader or part of the other, as that is beyond the scope of this discussion. The point is that ethical arguments and arguments about justice are not (always) the same (Wienhues 2017). Appreciating the nature of the relationship between ethics and justice is what is important, and the possibility of conflict between ethical principles and some principles of justice is not of interest here, as such conflicts are also expected *within* either of these two categories. Further, the concern that ethical arguments and arguments about justice may be conflated is not of major concern as in some cases this could be as a result of

---

[7] An ethnic group of people in Ethiopia.

overlaps, or of the inextricable links between ethics and justice. Consider for instance when Rolston III writes

> … Wenz distinguishes between a theory of ethics and a theory of justice. A theory of ethics asks what is of direct moral concern and how it is of concern. A theory of justice asks what is a fair allocation of benefits and burdens among those beings who are of direct moral concern[8] (1988: 149)

If we take into account the understanding that ethical concerns and justice overlap, what matters is the significance of the relationship between the two spheres of concern. In relation to the above quote, one may observe as Rolston does that "a theory of justice is a subset of a theory of ethics, since some moral questions are not about distributing benefits and costs" (ibid. 149). Alternatively, we may say that justice is one of the moral values (principle/virtue) which again makes it a subset of ethics. However, it does not necessarily follow from this that the principles of justice are inferior to ethics. The understanding in this discussion is that ethical concerns can be supplemented by principles of justice. This is because concerns about justice can be highly specific and therefor more pressing. Justice is often tied to what has happened whereas ethics relies more on what should happen. To appreciate some of the challenges the relationship between ethics and justice poses for Western environmental ethics, the next section explores some of the disagreements between deep ecology and social ecology.[9]

13.5   Deep Ecology Versus Social Ecology

Deep ecology as seen from some of its basic principles of the platform pushes ecological concerns toward other living things. For example, the first principle of the deep ecology platform states: "The well-being and flourishing of human and nonhuman life on Earth have intrinsic value in themselves (synonyms: intrinsic value, inherent value). These values are independent of the usefulness of the nonhuman world for human purposes". The fourth principle also states that the flourishing of nonhuman life requires a substantial decrease in human populations (Devall and Sessions 2012: 146). In contrast, social ecology, like the environmental justice movement, brings to the fore fundamental concerns about social justice and how these relate to environmental problems. It pushes the concept of ecology and related concerns in the direction of human society and the principles to which social ecology appeals relate well to the concept of social justice.

I should also note here that the disagreements between social ecology and deep ecology are wide ranging.

---

[8]This perspective appears to imply that in order to determine what is just, we must first determine what is moral. There can be a challenge therefore if what is considered just turns out or appears to be immoral.

[9]In dealing with some of the disagreements between social ecology and deep ecology we will have to deal also with some disagreements between the principles of justice and ethics.

> The differences between these two tendencies in the so-called "ecology movement" consist not only in quarrels over theory, sensibility, and ethics. They have far-reaching *practical* and *political* consequences on the way we view nature, "humanity", and ecology. Most significantly, they concern how we propose to *change* society and by what *means* (Bookchin 2012: 166).

Addressing all the disagreements between social ecology and deep ecology is beyond the scope of this discussion. However, the fact that social ecology and deep ecology offer different explanations for the root cause of environmental problems is not in itself a problem given the complexity of the environmental challenges we face.

Apart from concerns about the intrinsic value of nonhuman nature the differences in principles here also emanate from the respective orientation of each of these approaches in relation to the principles of ethics and justice. Deep ecology is concerned about the prevailing Western human attitudes toward nonhuman nature and the need to change these attitudes whereas social ecology is primarily concerned about institutions in society that perpetuate the dominance of humans over one another and nonhuman nature. For social ecologists the problem lies in hierarchical structures in society and it is these that should be removed in order to free both human beings and nonhuman nature from exploitation. Of the two we can see that social ecology is inclined more toward justice whereas deep ecology sees the environmental crisis is an ethical crisis requiring an ethical transformation of people.

In the context of this discussion, an appreciation of the emphasis placed on harmonious relations does not require choosing between social ecology and deep ecology. Focusing on harmony broadens the scope to carter for, and unifies, the concerns raised from these different perspectives. In this case, concerns about environmental justice and ethics that do not take into account the wellbeing of nonhuman life (or at least some of it) are either insincere or not just comprehensive enough. Besides, if the emphasis is on harmonious relations, accounting for the wellbeing of nonhumans does not call for equality among humans and nonhumans. In fact, there is no need to even create the impression that the survival fauna and flora is more important than the wellbeing of humans and especially the poor. From the perspective of the African context of putting emphasis on harmonious relationships, one can argue for the broadening of the concept of environmental justice without getting entangled in the disagreements that have characterised the debate between deep ecology and social ecology.

In arguing for a broadening of the concept of environmental justice it is worthwhile to acknowledge the distinction between environmental justice and ecological justice. "Ecological justice is the idea of doing justice *to* nature and forms the counterpart to environmental justice which is concerned with justice between humans with regard to nature" (Wienhues 2017: 2; cf. Low and Gleeson 1998). In view of this distinction between environmental justice and ecological justice, this discussion will focus on environmental justice and argue that a broader view of this notion is applicable to nonhuman beings. In this sense environmental justice is not simply an issue between human beings with regard to nature, but also between humans and nonhuman beings.

The reason why I do not wish to focus on ecological justice (in the sense of doing justice to nature) is twofold. First, I do not suppose that the term "environmental" is inadequate if the aim is to include nonhuman beings in "the community of justice" given that all living things inhabit the environment in some form or other. Rather, the inadequacy, on this account, lies in the predominant conception of environmental justice in purely anthropocentric terms. However, apart from the inclusion of non-human beings in the realm of justice, I do understand why one would argue that the term environmental justice may not be adequate to capture concerns about doing justice to nature. The term nature is much broader and complex than the concept of environment.

Secondly, the dualism of man versus nature is not clearly reflected in African ontology. As a result there seems to be a lack of basis upon which we can address humans and nature separately or to treat human beings as being independent of the rest of nature. A discrete conception of nature in African traditional thought is also difficult to come by. In view of the above, it wold not be necessary for me to devote much attention to nature separately, unless it is required indirectly to provide the context for the need for harmony as portrayed in the African view of ontology and justice. The conception of justice as harmony not only among humans but also between humans and nonhumans is essential to an African conception of environmental ethics.

References

Attfield, R. 2003. *Environmental Ethics*. Cambridge: Polity Press.

Beckerman, W., and J. Pasek. 2010. In Defence of Anthropocentrism. In *Environmental Ethics: The big questions*, ed. D.R. Keller, 83–88. Wiley-Blackwell.: Sussex.

Behrens, K.G. 2011. African Philosophy, Thought and Practice and Their Contribution to Environmental Ethics. Ph.D. Thesis, University of Johannesburg.

Bookchin, M. 2012. Social Ecology Versus Deep Ecology. In *Environmental Ethics: Readings in Theory and Application*, ed. L.P. Pojman and P. Pojman, 165–175. Cengage Learning.: Wordsworth.

Callicott, J. 1994. *Earth's Insights. A Survey of Ecological Ethics from the Mediterranean Basin to the Australian Outback*. Berkeley: University of California Press.

Devall, B., and G. Sessions. 2012. Deep Ecology. In *Environmental Ethics: Readings in Theory and Application,* ed. L.P. Pojman and P. Pojman, 143–148. Wordsworth, Cengage Learning.

Dobson, A. 1998. *Justice and the Environment: Conceptions of Environmental Sustainability and Dimensions of Social Justice*. Oxford: Oxford University Press.

Ekwealo, C.J. 2012. NduMmiliNduAzu (Live-And-Let-Live): African Environmental Ethics. *Journal of African Environmental Ethics and Values*. 3: 90–106.

Ferré, F. 2010. Persons in Nature: Toward an Applicable and Unified Environmental Ethics. In *Environmental Ethics: The Big Questions*, ed. D.R. Keller, 154–160. Wiley-Blackwell: Sussex.

Finger, M., and F. Zorzi. 2013. Environmental Justice. *UFRGSMUN/UFRGS Model United Nations Journal* 1: 222–243.

Gyeke, K. 2011. African Ethics. In *The Stanford Encyclopedia of Philosophy*, ed. E.N. Zalta. https://plato.stanford.edu/archives/fall2011/entries/african-ethics/.

Hargrove, E. 2003. Weak Anthropocentric Intrinsic Value. In *Environmental Ethics: An Anthology*, ed. A. Light and H. Rolston III, 175–190. Malden, MA: Blackwell Publishing.

Holbrook, D. 2009. The Consequentialist side of Environmental Ethics. In *The Environmental Responsibility Reader*, ed. M. Reynolds, C. Blackmore, and M.J. Smith, 52–59. London: Zed Books/The Open University.

Honneth, A. 1995. Integrity and Disrespect: Principles of Morality Based on the Theory of Recognition. *Political Theory* 20: 187–201.

Ibanga, F.D. 2016. Logical and Theoretical Foundations of African Environmental Ethics. *Africology: The Journal of Pan African Studies*. 9 (9): 3–24.

Ikuenobe, P.A. 2014. Traditional African Environmental Ethics and Colonial Legacy. *International Journal of Philosophy and Theology*. 2 (4): 01–21.

Jamieson, D. 2008. *Ethics and the Environment: An Introduction*. Cambridge: Cambridge University Press.

Kelbessa, W. 2005. The Rehabilitation of Indigenous Environmental Ethics in Africa. *Diogenes* 207: 17–34.

Korsgaard, C.M. 1983. Two Distinctions in Goodness. *The Philosophical Review* 92 (2): 169–195.

Low, N., and B. Gleeson. 1998. *Justice, Society and Nature*. London: Routledge.

McDonald, D.A. 2002. What is Environmental Justice? Introduction. In *Environmental Justice in South Africa*, ed. D.A. McDonald, Athens, 1–12. Ohio: Ohio University Press.

Martell, L. 2009. On Values and Obligations to the Environment. In *The Environmental Responsibility Reader*, ed. M. Reynolds, C. Blackmore, and M.J. Smith, 28–39. London: Zed Books/The Open University.

Metz, T. 2007. Toward an African Moral Theory. *The Journal of Political Philosophy*. 15 (3): 321–341.

Norton, B.G. 2003. Environmental Ethics and Weak Anthropocentrism. In *Environmental Ethics: An Anthology*, ed. A. Light and H. Rolston III, 163–174. Malden, MA: Blackwell Publishing.

O'Neill, J. 2003. The Varieties of Intrinsic Value. In *Environmental Ethics: An Anthology*, ed. A. Light and H. Rolston III, 131–142. Malden, MA: Blackwell Publishing.

Peterson, A.C. 2013. Articulating Moral Bases for Regional Responses to Deforestation and Climate Change: Africa. *William & Mary Environmental Law and Policy Review*. 38 (1): 81–117.

Rawls, J. 1972. *A Theory of Justice*. Oxford: Claredon Press.

Rolston, III, H. 1988. *A Review of Peter S. Wenz's Environmental Justice*. Albany: State University of New York Press.

Tangwa, G. 2004. Some African Reflections on Biomedical and Environmental Ethics. In *A Companion to African philosophy*, ed. K. Wiredu, 387–395. Oxford: Blackwell publishers.

Wienhues, A. 2017. Sharing the Earth: A Biocentric Account of Ecological Justice. *J Agric Environ Ethics*. (Published online).

Young, I.M. 1990. *Justice and the Politics of Difference*. Princeton, NJ: Princeton University Press.

Zimmerman, M.J. 2010 Intrinsic vs. Extrinsic Value. *The Stanford Encyclopedia of Philosophy*. https://plato.stanford.edu/archives/win2010/emtries/value-intrinsic-extrinsic.

Chapter 14
Expanding Nussbaum's Eighth Capability Using African Environmental Ethics

Jessica van Jaarsveld

Abstract This chapter looks at Martha Nussbaum's capabilities approach and finds ways that it can benefit from engaging with African environmental ethics. Nussbaum's approach, which has a growing influence on human wellbeing discourse, lists ten capabilities that she claims all governments must make available to their people at a threshold level (at least) in order for them to lead flourishing lives. Among them, the capability at number eight termed "other species", refers to the ability to live with concern for and in relation to the world of nature. Nussbaum does not go into much further detail regarding this capability, and so I compare and contrast three ways in which this eighth capability can be conceived; an anthropocentric, an ecocentric and a traditional African environmental way. I find that of the three, African environmental ethics offers the most satisfactory way in terms of its theoretical and practical implications. This view entails acknowledging our situatedness within a community of all living things, and respects the consequent call for harmonious relations. This chapter delivers an exposition of an under-explored capability on Nussbaum's list and a defence of the advantages that African environmental ethics affords in this regard.

14.1 Introduction

The Capabilities Approach (CA) to human development has been increasingly influential in recent decades. Originally developed by Amartya Sen, the capabilities approach has moved development theory away from purely economic conceptions to more holistic accounts, in which freedom and a person's ability to live the kind of life that they value are the focus of attention. Many theorists have followed Sen, further developing the CA, with Martha Nussbaum being one of the most well-known and influential. Nussbaum offers an account that differs from Sen's in that she formulates a list of ten central human capabilities that she says all humans must have at a mini-

J. van Jaarsveld (✉)
University of Johannesburg, Johannesburg, South Africa
e-mail: jessi@stefduplessis.com

© Springer Nature Switzerland AG 2019   205
M. Chemhuru (ed.), *African Environmental Ethics*, The International
Library of Environmental, Agricultural and Food Ethics 29,
https://doi.org/10.1007/978-3-030-18807-8_14

mum level in order to lead flourishing lives, while Sen avoids such lists. Beginning with Life and Bodily Health and Bodily Integrity, Nussbaum's list includes those things that she deems crucial to human flourishing.

The approach is now well-established, so much so that "the influence of the CA has now exceeded Sen's and Nussbaum's own work and become a somewhat autonomous force in development studies" (Poolman 2012: 367). The CA is used in welfare economics, social policy and political philosophy and, as a framework for human wellbeing, it can be used to assess poverty and inequality and to design and evaluate policies accordingly.

Nussbaum's eighth capability on her list of ten, "Other Species" refers to "being able to live with concern for and in relation to animals, plants, and the world of nature" (Nussbaum 2011: 34). This capability makes Nussbaum's approach fairly unique in that it explicitly makes mention of the role that living in relation to the natural environment plays in human flourishing. However, what exactly this capability is referring to is left unspecified by Nussbaum. This leaves it open to a multitude of interpretations, considering that different positions within environmental ethics would offer contrasting conceptions of what it means to live with concern for and in relation to nature.

While Nussbaum's list is intended to only be an abstract outline that thus allows for multiple realisability, we should aim to use it as a basis for a theory of development that best moves the earth towards a stable, humane and habitable future. Different conceptions of Nussbaum's eighth capability may perform differently in this regard, and so there is a need to assess which theory may offer the best understanding in terms of its theoretical and practical implications.

In light of this, I will be looking at three potential theories for understanding what it may mean to be "able to live with concern for and in relation to animals, plants, and the world of nature" (Nussbaum 2011: 34). I look first at the two dominant, and fundamentally opposite, positions within environmental ethics, namely anthropocentrism and ecocentrism. I then look at African environmental ethics, which, though often accused of being anthropocentric, can actually be seen as occupying a middle ground between anthropocentrism and ecocentrism.

I show that African environmental ethics may offer the most attractive way to understand Nussbaum's capability, as employing this position offers both theoretical and practical benefits. It supports the formation of policies that can guide a sustainable use of the environment, without drastically relegating human needs.

This is the first time that African environmental ethics has been used to expand on Nussbaum's approach. It is useful to flesh out Nussbaum's environmental capability in this way because Nussbaum's theory of development is highly influential, and increasingly so, and so grappling with underexplored areas of her work may offer new and helpful insights into how we may best enhance human flourishing for all people. This may take us a step closer to having the right tools to navigate human life through the unchartered territories of the anthropocene. The looming threats to our natural environment place importance on our need to grapple with the ways that the environment affects human flourishing, and this may set the stage for future work that investigates how African environmental ethics can enter capabilities discourse.

I begin by outlining and contextualising Nussbaum's capabilities approach in Sect. 14.2. I then show the way in which her eighth capability is not fully clarified, and explain the need to flesh this capability out. In Sect. 14.3 explain the three positions that I will be comparing in terms of how they conceptualise what it means to live with concern for and in relation to the world of nature; anthropocentrism, ecocentrism and African environmental ethics. Section 14.4 discusses the benefits afforded by employing an African environmental ethic, and I conclude that it is the most attractive position from which to understand Nussbaum's eighth capability.

Before beginning it is necessary to note some limitations and clarifications. When speaking of an "African environmental ethic" I am of course not claiming that there exists one homogenous set of beliefs across the—very large and diverse—African continent. However, it is possible to refer to "African" perspectives in the same way that it is common practice to refer to "Western" views. As Tangwa (2006: 388) explains, one can use the term "African" in the same way that it is widely accepted that one can use the term "Western", that being "without any necessary implication that some differences or exceptions may not be found within what is thus bracketed".

Despite the noteworthy diversity of the continent, Tangwa (1996:186) calls it "no secret" that Africans share a common world-view and outlook on life, underpinned by similar philosophies and practices. For instance, that land belongs to all, living and dead, and must be protected and cared for as such is a value that "cuts across all ethnic groups in Africa" (Omari 1992: 174). As another example, Murove (2009a: 26) notes that many scholars have identified "interrelationality" as being the feature that "best sums up African ethics". It is therefore justifiable to discuss "African" environmental ethics without being criticised for making unfounded generalisations.

It must also be noted that the positions I will be discussing do of course not exhaustively encompass all positions within environmental ethics, but it would not be feasible to discuss every position that there is here. Specifically, by looking at the views on the two extremes I can show how positions would, in general, respond to Nussbaum's eighth capability based on where they roughly lie within the debates of environmental ethics. It is a significant simplification, but it is a useful starting point for future work. It also serves to situate and explore African environmental ethics, which, up until recently, has not received much attention within the field. African ethics has been represented as nothing more than a savage ethics, claiming that "there is nothing authentic to be learned from African contextual realities" (Murove 2009a: 17), but this is a significant misrepresentation and unfounded dismissal of a valuable, insightful and thoroughly developed ethical theory that warrants attention.

Therefore, part of this project is to highlight the benefits that would follow from our developing an African environmental ethical perspective. By discussing the different theoretical and practical implications of the three positions, I hope to show that an African environmental ethic may offer the most attractive way to understand Nussbaum's eighth capability. Metz (2016) offers a similar sort of exposition regarding recent philosophical approaches to social protection. He compares and contrasts the philosophies of the Capabilities Approach and *ubuntu* and assesses the theoretical and practical implications of both as they pertain to social protection. His conclusion is that he tends "to find *ubuntu* more attractive or at least worth taking seriously as a rival to its more influential competitor" (Metz 2016: 146).

I hope to proceed in the same way, showing that when it comes to unpacking Nussbaum's eighth capability, African environmental ethics is the most attractive of the three positions within environmental ethics that I will be looking at (the other two being anthropocentrism and ecocentrism), or at the very least to show that it is, as Metz found with *ubuntu* and social protection, worth taking seriously as a rival to its more influential competitors.

14.2 Nussbaum's Capabilities Approach

The capabilities approach in general represents a shift in thinking regarding human development. Traditionally, development has been viewed mainly in economic terms with many definitions of development relying on economic measures such as Gross National Income per capita (GNI p.c.). Since the 1980's, however, there has been a realisation that indicators of development should also encompass non-economic dimensions. In coming to see development in more multidimensional terms, new and broader indicators have been created.

The shift in thinking to incorporate non-economic dimensions has been largely influenced by the growth of capabilities approaches to development. The capabilities approach finds its roots in the work of Amartya Sen. Sen (2003) draws attention to the fact that economic growth should only be an "intermediate goal" with the ultimate aim being the enrichment of human lives. Following Sen, Nussbaum (2009: 212) points out that there are many aspects that contribute to quality of life that do not automatically follow from economic growth. Nussbaum has contributed a great deal to the progress of development theories and, with Sen, has promoted the shift towards a capabilities approach and away from purely economic frameworks for development. Nussbaum's approach has a growing influence on human wellbeing discourse.

Consequently, Nussbaum (2000: 5) aims to formulate an account of what governments ought to do in order to uphold the human dignity of all people. Her focus is on what people are actually able to do and to be, in accordance with "an intuitive idea of a life that is worthy of the dignity of the human being" (Nussbaum 2000: 5). Specifically, Nussbaum formulates a list of ten "central human capabilities" that are the minimum capabilities required in order for a person to flourish. These are outlined below in a summarised form:

1. *Life*. Being able to live to the end of a human life of normal length…
2. *Bodily Health*. Being able to have good health… to be adequately nourished; to have adequate shelter.
3. *Bodily Integrity*. Being able to move freely from place to place; to be secure against violent assault…
4. *Senses, Imagination, and Thought*. Being able to use the senses, to imagine, think, and reason—and to do these things in a "truly human" way…

5. *Emotions.* Being able to have attachments to things and people outside ourselves…
6. *Practical Reason.* Being able to form a conception of the good and to engage in critical reflection about the planning of one's life…
7. *Affiliation.* (*A*) Being able to live with and toward others… (*B*) Having the social bases of self-respect and non-humiliation…
8. *Other Species.* Being able to live with concern for and in relation to animals, plants, and the world of nature.
9. *Play.* Being able to laugh, to play, to enjoy recreational activities.
10. *Control over One's Environment.* (*A*) *Political.* Being able to participate effectively in political choices that govern one's life… (*B*) *Material.* Being able to hold property… and having property rights on an equal basis with others…
(Nussbaum 2011: 33–34)

According to Nussbaum (2000: 71), it is the duty of every government to guarantee its citizens a threshold level of the capabilities above. If people consistently fall below this threshold level then it is tragic, unjust, and demands urgent attention. The list of the central capabilities can thus be used to determine a set of "basic constitutional principles that should be respected and implemented by the governments of all nations" (Nussbaum 2000: 5).

A crucial aspect of Nussbaum's (2000: 77) account is that the "items on the list are to some extent differently constructed by different societies". She explains by saying that a key feature of the list's structure is that it allows for "multiple realizability", meaning that each individual capability can be specified accordingly to localised cultural beliefs. Nussbaum's (2000: 77) capabilities approach is thus "designed to leave room for a reasonable pluralism in specification".

Nonetheless, there must be some starting point from which the capability is understood since if states are expected to use the capabilities as constitutional principles, doing so is only possible if there is a general understanding from which to begin. For the most part, there is a decent degree of clarity in this regard. Certain capabilities, such as Life and Bodily Health can be readily understood. For the other capabilities that may not be as straightforwardly understood, Nussbaum offers detailed explanations. For example, the fourth capability is listed by Nussbaum with the following, lengthy description which was only summarised above:

> *Senses, Imagination, and Thought.* Being able to use the senses, to imagine, think, and reason—and to do these things in a "truly human" way, a way informed and cultivated by an adequate education, including, but by no means limited to, literacy and basic mathematical and scientific training. Being able to use imagination and thought in connection with experiencing and producing works and events of one's own choice, religious, literary, musical, and so forth. Being able to use one's mind in ways protected by guarantees of freedom of expression with respect to both political and artistic speech, and freedom of religious exercise. Being able to have pleasurable experiences and to avoid nonbeneficial pain.
>
> (Nussbaum 2011: 33)

Emotions, Practical Reason and Affiliation (the fifth, sixth and seventh capabilities respectively) are similarly explained at length. However, the eighth capability, Other

Species, is simply stated as "Being able to live with concern for and in relation to animals, plants, and the world of nature" (Nussbaum 2011: 34).

Problematically, this eighth capability may be understood in a variety of ways. While Play (number nine) is also just listed, as seen above, as "Being able to laugh, to play, to enjoy recreational activities", there are not multiple positions, defended passionately by numerous branches of scholarly thought, regarding what it means "to play". Contrastingly, within the active and growing field of environmental ethics, there is an array of positions whose proponents do contend how one ought to engage with the environment. They may understand Nussbaum's eighth capability differently based on which position they hold.

These differences in understanding may have significant consequences. This is so because governments will develop different types of environmental protection based on varying understandings of the capability, and some forms of protection are better than others, as will be discussed. This does not detract from the multiple realisability of the list, but there are, after all, limits as to how different state-specific thresholds may be. Nussbaum (2007a: 180) makes this point when she explains that states may appropriately debate whether their school-leaving age should be seventeen or nineteen, but entertaining an age of twelve would not be acceptable anywhere. There are certain standards by which we can judge whether or not one understanding of the environmental capability is better. If a framework allows for the widespread destruction of ecosystems, for instance, it is likely to be an unsatisfactory framework.

Furthermore, considering that the approach is meant as an abstract outline, where "each nation, of course… sets a threshold to establish an adequate level of support" (Nussbaum 2007b: 16), it is the duty of each state to determine what type of environmental conditions are necessary to ensure their citizens enjoy a threshold level of their capabilities. As such, it would be helpful to provide the theoretical tools needed to establish this level. In other words, we should try to find a framework that offers the best way of conceiving of Nussbaum's environmental capability so that state's have assistance in guiding them towards ensuring that the are providing what is needed for their citizens to flourish.

In her work, Nussbaum does not offer significant explanation as to how this capability should be comprehended. It is significant that she has included an environmental capability, but what it actually entails has not been dealt with in any serious detail; Nussbaum

> has distinguished herself from many liberal political theorists by recognizing relationships to non-human life as a core component of human flourishing… However, she has left it to others to specify the theory's implications for understanding the role of environmental relationships in human and non-human flourishing and for establishing how to balance, prioritize, and make trade-offs between the capabilities of different species.
>
> (Holland and Linch 2016: 416)

Therefore, it would be useful to look at some of the potential ways that Nussbaum's eighth capability may be further developed. This will allow us to flesh out what it may mean to live with concern for and in relation to plants, animals and the world of nature, and to assess whether certain understandings are more attractive than others. The obvious place to find a theory capable of expanding what this capability entails would be within environmental ethics, since it is an area of philosophy that investigates how humans should interact with the natural environment and with its nonhuman constituents.

Willott and Schmidtz (2002: xii) say that environmental ethics involves the application of normative ethical theories to a specific set of practical problems, and asks questions about what we owe each other, and what, if anything, we owe to non-human entities in light of our ecological context. As a central question of the field, an environmental ethicist may ask, "What should be our attitude toward nature?" (Willott and Schmidtz 2002: xiii). Clearly environmental ethics is the right general starting point to look for a description of "living with concern for and in relation to animals, plants, and the world of nature".

While it may be safe to say that all environmental ethicists would agree with the claim that human flourishing involves living with concern for and in relation to nature, why they believe this to be the case and how they interpret the claim may differ significantly. I will therefore be looking at three positions within environmental ethics to show how these positions would interpret and apply Nussbaum's eighth capability. The first two positions represent opposite stances in one particular debate that has characterised the field of environmental ethics. This debate involves the question of whether or not nature possesses intrinsic value, and it "has launched a thousand metaethical and metaphysical ships in environmental ethics" (Light 2002: 426).

Brennan and Lo (2016: §1) explain the distinction between instrumental and intrinsic value. They show that instrumental value assigns a thing with value based on whether or not that thing contributes to some other ends. Intrinsic value, on the other hand, refers to the way that a thing can be valuable as an end in itself, and not because it contributes to some other ends. A human, for instance, is regarded as having intrinsic value but would also be said to have instrumental value if they were, for instance, a teacher who could be seen as instrumentally valuable to someone looking to acquire knowledge. Something that has intrinsic value generates a moral duty that commits moral agents to its protection.

Anthropocentricism, the first of the three positions I will be discussing, holds that humans alone have moral standing and are the only holders of intrinsic value. In contrast, nonanthropocentrism, the second of three positions under discussion, views at least some non-human entities as also having intrinsic value and moral standing, "either because some nonhumans have a capacity for self-conscious moral agency, or because the capacity for self-conscious agency is not the only basis for moral standing" (Willott and Schmidtz 2002: xviii). Environmental ethics originally positioned itself as a new discipline based on a rejection of the dominant, traditional anthropocentric position of Western ethical theories (Light 2002: 428).

I will take an example of an anthropocentric and a non-anthropocentric theory to show the implications of each when used to understand Nussbaum's environmental capability. I then look at the third position, namely traditional African environmental ethics and show how it could be used to comprehend Nussbaum's eighth capability, finding that it offers multiple benefits that the other two views do not. African environmental ethics has in the past been categorised as being anthropocentric, but

I will show that it is in fact a sort of middle ground between anthropocentrism and ecocentrism, making the three distinct philosophies.

14.3   The Three Positions

I begin by outlining three positions from which one can approach Nussbaum's eighth capability. Firstly, let us imagine an economist with no affinity for nature beyond its instrumental value. He may agree that human flourishing involves having concern for and living in relation to nature. To him, one should be concerned for nature in so far as it supports human needs and wants. Ensuring that nature be able to meet our needs for food, shelter and so on would very much entail "concern". He would be deeply concerned by a crop failure that would cripple and export-oriented economy and leave thousands of people short of food, for example.

Similarly, his living in relation to nature may merely involve the ways that his life and the ecosystem services that support his life intersect. After all, a relation may mean nothing more than a connection, referring only to the way that one thing effects or has relevance to another. He breathes out carbon dioxide, plants convert this into oxygen which he breathes in, and so the "relation" continues.

Secondly, as an example of a strongly nonanthropocentric position, the Deep Ecology movement rejects the anthropocentric "man-in-environment" image and instead sees all organisms as "knots in the biospherical net or field of intrinsic relations" (Naess 1973: 95). In this net, all organisms are fundamentally determined by their relation to each other, and each has an *equal right to live and blossom*" (Naess 1973: 96. Emphasis in original). Humans have mistakenly seen themselves as having a master-slave relation with the world around them, Naess continues, and this has resulted in the "alienation of man from himself" since his focus should be on coexistence and cooperation rather than exploitation and suppression.

If we were to understand Nussbaum's eighth capability from the perspective of deep ecology, living in relation to the world of nature would be in a far more fundamental sense than for the economist. The relation for the deep ecologist is tied to one's very identity. Similarly, one would live with concern for nature in a more extreme sense, as this concern would not be motivated by self-interest, but by the belief that all beings have an equal right to flourish. The ideal would be to have equal concern for oneself as for all forms of life, since as deep ecologists believe, "all organisms and entities in the ecosphere, as parts of the interrelated whole, are equal in intrinsic worth" (Devall and Sessions 2002: 122).

The third position is that of African environmental ethics, and I propose that this outlook regarding the human-nature interaction offers a particularly apt way to conceptualise Nussbaum's eighth capability. This is so because the notions of living with concern for and in relation to the world of nature is foundational in African environmental ethics. This finds its roots in the—particularly sub-Saharan indigenous—African notion of what it means to exhibit human excellence, that being to properly encompass the ideals of *Ukama* and *Ubuntu*.

As Murove's (2009b: 315) explains, *Ukama* is a Shona word meaning relatedness, while *Ubuntu* "implies that humanness is derived from our relatedness with others" and is found in Zulu, Xhosa, Sotho and Tswana. The relationality encompassed in *Ukama,* Murove continues, is in part made manifest in *Ubuntu* as *Ubuntu* maintains that individual flourishing is only possible when a person lives in relation to the community. Murove (2009b: 323) says that a person who fails to recognise "the all-pervasive reality of interdependence" would lack humanness.

Ramose (2009: 308) also explains that the notion of *Botho* (humanness) is epitomised in the Sotho proverb, which can be found in almost all indigenous African languages; *motho ke motho ka batho.* Ramose says the proverb means "to be human is to affirm one's humanity by recognising the humanity of others". Ramose notes that this indicates the "mutual foundedness" of individuals and the community, where both must recognise their complementary natures if they are to fulfil their respective purposes. Bujo (2009: 285) similarly states that one should understand the African person as being "characterised by interrelationships".

The two concepts of *Ukama* and *Ubuntu*/*Botho*, though, apply to more than just other people. They provide the basis for the belief that human well-being is essentially tied to the human "dependence on, and interdependence with, all that exists" (Murove 2009b: 315). The kinds of relationships entailed by *Ukama* and *Ubuntu* are applicable between humans and the universe as a whole. In other words, since African ethics, and African environmental ethics as a result, is founded on the concepts of *Ukama* and *Ubuntu*, there is a crucial interrelatedness between people, as well as between people and the natural environment.

Clearly, African environmental ethics, like Nussbaum's eighth capability, promotes living with concern for and in relation to the environment. Murove (2009b: 324) makes this point explicitly when he states: "there is no division between human society and other living things. Human existence is only meaningful when seen as a continuum with all else that exists". The acknowledgement that everything exists in mutual interdependence necessarily entails a concern for the environment and all of its components. Human well-being, as Murove (2009b: 330) says, "cannot be fully realised outside relatedness with the natural environment".

Peterson (2004: 169) notes this when he says that "any African environmental ethic rests on the same base that supports all African traditions-that of communalism". It can be seen that the African concepts of *Ukama* and *Ubuntu* lead to an ecologically sensitive orientation to the world, as the balance between all that constitutes existence must be respected and upheld. African ethics provide a paradigm of how humans are to exist in harmony with the natural environment, embracing togetherness "in all spheres of existence- social, spiritual, economic and ecological" (Murove 2009b: 329).

In other words, Africans live in a "close relationship with the entire cosmos" (Bujo 2009: 281). Peterson (2004: 168) describes the relationship between humans and nature in African thought (specifically Central African) as being a "both/and dialectical" rather than an "either/or dualism". Tangwa (2006) also provides a useful term to summarise the traditional African relationship with nature by calling it "eco-bio-communitarian". Tangwa explains that the term "eco-bio-communitarian" captures the way in which the traditional African outlook entails the recognition and acceptance of the way in which humans, plants, animals and the earth as a whole are inextricably interdependent. Given that humans live in inextricable interdependence, "human existence could break down if the cosmos were neglected" (Bujo 2009: 285). As such, humankind should remain extremely cautious of not allowing the world in which they find themselves to become damaged.

As Peterson (2004: 169) explains, there exists a bondedness between all the members of the common fabric of life, which in turn entails that we respect and a take responsibility for these members. As the fabric of life is one piece, "connections within the fabric have to be maintained" (Peterson 2004): 169. The result is that individual well-being is tied to ensuring the well-being of others, human and non-human. Consequently, traditional African societies were based on a "balanced ecosystem; people and nature interacted in such a way that the harmony between them was maintained" (Omari 1992: 169). The above discussion should make clear the way in which African environmental ethics would conceive of living with concern for and in relation to animals, plants and the world of nature.

This African position can be seen as a middle ground between the anthropocentric and ecocentric philosophies previously discussed. Firstly, the similarities to deep ecology are quite clear. The African notion of the web of life is similar to the deep ecologists conception of the biospherical net. Both conceive of humankind and the rest of the universe as foundationally relational. However, there is a significant difference between them. While deep ecology views the intrinsic worth of all entities as being equal, "without feeling the need to set up hierarchies of species with humans at the top" (Devall and Sessions 2002: 122), African environmental ethics encompasses the African commitment to a hierarchy of Being.

In this hierarchy, which forms a chain of beings, God is at the apex, followed by "the ancestors, then humankind, and the lower forces, animals, plants, and matter" (Teffo and Roux 1998: 138). There is a recognized difference between plants, animals, humans and spirits (Tangwa 2006: 389). In African ethical thought, we can recognise the difference between humans and non-human animals. We can and should be co-creators who "play a creative role in shaping the future of the natural and social evolutionary process" (Peterson 2004: 172). As such, we are offered a middle way between anthropocentrism and ecocentrism, avoiding the either/or debate by instead focusing on the "bondedness of all forms of life" (Peterson 2004: 172).

Behrens (2010: 466) similarly suggests that the focus on interrelatedness in African environmental ethics is best seen as a rejection of anthropocentrism, but as something close to, and yet not entirely the same as, holist perspectives.

> Since, on this African view, moral value is located in harmonious relationships with living beings, and not in some characteristic possessed by individual organisms, or in groups or wholes such as species or ecosystems, it seems that this perspective shares some characteristics with both holism and individualism, yet is also distinct from both.
>
> (Behrens 2010: 479).

While holism and deep ecology are not necessarily equivalent, Behrens's distinction here would apply to the version of deep ecology that I have discussed.

14.4 The Advantages of Employing African Environmental Ethics

There are various benefits that result from African environmental ethics falling between anthropocentrism and ecocentrism. Firstly, this seems to be the position that is most consistent with the other commitments of Nussbaum's account. The starkly anthropocentric position does not fit well into Nussbaum's overall conception. I believe it to be fairly clear that Nussbaum had more in mind when she stated that human flourishing involves living with concern for the world of nature than purely having concern for it as a result of its instrumental value.

Nussbaum (2011: 162) advocates applying her notion of capabilities to animals, saying that all animals are entitled to flourish as the kind of creature that they are, "reaching a threshold level of opportunity for a life characteristic of their kind". In light of this, I think she clearly intended to capture the sort of concern and relation that goes beyond instrumentality. It is telling that she did not include "being able to live with concern for and in relation to lampshades, coffee mugs and the world of stationery" on her list because there is something about the natural world that we tend to value more intrinsically than the objects sitting on our desks, whether or not we can successfully defend this in theory.

It similarly does not seem to be the case that her account would represent an ecocentric view since it is, after all, a conception of *human* flourishing. Clearly, it recognises some kind of a distinction between the flourishing of humans and nature at large, otherwise it would be designed as an account of the flourishing of the biospherical net. Her view seems to fit somewhere in between anthropocentrism and ecocentrism, and as such an African environmental ethic may offer the best way to understand her eighth capability.

Secondly, though anthropocentric in some sense, African environmental ethics withstands the major criticisms levied against anthropocentrism. For instance, Routley[1] (1973) famous argument of the "last man" stands to show what is unsatisfactory about anthropocentric positions. Routley (1973: 19) develops a thought experiment in which there has been a world-wide catastrophe, and there remains only one last surviving man, who then goes about "eliminating, as far as he can, every living thing, animal, or plant". Considering that his elimination of natural entities does not stand to affect humans in any way (since he will soon die and there will be no one after him to experience the effects), Routley goes on to explain that what the last man does cannot be considered wrong from a human centred theory of value. However, there is a strong intuition that what he does is wrong. This leads Routley (1973: 23) to conclude that "human interests and preferences are far too parochial to provide a satisfactory basis for deciding on what is environmentally desirable".

African environmental ethics, however, would certainly not suggest that it is acceptable to destroy the natural world, even in the absence of humans. The last man would be no less bound to respect harmonious relations between himself and

---

[1] Now Richard Sylvan.

the natural world, and destroying every remaining form of life would be a gross vio-lation of the notion of Ubuntu as it pertains to his relation with the biotic community.

As Norton (1984: 135) points out, there are in fact two sorts of ways that a value theory can be anthropocentric, a strong and a weak way, where only the for-mer involves the "extractive and exploitative reasons". The latter can in fact offer a "framework for developing powerful reasons for protecting nature" (Norton 1984: 135). There is a growing attempt to develop theories that involve a weak anthro-pocentricism, or what Brennan and Lo (2016: §1) also call "enlightened anthro-pocentrism". Enlightened anthropocentric position can provide an adequate moral basis for practical environmental protection, and African environmental ethics seems to be anthropocentric in this sense.

Thirdly, while anthropocentrism has been blamed as the root cause of the cur-rent environmental crises facing the world, this may not apply to the anthropocen-trism found in African environmental ethics. Exploitation and depletion of natural resources, destruction of the ozone layer, loss of biodiversity, pollution, species loss, and so on, are said to all be caused by the underlying belief that humankind has dominion over nature and can use and abuse it to satisfy its needs and wants. How-ever, African environmental ethics does not allow for unnecessary exploitation of the natural world, related to the fact that it is only anthropocentric in a weak or enlightened sense.

Kelbessa (2014: 48) speaks about how the environmental ethics of the Oromo of Ethiopia teaches that humans must look after domestic animals, saying that "do-mestic animals should not be severely maltreated. They should be allowed to graze healthily and continue to exist". The Oromo have also developed laws with accompa-nying punishments that ensure that domestic animals are not exposed to unnecessary cruelty. As an example, the Borana Orama have a law which states that a person is fined thirty head of cattle if found to have intentionally or accidently beaten a horse, mule or donkey that resulted in the animal's death (Kelbessa 2014: 49).

Though there is a recognised difference between humans, animals, plants and so on, this difference does not imply that humans have any special privilege allowing them to "subdue, dominate, and exploit the rest of creation" (Tangwa 2006: 390). It is believed that God makes animals, plants and the inanimate parts of the environment available for humankind to use, but Bujo (2009: 290) notes that this does not result in people being allowed to "treat the lesser forms of being arbitrarily". Rather, there is an attitude of "respectful coexistence" (Tangwa 2006: 390).

Fourth, Nussbaum's list was not designed with the intention of it being only food for thought. It is supposed to be practically useful, and a model for develop-ing constitutional principles. As Nussbaum (2011: 46) herself says, "development economics is not just an academic discipline; it has wide-ranging influence on our world. Reigning theories in the field influence the choices of political leaders and policy-makers". Policies may well be designed according to an understanding of Nussbaum's approach, and there would be vastly different types of environmental protection that would follow from differing interpretations of her capability. If it were interpreted by the instrumental-valuing economist, there would be no constitutionally supported protection against species extinction, loss of biodiversity and so on, assuming such events did not have significant effects on material human needs.

On the other extreme, if understood from the perspective of ecocentrism, then policies would be designed to radically reign in humankinds' use of nature, which would involve aiming to massively reduce human population size and to fundamentally change the structures of society. The public reception to such policies can be readily anticipated. Fairbanks (2010: 80) for one notes that the capitalist, consumer culture dominant today, especially in the United States, makes it exceptionally difficult—if not impossible—to successfully foster beliefs that attribute environmental value in a nonanthropocentrically motivated way.

Light (2002: 427) similarly explains that abstract arguments attempting to prove the intrinsic value of nature are too far removed from the types of arguments that morally motivate people to act in an environmentally conscious way. Instead, a practically realisable way of understanding Nussbaum's environmental capability "must allow that human beings belong on the planet too" (Hettinger 2002: 114).

Fifth, by employing a traditional African conception to further engage with Nussbaum's approach, there is an added benefit that follows. When looking for ways to respond to the environmental crisis, it can be helpful to look beyond Western views. Since the challenges facing the earth affect all humans globally, "it would therefore be a great mistake to think that the solution to these problems should be left to the Western world" (Tangwa 2006: 393). There is much that Western theories could gain from looking to indigenous and traditional theories. Kalu (2001: 244) speaks about the need to return to old values in order to face current development challenges, thereby "inspiring a greater respect for the land and its resources as something sacred". Kalu goes on to quote Northrop Frye when he said that the guide to the future is through a rearview mirror.

While it may not be fair to declare from the outset that Western or modern theories are inadequate to deal with the global environmental situation, African environmental ethics has been shown to come out on top for a variety of reasons as discussed above. Since this is the case, we can say that it is an added bonus that it happens to be a non-Western view that has been found to be most attractive, as it can contribute a perspective that has perhaps not yet been explored by Western theories. As Tangwa (2006: 391) notes, "African culture could, perhaps, show the way back to those natural human values that Western culture has sacrificed to the god of technology and industrialization and commerce, if, indeed, it ever had them".

14.5 Conclusion

This chapter has set out to show that African environmental ethics offers the most attractive way to conceptualise Nussbaum's eighth capability, or at least that should be taken seriously as a way to understand what it means to live with concern for and in relation to the world of nature. By adopting this position we are able to conceive of our relation with the environment in more than instrumental terms, but we are similarly still able to use and interact with nature in ways that are not excessively exploitative. It offers a middle ground between anthropocentrism and ecocentrism, and is theoretically and practically powerful as a result. Nussbaum has left it open to theorists to disentangle exactly what her eighth capability may mean and to determine its implications for policies. When attempting to do just that, it can be seen that African environmental ethics may hold the most promising position from which to begin.

References

Behrens, Kevin. 2010. Exploring African Holism with Respect to the Environment. *Environmental Values* 19 (4): 465–484.

Brennan, Andrew and Lo, Yeuk-Sze. 2016. Environmental Ethics. In *The Stanford Encyclopedia of Philosophy (Fall 2016 Edition)*, ed. Edward N. Zalta, Available at http://plato.stanford.edu/archives/fall2016/entries/ethics-environmental/.

Bujo, B. 2009. Ecology and Ethical Responsibility from an African Perspective. In *African Ethics: An Anthology of Comparative and Applied Ethics*, ed. M.F. Murove, 281–296. Pietermaritzburg: Interpak Books.

Devall, Bill, and George Sessions. 2002. Deep Ecology. In *Environmental Ethics: What Really Matters, What Really Works*, ed. D. Schmidtz and E. Willott, 120–126. New York: Oxford University Press.

Fairbanks, Sandra Jane. 2010. Environmental Goodness and the Challenge of American Culture. *Ethics and the Environment* 15 (2): 79–102.

Hettinger, Ned. 2002. The Problem of Finding a Positive Role for Humans in the Natural World. *Ethics & the Environment.* 7 (1): 109–123.

Holland, Breena, and Amy Linch. 2016. Cultivating Human and Non-Human Capabilities for Mutual Flourishing. In *The Oxford Handbook of Environmental Political Theory*, ed. T. Gabrielson, H. Cheryl, J.M. Meyer, and D. Schlosberg. Edited Oxford: Oxford University Press.

Kalu, Ogbu U. 2001. The Sacred Egg: Worldview, Ecology, and Development in West Africa. In *Indigenous Traditions and Ecology: The Interbeing of Cosmology and Community*, ed. John A. Grim, 225–247. Cambridge: Distributed by Harvard Press for the Center for the Study of World Religions, Harvard Divinity School.

Kelbessa, Workineh. 2014. Can African Environmental Ethics Contribute to Environmental Policy in Africa? *Environmental Ethics* 36: 31–61.

Light, Andrew. 2002. Contemporary Environmental Ethics from Metaethics to Public Philosophy. *Metaphilosophy* 33 (4): 426–449.

Metz, Thaddeus. 2016. Recent Philosophical Approaches to Social Protection: From Capability to *ubuntu*. *Global Social Policy.* 16 (2): 132–150.

Murove, M.F. 2009a. Beyond the savage evidence ethic. In *African Ethics: An Anthology of Comparative and Applied Ethics*, ed. M.F. Murove, 14–32. Pietermaritzburg: Interpak Books.

Murove, M.F. 2009b. An African Environmental Ethic Based on the Concepts of *Ukama* and *Ubuntu*. In *African Ethics: An Anthology of Comparative and Applied Ethics,* ed. M. F. Murove, 315–331. Pietermaritzburg: Interpak Books.

Naess, Arne. 1973. The shallow and the deep, long-range ecology movement. A summary. *Inquiry* 16 (1): 95–100.

Norton, Bryan G. 1984. Environmental Ethics and Weak Anthropocentrism. *Environmental Ethics* 6: 131–148.

Nussbaum, Martha C. 2000. *Women and Human Development: The Capabilities Approach.* New York: Cambridge University Press.

Nussbaum, Martha C. 2007a. *Frontiers of Justice: Disability, Nationality, Species Membership.* Cambridge: The Belknap Press of Harvard University Press.

Nussbaum, Martha C. 2007b. Foreword: Constitutions and Capabilities, 'Perception' Against Lofty Formalism. *Harvard Law Review* 121 (4): 4–97.

Nussbaum, Martha C. 2009. Creating Capabilities: The Human Development Approach and Its Implementation. *Hypatia* 24 (3): 211–215.

Nussbaum, Martha C. 2011. *Creating Capabilities: The Human Development Approach.* Cambridge: The Belknap Press of Harvard University Press.

Omari, C.K. 1992. Traditional African Land Ethics. In *Ethics of Environment and Development: Global Challenge, International Response*, ed. J.R. Engel and J.G. Engel, 167–175. London: Bellhaven Press.

Peterson, R.B. 2004. Central African Voices on the Human-Environment Relationship. In *This Sacred Earth: Religion, Nature, Environment*, 2nd ed, ed. R.S. Gottlieb, 168–174. New York: Routledge.

Poolman, Clare. 2012. Humanity in the Capabilities Approach to Development. *POLIS Journal* 7: 366–408.

Ramose, M.B. 2009. Ecology through *Ubuntu*. In *African Ethics: An Anthology of Comparative and Applied Ethics*, ed. M.F. Murove, 308–314. Pietermaritzburg: Interpak Books.

Routley, Richard. 1973. Is There a Need for a New, an Environmental, Ethic? In *Proceedings of the 15th World congress of Philosophy*, 1973, vol. 1, 205–10.

Sen, Amartya. 2003. Development as Capability Expansion. In *Readings in Human Development*, ed. S. Fukuda-Parr and A.K.S. Kumar. New York: Oxford University Press.

Tangwa, G.B. 1996. Bioethics: an African perspective. *Bioethics* 10 (3): 183–200.

Tangwa, G.B. 2006. Some African Reflections on Biomedical and Environmental Ethics. In *A Companion to African Philosophy*, ed. K. Wiredu, 387–395. Oxford: Blackwell Publishing.

Teffo, Lesiba J., and Abraham P.J. Roux. 1998. Metaphysical Thinking in Africa. In *Philosophy from Africa: A Text with Readings,* ed. Peter H. Coetzee and Abraham P. J. Roux, 134–148. Johannesburg: International Thomson Publishing Southern Africa.

Willott, Elizabeth, and David Schmidtz. 2002. Why Environmental Ethics? In *Environmental Ethics: What Really Matters, What Really Works*, ed. David Schmidtz and Elizabeth Willott. Oxford: Oxford University Press.

Part V
Questions of Animal Rights in African Philosophy

Chapter 15
Moral Status of Non-human Animals from an African Perspective: In Defense of Moderate Anthropocentric Thinking

Dennis Masaka

Abstract In this chapter, I argue that although African environmental ethics has been considered in some quarter as decisively anthropocentric in orientation, I differ slightly with this common conception and argue that it might be viable to consider it as moderately anthropocentric. I will then proceed to give reasons why I think so. At the same time, I do not intend to portray African environmental ethics as decidedly non-anthropocentric, that is, as moving towards considering non-human animals as morally equal to human beings. This is precisely out of the realisation that such an ideal relation seems not to be the objective of establishing harmonious co-existence between human beings and non-human animals. In defending the moderate anthropocentric view as the character of African environmental thinking, I am trying to suggest how it could be understood differently from its common conception as either decidedly anthropocentric or non-anthropocentric. For reasons of closer familiarity, I will use some examples from Zimbabwean environmental ethical perspective as I seek to defend the position that the moderate anthropocentric view seems to be a viable representation of the relations between human beings and nonhuman animals in African environmental ethics.

15.1 Introduction

In some quarters, the relation between the indigenous people of Africa and non-human animals has often been conceived as decisively anthropocentric (*see* Kelbessa 2005: 21; Ikuenobe 2014: 1; Okoye 2014: 139) meaning to say that only human beings are considered as the only bearers of intrinsic value and, therefore, as deserving to be treated with dignity and respect. *The thinking here is that African environmental ethics does not seem to regard non-human animals and the environment in general as entities that deserve to be accorded some rights and inherent value* (Callicott 1994: 158). *I seek to challenge this thesis mainly because it appears that the indigenous*

D. Masaka (✉)
Great Zimbabwe University, Masvingo, Zimbabwe
e-mail: dennis.masaka@gmail.com

© Springer Nature Switzerland AG 2019
M. Chemhuru (ed.), *African Environmental Ethics*, The International
Library of Environmental, Agricultural and Food Ethics 29,
https://doi.org/10.1007/978-3-030-18807-8_15

people of Africa indeed extend[1] *some moral status to non-human animals and the environment.*

Yet some have tended to regard the indigenous people of Africa's relations with non-human animals as decidedly non-anthropocentric, that is, as oriented towards treating non-human realities as their moral equals (Chuka 2012: 272). I do not subscribe to this position either for the prime reason that it is inconceivable to think of such levels of parity between human beings and non-human beings especially when one refers to the real world of relations between these two groups of beings. I argue that though this level of parity is believable, it is unattainable. What it means is that in this chapter, I am not accepting both the radical anthropocentric and non-anthropocentric positions as the only available alternative positions for explaining the relations between human beings and non-human animals in Africa.

In place of these dominant and common positions, I offer a slightly different perspective and argue that human beings' relations with non-human animals is neither decisively anthropocentric nor non-anthropocentric but may be conceived as falling within the category of moderate anthropocentric relations. Though there are some who have defended the position that is similar to the one that I am defending in the present chapter (*see* Hassoun 2010: 27), I feel that by conceiving African environmental ethics as moderately anthropocentric, I intend to understand it differently from how it is presently understood. I then proceed to given reasons why I think so. I will argue that the moderate anthropocentric view seems to be a viable understanding of the relations between human beings and nonhuman animals in African environmental ethics in general. My view is that some rights can still be extended to non-human animals and the environment even when they are not necessarily considered as "moral equals" with human beings.

Though, I subscribe to the moderate anthropocentric view as the defining character of African environmental ethics, I still think that African environmental ethics extends some rights to non-human animals. In this chapter, by rights, I mean some entitlements both negative and positive that ought to be extended to non-human animals and the rest of the environment such as the right to life, the right to a livable environment and the right not to be abused. My conception of rights is essentially broader than that of Rolston, III (1996: 165) who limits rights to human beings only when he claims that "rights is a way of celebrating and guarding what is essentially human." My view is that an African environmental ethic understood as moderately anthropocentric might still allow extension of some rights to non-human animals.

---

[1] I find it necessary, from the onset, to justify why I think that it is human beings who actually extend some moral value to non-human animals. Even though it might be acceptable that they indeed have inherent value independent of what human beings consider them to be, I still think that it is human beings who speak about such values based on their thoughts about non-human animals and their moral status. Because human beings are the ones who pronounce certain segments of or the environment as a whole as having moral value, I maintain that it is proper to speak of human beings extending moral status to them. The thinking that non-human animals have moral status independent of what human beings consider them to be, and that perhaps that they consider themselves as having inherent value might be subject to debate especially if one considers that it is not non-human animals' perspective that is at play here but that of human beings.

I start by noting that the relation between human beings and non-humans in Africa is often conceived as decisively anthropocentric in nature. I will attempt to highlight what I consider the reasons in defense of this common contention and their relative plausibility. Yet there are some who would want to consider this relation as non-anthropocentric. I will discuss this contention in the second section. In the third section, I attempt to show why I think that this relation is neither decidedly anthropocentric nor non-anthropocentric. I then suggest that perhaps it is viable to conceive of this relation as moderately anthropocentric in orientation and import. I will give reasons for holding this position. My view is that holding this position does not necessarily discount the possibility of non-human animals having moral status and rights that human beings ought to respect and uphold.

15.2 Relations Between Humans and Non-human Animals as Anthropocentric

In this section, I seek to consider the view that has gained currency in some quarters that African environmental ethics is decidedly anthropocentric in terms of its orientation and import in the sense that it appears to confer inherent value to human beings only while at the same conferring instrumental value to the environment and what is in it (Horsthemke 2015: 93; Chemhuru 2017: 17). The objective is to establish reasons for such a contention and my reasons for thinking that such a perspective does not seem to reflect the import of African environmental ethics. In particular, with respect to the relations between human beings and nonhuman animals, African environmental ethics has been conceived as principally human-centred for the reason that it prioritises the interests of human beings over those of non-human animals and the environment in general.

The assumed anthropocentric nature of African environmental ethics is often conceived as in conflict with the non-anthropocentric view. And at times, the very existence of African environmental ethics is contested. As Callicott (1994: 156) argues, "on the other hand, mention of African culture evokes no thoughts of indigenous African environmental ethics." Even when its existence is accepted, the tendency has been to regard it as fundamentally centred on the pursuit of human interests at the expense of those of non-human animals and the environment in general. In this respect, Callicott (1994: 158) argues that:

> African thought orbits, seemingly, around human interests. Hence one might expect to distill from it no more than a weak and indirect environmental ethic, similar to the type of ecologically enlightened utilitarianism, focused on long-range human welfare.

What can be discerned from Callicott's (1994: 158) characterisation of African environmental ethics is that the indigenous people of Africa may not have an ethic that takes into consideration the welfare and wellbeing of the environment and what is in it. Callicott's (1994: 158) use of term "seemingly", in characterising the indigenous people of Africa's supposed commitment to the environment or lack of it might mean that he is not so sure that indeed African environmental ethics is fundamentally anthropocentric.

In my view, it might turn to be the case that there are no people in this world who are exclusively anthropocentric in terms of their relations with the environment. Now, it might be necessary to attempt at defining the anthropocentric view. In fact, what I refer to as the anthropocentric view is commonly referred to as the "anthropocentrism". As defined by Goralnik and Nelson (2012: 145):

> anthropocentrism literally means human-centered, but in its most relevant philosophical form it is the ethical belief that humans alone possess intrinsic value. In contradistinction, all other beings hold value only in their ability to serve humans, or in their instrumental value. From an anthropocentric position, humans possess direct moral standing because they are ends in and of themselves; other things (individual living beings, systems) are means to human ends.

For the purposes of this chapter, I will use the term "anthropocentrism" sparingly because of the supposed immutability that seems to subsist in any concept that is considered as an "-ism" (see Ramose 2009: 308). In light of this, I prefer to use the term "anthropocentric view" as opposed to "anthropocentrism". I would like to understand the anthropocentric view as a position that privileges human beings with intrinsic worth while the environment and what resides in it, are taken as having instrumental value. This may not be taken to mean that human beings are bound not to extend some respect to the environment though. A thing or being has intrinsic worth if it is important in itself. It is a being that ought to be treated with dignity and respect. On the other hand, a being has extrinsic or instrumental value if it is not important in itself but derives its importance by virtue of it being of use to a being that has intrinsic worth. So, its value or importance does not really reside in itself but in terms of how it could be used to advance or attain the goals and interests of a being that has intrinsic worth. If non-human animals were understood as having instrumental value, it would then mean that they would become important barely by virtue of their value as mere means to human beings' purposes.

However, it might be contestable to regard African environmental ethics as exclusively anthropocentric especially in the light of the fact that, to some extent, non-human animals and the environment in general appear to be granted some level of intrinsic and moral importance as entities that ought to exist independent of human beings. I want to think that some level of dependency of human beings on non-human animals and the environment in general could not be taken as implying that human beings are then expected to consider them as having instrumental value. Perhaps, when we consider human beings and how they depend on the environment in general as part of the workings of the ecosystem, then it might not be viable to consider their actions and non-actions as exclusively human-centered. Their use of the environment could be understood as quite in line with the proper function of the ecosystem. In this light, I argue that it might be prejudicial to argue as Callicott (1994: 158) does in regard to the assumed character of African environmental ethics especially when one considers that any environmental ethic that is in existence is an outcome of human creation.

The fact that any environmental ethic is a creation of human beings is important in understanding the relations that presently subsist between human beings and non-human animals. Is it then possible for humans to construct such an environmental ethic that ushers the supposed ideal parity and fairness that would ensure the expected co-existence between human beings and non-human animals? My take is that neither the indigenous people of Africa nor any other peoples from other geopolitical centres may produce such an environmental ethic. As Chemhuru (2017: 17) argues, "rather, totally rejecting anthropocentric environmental ethics would be unreasonable and problematic." In this regard, since any environmental ethic that is supposed to govern the interaction between human beings and non-human animals is crafted by humans, it might be too hopeful to expect it to be impartial to the levels that some might want. Even though a given environmental ethic may extent moral consideration to non-human animals and the environment in general, the ideal impartiality in terms of the worth extended to both human beings and non-humans may not be attainable.

The tendency might be for human beings to define and design the environmental ethic in such as way that it places their interests higher than those of non-human animals and the environment in general. Since such an environmental ethic is a product of human beings and how they seek to see the status of the environment in relation to human beings, it could be expected to favour the interests of its authors, that is, human beings. This is expected given the rather "innate" attribute of human beings to favour their interests over those of any other realities. I think that it is not peculiar to Africa that an environmental ethic is a human pronouncement on how humans ought to relate to the environment in general. Even though the levels of concern for the environment may differ from place to place and from time to time, it might be presumptive to regard African environmental ethics as exclusively anthropocentric in nature. Yet, as I argue, perhaps only gods might be in a position to design such an environmental ethic that enables the ideal levels of dignity and respect to be extended to both humans and non-human animals.

In fact, by virtue of its naming as "environmental ethics", it might mean that it is human beings' perspective on how they ought to relate to the environment in their day to day existence. In this light, environmental ethics so conceived is not an outcome of dialogue or a contract of some kind between human beings and the environment leading to a consensual position of an ethic that ought to govern their relations, if at all such a dialogue is possible. So, the so-called "environmental ethics" could be nothing more than a one-directional perspective of how human beings consider as their view of how they have to relate to non-human animals and the environment in general. Is it then reasonable to expect human beings to design an ethic that informs their relation with the environment that is objective and unbiased? I do not think so. In this respect, it is necessary to distinguish between what is ideal and what is achievable. It might sound ideal and fashionable to consider non-human animals as deserving the same kind of moral status that is extended to human beings.

Yet it has been largely proven impossible to attain such levels of moral equality anywhere. Perhaps what might be achievable could be try to lessen the gap between human beings and non-human animals in terms of the dignity and respect extended to them: a gap that seems to favour human beings. And what could be ideal and unachievable is to pretend that the elusive parity between human beings and non-human animals can be attained. I will pursue this argument later in this chapter.

Given the foregoing, it might be necessary to challenge the extent to which the indigenous people of Africa consider the welfare and wellbeing of non-human animals as inherently important and worth of respecting. In real terms, the complaints about the anthropocentric view seem to be focused on its tendency to extend marginal moral status to non-human animals and not with total disregard of their moral status altogether. Perhaps this issue can be debated as one seeks to establish the extent to which a given environmental ethic could be said to give sufficient or insufficient attention to non-human animals. In this light, it appears contentious to regard any environmental ethic as exclusively, "human-centred" (Hayward 1997: 57).

That being the case, the understanding of some theories of environmental ethics as "human-centered" could be put to question especially when one considers that, throughout history, humans themselves have not shown some serious intentions and commitment to establish moral parity between and among themselves. If anything, there is evidence of asymmetrical relations within and across human races and ethnic groups based on the assumed superiority and privilege of one group of people over the others. As Hayward (1997: 121) argues:

> on the contrary, a cursory glance around the world would confirm that humans show a lamentable lack of interest in the well-being of other humans. Moreover, even when it is not other humans whose interests are being harmed, but other species or the environment, it would generally be implausible to suggest that those doing the harm are being 'human-centred'.

To uncritically understand an environmental ethic as "human-centred" would give the impression that such an ethic is focused on fulfilling the interest of the whole genus of human beings per se. But, as shown by Hayward (1997: 121; *see also* Callicott 1980: 313), such generalisations are not warranted.

It might actually turn out that even if we are to regard environmental ethics as human-centred, very few from the genus of human beings are benefitting from the irresponsible use of the environment (Burchett 2014: 121). As Rolston, III (1996: 162) argues, "those who are not at peace with one another find it difficult to be at peace with nature and vice versa. Those who exploit persons will typically exploit nature as readily-animals, plants, species, ecosystems, and Earth itself." Yet, I maintain that, it might not be correct to deny completely the fact that human beings indeed show some level of moral concern for non-human animals and the environment in general. In this light, I think that an anthropocentric view understood as a "human-centred" position that totally disregards the welfare and wellbeing of non-human animals (Burchett 2014: 122) does not reflect African thinking about the environment. Yet, some might want to understand African environmental ethics as decidedly non-anthropocentric. I now proceed to present this position. I will share my reservations with such a position thereafter.

15.3 Conceiving Relations Between Humans and Non-human Animals as Non-anthropocentric

In response to the thinking that African environmental ethics is anthropocentric, some who are sympathetic to this ethic have argued that it is actually non-anthropocentric in terms of its treatment of non-human animals and the environment in general (Chuka 2012: 272). I will pursue this thesis here. I will later offer my reservations with such a position. By definition, non-anthropocentrism means the view that human beings and non-human animals have values inherent in themselves as separate entities that ought, as of necessity, to be respected and accepted as such.

As Kelbessa (2015: 143–144; *see also* 2005: 19) argues, "…non-anthropocentric ethics teaches that other beings, in addition to human beings, have value in themselves. Human beings are required to sacrifice some of their well-being out of consideration for the value of animals, species, and ecosystems." The thinking that African environmental ethics is non-anthropocentric could be intended to create the kind of relations between human beings and the environment that treats them as equal in terms of moral importance and perhaps inherent value. I think that if the non-anthropocentric view is conceived as a negation of the anthropocentric view, then perhaps it ought to be conceived as speaking to the need to bestow intrinsic worth to non-human animals that continue to be sidelined from the genus that ought to be treated as such. That being the case, the non-anthropocentric view ought to be seen as reversing the supposed mistakes that the anthropocentric view makes with respect to how human beings relate to non-human animals and the environment in general.

Yet, as I argue, there is a sense in which the assumed non-anthropocentric stance of African environmental ethics does not reflect African thinking about the environment (Grim 1997: 145). Perhaps, to my knowledge, the lack of some published works that decidedly spell out African environmental ethics as keen on extending intrinsic worth to non-human animals and the environment at large could distract efforts to build a strong case for a non-anthropocentric African environmental ethics in present day Africa. I will tap into the some works that are in existence as I seek to extract the implied non-anthropocentric stance of African environmental ethics and perhaps give credence to the view that African environmental ethics is often conceived as non-anthropocentric.

Though the temptation could be to envisage the extension of exclusive inherent value to non-human animals, this might not be possible given the apparent interdependence of human beings and non-human animals. For example, in as much as human beings depend on non-human animals for say food, there is also a sense in which some non-human animals depend on human beings for food. Perhaps, this could be conceptualised as the workings of nature. Nevertheless, this might not be taken as implying that both human beings and non-human animals are expendable and devoid of intrinsic moral value. I think that a non-anthropocentric view might not be construed as advocating for the total non-use of nonhuman animals and the environment in general for human purposes. Conceived thus, such a non-anthropocentric view might not do justice to the workings of nature which seems to dictate that beings found in the environment are interdependent on each other for their respective sustenance, welfare and wellbeing.

But, even if it is acceptable that human beings and nonhuman animals are dependent on each other for their sustenance, I think that it is also important to consider that non-human animals have inherent moral value independent of whatever actual or perceived use to human beings. I would like to think that this understanding of a non-anthropocentric ethics is quite reasonable. It is also worth noting that "according to some indigenous people, the non-human world is not only considered to be instrumentally valuable, it has its own inherent value given to it by God. So, human beings are not permitted to destroy it for whatever reasons they wish" (Kelbessa 2015: 145). Kelbessa (2005: 21) refers to the Oromo of Ethiopia in order to show that Africans do not only respect the wellbeing of human beings but also that of non-human beings. In this light, I am tempted to consider Kelbessa's (2015: 21) contention here as inclined towards a non-anthropocentric view of African environmental ethics.

Though the source of this inherent value may not be *one* given that some might think that nonhuman animals have inherent value by virtue of having life, one important lesson that might be derived from Kelbessa's (2015: 145) position is that non-human animals ought to be treated with dignity and respect because they do have intrinsic worth. The implication of such a position is that human beings ought not to treat non-human animals and the environment in general as their morally inferior counterparts. The rank ordering of entities in the environment that places human beings as having dominion over the rest of the environment would thus fall away if some level of parity between human beings and nonhuman animals were to be established. As a result, a decidedly instrumental use of non-human animals for human purposes would become untenable.

However, it remains to be seen whether some beings in the environment are bound by the same commitment to respect the inherent value immanent in their kind, the rest of the environment and in human beings. Granted that this is possible and attainable, perhaps the relations between human beings and the environment in general would lead to a scenario that is closer to a non-anthropocentric interdependence of beings in the environment.

In the light of the foregoing, could it be possible then to think of the non-anthropocentric view as a viable position that could be used to extend inherent moral value to non-human animals in Africa? While the non-anthropocentric view appears convincing as a basis for extending inherent value to non-human animals, there is a sense in which what it seeks to achieve is largely unachievable. In my view, it appears to be the character of human beings' relations with non-human animals that their interests are given precedence over those of non-human animals. Even though this might not necessarily mean the disregard of the interests of non-human animals all together as one seeks the attainment of human interests, still it appears as if human beings are primarily motivated by the desire to pursue human interests and perhaps less on extending moral consideration to non-human animals. And in my view, this perspective seems not to be defined by geography but appears to be the character of human beings' relation with non-human animals across cultures. I now proceed to defend it. I refer to it as the "moderate" anthropocentric view. I consider it as perhaps the most viable position that might be closer to a description of the relations between human beings and the environment in African environmental ethics.

15.4 In Defense of the "Moderate" Anthropocentric View

Much of what has been written about African environmental ethics either classifies it as decidedly anthropocentric or as non-anthropocentric. Yet, so far, I have argued that both the anthropocentric and non-anthropocentric views appear not to reflect the true or closer picture of what African environmental ethics is. Perhaps a compromise position that I call "moderate" anthropocentric view might turn out to be a closer description of the relations between human beings and non-human animals in African environmental thinking. I now proceed to give reasons why I think the "moderate" anthropocentric view could be a viable description of African environmental ethics. In doing so, examples from the indigenous people of Zimbabwe are going to be invoked in partly justifying my contention that African environmental ethics is "moderately" anthropocentric. With in mind the fact that Africa is home to diverse people who may have, in some sense, diverse ways of relating to the environment, I think that, in a fundamental sense, there remains a lot in terms of the general orientation of African environmental ethics that is shared by these peoples across Africa.

By "moderate" anthropocentric environmental ethic, I mean an ethic that is significantly focused on promoting human interests but at the same time concerned about some interests and rights of non-human animals and the environment in general. In such an ethic, human interests are given preferential consideration while those of the rest of the environmental are albeit respected but may be set aside in pursuit of human interests. Indeed, the interests and rights of non-human animals and the environment are respected but may not necessarily be equated to human interests and rights.

In this light, I take the philosophy of *ubuntu*, whose foremost exponent is Ramose (1999), and the philosophy of *ukama*, as expounded by Murove (2009), as positions that, to some extent, could be invoked to support the moderate anthropocentric view that I defend in this chapter. In espousing the concept of *ubuntu*, Ramose (2009: 308–309) considers it a "humanness" which thus understood opens possibilities for motion and change to the way things are presently conceived or are. In this light, humane relations ought to guide interactions between the individual and others in the community. For Ramose, *ubuntu* entails the principle of wholeness whereby an individual is incomplete without others. And by extension:

> the principle of wholeness applies also to the relation between human beings and physical or objective nature. To care for one another, therefore, implies caring for physical nature as well. Without such care, the interdependence between human beings and physical nature would be undermined. Moreover, human beings are indeed an intrinsic part of physical nature although possibly a privileged part. Accordingly, caring for one another is the fulfilment of the natural duty to care for physical nature too. The concept of harmony in African thought is comprehensive in the sense that it conceives of balance in terms of the totality of the relations

that can be maintained between and among human beings, as well as between human beings and physical nature. The quest for harmony is thus the striving to maintain a comprehensive but specific relational condition among organism and entities (Ramose 1999: 309).

A critical reading of this quoted passage might give the impression that though some level of concern could be extended to the physical world, human beings require special treatment compared to the rest of the physical world by virtue of being its "privileged" part. In fact, caring relationships between and among human beings appear to be given first grade rating while the caring of the physical nature proceeds and is anchored on it.

Yet, having a "natural duty" to care for the physical world might entail responsibility that ought to be carried out without prejudice. Nevertheless, another reading of the same passage might imply that if human beings are possibly the source of the moral code that ought to guide their interaction with non-human animals, then perhaps they themselves ought to treat each other with dignity and respect. The reasoning here is that if some level of parity between human beings were to be established, then perhaps, as a collective they could then have a firm commitment to the extension of some inherent value to both human and non-human beings. As I have argued earlier, this appears to be a hindrance to the commitment to genuine extension of intrinsic status to non-human animals and the environment in general. In fact, prejudicial treatment of other human beings along the lines of race, ethnicity, gender, physical and mental status continues to characterise the human race.

Perhaps, human beings, as self-appointed authors of the environmental ethic that extends moral consideration to non-human animals ought, as part of efforts to establish moral parity between different parts of the environment, to ensure that inherent value is also extended to humanity irrespective of race, ethnicity and gender. By arguing thus, I am not subscribing to the thinking that non-human animals and the environment in general, as it, were ought to be given second thought when it comes to treating them as entities that deserve to be accorded inherent value. In fact, in some quarters, it appears that non-human animals and the rest of the environment are treated qualitatively better than is done to some humans. Yet, the objective of a non-anthropocentric ethics is to establish parity in terms of inherent value extended to various parts of the environment in a relational way. But for this to be attainable, it is necessary to put to question human beings' claim that they occupy the centre of the universe and thereby deserving some privileged treatment (Ramose 2009: 311).

Closely connected to Ramose's (1999) philosophy of *ubuntu* is Murove's (2009) philosophy of *ukama*. A brief overview of Murove's (2009) philosophy of *ukama* might be necessary before I attempt to establish how it and Ramose's (1999) philosophy of *ubuntu* could be employed in defense of moderate anthropocentric view that I plead for here. For Murove (2009: 316), *ukama* is the Shona word for "relatedness" and can be joined with *ubuntu* to produce an ethical position that takes into consideration the interests of both human beings and the environment in general. As Murove (2009: 315–316) argues:

when these two concepts are compounded, together they provide an ethical outlook that suggests that human well-being is indispensable from our dependence on, and interdependence with, all that exists and particularly with the immediate environment on which all humanity depends. Were this to be developed as an environmental ethic appropriate to the contemporary world it would inspire people north and south to combat threats of pollution and environmental degradation.

A combination of the two is considered to produce bright promises of indissoluble solidarity between human beings and the natural world. A point that both Ramose (2009) and Murove (2004: 207) seem to share is the relational nature of humanity's co-existence with the environment. Yet, as I will argue, in their conception of human beings' relation with nature, they both seem to consider human beings as superior "partners" in this co-existence. An elaboration might be necessary here. In the case of Ramose (2009: 309), human beings are indeed part of the physical nature but they are perhaps its "privileged" part. If the relation between human beings and nature is understood thus, then perhaps human beings are, to some degree, superior to the rest of the environment. Perhaps, this might not necessarily mean that they deserve differential treatment from the one accorded to non-human animals and the environment in general. Yet, if human beings are a "privileged" part of the physical nature, then perhaps, they may require some level of treatment that may not necessarily be extended to the rest of the environment.

Whereas for Murove (2009: 317), "among Africans, *Ukama* provides the ethical anchorage for human social, spiritual and ecological togetherness." However, it remains to be established whether by this reasoning, inherent value could possibly be extended to non-human animals and the environment in general through the philosophy of *ukama* understood as "relatedness". It is important to note that Ramose (2009: 309) also speaks of the importance of caring relations between human beings and the physical world. One could be tempted to think that *ubuntu* and *ukama* can be used to defend the moderate anthropocentric view. The reasoning here is that the caring relations between human beings and the physical world could lead to the extension of some moral status to non-human animals without necessarily seeing them as human beings' moral equals.

Yet, its pronounced emphasis on human relations has led some into thinking that African environmental ethics is decidedly anthropocentric in orientation and import (Behrens 2010: 468). A good example is Horsthemke (2015: 11) who argues that "in fact, in focusing exclusively on human beings, *ubuntu* is by definition anthropocentric, as is the slogan *batho pele*-'people first'." Such a contention appears quite viable and reasonable especially if one considers that *ubuntu* and its cognates such as *ukama* are primarily concerned with human relations and secondarily with relations between human beings and the environment at least as implied in Ramose (2009) and Murove's (2009) relational thesis. I do not necessarily think that the indigenous people of Africa who have constructed and are informed by the philosophy of *ubuntu* and *ukama* are decidedly anthropocentric in their treatment of the environment in general. What could be contestable is the extent to which a viable and sound environmental ethic could be said to proceed and flow from the brilliant philosophy of *ubuntu* and *ukama*. I think *ubuntu* and *ukama* may not be viable basis for constructing relations that are anchored on the imperative to extent some moral status to both human beings and the environment.

That being the case, the relations between human beings and the environment might require further substantiation so that it becomes clear how such relations really captures the spirit of *ubuntu* and *ukama*. In other words, there is still much to be done in transferring an inter-human ethic to the sphere of human beings' relations with non-human beings. As Rolston, III (1998: 124) argues, "nature is amoral; the moral community is interhuman." I would like to think that *ubuntu* and *ukama* ought to involve and invoke some level of reciprocity between and among the "related" beings. Perhaps, such reciprocity might only be possible between beings that have certain fundamental qualities in common. In addition, it ought to proceed and be anchored on dialogue between parties to the relation: a requirement that I think may not be attainable.

Granted that such dialogue is unattainable, it might then turn out to be a challenge to talk of relations between human beings and the environment in the sense in which I understand the term in this chapter. But, as I have argued earlier, any environmental ethic that is presently in existence do not seem to be a product of dialogue between human beings and the environment. Now, supposing my claim is acceptable, it might turn out that the assumed relations between human beings and the environment are none other than purely human constructs. Yet, *ubuntu* and *ukama* may not grant that moral equality to non-human animals and the environment as those who are sympathetic to the non-anthropocentric discourse might want to argue. At the same time, it appears contestable to assume that African environmental ethics does not at all extend some moral status to non-human animals.

A reference to a Shona proverb that, in its literal sense, pits human beings and non-human animals might help in justifying my contention here. This proverb goes: "Hapana chembwa tenzi wararira mutakura" which might be translated to mean "nothing is left for the dog if its master had to eat boiled grains as supper". In the context of the present discussion, I am not much interested in the deeper or hidden meaning of this proverb but with its literal import. Though in its deeper meaning, it might be understood as implying that in times of deprivations, the powerful and the mighty may prioritise their interests over those of the weaker ones, understood literally, this proverb seem to imply that when the worst comes to the worst, it is the interest of the non-human animals, and in this case, that of the dog that might be sacrificed. In its literal understanding, this proverb imply that the clinical parity between human beings and non-human animals that some envisage as the ideal might turn out to be far-fetched. Nevertheless, I do not think that this could be taken as implying that non-human animals are not entitled to be treated with dignity and respect even though the ideal parity between human beings and non-human animals that we may yearn for may not necessarily be possible in real life situations.

Indeed, among the indigenous people of Zimbabwe, human beings and non-human animals are not taken as moral equals per se. It appears that both are considered as having lives that are important in themselves though we may not rule out the temptation to value non-human animals and the environment in general in terms of how they could enhance human welfare and wellbeing. I would not take this as implying that African environmental ethics is decidedly anthropocentric in terms of its orientation and import. In fact, I want to think that perhaps, within the kingdom of non-human animals something similar to the anthropocentric perspective might characterise how they see human beings. Proceeding from the example of the dog, I think that the indigenous people of Zimbabwe in particular and Africa in general would want to or indeed consider non-human animals as beings whose interests are ranked lower than those of human beings. Yet, this cannot be taken as implying that they are necessarily excluded from the genus of beings that deserve to be treated with some level of dignity and respect. Analogically, even within the community of human beings, there are times when the interests of some human beings are sacrificed in pursuit of the interests of other beings. But, this might not necessarily mean that such human beings do not have moral status.

I take taboos as one of the sources of a sound environmental ethical thinking among the indigenous people of Zimbabwe and indeed elsewhere in Africa for the reason that they try to extend some moral status to non-human animals and the environment in general. This respect is not wholly tied to or defined by human interests. This respect is attained by attaching some form of misfortune, punishment or threat of it for those who may dare violate what I will regard as environment-related taboos. The fear of punishment will dissuade those who are wont to mistreat non-human animals and the environment in general. As a result, some level of respect is extended to non-human animals and the environment. Threats of misfortunes and punishment are invoked as possible outcomes for those who may be tempted to violate some rights of non-human animals and the environment. Though it may be contested that such misfortunes or punishments will indeed visit the culprits, my experience with the indigenous people of Zimbabwe, for example, at least shows that people are generally not keen in trying to put to test these taboos by violating them. So, in a sense, taboos can be used as a source of constructing a sound ethic that bestows some level of intrinsic worth to non-human animals and the rest of the environment.

In addition, the ascription of totems that identifies some groups of people with certain non-human species or other parts of the environment have been cited as another way of safeguarding the interests of the non-human beings and the rest of the environment among the indigenous people of Africa and elsewhere. It has been argued that the ascription of totems has the effect of creating some kind of harmonious and respectful co-existence between human beings and non-human animals and the environment. As Mangena (2015: 4) argues, "…the idea of totemism that motivates human beings to want to appropriate animal traits like courage, humility and cunningness shows that Zimbabweans are generally not anthropocentric in character." I take Mangena's (2015: 4) thesis as inclined towards the moderate anthropocentric view of African environmental ethics that I defend in this chapter. Yes, the rights of non-human animals and the environment in general might matter but if we are to be honest with facts on the ground, it is far-fetched to conceive of African environmental ethics as inclined to consider human beings and non-human animals as moral equals. Yet, at the same time, it appears quite reasonable to argue that African environmental ethics' relative bias towards human beings, does not at all totally discount the fact that non-human animals and the environment in general are entitled to rights *albeit* as mediated by human beings.

15.5   Conclusion

In this chapter, I have argued that African environmental ethics is neither decidedly anthropocentric nor non-anthropocentric in orientation and import as some would want to think. The position that I have actually defended here is that African environmental ethics might best be described as moderately anthropocentric. This conclusion is out of the realisation that in the real world of interaction between human beings and non-human animals, human beings are not necessarily inclined to create the kind of moral parity between them and non-human animals. I noted that, though it appears fashionable to consider an environmental ethic as intent on establishing moral equality between human beings and non-human animals, this could be a moral ideal that is yet to be realised if at all it is to be. I have stated that this does not necessarily mean that non-human animals and the environment in general are altogether denied some rights and some moral status.

References

Behrens, K. 2010. Exploring African Holism with Respect to the Environment. *Environmental Values* 19: 465–484.

Burchett, K. 2014. Anthropocentrism and Nature: An Attempt at Reconciliation. *Teoria* 2: 19–137.

Callicott, J.B. 1980. Animal Liberation: A Triangular Affair. *Environmental Ethics* 2: 311–338.

Callicott, J.B. 1994. *Earth's insights: A survey of ecological ethics from the Mediterranean basin to the Australian outback.* Berkeley: University of California Press.

Chemhuru, M. 2017. Elements of Environmental Ethics in Ancient Greek Philosophy. *Phronimon* 18: 15–30.

Chuka, O.A. 2012. From Traditionalism to Modernism: A Study of the Problem of Environment in Africa. *Open Journal of Philosophy* 2 (4): 272–276.

Goralnik, L., and M.P. Nelson. 2012. Anthropocentrism. In: *Encyclopedia of Applied Ethics*, 2nd ed., vol. 1, ed. R. Chadwick, 145–155. San Diego: Academic Press.

Grim, J.A. 1997. Indigenous Traditions and Ecological Ethics in 'Earth's Insights. *Worldviews* 1 (2): 139–149.

Hassoun, N. 2010. The Anthropocentric Advantage. *Research Showcase @ CMU* 1–44.

Hayward, T. 1997. Anthropocentrism: A Misunderstood Problem. *Environmental Values* 6 (1): 49–63.

Horsthemke, K. 2015. *Animals and African Ethics.* New York: Palgrave Macmillan.

Ikuenobe, P.A. 2014. Traditional African Environmental Ethics and Colonial Legacy. *International Journal of Philosophy and Theology* 2 (4): 1–21.

Kelbessa, W. 2005. The Rehabilitation of Indigenous Environmental Ethics in Africa. *Diogenes* 207: 17–34.

Kelbessa, W. 2015. Indigenous Knowledge and Its Contribution to Biodiversity Conservation. *UNESCO* 143–152.

Mangena, F. 2015. How Applicable is the Idea of Deep Ecology in the African Context? *Filosofia Theoretica: Journal of African Philosophy. Culture and Religions* 4 (1): 1–16.

Murove, M.F. 2004. An African Commitment to Ecological Conservation: The Shona Concepts of *Ukama* and *Ubuntu. The Mankind Quarterly* XLV (2): 195–215.

Murove, M.F. 2009. An African Environmental Ethic Based on the Concepts of Ukama and Ubuntu. In *African Ethics: An Anthology of Comparative and Applied Ethics*, ed. M.F. Murove, 315–331. Scottsville: University of KwaZulu-Natal Press.

Okoye, C.A. 2014. An Evaluation of the Evolved African Conception of the Environment. *African Identities* 12 (2): 139–151.

Ramose, M.B. 1999. *African philosophy through Ubuntu*. Harare: Mond Books.

Ramose, M.B. 2009. Ecology Through Ubuntu. In *African Ethics: An Anthology of Comparative and Applied Ethics*, ed. M.F. Murove, 308–314. Scottsville: University of KwaZulu-Natal Press.

Rolston III, H. 1996. Earth Ethics: A Challenge to Liberal Education. In *Earth Summit Ethics: Toward a Reconstructive Postmodern Philosophy of Environmental Education*, ed. J.B. Callicott and F.J.R. da Rocha, 161–192. Albany: State University of New York Press.

Rolston III, H. 1998. Challenges in Environmental Ethics. In: Environmental Philosophy: From Animal Rights to Radical Ecology, 2nd ed., Michael E. Zimmerman, J. Baird Callicott, George Sessions, Karen J. Warren, and John Clark, 124–144. Upper Saddle River, NJ: Prentice Hall.

Chapter 16
Animal Rights and Environmental Ethics in Africa: From Anthropocentrism to Non-speciesism?

Kai Horsthemke

Abstract The claim is frequently made on behalf of African moral beliefs and customs that African cultures do not involve objectification and exploitation of nature and natural organisms, unlike Western (or Northern) moral attitudes and practices. Through exploration of what kind of moral status is reserved for other-than-human animals in African ethics, I argued in my recent book *Animals and African Ethics* that moral perceptions, attitudes and practices on the African continent have tended to be resolutely anthropocentric, or human-centred. Although values like *ubuntu* (humanness) and *ukama* (relationality) have, in recent years, been expanded to include non-human nature, animals characteristically have no rights, and human duties to them are almost exclusively 'indirect'. Taking into account the brutal and dehumanising ravages of colonialism, racism and political, cultural and moral apartheid that Africans have historically been subjected to, it does not seem to be wholly off the mark to invite people in sub-Sahara Africa, especially, to reflect on an even longer, more deeply-entrenched historical process of discrimination, oppression and exploitation, namely that of species apartheid. Yet, adoption of a more enlightened stance *vis-à-vis* the non-human world and animals in particular would almost certainly involve giving up the moral anthropocentrism that characterises many attitudes and practices on the African continent. This need not entail surrendering what is arguably at the core of sub-Saharan morality—the emphasis on community and harmonious communal relationships. 'I am because we are' could reasonably be interpreted as not being confined to the human realm, as transcending the species barrier. I have in mind here something like a relational approach to animal rights and environmental ethics that is neither anthropocentric nor speciesist. The multifarious historical and geographical relationships we have with other-than-human animals give rise to a multitude of moral obligations that differ according to the kinds of relationships we find ourselves in. There is an increasing awareness among African scholars of the untenability of a rigidly species-governed 'us-against-them' thinking, that anthropocentrism shares many relevant features with ethnocentrism, and that speciesism

K. Horsthemke (✉)
KU Eichstätt-Ingolstadt, Eichstätt, Germany
e-mail: kai.horsthemke@gmail.com

© Springer Nature Switzerland AG 2019
M. Chemhuru (ed.), *African Environmental Ethics*, The International
Library of Environmental, Agricultural and Food Ethics 29,
https://doi.org/10.1007/978-3-030-18807-8_16

is relevantly like racism. It is my aim in the proposed contribution to explore these ideas and conceptual tools in more detail.

16.1 Introduction: African Attitudes Towards Non-human Nature

The claim has frequently been made on behalf of African moral beliefs and customs that African cultures do not involve objectification and exploitation of nature and natural organisms, unlike Western (or Northern) moral attitudes and practices. For example, in the words of Zimbabwean novelist Chenjerai Hove, Africans

> Have neither catalogued nature nor pinned it down and preserved it in formaldehyde. We see it differently and speak to and about it differently. (Quoted in Grill 2003: 363[1]; my translation)

The most comprehensive account of traditional African perceptions of and interaction with the non-human world has been provided by Mutwa (1996), who stresses that in the past, Africa people did not regard them selves as being above the animals, birds, fish and trees. Through exploration of what kind of moral status is reserved for other-than-human animals in African ethics, I argued in my recent book (Horsthemke 2015) that moral perceptions, attitudes and practices on the African continent have tended to be resolutely anthropocentric, or human-centred. Although values like *ubuntu* (humanness) and *ukama* (relationality) have, in recent years, been expanded to include non-human nature, animals characteristically have no rights, and human duties to them are almost exclusively 'indirect'.

Taking into account the brutal and dehumanising ravages of colonialism, racism and political, cultural and moral apartheid that Africans have historically been subjected to, it does not seem to be inappropriate to invite people in sub-Sahara Africa, especially, to reflect on an even longer, more deeply-entrenched historical process of discrimination, oppression and exploitation, namely that of species apartheid. There is an increasing awareness among African scholars of the untenability of a rigidly species-governed 'us-against-them' thinking, that anthropocentrism shares many relevant features with ethnocentrism, and that speciesism is relevantly like racism. It is my aim in the proposed contribution to explore these ideas and conceptual tools in more detail. Before I do so, I briefly survey the aspects and elements of African ethics that prompted my initial diagnosis of anthropocentrism.

---

[1]Bartholomäus Grill, a long-time Africa correspondent for the German weekly newspaper *Die Zeit*, does not provide a source here. While I have not been able to find this quotation or anything resembling it in English, I rely here on the accuracy of Grill's initial translation into German and assume it reflects Hove's actual view.

16.2 A Survey of African Ethical Concerns Regarding Animals and the Environment

16.2.1 African Creation Myths and the Hierarchy of Being

Many diverse creation myths have been transmitted over many centuries through the living, immediate medium of African orality. While these creation myths are distinct from one another, there are certain commonalities between African religions. For example, the hierarchy of beings invariably places animals in an inferior position to humans. Morality is a matter of human relationships, with God, the ancestors (IsiZulu:*amadlozi*) or 'living dead' (IsiZulu:*abaphansi*) and non-human creation. The ancestors play a vital role in the lives of Africans in that they act as a link between God and living human beings. They are consulted regularly during ceremonies at which animals are routinely slaughtered. Failure to engage in such sacrificial activities is believed to provoke the wrath not only of the ancestors but also of God (see Mbiti 1969; Taringa 2006).

16.2.2 The African Ritual of Animal Slaughter

Rituals of sacrificial slaughter constitute a widespread practice on the African continent, as a part of all kinds of religious, traditional or cultural ceremonies. This was most starkly demonstrated in the recent killing of a sheep on Clifton Beach in Cape Town, for the alleged purpose of cleansing the terrain of colonial subjugation. Sacrifices and offerings may be directed not only to God but also to the spirits and the ancestors, for purposes of healing, to revive or restore relationships between the living and the ancestors, on the one hand, and the spiritual world, on the other. Living human beings communicate with the dead by regular sacrifice and invocation. The kind of animal to be slaughtered varies with the respective social and economic circumstances (see the CRL reports of 2002 and 2009, respectively).

16.3 Traditional African Perceptions and Current Practices—Taboos, Totemism and Spiritualism

Traditional African perceptions of and interaction with the non-human world usually emphasise that in the past, Africa people did not regard themselves as being above the animals, birds, fish and trees. Yet, carefully analysed, it is evident that the 'value' of, and basis of 'respect' for, wild animals—like domestic animals—is determined by their function in the lives of human beings, their purpose and the use to which they are put by human beings, more often than not guided by superstition. Thus,

Munamato Chemhuru and Dennis Masaka's account of taboos in Shona environmental ethics (2010; see also Taringa 2006) illustrates a manifestly anthropocentric
ethic of sustainable use of non-human resources. 'Taboos' here, correctly seen, are
the expression of human superstition and have little to do with the animals themselves. The taboos placed on killing certain animals are frequently arbitrary, and one
clan's totem animal often turns out to be another clan's favourite 'bush meat'.

16.4   *Ubuntu/Botho/Hunhu* and Non-human Animals

There have been various attempts in recent years to employ *ubuntu/botho/hunhu* as
a locus for "fostering human respect for the environment" (Makgoba 1996: 23), as
an orientation "towards balance and harmony in the relationship between human
beings and the broader be-ing or nature" (Ramose 2002: 326), and as "an expression of interconnectedness between people themselves, and between people and the
biophysical world" (Le Grange 2012: 63). Catherine Odora Hoppers maintains that

> such a philosophy … does not seek to conquer or debilitate nature as a first impulse. This
> can be contrasted, for instance, with … the mechanistic conception of reality …

Ubuntu ethics

> stresses instead the essential interrelatedness and interdependence of all phenomena – bio-
> logical, physical, psychological, social and cultural. Indigenous cosmology centres on the
> co-evolution of the spiritual, natural and human worlds. … Experiences from indigenous
> communities in other parts of the world emphasise the fact that knowledge is relationship,
> and relationship brings with it responsibilities and obligations and extends into ecological
> practice. (Odora Hoppers 2005: 4–6)

The African principle of human interdependence states that a human being
depends on human beings to be a human being: *Umuntu ngumuntu ngabantu*, or
Motho ke motho ka batho, or *Munhu munhu navhanhu*: "I am because we are" (see
Mbiti 1969: 108–109; Menkiti 1984: 171, 179; Mangena 2012: 11). It would appear
that the envisaged concern for non-human nature and the environment could be fos-
tered only on the basis of human benefits and would therefore not amount to any
acknowledgement of the intrinsic value of nature or the environment. Nor could the
principle in question constitute a basis for 'respect' or a "harmonious relationship"
with members of non-human species. That is, the prime and direct beneficiaries of
such a relationship or 'respect' must be human beings, whether as agents or recip-
ients. In fact, in its etymological focus on human beings, *ubuntu* is by definition
anthropocentric. At best, then, the principle(s) in question yield what is generally
referred to as an 'indirect-duty view' regarding other animals. Moeketsi Letseka has,
perhaps unwittingly, indicated the gulf that exists between *ubuntu/botho/hunhu* and
concern for animals:

> Consider … the case of an offence on which everyone agrees that it is heinous and an affront
> to *botho* or *ubuntu*, such as repeatedly raping an eighty-year-old grandmother or a six-year-

old girl. To express their displeasure community folk might utter statements like: 'He is not a person but a dog' [or] 'Oh God, he is an animal'. (Letseka 2000: 186)

The questionable move of equating rapists and animals like dogs might be excused as reporting an unreflective popular perception, but it arguably points to something deeper—namely the view that animals occupy a territory untouched by ordinary moral concerns and considerations: indeed, an amoral realm.

16.5 *Ukama* and African Environmentalism

Perhaps it is uncharitable to focus exclusively on *ubuntu*—which constitutes an improvement on egoism but is still decidedly anthropocentric—as exemplifying African ethical attitudes towards animals. According to moral theorists, Africa has additional conceptual resources that might help address questions around direct ethical responsibility regarding non-human nature, resources that involve an extension of the traditional ideas of 'relatedness' and 'relationality'. Whereas some thinkers emphasise African holism, "solidarity with creation as a whole" and "cosmic community" (Bujo 2009: 284, 296), an ethic of "nature-relatedness" (Ogungbemi 1997) or "eco-bio-communitarianism" (Tangwa 2004), others draw on the notion of *ukama* originating in Zimbabwe (Murove 2004, 2009: 315–316; Prozesky 2009: 302; Le Grange 2012: 61–62). Unlike *ubuntu*, *ukama* asserts that a person can be a person in, with and through not just other people (those who are still alive as well as ancestors) and but also in, with and through the natural environment. Tellingly, however, the "closeness" in question derives from an animal being used, first and foremost, for human ends and purposes. Thus, Bénézet Bujo's notions of "cosmic community" and of the relationality of all life, and of holism *tout court*, remain perfectly compatible with a largely instrumental view of non-human nature. Segun Ogungbemi's ethic of "nature-relatedness" is located in the "ethics of care" that characterised traditional African society. It recognises that human existence necessarily depends on the natural world, and it is because of this reliance that humans must treat the environments in which they live with due respect—for the sake of current human and future well-being, not because of any intrinsic value or dignity animals and the natural environment may possess. Similarly, although Godfrey Tangwa speaks of a tendency towards cosmic humility and cautiousness "in their attitude to plants, animals, and inanimate things" (389) on the part of ordinary Africans, and although the "traditional worldview … does not suppose that human beings have any mandate or special privilege, God-given or otherwise, to subdue, dominate, and exploit the rest of creation", he mentions "frequent offerings of sacrifices to God …" (389–390). What do these offerings of sacrifices comprise, if not "plants, animals, and inanimate things"? How is the traditional "live and let live"-attitude to be squared with the anthropocentrism of ordinary Africans and their "contribution to environmental hazards", as identified by Ogungbemi (Ogungbemi 1997: 204)?

A further, important question concerns *umuntu*'s actual responsibilities with regard to non-human nature. The mere moral injunction to harmonise humanity's behaviour with the natural environment does not tell much about *umuntu*'s concrete, specific responsibilities and duties. In fact, the imperative of 'harmonisation' could be—and indeed has been—considered compatible with, perhaps even to require, the bare-handed slaughtering of bulls, for the sake of 'good relations' between *umuntu* and *amadlozi*, and even 'future generations'. Insofar as *ubuntu* and *ukama* have any action-guiding content at all, this is unlikely to have any primary, direct beneficiaries other than human beings. Therefore, like *ubuntu*, *ukama* and most of the environmentalist positions it engenders remain anthropocentric.

16.6   Animals and the Law in East, West and Southern Africa

Moving beyond traditional African perceptions and attitudes and into post-colonial Africa, what—if any—are the legal provisions made for the welfare and protection of individual animals? It is evident that an anthropocentric approach is implicit in the legal systems, particularly in those legal norms that underpin emerging animal welfare concerns and environmental law norms. A survey of ethics protocols and guidelines for the use and transport of non-human animals in "livestock production" and scientific research in East, West and Southern Africa (see, for example, Nyika 2009) demonstrates that, although there is some lip service to the 'intrinsic value of animals', the extant formulations evidently leave interpretation of what is seen to count as "humane treatment", "prevention of cruelty" and "the unnecessary killing of animals" wide open.

Anthropocentrism characterises not only traditional African perceptions and world-views and current East, West and Southern African legal systems; it also pervades post-apartheid and post-colonial environmental politics, explicitly so. That the adoption of an anthropocentric agenda is politically expedient is not in doubt. The interesting question whether it is ethically defensible is unfortunately beyond the brief of the present chapter. (I deal with this problem in depth in Horsthemke 2010 and again in Horsthemke 2015: 124–146.)

16.7   The African Case for and Against Anthropocentrism

As this brief survey of the various African views and considerations demonstrates, tendencies vary (very broadly) from (1) more or less out spoken human-centredness and more or less qualified endorsement of human moral superiority via (2) lip service to environmental or animal-friendliness, while humans remain the measure of all things and at the centre of ethical concern and deliberation, to (3) outright rejection of moral anthropocentrism and explicit pro-animal attitudes. It is the middle group that often constitutes the greatest challenge to the critical reviewer, in terms of having top in point not only the deficiencies of the respective views but also the reasons why an environmental-friendly view may not necessarily (indeed, often does not) incorporate any direct concern for individual non-human animals. For one thing, the critical reviewer may not want to be little or discourage the ethical progress and advancements, however small and tentative, that have been made. For another, suggesting a radicalisation in environmental and pro-animal thought and practice may seem to threaten or at least minimise the distinctly African contribution to the ethical debates in question. This is arguably where a sustained focus on the last group becomes all-important, in attempting to determine what values and other conceptual and practical resources exist in African awareness not to ameliorate but to bring about substantial changes in the conditions under which them any billions of animals live (and die) on the continent.[2]

The theoretical positions of the first group (1) range from open endorsement of anthropocentric ethics via in difference to hostility, with frequent cautions about the dangers of allocating any sort of moral space, let alone rights, to non-humans. Thus, after asserting that the various rights implied by duties of justice (characteristically owed to persons) and that "the possess or of the rights in question cannot be other than a person" (Menkiti 1984: 177), Ifeanyi Menkiti states that this interpretation rules out "some dangerous tendencies currently fashionable in some philosophical circles of ascribing rights to animals" (ibid.). "The danger", as he sees it,

> is that such an extension of moral language to the domain of animals is bound to undermine, sooner or later, the clearness of our conception of what it means to be a person. The practical consequences are also something for us to worry about. For if there is legitimacy in ascribing rights to animals then human beings could become compelled to share resources with them [,… such as] equally deserving cats and dogs. Minority persons might then find them selves the victims of a peculiar philosophy in which the constitutive elements in the definition of human person hood have become blurred through unwarranted extensions to non-human entities. (ibid.)

Reginald Oduor, too, struggles to make any sense of the notion of animal rights:

> With regard to the possible relationship between struggles against slavery and against the oppression of women on the one hand and animal rights on the other, I personally do not see one. This is due to the fact that the women and the former slaves consciously participated in the struggles for their liberation. On the other hand, the animals cannot be properly said to participate in the struggle for their rights; instead, humans have taken it upon them selves to act on behalf of the animals. This is not to imply that humans have a right to mistreat animals: I think that the fact that human beings are rational obligates them to be responsible in their treatment of all sentient beings. (Oduor 2012: 9)

---

[2]In other words, I share the concerns expressed by many animal rights advocates that focus on 'animal welfare' is likely to be counterproductive, in that it serves to legitimate current abusive practices, is not committed to acknowledgement of the inherent value (let alone moral rights) of animals and secures fairly negligible benefits for the latter. (See Donaldson and Kymlicka (2011: 2–3). See also Eloff (2013), for a radical liberationist rejection of the ideas of both 'welfare' and 'rights', with regard to questions concerning animals. On the distinction between animal rights and animal welfare from a largely African agricultural perspective, see Coetzer and Goldring 2005.)

A part from the fact that "responsibility" remains wide open to interpretation, it is not difficult to see that for Oduor any such obligation "to be responsible in their treatment of all sentient beings" is not a directly owed to animals. It flows directly from the fact of our (human) rationality. Although Metz (2012, 2014) endorses neither anthropocentrism nor speciesism, he does provide the anthropocentrist with certain tools. Most significantly, he argues not only that animals cannot be the subject of communion and do not have a "dignity" but also that, in cases of genuine conflict of interests, relevantly disabled human beings should always take precedence of non-humans (Horsthemke 2015: 85–92). Yet, he also furnishes a telling response to arguments like those advanced by Menkiti and Oduor: to extend considerations of morality, justice, rights etc. only to (a community/communities of) 'persons' is unwarrantedly parochial.[3] The Chewa proverb *Kalikhokha nikanyama; tuli tuwili nituwanthu* ("What is alone is a brute animal; whatever or whoever has a partner/neighbour is a human being"; see Kaphagawani 2004: 337) indicates a profound ignorance of the nature and character of social animals. A similar misconception underlies the claim that what "clearly demarcates humanity from animality" is human possession not only of intelligence but also of "the heart" (Kaphagawani 2004: 339; Kagame 1989: 36). Intelligence is demonstrated in the essentially human ability to reflect and meditate on the data of their senses, to "compare the facts of knowledge" human beings have acquired, and "to invent something new by combining previously acquired knowledge" (Kagame 1989: 36). "The heart", on the other hand, refers to personality: "in the heart lies the personality of man … It is by which this man is himself and not another" (Kagame 1989: 36). Personality is what characterises human beings; it is also "one of the criteria for distinguishing one person from another" (Kaphagawani 2004: 339). One might point out that this just shifts the problem: for now we want to know what exactly constitutes "personality". Perhaps we might associate personality with *moral* personality, along the lines already suggested by Menkiti (1984). But why does this involve a *misconception*? For one thing, intelligence and personality (even moral personality and agency) are not matters of 'all-or-nothing'. They are possessed in varying degrees by *both* human beings *and* animals. Mentally impaired humans and children have these abilities to comparatively lesser degrees than so-called 'normal' adult human beings, and some non-human animals have these abilities to comparatively higher degrees than *both* certain human beings *and* certain other animals.

Returning to the diagnosis of different African positions with regard to non-human nature, the 'middle group' (2) is constituted by the writings and views of those who adopt an environmentally friendly and/or non-anthropocentric stance but whose positions turn out, on careful scrutiny, implicitly or explicitly to give human beings pride of place in a single moral hierarchical arrangement. These include the accounts seeking to accommodate animals, on traditional religious and/or cultural grounds, furnished for example by scholars like Ramose (2009), Mutwa, Ogungbemi, Mangena (2012, 2013), Tangwa, Metz (2012, 2014), Bujo, Murove (2009) and Prozesky (2009). By contrast, genuinely non-anthropocentric approaches (what I referred to

---

[3]I have dealt in depth with these issues elsewhere (see Horsthemke 2010).

as group 3 above) are arguably provided by Masiga and Munyua (2005), Behrens (2008, 2014) and Kelbessa (2005, 2014), as well as Ojomo (2011) and Nneji (2010). For the remainder of this chapter, I will focus on the latter contributions as containing the seeds for an enlightened moral stance with regard to animals and non-human nature as a whole.

Masiga and Munyua's essay (2005) is a critical, albeit largely empirical account of the current state of "animal welfare" in Africa. Their survey pre-dates Nyika's (2009) concerns about inadequate ethics protocols and guidelines for the use and transport of non-human animals in "livestock production" and scientific research in sub-Sahara Africa and, indeed, provides an alarming account of abuse in livestock production and handling along stock routes and in slaughterhouses (pertaining especially to poultry, dairy cattle, pigs and goats), of animals used for transport and ploughing (horses, donkeys, mules, camels and steers), in the treatment of companion animals (like cats and dogs) and also of wild animals in zoos and open areas like parks and reserves. Regarding the latter, unlike for domestic animals, "there are no societal and cultural norms or set standards of care for wildlife" (Masiga and Munyua 2005: 582). Not only are wild animals threatened by the lucrative exotic animal and bush meat trade but they are also 'controlled', captured and killed with means that often entail protracted suffering. In contradiction to claims by indigenous knowledge advocates, Masiga and Munyua also provide sobering descriptions of so-called "ethnoveterinary practices" and the suffering they involve (583–584):

> In Africa, castrations can be performed as an open or closed procedure. To perform an open castration, the scrotum is cut open with a sharp instrument and the testicle is exteriorised and subsequently twisted and stretched until it tears off. To perform a closed castration, the spermatic cords from both testicles are hammered with a mallet or a club to block the *vas deferens*. In contrast, to increase the virility of an animal, the same procedure is conducted, but only one spermatic cord is blocked.

> To prevent repeated uterine prolapses, a fold of skin on the back of an animal at the level of the sacrum is stapled using a sharpened stick. This causes the back of the animal to arch downward, which, in turn, causes the uterus to fall into the abdomen. To retain a prolapsed uterus, a similar technique is used whereby the size of the vulva is reduced using either strings or sharpened sticks.

> While animal handlers in Africa are proficient at performing these techniques, analgesics and anaesthetics are not used, which results in pain and suffering for the animals.

Regarding research and laboratory animals, the authors lament the fact that in most African countries "there are no policies and legal frameworks in place to support the initiatives" that pertain to research and development work:

> To compound the situation, in countries like Kenya and other former British colonies, the legal system criminalised animal abuse without any provisions for community awareness or education about animal welfare. The situation is made worse by the fact that the research and training institutions are governed by different statutes that protect them from the scrutiny of external parties (i.e. the institutions are only subject to reviews by internal animal welfare and ethics committees). Furthermore, the internal committees, which are often subservient to the directorate, do not have the capacity and/or authority to perform self-inspections or enforce regulations, which makes them essentially powerless. (584)

Although their survey is hard-hitting and graphic, the recommendations made by Masiga and Munyua unfortunately do not transcend basic welfarist objectives: regular reviews of existing legislation, monitoring and reduction of instances of animal abuse, increasing community awareness and "promoting … community involvement in and education about animal welfare issues", and promoting "training in animal welfare for service providers in veterinary practice, livestock production, and wildlife management" (585).

Nneji emphasises the need for human beings to put them selves into the position of animals, in order for an appropriate awareness to be brought about or attained:

> Using imaginative empathy we will very much appreciate the clarion call for environmental ethics. If humans can swap life with animals and other sentient beings, the call for environmental protection and conservation will sink in well into human consciousness. (Nneji 2010: 40)

In this regard, Kelbessa (2005) too refers to the symbolic and ethical reservoir in African indigenous traditions that ensures respect and compassion for other living creatures. He nonetheless warns that not all indigenous knowledge (see, for example, Le Grange 2004) should be seen as being environmentally friendly.

Building his "African relational environmentalism" (Behrens 2014) on the ideas of Tangwa, Bujo, Murove and Metz, Behrens seeks to counter the common assumption that African moral thought and practice is inherently anthropocentric (Behrens 2014: 64). He contends that a promising African account of moral considerability can be derived from a communitarian foundation—especially, as Behrens understands it, an African emphasis on the interrelatedness or interconnectedness between everything in nature (65). The idea is that natural entities (present, past and future human beings, animals, plants, communities like species and whole ecosystems, even inanimate natural objects) are all bound up in a "web or fabric of life" (76). It is neither the individuals nor the community that are given moral priority (66), but rather the relations that exist between them, the fact of their harmonious (co)existence (76). From these considerations, Behrens concludes that all living things, by virtue of their existing in harmonious relations with one another, are morally considerable. It follows, he says, that human beings have a moral obligation to live in harmony with the rest of nature and to respect all natural objects. In the case of natural entities like rivers and inanimate objects, this obligation cannot be direct; nor can it be, says Behrens, in the case of metaphysical ideas like ancestors and spirits (77–81). But normal adult human beings are nonetheless bound up in relationships with all these entities that could be harmonious or disharmonious. Insofar as the former are preferable to the latter, this is sufficient for grounding not only moral considerability but also moral responsibility, whether direct or indirect.

Although Behrens sometimes argues that it is the entities themselves that matter morally (be they individuals or groups/species), a thorough-going relational theory would have to give moral priority to the *relations* between entities, to the fact of their interconnectedness, of belonging to a web of life. This lack of clarity means that he may face a concern similar to the one I raised with respect to Metz's relational ethic (Horsthemke 2015: 89): that moral standing is determined by something *outside* those who can reasonably be said to possess it. In other words, how can "belonging to a web or fabric of life" also bestow moral considerability on the *entities* in question and not only on the *relation(s)* between them? Although Behrens appears to distance himself from Metz's conclusion that many animals, plants and inanimate natural entities cannot be morally considerable, the question arises whether his African relational environmentalism is really egalitarian in a way Metz's theory is not, or whether it also allows for differing degrees of moral considerability. At least on the face of it, Behrens seems careful to avoid any charge that he is invoking any hierarchical arrangement here, with human beings once again occupying moral pride of place.

What is noteworthy about the theories advanced by both Metz and (to a lesser extent) Behrens is that they seek to demonstrate the practical implications of their accounts of moral status and considerability, respectively, and to establish the content of moral obligations, on the grounds of their respective African ethics. By contrast, Philomena Ojomo claims that authors like Ogungbemi and Tangwa fail to raise let alone discuss some fundamental questions. One of these concerns "the nature of African obligation and the role of the relationship between Africans ([including] non-Africans in Africa…) towards … future generation[s] in Africa, sentient beings, non-human animals, [the] African environment in particular and nature in general". Another concerns "the political, cultural, economical, educational, legal, and moral imperatives to be taken into consideration in the construction of an African environmental ethics in order to salvage the African environment from further deterioration" (Ojomo 2011: 111). However, while Ojomo at least raises these questions, she provides no answers—which is arguably the greatest shortcoming of an otherwise promising contribution.[4]

16.8   Towards a Non-speciesist Africa?

When Bishop Desmond Tutu, in his foreword to *The Guide to Animal Protection* (Tutu 2013: xv), refers to "other issues of justice", he takes these to apply not only to human beings but also to "the world's other sentient creatures". "Even when faced with human problems" that "fight for our attention in what sometimes seems an already overfull moral agenda", we should not overlook "instances of injustice", i.e. "the abuse and cruelty we inflict on other animals" (ibid.).

I am happy to concede that anthropocentrism, whether this involves the view that only human beings merit moral treatment or the view that any human is necessarily

---

[4]In an earlier paper, Ojomo cites biocentrism as maintaining that

> all life forms are "moral patients" - entities to which we should accord moral consideration. We therefore have a duty towards all forms of life. It is its *telos (purpose)* that gives each individual organism inherent worth, and all living organisms possess this worth equally because all individual living beings have their *telos*. (Ojomo 2010: 53)

It is not clear, however, whether and to what extent this reflects her own view.

superior to/more significant morally than any other animal, is not an *essential* constituent of African morality. I hope to have indicated above that there exist several resources in African philosophical thinking for deriving a non-anthropocentric and non-speciesist ethical orientation. Adoption of a more enlightened stance *vis-à-vis* the non-human world and animals in particular would almost certainly involve giving up, or at least rigourous critical reflection upon, many of the attitudes and practices on the African continent. This need not entail surrendering what is arguably at the core of sub-Saharan morality—the emphasis on community and harmonious communal relationships.

If I am to provide compelling grounds for an enlightened pro-animal stance on the basis of African ethical considerations, then I must acknowledge that sub-Saharan morality is not individualist and, therefore, likely to be less open initially to individual-rights-based, 'subject-of-a-life'-type considerations than certain mainstream, animal-centred ethics. I say 'initially' because, ultimately, community and harmonious communal relationships derive their essential meaning from the existence of individuals, or individual selves. Apart from the "great goods" referred to by Tutu (1999: 35)—social harmony, friendliness, and community—mention has been made of imaginative empathy, compassion[5] and respect, as well as interrelatedness or interconnectedness between everything in nature. Among Native Americans, these values find expression in the Lakota phrase *Mitakuye oyasin* or the Cree concept of *wahkohtowin* ("All is related"; "We are all related"), both of which refer to the self in relation, the self being defined relationally. "I am because we are" could reasonably be interpreted as not being confined to the human realm, as transcending the species barrier. I have in mind here something like a relational approach to animal rights and environmental ethics that is neither anthropocentric nor speciesist. The multifarious historical and geographical relationships we have with other-than-human animals give rise to a multitude of moral obligations that differ according to the kinds of relationships we find ourselves in.

That said, I do think that partiality is not morally insignificant. Personal relations matter. For instance, in cases of conflict such as in the scenario imagined by Metz (2017), I would have good reason to give preference to *my* pig over a complete human stranger, let alone one of comparable, porcine intelligence and capacity to commune (bearing in mind that pigs are highly intelligent and sensitive animals). I may also have excellent reasons to give preference to a pig over a person of dubious moral convictions or questionable political affiliation. If both the pig and the other human being are, equally, strangers to me, I may well choose to kill the pig—however, I may also choose to hand over the gun and to forgo the questionable pleasure of ingesting another individual's flesh. But these are claims about agents' motivation, emotional attachments, etc.—they do not bear on the moral status of the 'object' of agency, the moral recipient. I do not think that choice in extreme situations must necessarily be

---

[5] It should be noted that sympathy (compassion) and empathy, both singled out by Kwasi Wiredu as the "very foundation of morality" (see Masolo 2004: 496), concern individuals—and *not* collectives or communal entities.

guided by categorical judgement, by an appeal to overarching ethical principle. I am unsure whether this even possible.

As is indicated by the wealth of contributions to this symposium and edited volume, there appears to be a growing awareness among African scholars of the untenability of a rigidly species-governed 'us-against-them' thinking, that anthropocentrism shares many relevant features with ethnocentrism, and that speciesism is relevantly like racism—all of which fills me with (admittedly reluctant) optimism about our relationships with non-humans on the African continent and perhaps even on this planet. Our task, as philosophers and as human beings, is a formidable one that requires imagination as well as intellectual honesty and practical consistency. Being for animal rights and being for human rights is part of the same moral fabric. One cannot consistently reject speciesism if one does not also vehemently oppose racism and sexism. Furthermore, opposition to racism and sexism is superficial without any commitment to end the wrongs suffered by countless numbers of animals each day—a commitment that may require making fundamental changes in one's lifestyle.

References

Behrens, K.G. 2014. An African Relational Environmentalism and Moral Considerability. *Environmental Ethics* 36 (1): 63–82.

Behrens, K.G. 2008. *Tony Yengeni's Ritual Slaughter: Animal Anti-cruelty vs. Culture*. MA Research Report/University of the Witwatersrand. http://wiredspace.wits.ac.za/jspui/bitstream/10539/6087/1/BehrensMAEPReportFeb08.pdf. Accessed 29 Oct 2014.

Bujo, B. 2009. Ecology and Ethical Responsibility from an African Perspective. In *African Ethics: An Anthology of Comparative and Applied Ehics*, ed. M.F. Murove, 281–297. Scottsville: University of KwaZulu-Natal Press.

Chemhuru, M., and D. Masaka. 2010. Taboos as Sources of Shona People's Environmental Ethics. *Journal of Sustainable Development in Africa* 12 (7): 121–133.

Coetzer, T.H.T., and J.P.D. Goldring. 2005. Animal Rights and Animal Welfare. In *Ethics in Agriculture: An African Perspective*, ed. A. Van Niekerk, 83–100. Dordrecht: Springer.

CRL Rights Commission (Commission for the Promotion and Protection of the Rights of Cultural, Religious & Linguistic Communities). 2002. *Act No. 19*. http://www.crlcommission.org.za/docs/CRLACT.pdf. Accessed 23 Dec 2014.

CRL Rights Commission (Commission for the Promotion and Protection of the Rights of Cultural, Religious & Linguistic Communities). 2009. *Guidelines Report on the African Ritual of Animal Slaughter*, 1–16. http://www.crlcommission.org.za/docs/rpd/Report%20Slaughter%20Guides%20reprint.pdf. Accessed 29 Oct 2014.

Donaldson, S., and W. Kymlicka. 2011. *Zoopolis: A Political Theory of Animal Rights*. Oxford: Oxford University Press.

Eloff, A. 2013. *Rites of the Nomads: From Animal Rights to Nomadic Ethics*. http://www.academia.edu/4908260/Rites_of_the_nomads_from_animal_rights_to_nomadic_ethics. Accessed 9 Feb 2015.

Grill, B. 2003. *Ach, Afrika. Berichte aus dem Inneren eines Kontinents*. Berlin: Siedler.

Horsthemke, K. 2010. *The Moral Status and Rights of Animals*. Johannesburg: Porcupine Press.

Horsthemke, K. 2015. *Animals and African Ethics*. Basingstoke: Palgrave MacMillan.

Kagame, A. 1989. The Problem of 'Man' in Bantu Philosophy. *Journal of African Religion and Philosophy* 1: 35–40.

Kaphagawani, D.N. 2004. African Conceptions of a Person: A critical survey. In *A Companion to African Philosophy*, ed. K. Wiredu, 332–342. Oxford: Blackwell.

Kelbessa, W. 2005. The Rehabilitation of Indigenous Environmental Ethics in Africa. *Diogenes* 52: 17–34.

Kelbessa, W. 2014. Can African Environmental Ethics Contribute to Environmental Policy in Africa? *Environmental Ethics* 36 (1): 31–61.

Le Grange, L. 2004. Western Science and Indigenous Knowledge. *South African Journal of Higher Education* 18 (3): 82–91.

Le Grange, L. 2012. *Ubuntu, Ukama* and the Healing of Nature, Self and Society. *Educational Philosophy and Theory* 44 (S2): 56–67.

Letseka, M. 2000. African Philosophy and Educational Discourse. In *African Voices in Education*, ed. P. Higgs, N. Vakalisa, T. Mda, and N. Assie Lumumba, 179–193. Lansdowne: Juta.

Makgoba, M.W. (1996). In Search of the Ideal Democratic Model for SA. *Sunday Times*, 27 Oct 23.

Mangena, F. 2012. Towards a *Hunhu/Ubuntu* Dialogical Moral Theory. *Phronimon* 13 (2): 1–17.

Mangena, F. 2013. Discerning Moral Status in the African Environment. *Phronimon* 14 (2): 25–44.

Masiga, W.N., and S.J.M. Munyua. 2005. Global Perspectives on Animal Welfare: Africa. *Revue Scientifique et Technique (International Office of Epizootics)* 24 (2): 579–586.

Masolo, D.A. 2004. Western and African Communitarianism: A Comparison. In *A Companion to African Philosophy*, ed. K. Wiredu, 483–498. Oxford: Blackwell.

Mbiti, J.S. 1969. *African Religions and Philosophy*. Nairobi & London: Heinemann.

Menkiti, I.A. 1984. Person and Community in African Traditional Thought. In *African Philosophy (Originally Published 1979)*, ed. R. Wright, 171–181. New York: University of America Press.

Metz, T. 2012. An African Theory of Moral Status: A Relational Alternative to Individualism and Holism. *Ethical Theory and Moral Practice* 15 (3): 387–402.

Metz, T. 2014. A Relational Theory of Animal Moral Status. Paper presented in an Ethics Colloquium at the Lichtenberg-Kolleg/Göttingen Institute of Advanced Study, University of Göttingen, Germany, 2 Dec.

Metz, T. 2017. How to Ground Animal Rights on African Values: Reply to Horsthemke. *Journal of Animal Ethics*, 7 (2, Fall): 163–174.

Murove, M.F. 2004. An African Commitment to Ecological Conservation: The Shona Concepts of *Ukama* and *Ubuntu*. *Mankind Quarterly* 45 (2): 195–215.

Murove, M.F. 2009. An African Environmental Ethic Based on the Concepts of *Ukama* and *Ubuntu*. In *African Ethics: An Anthology of Comparative and Applied Ethics*, ed. M.F. Murove, 315–331. Scottsville: University of KwaZulu-Natal Press.

Mutwa, C. 1996. *Isilwane: The Animal*. Cape Town: Struik.

Nneji, B. 2010. Eco-Responsibility: The Cogency of Environmental Ethics in Africa. *Essays in Philosophy* 11 (1): 31–43.

Nyika, A. 2009. Animal Research Ethics in Africa: An Overview. *Acta Tropica* 1125: S48–S52.

Odora Hoppers, C.A. 2005. *Culture, Indigenous Knowledge and Development: The Role of the University*. Johannesburg: Centre for Education Policy Development (CEPD), Occasional Paper No. 5: 1–50.

Oduor, R.M.J. 2012. African Philosophy and Non-Human Animals: Reginald M.J. Oduor Talks to AntenehRoba and Rainer Ebert. https://www.uta.edu/philosophy/faculty/burgess-jackson/Interview.pdf. Accessed 22 Sept 2014.

Ogungbemi, S. 1997. An African Perspective on the Environmental Crisis. In *Environmental Ethics: Readings in Theory and Application*, 2nd ed, ed. L. Pojman, 330–337. Belmont/CA: Wadsworth.

Ojomo, P.A. 2010. An African Understanding of Environmental Ethics. *Theory and Practice: A Journal of the Philosophical Association of Kenya (PAK)* 2 (2): 49–63.

Ojomo, P.A. 2011. Environmental Ethics: An African Understanding. *The Journal of Pan African Studies* 4 (3): 101–113.

Prozesky, M.H. 2009. Well-Fed Animals and Starving Babies: Environmental and Developmental Challenges from Process and African Perspectives. In *African Ethics: An Anthology of Comparative and Applied Ethics*, ed. M.F. Murove, 298–307. Scottsville: University of KwaZulu-Natal Press.

Ramose, M.B. 2002. The Ethics of *Ubuntu*. In *Philosophy from Africa*, 2nd ed, ed. P.H. Coetzee and A.P.J. Roux, 324–330. Cape Town: Oxford University Press Southern Africa.

Ramose, M.B. 2009. Ecology Through *Ubuntu*. In *African Ethics: An Anthology of Comparative and Applied Ethics*, ed. M.F. Murove, 308–314. Scottsville: University of KwaZulu-Natal Press.

Tangwa, G. 2004. Some African Reflections on Biomedical and Environmental Ethics. In *A Companion to African Philosophy*, ed. K. Wiredu, 387–395. Oxford: Blackwell.

Taringa, N. 2006. How Environmental is African Traditional Religion? *Exchange* 35 (2): 191–214.

Tutu, D. 1999. *No Future Without Forgiveness*. New York: Random House.

Tutu, D. 2013. Foreword: Extending Justice and Compassion. In *The Global Guide to Animal Protection*, ed. A. Linzey, xv. Urbana/Illinois: University of Illinois Press.

Chapter 17
Decolonizing Human-Animal Relations in an African Context: The Story of the Mourning Elephants

Angela Roothaan

Abstract In 2012, elephants from two separate herds walked about twelve hours to hold what seemed to be a vigil for their deceased rescuer, South African conservationist Lawrence Anthony. Their story was met with reactions varying from intrigue to disbelief, as standing ideas on non-human animals forbid us to think they might outdo humans in their capacity to sense the death of a close one, even across species-boundaries. In my chapter this story will be the starting point to critically address Western dominated philosophical views of human-animal relations, and explore it for its potential for a new philosophical environmentalism starting from an African context. The story holds several important elements that will be analyzed consecutively and will provide arguments for decolonized human-animal relations. First: the elephants' behavior has to be understood in the historical context of troubled human-elephant encounters, as well as land dispossession in (neo-) colonial contexts. Second: their 'family relationship' to the person who granted them asylum in his private nature reserve asks us to transcend the 'colonial' othering of non-human animals. Third: the elephants' potential to sense the dying of a 'relative' invites us to acknowledge distant 'feeling' perception, which is acknowledged in traditional, 'shamanistic' epistemologies. All three elements lead to understanding and accepting human perception and agency to be continuous with that of non-human animals rather than radically different. This chapter will make use of multi- and inter-disciplinary decolonizing approaches (Bamana, Kohn, Murombedzi, Plumwood).

The world is full of persons (people if you prefer), but few of them are human

The world is full of other-than-human persons

The world is full of other-than-oak persons

The world is full of other-than-hedgehog persons

The world is full of other-than-salmon persons

An adapted version of this chapter will be published in Roothaan (2019).

A. Roothaan (✉)
Vrije Universiteit Amsterdam, Amsterdam, The Netherlands
e-mail: acmroothaan@casema.nl

© Springer Nature Switzerland AG 2019
M. Chemhuru (ed.), *African Environmental Ethics*, The International
Library of Environmental, Agricultural and Food Ethics 29,
https://doi.org/10.1007/978-3-030-18807-8_17

The world is full of other-than-kingfisher persons
The world is full of other-than-rock persons...

Graham Harvey, *An Animist Manifesto* (2012).

17.1   Introduction

In 2012, elephants from two separate herds walked about twelve hours to hold what seemed to be a vigil for their deceased rescuer, South African conservationist Lawrence Anthony. Their story was met with reactions varying from intrigue to disbelief, as standing ideas on non-human animals forbid us to think they might outdo humans in their capacity to sense the death of a close one, even across species-boundaries—not to mention that they would intentionally perform a mourning ritual.

In my chapter this story will be the focus point to critically address Western dominated philosophical views of human-animal relations, and explore alternative ontologies for their potential for a new philosophical environmentalism starting from an African context. At a point in time where environmental concerns are gaining more and more civil and public attention in African countries, environmentalism as such should be decolonized. Whereas mainstream conservationalism is secularist, human-centered, and technology-focused, it might reproduce the attitudes that created so many of the environmental problems that face humanity in our present times. Therefore it is necessary to take a step back from solution-centered environmental discourse, and subscribe to the aim of widening ontological frameworks—in order to include alternative perceptions of nature (in this case more specifically non-human animals) in such discourse.

To this effect I will critically address mainstream conservationalist environmentalism focused on non-human animals, and propose, alternatively, a dialogical intercultural frame of thought, which will address the politics of epistemologies, thus allowing the negotiation of varying views of nature. The upshot of this approach will be to forego the idea that any 'system of thought' can ever capture the essence of things in a definitive manner, while simultaneously avoiding a relativistic position, by maintaining that the phenomena we perceive are real.

The story of the mourning elephants holds several important elements that bring us to the kind of open-ended reflections at which this investigation aims. Their analysis and discussion will add to a decolonization of human-animal relations—which should be the foundation for a postcolonial environmental approach. Decolonization will thus be extended from the sphere of relations between humans to relations of humans to non-human animals (Plumwood 2003; Roothaan 2017).

The elements that will be looked into are: (1) the historical context of troubled human-elephant encounters, as well as land dispossession in (neo-)colonial contexts, adding background to the elephants' behavior; (2) their 'family relationship' to the person who granted them asylum in his private nature reserve, inviting us to transcend the 'colonial' othering of non-human animals; (3) the elephants' potential to sense the dying of a 'relative', problematizing the mainstream denial of distant 'feeling' perception, which is acknowledged in traditional, 'shamanist' or spirit ontologies.

To conclude this chapter, I will show that all three elements lead to understanding and accepting human perception and agency to be continuous with that of non-human animals, contesting thus the idea of the human-animal divide. It will also be made clear that we can only arrive at such a view in a philosophically convincing manner by acknowledging the need to negotiate our epistemologies in the political realm.

17.2 Decolonizing Human-Animal Relations

The goals of wildlife conservation, on international, national as well as local policy levels, have long stopped to be just an (neo-colonial) interest from concerned Westerners trying to address the side effects of global trade and industrialization. Even though a certain evangelizing and patronizing approach, smacking of the ideology of civilization that went hand in hand with colonialist projects, is not absent from the many reports of NGO's and intergovernmental organizations working for the preservation of the natural richness of the earth—the research as well as the preservation work itself is just as well initiated by politicians, entrepreneurs and academics from formerly colonized countries. This means that the 'decolonization' of which I speak here is not meant to make a plea for transferring initiatives and programs from the hands of former colonizers to the formerly colonized—that is already taking place. The point I will make here addresses the fact that traditional, spiritual, shamanist[1] worldviews with which conservationist initiatives may have to deal when working in rural areas have never entered in environmentalist discourse as equal epistemic options. Before they can be considered thus, the dominant and dominating secularist worldview would have to be opened up to the politics of epistemologies at work in the environmental discourse.

With 'politics of epistemologies' I refer to the issue that certain descriptions of the conditions of true and valid knowledge dominate others by means of power systems regulating human investigation. While making a plea for an open, democratic discourse on knowledge within the limits of 'valid knowledge', hegemonic knowledge systems have always excluded criticisms of the conditions of validity of that same democratic forum. As a consequence, we may see elements of shamanist ontologies enter conservationist reports, but only within the strict confines of what counts as valid knowledge. Valid knowledge is understood to recognize the modernist categories of space and time and causality, of mind and matter, and to be technologically applicable for purposes of conservation of certain species or landscapes that are negotiated with the economies of tourism, industrial agriculture, mining and the production of items for global and local markets.

For an example of the above, let us refer to a report in which elephant protection plays a role. In a recent article in the *International Journal of Natural Resource*

---

[1]A concept which I will use transculturally, cf. Roothaan (2015), 141–2.

Ecology and Management (2017) Abugiche, Egute and Cybelle describe that where traditional taboos to hunt and eat elephants are still remembered and partially adhered to (Abugiche, Egute, Cybelle: 64–65), this may be played upon to ensure future protection of the animal. They describe this as follows: "There is need for new and holistic wildlife conservation policies that will blend traditional systems of regulation, myths, rituals, and perception with existing wildlife legislation in the country to enhance conservation […]" (ibid. 66). We see here, as well as in similar publications (cf. e.g. Hens 2006), that only the effects of traditional worldviews for conservationist practices are being considered, whereas the epistemic content of those worldviews, and thus their focus on a certain relationship with the elephants, is being ignored. This has several important consequences. Not only may it be questioned how taboos can uphold their power over peoples' actions when they are cut lose from the original epistemic frame from which they stem, but more importantly this approach leaves the idea of 'conservation' as such—an idea that functions within a colonial worldview of human control over the earth and its creatures—undiscussed.

An environmentalist philosopher who has systematically discussed the politics of epistemologies—in a bid to decolonize our relationship with nature—is the late Val Plumwood.[2] In a 2003 article, she offers several conceptual instruments to step out of what she calls colonial and centrist relationships. Centrism, in my own analysis, is the frame that treats a specific worldview as the center from which to understand the world—it floats on an implicit and ideally invisible power relationship—preventing that alternative worldviews can take themselves serious and enter into full negotiations with the center. This is how Euro-American imperialism worked and still works, be it through political, military, economic, or cultural means. It makes those who adhere to non-modernist worldviews take an apologetic stance, or to present their knowledge systems in prefabricated categories of the center—such as 'mythology', 'magic' or even one I will use here for lack of a better one: 'traditional'. A deconstructive approach can help us where we can hardly avoid such categories (if we want to indicate that they refer to an alternative to the modernist worldview)—to loosen their grip on our colonized minds. Such an approach is taken by Jacques Derrida in his famous essay *The Animal that therefore I am (more to follow)* (Derrida and Wills 2002). Plumwood, however, doesn't take the road of deconstruction, but while accepting the philosophical use of oppositional categories, tries to enrich the concepts in which is spoken of the 'alternative' worldviews, thereby making them ready to hold to their own centre from where they understand the world.

Thus she speaks, instead of 'non-human' nature of 'more-than-human' nature (thereby decentering the human) (Plumwood 2003, 52). She proposes that we should resist the 'backgrounding' of humanist centrism, and 'foreground' the more-than-human instead—which then leads to viewing the human being as just one of the different agents peopling the earth (Plumwood 2003, 61). In the context of Aus-

---

[2]Crucial to her later work in environmental ethics has been her experience, in 1985, of being attacked by a crocodile in the Australian wetlands where she was canoeing. The rare combination of someone surviving such an attack, and that person being a philosopher, has left us with completely new anthropological insights on what it means that human beings are ecologically meant to be prey, just like other hunted animals. Cf. Plumwood (1995).

tralian nature she insists that we refrain from speaking of it in terms of 'wilderness', as this ignores the impact of indigenous peoples (their agency) on their environment (Plumwood 2003, 62). Here she touches on the interrelatedness of colonializing relations of 'centrists' and decentered 'indigenous' peoples on the one hand and the same relations between human and non-human (more-than-human) 'earth others'. Discussing postcolonial and deconstructive approaches I have argued elsewhere that where a Euro-American hegemonic outlook treats only certain humans (modern, white, especially male ones) as 'really' human, dehumanization of non-western peoples reinforces the diminishing of their worldviews, especially where these recognize the personhood of non-human animals (Roothaan 2017). Plumwood shows how Eurocentrism also denies positive qualities to non-European landscapes. In her example it is the Australian landscape that is viewed as "[…] as a deficient, empty land, a mere absence of the positive qualities of the homeland" (Plumwood 2003, 65). In fact, such emptying out concerns non-western humans, non-human animals, and even non-animal 'others' such as rocks, plants, and rivers:

> In the colonizing framework, the Other is not a positively-other-than entity in its own right, but an absence of the self, home or centre, something of no value or beauty of its own except to the extent that it can be brought to reflect, or bear the likeness of, home as standard. (Plumwood 2003, 65)

Although her account is of the Australian case, where the indigenous Aboriginal people have maintained that their experience of the world is one in which the land is central, being the sacred and narrative subject from which human narrative and action depend, it can be taken as a paradigm to study other places where Western centrism has suppressed and ignored views that consider human beings as co-dependent with other beings. Especially her claim to treat 'Earth others' as agents and narrative subjects in their own right could help to philosophically open up to a story as the one which is taken here as our point of departure—that of the mourning elephants.

17.3   Troubled Encounters

When we investigate the story of the elephant herds that came to pay tribute to their rescuer Lawrence Anthony, it is important to avoid to let it 'youtubify' our response in a simplistic emotional manner. The story namely has many elements that evoke the centrisms that are at the root of our troubled relationships with animals such as elephants. We like to cry for dead persons who remind us of our own beloved mourned ones, we are moved by the type of the rescuing hero—especially when he is a white male, who with his rational and responsible foresight, as well as his high morals, counters the cruel and chaotic effects of unbridled growth of human occupation of 'wild' nature in African societies—to preserve a beautiful animal that otherwise would perish. As sympathetic a person as Lawrence Anthony himself might have been (and we have to admire his openness to listen and speak to the elephants that were pushed out of their natural lands)—when we focus on him as an elephant-whisperer, or as a savior of natural wildlife, we tend to background the complexities of the settler society in which the animals in this case were pushed to aggression.

Anthony himself has stressed in his 2009 book on his work with elephants, that the conversationist efforts he developed in his wildlife park Tula-Tula (which were the former hunting grounds of Zulu king Shaka) are in cooperation with 'local people', whom he tried to get involved in wildlife preservation and thus giving them jobs. The term 'local' should make us suspicious. Here we find a description that already marks certain people (and, implicitly, their aims and ideals as well) as 'local'—over against the 'higher' national or transnational efforts of people like Anthony himself. Of course it were transnational economies that brought wildlife under threat in the first place, through their colonialist endeavours and the legal and political structures they left behind. The question regarding elephant (or any form of wildlife) conservation should therefore perhaps not be how to integrate locals in growing industries like eco-tourism and nature preservation, but rather how the effects of national and transnational economies that aim to create 'progress' by furthering material wealth could be curbed as such. The elephant herd that was saved from being shot by Anthony, would not have been in their situation in the first place, had not a certain part of the human race at one point in history declared that it possessed certain pieces of land and could control all living beings (including 'local' human beings) that were on it. After that event wild animals have to be 'protected' by fencing off pieces of land, also with 'local' people on them, that are then artificially singled out from the 'normal' use and abuse of the earth 'outside'.

When one zooms in on what lies behind so many animal conservation stories, as Hector Magome and James Murombedzi have done in their work on the political and legal issues at stake in the management ownership of national parks, the complexities at the ground come into view. Discussing several cases from countries in Southern Africa such as Zimbabwe, Namibia and especially South Africa, they analyze the troubled relations between governments, private owners and local communities that form the net in which all together, the original human inhabitants, the newcomers, the non-human animals and non-animal others are caught. When one looks at the very historical circumstances that formed society in South Africa, one sees elements that prefigure the complications surrounding wildlife and nature reserves.

> [...] land dispossession in South Africa was based upon apartheid policy, a racially based separate development strategy that was designed by government to advance and benefit the interests of its minority white citizens at the expense of its majority black people. Although colonial influence in South Africa dates back to 1652, when the first European settlers arrived, the land conquest was institutionalized when the apartheid government passed the Natives' Land Acts of 1913 and 1936, which restricted land ownership by black people to just 13 per cent of the country's total land area. The land set aside for black people consisted of fragments scattered in selected areas of the country, first called 'native reserves' and later 'homelands'. This land was, with few exceptions, infertile and thus agriculturally unproductive. This situation forced many black males into the migrant labour system of the gold mines. (Magome and Murombedzi 2003, 109)

While land rights were differentiated as private (mostly white owners), national (the state, that under apartheid was organized towards benefiting the whites) or communal (good enough for local people), along an axial line of a center and its peripheries therefore—non-human others were kept out of the balance altogether. Just until many species threatened to go extinct and people with power started to realize they had to do something about it.

In his article on the 'devolution' of wildlife management, Murombedzi provides further analysis of how post-colonial political, legal and organisational structures are no ideal frames to negotiate the needs of impoverished and often culturally and geographically uprooted 'indigenous' people, versus those descendants of the colonialists whose rights are often still served best by those structures. In South Africa e.g. policy makers have to deal with the dual system of land ownership:

> Southern Africa today, and especially Zimbabwe, South Africa and Namibia, is characterized by a distinctive dual land-tenure system, with individual freehold tenure for a 'modern', mostly white, farming sector and 'communal tenure' for the 'traditional', exclusively black, farming sector. (Murombedzi 2003, 138)

Present day wildlife management has to try to involve the rights and needs of local peoples, whose traditional legal systems often aren't even officially recognized—which creates, next to population growth, the growing predominance of factors such as Chinese consumerism in African markets, and an increasing desire of wealthy tourists from all over the world to see 'pure' 'African' nature: complicated issues, in which wildlife itself is unwillingly entangled. It is within such contexts that the story of Anthony's elephants, who were threatened to be killed off because they were repeatedly trying to escape from their original wildpark and saved by him from that fate, should be understood.

17.4   Mourning Elephants as Moral Agents

Individuals such as Plumwood and Harvey (from whose 'Animist Manifesto' I took the motto above this chapter) have shown us that you don't have to belong to an 'indigenous' people to be open to non-human others that speak and act, that tell about things, that mourn and perhaps even worship. In a world and time in which modernism has reached all corners of the earth and in which—albeit to different levels—we are all subject to humanist centering and estrangement from nature, as present in our dependency of globalizing streams of consumer goods like clothes, processed foods and industrially produced medicines, it is a complicated issue in general to get to really acknowledge non-human animals as our likes, as agents and narrative subjects. Besides the growing material dependency of people from *all* cultures, the cultural and religious missionizing projects that went along with colonialism have also led to curvy roads for those who want to recuperate alternative approaches to animals. An example is to be seen in the life of the Congolese former catholic missionary in Mongolia Gaby Bamana—who, after long years of trying to convert Mongolians, came to the conclusion that he couldn't be successful in bringing them away from their shamanist worldview—as he couldn't do what Europeans had done to his own ancestors. This experience made him turn to a new career as a researcher in cultural anthropology, trying to understand the spirit ontology of the Mongolian herders, that draws quite different lines distinguishing 'humans' and 'animals' than usual in the Western view:

> Analysis of research conversations I conducted and observations I made between 2010 and 2011 suggests that, in spite of the difference in species, herders considered dogs to be kin to humans (*neg yas*) because dogs are believed to share the same ontological nature as humans (*negtöröl*). Thus, dog and human spirits are connected (spiritual analogy), and one practical implication of such connection is the social relationship of solidarity in everyday life. (Bamana 2014, 2)

Bamana investigates why dogs have a special place in Mongolian herder culture. In contrast to horses, for instance, who are also favored domestic animals, only dogs have personal names. He finds that in a special way dogs are thought to be relatives of humans, and this not in an abstract metaphorical manner, but—it is believed—because they share their ontological substance, their spiritual essence, with humans. Dogs and humans, according to the herders, can be reincarnated into each other and share a mythological/spiritual descent. In the work of another present day anthropologist, Eduardo Kohn, we find an attempt at further philosophical explanation of interspecies relations in Amazonian shamanist cultures, that recognize relations that go beyond the modernist human-animal divide. Here too, we find human beings having a special relationship with dogs, who hunt with and for them (Kohn 2013, 131 and further). The people studied by Kohn analyze the dogs' dreams as foretelling knowledge, like they do their own—and in doing so, they develop ways of communication that are open to diverse ways of giving meaning to events.

Elephants, one might say, are a completely different matter from dogs—as canines have lived together with humans for tens of thousands of years, while elephants up to this day are so called 'wild' animals. Wild here meaning not that they don't have socially regulated behavior amongst themselves, but that there is no standing social relation between their own and human societies. When we meet an elephant we will have to first negotiate how we will communicate with each other, so to speak, whereas with domestic and farm animals there are already inherited patterns of communication in place. In the story of Anthony's first encounter with the frustrated and angry elephants it is precisely his talent to do this which made him succeed in his effort to move the herd to his land where they could live without coming into further conflict with humans. In his book *The Elephant Whisperer* (Anthony and Spence 2009) it is described how Anthony, trying to convince the angry elephants to abstain from destructing the fence, speaks to the matriarch of the group, in English, making a guess that she will understand the tone of his voice, or that somehow his intent will come across. And it seems it did, because the elephants calmed down after he told them that their only chance at life and safety (their original matriarch had been recently shot) was to cooperate with him.

Of course many people are amazed at his courage to stand before an angry animal that could easily kill him and try to speak to it. We should not stop at such amazement however, but explain what it was that made his attempt at interspecies communication (to speak trans-species pidgin, as Kohn calls it—Kohn 2013) possible. One of the possibility conditions of such a communication should be the understanding, the belief or trust, that the elephant is not totally alien to me. That there is some kind of kinship, may we think of it in evolutionary terms, that we share a biological ancestor and are 'built', and wired, in similar ways—or in terms of a spiritual common ancestry as in the case of the Mongolian dog-herder relationship. Another is, however, the understanding that elephants have agency, and therefore, intentionality: that they can show deliberate behavior, and are not just driven by 'animal instincts' as philosophers and scientists alike used to think for a long time.

Nowadays science is opening up to ascribing intelligence, intentionality, deliberation and agency to a growing range of species. In science, however, one can only maintain such ideas after hypotheses (that might spring from philosophical/theoretical renewals like the ones made by Plumwood and the likes) have proven to be true according to observed behaviors. Empirical evidence is the criterion of scientific truths. That is why modern cultures, that take scientific results as their ontological measuring stick, have such a hard time to acknowledge and take seriously the knowledge of shamanist cultures. Even though a shaman or sage from such a culture can say that he *knows* that humans and dogs, or elephants for that matter, are related spiritually—because he *saw* it in his trance vision—such experience is not considered to be empirical evidence. Empirical evidence is restricted to controlled and repeatable observations. In an attempt to open up modern science and philosophy to spiritual knowledge, William James therefore spoke of the need for a 'radical empiricism' which would take seriously *all* kinds of experience (cf. Bordogna 2008).

As Deborah Rose, who works along the lines Val Plumwood set out, points out rightly, it is the epistemological questions concerning a shamanist approach that are presently the hardest to answer—which made Plumwood opt for a future-oriented, ethical approach of non-human others, with whom we share being of-the-earth, being earthlings:

> Most of her argument was laid out extensively in *Environmental Culture*. Here she put forward an interspecies ethic of recognition which depended on a particular stance toward the nonhuman world. That is, she was not making a set of truth claims about the world, but rather was asking what kind of stance a human can take that will open her to a responsive engagement in relation to nonhuman others. (Rose 2013, 97)

Although starting out from a concern about culture and identity rather than from ecological concerns, Nigerian philosopher Ekwealo likewise approaches his revaluation of traditional approaches to nature from a discussion of ethics. He calls his approach ecocentric and holistic, and propagates that a new, decolonized environmentalism should be built on a new, Africanized, ontology:

> Consequently, a correction of all environmental and human associations believed to be progressive would start on a philosophical level in which there would be an exercise in deconstruction of earlier metaphysical thinking and re-construction based on a new ontological foundation. It is only within this background that all ideas on conservation, sustainability, restoration and issues of peace, harmony and development would be possible. (Ekwealo 2017, 15)

Similarly, Michael Eze makes a plea for a new ethical approach to nature, and calls his version eco-humanism (cf. Eze 2017). Like Ekwealo, he argues for an African approach to nature, which takes all being as being enlivened by vital force, a concept they both take from Placied Tempels' 1945 book *Bantu Philosophy*. As Ekwealo puts it, "[…] Africans believe that 'force' or 'spirit' is all pervading energy in the universe irrespective of the form or nature of its manifestation" (Ekwealo 2017, 55). Here I will not go into the question of whether Tempels gave a valid rendering of all-African metaphysical viewpoints,[3] but will turn to the question that these proposals for a new, Africanized, environmental ethics (like Plumwood in her more universalizing work), leave undiscussed: how to critically review their background ontology from an epistemological viewpoint.

Connecting to the above, therefore, this way out of humanist centrism, omits to challenge the politics of epistemologies that sustain the colonialist frames that still dominate how we view knowledge, and therewith, reality. While animists, as Plumwood and others call themselves, or holists, as Ekwealo and also Eze call themselves, make important moves in the realm of ethics—they leave the politics of epistemology to the side. If our endeavor to revalue the earth and its others, decentering us, humans, and recentering the earth, ignores political epistemological questions, we leave the struggle for 'truth' untouched. In our search for the right values with which to approach the earth, we should not avoid to mention the struggles to turn real world politics around. And real political struggles as they are fought everywhere, be it around the Dakota pipeline in the US or the Bela Monte dam in Brazil, or around the damage to original forest being done by large scale logging and farming from Asia to Central Africa, are also struggles about truth. If we try to answer the question which view of the world is the true or the right one, it will affect how real world politics is being done.

17.5   Distant Feeling: The Reality of the Spiritual

A question which I didn't pose, nor answer yet is why I choose the term 'shamanist' over animist, to refer to what I consider to be real alternatives to the modernist interpretation of reality. As Rose points out, the term 'animist' originated with 19th century anthropologists, who aimed to create dualist descriptions of 'civilized' and 'primitive' peoples. The primitives were the animists, who, believing that everything (not just sentient beings, but all natural phenomena) is enlivened by a spirit, failed to recognize the fundamental difference between mind and matter, and between humankind and everything else (Rose 2013, 96). Present day academic animists therefore self-identify in a oppositional manner, rethinking the view of animated reality in a positive manner. It is not so much its origins which made me move from describing my interest as animist (which I did before) to shamanist—but the fact that 'animist' is an ontological indicator instead of an epistemological one. If we just recognize there to be varying ontologies (stretching thereby the claim present in the

---

[3] For a well-balanced review of Tempels' contribution to African philosophy, cf. Mosima (2016), 37–46.

singular use of the term), going together with cultural differences, we might easily slip in cultural relativism, and accept its side effect of letting existing power relations between knowledge systems remain in place. The term shamanist however, points to knowledge—and thus to epistemology. The shaman traditionally is the one who provides healing and direction for group members by entering upon a spirit journey.[4]

In order to tackle the politics of epistemologies, we should investigate the truth conditions of the spirit journey. To do so we should develop a wider epistemological model than the Kantian one, which restricts validity to those insights that keep to the boundaries of space, time and causality (cf. Roothaan 2012, 120). Shamanistic experience, now, does not do so—as the trance traveller crosses space without reckoning with time, and vice versa. Also causality does not seem to play a role, as the healing procedures of shamanist practice involve the possibility to put things that happened in the past (even among the ancestors) right, or attract events from the future to the now, as in the case of rainmaking or., e.g. the choice of a spiritual leader who is still an infant. The elephants in the case we are discussing seem to possess shamanistic abilities (in this description of them)—sensing across a distance, and possibly (although the descriptions from several media are not clear about this) even before the fact, the death of their 'friend'—as they are supposed to have arrived at his house the day after he passed, having walked a long distance.[5] These abilities seem to have been recognized in certain African epistemological systems—like in that of the San, as described in the collection of myths and stories about animals in Africa by Shelagh Ranger. Citing Peter Garlake, she writes how animals are thought to have shared humanness with the human race, before different species God gave them different roles and behaviors. Therefore

> Animals retain elements of their human past and nature; they conceive of themselves as human, are interested and involved in human affairs, will interfere in, help and hinder them. Animal behaviour is […] rational, purposive, directed by values and customs and institutions. Animals have language. Some practise sorcery. Their knowledge transcends that of humans in some areas […]. (Ranger 2007, 80)

This description has also something very specific to say about our case, for it continues—citing San people remarking that "'animals know all things', 'they know things that we don't', they know what is going to happen: 'an animal is a thing which knows of our death'" (Ranger 2007, 80). This would mean that not only elephants can have such knowledge, but all animals. Stories about the behavior of pets living with humans tend to confirm this. Like the one of the two dogs of a friend's husband, who was terminally ill. The dogs would come into his room regularly, but on the day

---

[4]Less accurately called a trance journey. Although the shaman induces his journey by entering a trance state, this is not the distinctive aspect of the phenomenon. It could be theoretically possible for certain individuals to make a spirit journey without the trance—to get spiritual knowledge so to speak directly, as is said of individuals who are extraordinarily wired to look into the spiritual realm (cf. Borg about Jesus).

[5]Now it becomes clear why I preferred the expression 'spiritual journey' to that of 'trance journey' for we do not know whether animals who show such abilities need to experience in a trance state. It might be possible that they, and human beings too, have this kind of knowledge while not leaving their everyday state of awareness.

that he was to die, they posted themselves at his bed, and stayed there the entire day until he was gone.

It is an important question how this kind of knowledge can be considered valid—we need wider conditions of possibility than the Kantian ones that restricts knowledge to that which can be known through the natural (empirical) sciences. The epistemology to measure knowledge like distant feeling and sensing death should take into account the wider reality of life: that of being in relation (as Plumwood also stresses) and that of realising things—an epistemology which I have named pragmatic-interactive—it measures knowledge for its potential for action-in-relation, or its "[…] furthering (in more or less successful ways) life as it is shared, and at the same time individually enjoyed" (Roothaan 2012, 128). Such an epistemology concurs with ideas of Plumwood *cum suis* that knowledge should be practice (future) oriented and should center relations instead of a certain species and its interest—but it goes beyond claiming this to be a right (moral) *standpoint*. It claims also to demarcate what is true and what is false epistemologically speaking.

The consequence of such an epistemological move now has to be that many aspects of the modernist humanist understanding of nature should be considered false, not furthering life as it is shared, nor as it is individually enjoyed—as they lead to extinction of our co-animals, to barren landscapes and to continuous sadness and fear in all those who do not belong to the centered group. Like it was the case with the elephant herd that was rescued by Anthony and his team. The turning point of the story how he rescued those elephants that broke loose continuously, and were about to be shot for it, lies in the efforts he made to talk to Nana, the matriarch of the herd, and to convince her that she should not fear while on his land (Anthony 2010, 64–79). Thus, the story is about more than preserving a group of elephants. It is more so about countering the view that only allows them to occupy the space of being a beautiful asset to nature, or a superfluous hindrance to human society—in both cases ignoring their own agency and potential for knowing about their oppressed situation.

17.6   Conclusion

What, now, has been the result of this analysis? It was the aim of this chapter to critically address Western dominated philosophical views of human-animal relations, and explore alternative ontologies for their potential for a new philosophical environmentalism starting from an African context. The story of the mourning elephants offered a good opportunity for this, as it finds itself at a crossroads of issues present in environmentalism. These issues are mainly those of

(a) the specific political, legal and organizational structures in previously colonized societies that form the frame of troubled human-elephant encounters, as it was shown referring to the works of Magome and Murombedzi.

(b) the questions concerning human-animal relations as such: can decentering the human animal help to understand the elephants' behavior over towards Anthony as towards a relative?

(c) the issue of the conditions of possibility (the politics of epistemologies) of 'shamanist' knowledge, more specifically of being aware of events beyond space and time, like the vigil of the elephants seems to imply.

In treating these different issues, I wanted to show the intertwinement of empirical (historical, legal, political, etc.), ethical and epistemological questions, being convinced that ethical approaches to real world issues should always also include awareness of the political backgrounds of these issues. In our case these political backgrounds imply the politics of things such as land-rights and democratic representation, but behind them they imply the politics of what may count as knowledge. I hope to have shown that an epistemological approach that adopts conditions of possibility based on interaction and life-enhancement, instead of the Kantian one that bases itself on causality, space and time, might support 'decentered' worldviews, such as the one of the San that entailed the knowledge that 'an animal is a thing that knows about our death'. Recognizing animals, to start with the elephants, to be capable of such knowledge, and of the intentional actions of compassion and giving back that are shown in their vigil for a human being they trusted, is then not just a nice ethical fringe on the dominant systems of power that go on to threaten life and well-being on this planet—but a critical act of resistance over against those systems. It would imply that we should listen more to what animals, being obviously wise and caring beings, have to say to us.

As a footnote to the above, we should recognize its implications—that not only non-human animals, like elephants, are capable of spiritual knowledge that defies space, time and causality, but that we, being animals also, have similar abilities. It seems however, that for the most of us, this kind of knowledge is harder to access than it is for more-than-human animals like the elephants, for all human cultures have developed varying strategies for inducing trance and/or meditative states in which such knowledge first can be accessed successfully.

References

Abugiche, A.S., T.O. Egute, and A. Cybelle. 2017. The Role of Traditional Taboos and Custom as Complementary Tools in Wildlife Conservation Within Mount Cameroon National Park Buea. *International Journal of Natural Resource Ecology and Management* 2 (3): 60–68. https://doi.org/10.11648/j.ijnrem.20170203.13. Accessed August 31, 2017.

Anthony, L., and G. Spence. 2009. *The Elephant Whisperer. Learning About Life, Loyalty and Freedom from a Remarkable Herd of Elephants*. London: Sidgewick & Jackson.

Bamana, G. 2014. Dogs and Herders: Mythical Kinship, Spiritual Analogy and Sociality in Rural Mongolia. *Sino-Platonic Papers* 245: 1–18.

Bordogna, F. 2008. *William James at the Boundaries. Philosophy, Science, and the Geography of Knowledge*. Chicago & London: The University of Chicago Press.

Derrida, J., and D. Wills. 2002. The Animal That Therefore I Am (More to Follow). *Critical Inquiry* 28 (2): 369–418. http://www.jstor.org/stable/1344276. Accessed February 12, 2011.

Ekwealo, C. 2017. *Ndu Mmili Ndu Azu. An Introduction to African Environmental Ethics.* Edited with Introduction by Diana-Abasi Ibanga. Surulere, Lagos: Redcom.

Eze, M.O. 2017. Humanitatis-Eco (Eco-Humanism): An African Environmental Theory. In *The Palgrave Handbook on African Philosophy*, ed. A. Afolayan and T. Falola. New York: Palgrave Macmillan (in print).

Harvey, G. 2012. An Animist Manifesto. *Philosophy, Activism, Nature* 9: 2–4.

Hens, L. 2006. Indigenous Knowledge and Biodiversity Conservation and Management in Ghana. *Journal of Human Ecology* 20 (1): 21–30. http://www.krepublishers.com/02-Journals/JHE/JHE-20-0-000-000-2006-Web/JHE-20-1-000-000-2006-Abstract-PDF/JHE-20-1-021-030-2006-1561-Hens-Luc/JHE-20-1-021-030-2006-1561-Hens-Luc-Text.pdf. Accessed June 9, 2017.

Kohn, E. 2013. *How Forests Think. Toward an Anthropology Beyond the Human.* Berkeley & Los Angeles/London: University of California Press.

Magome, H., and J. Murombedzi. 2003. Sharing South African National Parks: Community Land and Conservation in a Democratic South Africa. In *Decolonizing Nature. Strategies for Conservation in a Post-colonial Era*, ed. W.A. Adams and M. Mulligan. London/Sterling VA: Earthscan Publications Ltd., 108–134.

Mosima, P.M. 2016. *Philosophic Sagacity and Intercultural Philosophy. Beyond Henry Odera Oruka.* Leiden: African Studies Center.

Murombedzi, J. 2003. Devolving the Expropriation of Nature: The 'devolution' of Wildlife Management in Southern Africa. In *Decolonizing Nature. Strategies for Conservation in a Post-colonial Era*, ed. W.A. Adams and M. Mulligan, 135–151. London/Sterling, VA: Earthscan Publications Ltd.

Plumwood, V. 1995. Human Vulnerability and the Experience of Being Prey. *Quadrant* 29–34.

Plumwood, V. 2003. Decolonizing Relationships with Nature. In *Decolonizing Nature. Strategies for Conservation in a Post-colonial Era*, ed. W.A. Adams and M. Mulligan, 51–78. London/Sterling, VA: Earthscan Publications Ltd.

Ranger, S. 2007. *The Word of Wisdom and the Creation of Animals in Africa.* Cambridge: James Clarke & Co.

Roothaan, A. 2012. Why Religious Experience is Considered Personal and Dubitable—And What if it Were Not? In *Is Religion Natural?*, ed. D. Evers, M. Fuller, A. Jackelén, and T.A. Smedes, 117–129. London/New York: T&T Clark International.

Roothaan, A. 2015. The "Shamanic" Travels of Jesus and Muhammad: Cross-Cultural and Transcultural Understandings of Religious Experience. *American Journal of Theology & Philosophy* 34 (2): 140–153.

Roothaan, A. 2017. Aren't we Animals?: Deconstructing or Decolonizing the Human—Animal Divide. In *Are We Special?: Human Uniqueness in Science and Theology*, ed. M. Fuller, D. Evers, A. Runehov, and K.-W. Saether (Issues in Science and Theology). Springer.

Roothaan, A. 2019. *Indigenous, Modern and Postcolonial Relations to Nature. Negotiating the Environment.* London/New York: Routledge (forthcoming).

Rose, D.B. 2013. Val Plumwood's Philosophical Animism: Attentive Interactions in the Sentient World. *Environmental Humanities* 3: 93–109. http://environmentalhumanities.org/arch/vol3/3.5.pdf. Accessed August 31, 2017.

Part VI
Issues of Environmental Pollution in Africa

Chapter 18
Ethical Issues in Environmental Pollution: Multinational Corporations (MNCs) and Oil Industries in Tropical Regions—The Nigerian Niger-Delta Case

Kalu Ikechukwu Kalu and Konrad Ott

Abstract Multinational oil corporations (MNOCs) operating in the tropical region of the Nigerian Niger Delta have increasingly been accused of engaging in polluting and environmental degrading activities. The unsustainable issues of crude oil and gas exploitation by the MNOCs in this tropical region have been re-occurring episodes. The MNOCs' ability to carry out their operational act of crude oil exploration without taking responsibility for their actions have been characterized by associated environmental impacts that include, but not limited to environmental degradation, severe pollution, biota toxicity, ecological effects, loss of biodiversity, human health effects and gross abuse of human rights. There have been constant critics on the lack of MNOCs' adoption of an environmental sustainable approach that will avert issues of crude oil pollution and environmental degradation, and reduce human health consequences. Due to these corporate activities and potentially unethical practices associated with MNOCs, host communities, human rights groups and non-governmental organizations (NGOs) usually commence social movements against them. They agitate for the need of the MNOCs to adopt an appropriate attitude towards nature, human health and rights. Regarding MNOCs and the environmental protection in the Niger Delta, one fundamental question is: Do MNOCs have the "right" to cause environmental damage potentially resulting to loss of life and do they have an obligation to restore? This paper analyses the issues of oil and gas pollution problems emanating from the corporate act of the MNOCs in pursuance of sustainability, environmental and social justice for the environment and ecosystems of the oil-producing Niger Delta region.

Keywords MNOCs · Oil · Niger delta · Environment · Responsibility · Sustainability · Reparation and restoration

K. I. Kalu (✉) · K. Ott
Philosophisches Seminar der Christian-Albrechts-Universität zu Kiel, Kiel, Deutschland
e-mail: ikechukwu@philsem.uni-kiel.de

K. Ott
e-mail: ott@philsem.uni-kiel.de

© Springer Nature Switzerland AG 2019
M. Chemhuru (ed.), *African Environmental Ethics*, The International Library of Environmental, Agricultural and Food Ethics 29,
https://doi.org/10.1007/978-3-030-18807-8_18

18.1 Introduction

The discovery of oil deposits and oil industries in the topical region of the Nigerian resource-rich Niger Delta have been marred with some major variables—issues of environmental and social injustices, issues of responsibility and questions of sustainability. The aforementioned variables are results of potential immoral behaviours of the MNOCs impacts. The MNOCs' ability to carry out their crude oil exploratory activities without taking up responsibility for their business actions have impacted not only on the Niger Delta oil-rich host communities' human rights, human functional capabilities,[1] traditional economy[2] but have caused a host of harmful effects in the oil-producing natural environment such as environmental degradations, severe pollutions, biota toxicity, ecological effects, loss of biodiversity and global warming that transcends to climate change. The MNOCs have been associated with incessant environmental harms, ecological disaster of the marine ecosystems and organisms. Suffice it to postulate that the cause for these immoral behaviours and human rights problematic situation in the resource-rich Niger Delta lies in the governance gaps resulting from globalization (Ruggie 2008), which has to do with the scope and impact of economic forces and actors—MNOCs, and the capacity of the Niger Delta oil-rich to manage their adverse and unintended consequences. The governance gaps provide the laissez-faire and unrestricted environment for wrongful acts by the oil majors (being the core drivers of globalization phenomenon in the oil-producing Niger Delta) without adequate punishment or compensation (Ruggie 2008) from the Nigerian government. In moral philosophy, corporate acts that transgress issues of environmental and social justices, issues of responsibility and questions of sustainability are understood to be morally repugnant from an ethical perspective (Frederick 1999). This preliminary judgement must be substantiated by making the underlying principles (sustainability, justice) explicit and apply them correctly to a given case. Systems that establish the principles of what is morally right and wrong fall within the domain of normative ethics.[3] With regards to the MNOCs and environmental protection in the oil-producing Niger Delta, two fundamental ethical questions are involved, namely the questions of 'right' and 'moral responsibility': (a) *does the*

---

[1] In the work of Nussbaum (1999) "Sex and Social Justice", she enumerated some list of capabilities, which she calls 'threshold approach' for a decent quality of Livelihood, although Sen is not in conformity with such 'threshold approach'. However, Nussbaum justified her 'threshold approach' by saying "…that every person must be guaranteed realization of a minimum, basic level of each of these capabilities…this is a threshold approach, one that defines the minimum required in various fields in order for a person to live a full and free life in modern society." (Hananel and Berechman 2016: 80).

[2] The traditional economy of the resource-rich Niger Delta region is agrarian sector, which has to do with farming and fishing.

[3] Normative ethics helps in determining what we ought to do and helps justifying the actions that result from it. Normative ethics has to do with classical ethical theories and new ethical approaches. Classical ethical theories are Kantian deontology, utilitarianism, and contractualism and virtue ethics. While new ethical approaches are discourse ethics (as elaborated by Habermas) and capability approach (Sen and Nussbaum). Acts which are wrong or repugnant form the stated ethical theories are wrong or repugnant beyond reasonable doubt, which is known as argument from convergence.

MNOCs have the 'right' to cause environmental damage potentially resulting to loss of life and biodiversity and (b) *does the MNOCs have the 'moral responsibility' for restoring and rehabilitating the environment with the potential of increasing natural diversity for present and future generations?* An honest answer from most schools of thought to these questions will be an equivocal 'No' and 'Yes' respectively. However, the bottom-line is: there is the need for the MNOCs operating in the resource-rich Niger Delta to adopting an appropriate ethical attitude and principles towards human and natural environment. Whereby the MNOCs have acted against the ethical components of its mission statements, there should be compensatory justice that will take into consideration an act of compensation and in the case of the Niger Delta it entails restoration and reparation. This paper describes the Niger Delta geographic location, synopsis of the oil exploration, theoretical ethical reasons for compensatory justice that buttressed by (impact of oil exploration, pollution, poverty and human rights abuses, and ethical challenges in the Niger Delta). It equally articulates the issues of responsibility and sustainability in the Niger Delta, gives a proposal for political implementation that is followed by a conclusion.

18.2 Geography of the Niger Delta Tropical Region

The Niger Delta wetland is situated in the South-south and South-east geopolitical zones of the Sub-Saharan African Country of Nigeria and is a consortium of nine (9) Nigerian states (see Fig. 18.1) called "oil producing states" (Odunkoya 2006). It is a settlement to some 30 million humans, which is approximately 22% of the Nigerian population. The inhabitants are mostly local communities that depend primarily on the natural ecosystem for sustenance and livelihoods. They are into agrarian economy, but unfortunately oil exploitation constitutes adverse effects on the coastal landscapes, ecosystems and biodiversity (Boele et al. 2001). The wetland is geo-strategically located along the coastlines of the Atlantic Oceans. Within the Sub-Saharan Africa, it is the largest wetland estimating 20,000 km^2 (Tamuno and Edoumiekumo 2012). The wetland is naturally endowed with exhaustible or non-renewable resources (Kibert et al. 2012: 132) of crude oil and natural gas located both in *on-shore* and *off-shore*[4] oil fields (Saliu et al. 2007) and natural capitals (Ott et al. 2011: 13) for agriculture, forestry and fishing. The Niger Delta wetland has five ecological zones which include coastal zones, freshwater swamps, lowland rain-

---

[4]The on-shore and off-shore oil fields mean that the crude oil deposits are both on the land and in the sea. Exploration Drilling Production Solutions defines both as—On-shore "refers to the mainland. In exploration and production, "onshore" refers to the development of oil fields, gas deposits and geothermal energy on land." While off-shore has to do with "originally meant islands in the open sea belonging to a country. The term "offshore" means "off the coast". In oil and gas extraction, "offshore" refers to the development of oil fields and natural gas deposits under the ocean." http://exploration-production-services.de/en/home.html.

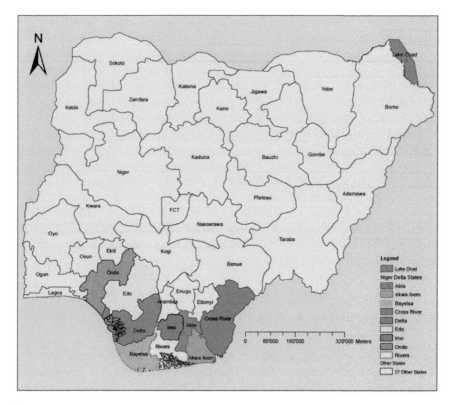

Fig. 18.1 Nigerian map showing the oil producing states of the Niger Delta (Ite et al. 2013: 79)

forests, mangrove swamps and barrier islands forests[5] and all makes the region one of the unique wetlands with marine ecosystem worldwide over (Kadafa 2012). The coastal zones and mangrove swamps of the Niger Delta are identified as the most important economically rich ecological zones amid the five main zones.

However, due to the harmful effects of oil exploitation, the Niger Delta oil-rich yearns for compensatory justice according to Polluter pays principle (PPP)[6] and this compensation entails (a) improving human capabilities and (b) natural capitals by means of restoration (strong sustainability).The Niger Delta natural capitals need

---

[5]Barrier Island forests have coastal area of the mangrove vegetation and tropical rainforest in the northern reaches of the delta.

[6]PPP is a famous environmentalist rules which demands that the monetary valuations (costs) of pollution ought to be bear by the person that precipitate the said or such pollution. Its objective is to holding the polluter accountable for the external monetary valuations (costs) occurring as a result of pollution created. It executes such functions like prevention and controlling of pollution and remediation, if pollution happens to occur.

Fig. 18.2 A prototype of the Niger Delta farmlands and ecosystem in Ogoni-land that has been devastated by crude oil spills (photograph by the authors)

restoration, remediation, clean-up and reparation of the damaged environment (see Fig. 18.2) in order to see if there will be some prospects for even organic agriculture.[7]

Although, there have been some environmental findings of the United Nations Environmental Programme (UNEP) report on acts of ecological restoration of some of the oil spill sites, but the prospects of rehabilitation of the damaged sites are not yet feasible due to the question of—*who will be morally responsible for the restoration of the damaged environments, the polluters, the beneficiaries or both*? This question gives rise to the dual principles of Polluter pays principle (PPP)[8] and Beneficiary pays principle (BPP)[9] and of which both are quite ad rems to the Niger Delta oil-rich.

---

[7] Organic Agriculture is a production system that sustains the health of soils, ecosystems and people. It relies on ecological processes, biodiversity and cycles adapted to local conditions, rather than the use of inputs with adverse effects. Organic Agriculture combines tradition, innovation and science to benefit the shared environment and promote fair relationships and a good quality of life for all involved (International Federation of Organic Agriculture Movements—IFOAM).

[8] See footnote number 6.

[9] The BPP concept advocates that the beneficiaries of the causal factor of the environmental pollution ought to be held responsible for its external costs and should subsequently be obliged to pay compensation to the victims of the externalities. Adherents of BPP believe that if a person, business organization or moral agent (beneficiaries) benefits from activities that injure others, the beneficiaries are morally bound to compensate the injured victims despite the possibility that the beneficiaries are not the causal factor of the injury.

18.3   Background of Oil Exploration

The discovery of crude oil in 1956 by an Anglo-Dutch firm called Shell-British Petroleum (then Shell D' Arcy) altered the economic landscape of the Nigerian reliance on agricultural export commodities for its foreign exchange earnings. A German company called Nigerian Bitumen Corporation was the first company that commenced the exploration of crude oil in Nigeria. Some literatures lend credence to this adventure:

> Petroleum exploration in Nigeria dates back to the first few years of this century. Organized marketing and distribution started around 1907 by a German Company, Nigerian Bitumen Corporation. (Ibeanu 2000: 21)

Unfortunately, the First World War thwarted their oil exploration activities (Nigerian National Petroleum Corporation News 2014).

However, the coming on stage of Shell D' Arcy in 1938 via a crude oil exploration licence that was extended to it by the then British colonial government in Nigeria to explore crude oil all through the Nigerian state was positive oriented (Nigerian National Petroleum Corporation News 2014). This crude oil exploration license illustrates the monopoly of Britain's imperial rights and hegemony over its colonies and on crude oil exploration. It was stated that with respect to Nigeria "the history of the oil industry is the history of imperialism."(Odunkoya 2006: 250).

Shell-BP was determined to explore crude oil in the Niger Delta. Thus, right from 1956, Shell-BP invested an enormous sum in its exploratory activities. It was reported that:

> Shell/D'Arcy has spent a total of 70,000 lb on its geological survey and on the cost of drilling of oil wells in the Niger Delta area. (Raji and Abejide 2013: 23)

Consequently, Shell-BP successfully struck the first oil deposit and subsequent drilling in 1956 in Oloibiri community in the present Bayelsa State (Kadafa 2012). It was in the same year of 1956 that Shell D' Arcy was renamed Shell-British Petroleum (Shell-BP).

Nigerian first export of crude oil was on the 17.02.1058. Shell-BP was instrumental to this milestone premier exportation. 1958 marked the genesis of 'petro-business' in the Niger Delta resource-rich region in particular and Nigeria in general (Odeyemi and Ogunseitan 1985). Shell-BP maintained the sole 'concessionary right' of crude oil exploration until 1960, when it was altered with the 'concessionary right' of oil exploration being extended to other foreign oil majors or MNOCs. Nigeria witnessed the oil boom in the 1970s and it became a member of Organization of Petroleum Exporting Countries (OPEC) in 1971 (Onyemaechi 2012). The Nigerian National Petroleum Corporation (NNPC)[10] was established in 1977.

---

[10]NNPC is a state owned oil corporation. It coordinates the public sector of the oil business while the multinational oil corporations (MNOCs) oversee the private sector. NNPC oversee the joint venture models between the Nigerian state and the MNOCs. As such, NNPC controls the upstream, midstream, downstream sectors and 14 subsidiaries of the Nigerian state oil business. http://nnpcgroup.com/AboutNNPC/CorporateInfo.aspx.

18.4 Impact of Oil Exploration

The ubiquitous presence of MNOCs in the Niger Delta oil-rich have generally promoted technological innovations, encourage an increase in foreign direct investments (FDI), investment capitals and trade flows into the oil-producing region in particular and Nigeria as a country. In fact, Nigeria has profited enormously from the crude oil exploration, discovery and subsequent production. This profit is premised on foreign exchange earnings and gross domestic revenue gained from its massive crude oil production and exports. On the other side, the existence of the MNOCs is being characterized by ethical challenges of human rights abuses and tremendous harmful effects on natural environment and biodiversity. The issue of moral entitlements are empirical evidences of ethical challenges of human rights abuses and catastrophic environmental impacts associated with oil exploitation in the Niger Delta. This issue of moral entitlements has to do with Nussbaum's list of ten human capabilities[11] which are quite peculiar to the Niger Delta oil-rich environment, where harmful effects due to oil pollution have reduce the capabilities of the people from effective functioning.

The Nussbaum ten listed capabilities (issue of moral entitlements) will be categorize in this paper under the capabilities of the resource-rich Niger Delta that are being impaired (impaired moral entitlements)[12] and those that are being violated (violated moral entitlements)[13] and aftermath we shall discuss three capabilities on each categorization as to enunciate the impact of oil exploratory activities.

18.4.1 Impaired Moral Entitlements

Life is the first Nussbaum 'threshold approach' under the impaired capabilities. The local communities of the Niger Delta ought to have high rate of life expectancy because of the natural endowments of the region, their good biodiversity with an ecosystems consisting of highly diversified species of flora and fauna and wonderful ecological structure. But the empirical situation in the region is a reverse opposite. A situational analysis shows evidence of low life expectancy because of heavy exposition of the inhabitants to toxic substances from the soil, water and air due to oil spills and natural gas flaring (which is a principle of causality, for there is a correlation between toxicity and life expectancy). Thus, the Niger Delta Development Com-

---

[11] In her work **Sex and Social Justice**, Martha Nussbaum listed the following ten capabilities she considers relevant to enhance performance and functions: Life, Bodily Health, Bodily Integrity, Senses, Imagination, and Thought, Emotions, Practical Reason, Affiliation, Other Species, Play and Control over one's environment.

[12] The capabilities we classified under the impaired moral entitlements are—Life, Bodily Health, Senses, Imagination, Thought, Emotions, Affiliation and Play.

[13] The capabilities we classified under the violated moral entitlements are—Bodily Integrity, Practical Reason, Other Species and Control over one's Environment.

Fig. 18.3 Oil spills sites in Ogoni-land of the Niger Delta, 22.01.2016 (Photo taken by the authors)

Fig. 18.4 Processing of cassava flakes near gas flaring sites in the Niger Delta (The Economist 2008) and (Heather 2012) respectively!

mission (NDDC) noted that incessant oil spills and gas flaring is reducing the life expectancy of the Niger Deltas to 40 s mostly in the mangrove swamps and barrier islands forests (Abidde 2017).

Bodily Health is the second Nussbaum 'threshold approach'. Local communities in the Niger Delta are supposed to be enjoying quality health due to the region's endowments with natural capitals; instead of suffering from increase in poor health. The images on oil spillages (see Fig. 18.3) and gas flaring in the Niger Delta region (see Fig. 18.4) depict the actual environmental situation in the Niger Delta. In the local communities of the Niger Delta, there exist a correlation between bodily health and life expectancy in the region.

Senses, Imagination, Thought (constructive reasoning) are the third Nussbaum 'threshold approach'. Constructive or positive reasoning ought to be the normal way of livelihood within the local communities of the Niger Delta. However, due to the nature of environmental injustice imminent in the region destructive or negative reasoning is the order of the day resulting to 'petro-violence' vis-à-vis arms and weapons proliferation (Isiaka 2010), emergence of militant groups, bunkering and kidnapping.

The capability of practical reason is distorted under such conditions. Destructive reasoning is the side effects of education. In any civilised society or environment, access to quality education plays an important role towards constructive reasoning and poverty emancipation. Quality education brings out the nature-nurture wisdom inherent in an individual thereby making the person to having good senses, quality thoughts and imagination. The situational analysis within the Niger Delta shows greater numbers of the local communities are still illiterate without accessibility to education. World Bank Report of 1995 corroborated by stating thus:

> Education levels are below the national average and are particularly low for women. While 76 percent of Nigerian children attend primary schools this level drops to 30 percent in some parts of the Niger Delta. (Oviasuyi and Uwadiae 2010: 120)

18.4.2   Violated Moral Entitlements

Bodily integrity happens to be the first Nussbaum 'threshold' capabilities that are being violated. There ought to be bodily integrity—freedom of movement, security, ability to have sexual pleasure—in the local communities, but the situational report seems to be the reverse opposite. The threshold of bodily integrity in the Niger Delta is more of a chain of social and immoral causality resulting from oil exploration and exploitation in the region. The impacts of environmental injustice in the Niger Delta have tremendously resulted to youth restiveness, which (Okorosaye-Orubite 2008: 1002–1013) defined as: "violent activities embarked upon by the youth to back up or press further the demands of the indigenes for a fairer deal in the crude oil business." Suffice it to state that the youth restiveness has transmuted into militant groups, hooliganism, kidnapping, oil bunkering and rapid increase in the number of weapons and ammunitions among the groups making the region to be "enmeshed in conflict and militancy" (Essien 2008: 294).

In the course of the militant groups' agitation for some fundamental human rights for livelihood and natural environment, most of the militants have taken to destructive agenda. This single act of the militants resulted to heavy militarization of the region by the MNOCs and Nigerian government in order to quell the disturbances of the militant groups and take absolute control of the oil explorations. This heavy militarization of the region has become a chain of social and immoral causality resulting to:

> Indiscriminate arrests, torture, rape and extrajudicial execution…contrary to the principles of increasing the wellbeing of the people of the Niger Delta and avoidance of adverse impacts. (ECCR 2010: 10)

Practical reason is classified as the second Nussbaum 'threshold' capabilities that are being violated. There is lack of adequate or functional educational systems that supposed to equip the Niger Delta youths with wholesome scientific and vocational skills or knowledge that would avail them the competency to compete for job within their locality. Practical reason is a product of functional education which is lacking in most local communities of the Niger Delta and its result has been youth restiveness and act of militancy. Functional education has its own contribution to the development of the psyche because it "develops the life of the mind that acts from the wholeness of organic life, with relation to practical life in the present and in the future" (Abraham 2011: 442). Functional education is one of the factors that sustain the capabilities of practical reason for it "enables the learner to gain thinking habits and develop the technical means needed in solving practical problems" (Abraham 2011: 442).

Other species is the third Nussbaum 'threshold' capabilities. As Halsband (2016) argues, the entitlement of being capable to live in concern and in relationship to a world of nature (Nussbaum) has strong implications for a human live that can endorse the beauty, fertility, and diversity of the non-human world. Empirical evidences currently show that an anthropogenic emission of oil extraction is a major threat to the anthropocentric capability to live in concern to a world of nature in the oil-rich region. Human interference such as MNOCs oil exploratory activities is quite harmful to the region's nature conservation and ecosystem. Either of the pervasive or directional anthropogenic changes or interference does occur in the form of ecosystem degradation or habitats pollution—both are ubiquitous in the local communities of the Niger Delta—thereby violating human capability to live in accordance with nature in the resource-rich region. Even if it is not clear, how the capability to live in concern for a natural world refers to biodiversity or how a threshold of this capability might be defined, it seems safe to argue that this capability is impaired and distorted under conditions of heavy environmental damage and pollution.

18.5   Pollution, Poverty and Human Rights Abuses

Predominantly the inhabitants of the local communities of the Niger Delta oil-rich states are farmers and fishermen. But due to the empirical diverse forms of oil and gas generated harmful effects, this traditional economy have become extremely difficult in all the oil and gas affected areas, and even drinking water has become scarce. Malnourishment and diseases are very common. The former president of the Movement of the Survival of Ogoni People (MOSOP)[14] Mr. Mitee on the 15.04.1999 at Port-Harcourt stated that:

> Lots of lands have been devastated by oil and drinking waters are left polluted. People inhale carbon dioxide and lots of lives have been lost due to pollution from spillages. (Eweje 2006: 27–56)

---

[14](Earth Rights International 1995–2015) asserted that MOSOP "is a human rights group founded in 1990 that is committed to using nonviolence to stop the repression and exploitation of the Ogoni and their resources by Shell and the Nigerian government. Upon its founding, MOSOP quickly garnered wide support and in 1993, at least half the total Ogoni population publicly supported the group. Ken Saro-Wiwa, founding member and president of MOSOP brought worldwide attention to the human rights violations committed against the Ogoni through international campaigning and his poignant writing. He was nominated for a Nobel Prize and awarded the Right Livelihood Award and the Goldman Prize for his environmental and human rights activism.".

The local communities' health and livelihood are in danger and being compromised due to the operations of the MNOCs. The environmental hazards exacerbated by the activities of the oil corporations in Niger Delta oil-rich present the most difficult enigma. Oil and gas exploration in the resource-rich region has proved more catastrophic to the environment than any other part of the world, where oil and gas is explored.[15] One of the reports noted that:

> Several major rivers are heavily polluted; farmlands are under acid rain and oil spills, and carbon dioxide emissions in the area are among the highest in the world. It has been calculated that some 45.8 billion kilowatts of heat are discharged into the atmosphere of the region from flaring, 1.8 billion cubic feet of gas every day. (Cited in Oviasuyi and Uwadiae 2010: 116)

The phenomenon of flaring gas is another harmful effect in the region. Albeit, there have been a decrement on the quantity of gas flaring now; but the quantity so far flared contributes to greenhouse emissions which invariably constitute climate change. Mr. Mitee stated thus:

> Apart from physical destruction to plants around the flaring areas, thick soot is deposited on building roofs of neighbouring villages. Whenever it rains, the soot is washed off and the black ink-like water running down the roofs is believed to contain chemicals which adversely affect the fertility of the soil. (Eweje 2006: 27–56)

For the Niger Delta local communities, the environmental, social and economic costs of the oil and gas explorations have been tremendous, rendering majority of the local communities to perpetual penury and misery due to the very fact that their traditional economy of farming and fishing have been hampered upon by the crude oil exploratory activities. Resultantly some of the host communities are challenging the performances of the MNOCs and that of the Nigerian government, positing questions like—*Could this oil income lead to sustainability for the local communities and the entire Niger Delta oil-producing environment?*

18.6 Ethical Challenges

The harmful effects of oil pollution in the oil-producing Niger Delta local communities portray "one of the clearest examples of the inhumanity of man to man" (Esikot and Akpan 2013: 11). The weighty nature of the environmental injustice and human rights abuse imminent in the Niger Delta is best enunciated in a Latin proverb—'*Homo homini lupus est*' meaning 'Man is a wolf to another man', which is in consonance with the Hobbesian description of the state of nature. The oil resources of the delta have turned from a prospect for prosperity to a curse, initiating and maintaining devil's circles by which many human capabilities of the overall population

---

[15]Due to numerous cases of oil spillages, some parts of the Niger Delta ecosystem do not contain or produce anything positive in terms of agricultural products. In fact some of the Niger Delta environments are ugly and often devastated or barely inhabitable place or area for they are completely without a particular quality or activity anymore.

have been impaired and degraded. Beside ecological disasters, the societal setting is full of despair, distrust, violence, and moral corruption of different kinds. Perhaps, ecological restoration activities may pave a way out of such devil's circles.

The ethical challenges of crude oil exploration and exploitation are predicated on the issue of environmental restoration and rehabilitation of the degraded environment at the aftermath of crude oil exploitations vis-à-vis the act of compensation for the victims of the harmful effects. *What ought to be done in the event of environmental degradation? Will the issue of compensation be the best alternate approach that will balance the hazardous effect of crude oil exploration and nature? What techniques of operation could be applied that will be sequential to ethical environmental care?* The rationale for these questions are because of the fact that the Niger Delta oil-rich ought to be having high rate of life expectancy and quality health due to the region's natural endowments. Unfortunately, empirical evidences postulate the opposite.

Due to the harmful effects of oil pollution, the immune systems of the inhabitants of the Niger Delta are being weakened for drinking toxic water and breathing poisonous chemicals. Of course most of the people are suffering from respiratory diseases, leukaemia, strokes, reproductive defects, skin problems, cancer, cholera and deformities in children are imminent. The Niger Delta is suffering from the concept of externality (Kibert et al. 2012: 130) and its externality is a negative externality due to the fact that they are bearing the cost of the MNOCs' business joint ventures with the Nigerian government which has adversely affected and it is still affecting them. In fact, the rate of environmental injustice and human rights abuse being meted out to the Niger Delta oil-rich region by the MNOCs demand concepts of restoration, rehabilitation and subsequently compensation where the need arises.

18.7   Issues of Responsibility

The issues of responsibility as it concerns MNOCs' corporate acts in the resource-rich Niger Delta has to do with ethical responsibilities—moral and social responsibilities being required or expected of corporations. An ethical responsibility demands a duty in pursuance of a morally correct path by the MNOCs in the course of their corporate acts; for they are required to have moral responsibility to the natural environment and social responsibility towards the host communities of the oil-producing Niger Delta who expects them to do the right thing, bearing in mind that the corporate existence vis-à-vis social licences to operate depends on the host communities.

As such the freedom to perform a corporate act is permissible and the ability to take up the responsibility resulting from such corporate action is ethical. The MNOCs operating in the Niger Delta oil-rich have the ability and capacity to carry out their operational act of crude oil extraction, however; they should be open to take ethical responsibilities resulting from their corporate acts. The MNOCs owe some degree of ethical responsibilities towards the welfare of their host communities and conservation of their natural environment. MNOCs are required to fully abide with human rights and environmental laws in the resource-rich Niger Delta. They are expected to act responsibly and avert some immoral behaviour. Responsibility entails duties of compensatory justice.[16] Compensatory justice demands restoration, sharp reduction of pollution, improving health conditions, education etc. The PPP[17] and BPP[18] are quite ad rem on this issue of responsibility because the MNOCs being the polluters and profiteer of the financial reward of the crude oil exploratory activities necessitate that they should bear the responsibilities of the costs of restoration of the damaged Niger Delta ecosystem and compensate the local communities of the Niger Delta oil rich where the need arises.

The issue of corporate responsibility (CR) falls within the ambient of ethical responsibility required of the MNOCs. In the CR context, the MNOCs are required to respond not only to their shareholders but also to other stakeholders. In the resource-rich Niger Delta, CR in business demands an inherent culture that is embedded and fundamentally rooted on ethical values and subsequent application of these ethical values to all business behaviours and functions by the MNOCs. These ethical values have to do with the procedural way business is being done (Institute of Business Ethics 2006). The MNOCs should be aware that the Niger Delta oil-rich know the social and environmental responsibilities expected and required of them "notwithstanding considerable disagreement about the meaning of the term—CR—and its various versions and implications" (Lodge and Wilson 2006: 72), of which Milton Friedman's famous referral doctrine that business has only one responsibility, maximization of profit for the stockholders of business (Friedman 1970) is amid the versions. We reject Friedman's definition due to its narrowness. Friedman even explained further that, this pursuance of profit for the stockholders should be within the ambient of ethical behaviour and environmental laws of the land (Friedman 1970). Of course the MNOCs should realize that John Elkington's phraseology of triple bottom line[19] should be a conceptual framework of their corporate business acts and they are expected to abide by the Kantian moral duty—(the deontological ethics)—as stated in the stakeholder theory of the modern capitalism otherwise known as Kantian capitalism.[20]

---

[16]Compensatory justice performs duties for correcting what ought to be taking into account as unjustified or undeserved injuries to persons or their possessions. It is a form of corrective justice and the idea is to furnish the person with 'a full and perfect equivalent' replacement of what (something) he or she has been deprived off.

[17]See footnote number 6 on the definition of Polluter pays principle (PPP).

[18]See footnote number 9 on the meaning of Beneficiary pays principle (BPP).

[19]John Elkington coined this phraseology—triple bottom-line (3BL). 3BL is a framework for measuring business performance. Pragmatically the concern of the triple bottom-line is that in a corporations reporting framework, it should take into account not only the financial outcome but also the environmental and social performances. The triple bottom-line has its focus not only on the economic prosperity, but also on environmental quality and social justice, which very often business tends to forget in its operational procedures. The idea of a triple bottom line proposes that for a corporation to operate in a society is not all about satisfying the stockholders via improved profits (the economic bottom line), rather taking into cognizance the social and environmental performances.

[20]Kantian capitalism has a normative moral claim that the Niger Deltas as stakeholders in the crude oil exploratory activities "has a right not to be treated as a means to some end, and therefore must

As such, the CR concept in the resource-rich Niger Delta region signify the commitment the MNOCs should make to its stakeholders in order to contribute to positive impacts while trying to reduce the negative aspects of their corporate acts. The ultimate achievement of CR has to do with core business activities; not considering that corporations have shifted from this idea of core business acts (required) to perceiving CR through the prism of voluntary and philanthropic gestures famously known as corporate social responsibility (CSR)—'public relations quick fix solution'. Of course, I should not deny the obvious that some MNOCs are not trying their best in the CSR concept but their frantic efforts of the CSR gestures are yet to produce some optimal dividends that are expected; when compared with their potential immoral practices and its impacts on human rights and natural environment of the Niger Delta oil-rich region vis-à-vis the MNOCs' respective mission statements regarding—honesty, responsibility, sustainability and stakeholder involvement.

18.8   Issue of Sustainability

The oil-producing Niger Delta cannot be talking of sustainability when the area has been marred with issues of human rights predicaments, social and environmental injustices resulting from the potential wrongful practices of the MNOCs. In fact, the issue of sustainability in the resource-rich region is enigmatic, for it is still at the realm of policy framework rather than reality. Ott asserts that the concept of sustainability "balances economic, ecological and social values in the principled pursuit of long term welfare." Whereas, the 2011 United Nations Environmental Programme (UNEP) report on Ogoni-land elucidates the empirical environmental situation of the oil-producing region where UNEP:

> …found severe and widespread contamination of soil and ground water across Ogoni land. In a number of locations public health was severely threatened by contaminated drinking water and carcinogens. Delta ecosystems such as mangroves had been utterly devastated. (UNEP 2016: 1)

From an ethical perspective, the concept of sustainability focuses on the members of the same generations, members of different generations and members of future generations on issues of environmental justice and equity with emphasis on natural resources (Ott 2008). This principle highlighted the ethical question on 'moral responsibility'. The concept of sustainability thus:

> …includes a principle according to which every human being has a moral right (entitlement) to satisfy his or her basic needs. Furthermore, it includes a principle of intergenerational fairness. (Ott 2008: 2)

This issue of sustainability signifies a 'long term dimension or welfare' with a special eye on natural capital, however pragmatically in the Niger Delta oil-rich the

---

participate in determining the future direction of the firm in which they have a stake." (Bowie 1999:10).

MNOCs confusingly defines it only from the prism of economic sustainability.[21] This seems to be a very weak sustainability concept. The MNOCs and the Nigerian government are required to play active role in capacity-building and development activities focusing on sustainability based decision making. This entails an ability or capacity of something to be maintained or sustain itself. It is about taking what we need to live now, without jeopardizing the potential for people in the future to meet their own needs (Ott 2008). This seems to be a strong sustainability concept. The resource-rich region's extensive forest reserves consisting of natural and plantation forestry need an act of conservation. The natural forest has lots of beautiful ecosystem services and freshwater swamps that provide foods—fish and other aquatic food such as crabs and other invertebrates. Also the natural forest is biodiversity hotspots which harbour a variety of important indigenous-economic trees such as mahogany tree (Swietenia macrophylla), iroko tree (Milicia excelsa) and achi tree (Brachystegia laurentii). These indigenous-economic trees are used as timber products, saw logs, fuel wood and chewing sticks. The biodiversity are habitats to many of the important faunal and flora, endemic or near-endemic mammal species and terrestrial vertebrates such as: bush pigs, monkeys, crass-cutters, hippopotamus and crocodiles. These entire ecological buffers of the Niger Delta require strong sustainability.

18.9   Proposal for Political Implementation

Amid all the enunciated deadlocks due to oil pollution, a real agenda for the oil-producing Niger Delta is a sine qua non in order to break the devil's circles in which people are locked in. This real agenda is a political proposal for there are explicit empirical evidences that the crude oil exploratory activities in the resource-rich Niger Delta are having some colossal impacts in the region. Of which the associated negative effects of the oil pollutions with regards to environmental victimization, human health and livelihood, violence and socio-economic costs in the oil-rich region are dreadful. Moreover, the Nigerian government seems to be weak to implement the Human Rights Council Agenda item 3[22] as to enforce the MNOCs to act in accordance with the principle of good field oil practices in the oil-rich region of the Niger Delta, as it is being practiced in some developed oil-producing countries like Norway, United States and Canada. In this present situation, the question begging for an

---

[21]Where economic sustainability is understood to mean "(i) remaining commercially viable (both now and ideally across future generations) and (ii) being able to sustain operations in the face of unexpected and severe events, such as the global financial crisis which struck in 2007/8 for example" (Broadstock 2016: 1).

[22]The UNITED NATIONS HUMAN RIGHTS COUNCIL in its Twenty-sixth session stipulated Agenda item 3 which focuses on "Promotion and protection of all human rights, civil, political, economic, social and cultural rights, including the right to development." Of which this Agenda item 3 is quite ad rem to the resource-rich Niger Delta situation. See the Human Rights Council resolution 5/1 of 18 June 2007, http://www2.ohchr.org/english/bodies/hrcouncil/docs/10session/ProvAgenda10session.pdf.

answer is: *which policy action ought to be adopted as to remedy the harmful effects and injustice, to take adequate account of the reparation of environmental damage and human rights, to achieve environmental sustainability and poverty reduction in the oil-producing Niger Delta?* This paper proposes a policy action for political implementation which might improve the overall situation and break out of the deadlock situation. This suggested policy action is policy proposal resulting from an ethical research cum analysis, justification of some crucial claims and a critical diagnosis of the overall Nigeria Delta oil-rich situations. The policy action has to do with an establishment of a commission for a policy change. It would be a joint implementation constitution of an epistemic/political community[23] [which is more inclusive] comprising of the following:—(a) Nigerian government, States, Locals—(b) MNOCs: experts on oil production—(c) Scientific board [which is strictly scientific, including humanities]—(d) UN-representatives (World Bank, UNEP), Organization of American States (OAS) and people involved in the Sustainable Development Goals (SDGs) process. This suggested approach would not just be more of the same previous initiatives but rather, it will be a total overhauling that requires beginning again[24] with a new viewpoint and line of action. It should not be based on incrementalism, instead a fresh start with too much history in the background. This political process of the suggested policy action should start with a great roundtable reconciliatory-conference, being organized perhaps by the World Bank and with the title—**Beginning Again: A Future for the Niger Delta**. The result of the reconciliatory-conference should be anchored on a—Declaration that defines common moral ground (commonly shared principles). The focusses of the commission's work shall be: (a) Phasing out gas flaring immediately, (b) Starting restoration and recovery measures (c) Reconciling opponents and safeguarding peaceful cooperation. This might open a pathway which could reconcile the SDG objectives with ecological restoration in a genuine peaceful post-colonial spirit.

18.10   Conclusion

This paper observed that it is quite obvious that the joint venture partnership between the Nigerian government and the MNOCs in the course of oil exploitation activities have not developed the oil-producing Niger Delta. Instead it has bred ruins, underdevelopment and unsustainability, environmental and social injustices. However, be

---

[23]Haas(1992) in his work "Introduction: Epistemic Communities and International Policy Coordination", p. 3, defines the concept of "epistemic community" as "a network of professionals with recognized expertise and competence in a particular domain and an authoritative claim to policy-relevant knowledge within that domain or issue-area.".

[24]The idea of "Beginning Again" is premised on Christian ethics, which demands that persons should try to make fresh starts, reconciliations and acceptance of guilt as a prerequisite for "Beginning Again", with the assumption that—we all have failed, let us try to live together as human beings and improve situations. A declaration of peace as "conditio sine qua non" ought to be the ultimate aim.

it as it may the proposed policy action for political implementation that has to do with a constituted epistemic/political community should define a common agenda based on some topical issues that have been affecting the Niger Delta oil-rich and then consent to what is obligatory and indispensable for development to forge ahead. For instance, curbing the harmful effects of oil pollution in the Niger Delta demands that the Nigerian government and the MNOCs should implement the 2011 UNEP Report that emphasizes a holistic cleaning-up of Ogoni-land vis-à-vis extending the restoration project to every part of the Niger Delta oil-rich. The Nigerian government as the duty bearers should see to it that victims of the harmful effects due to oil pollution are duly compensated. If individual compensation is unfeasible, collective compensation of local communities is appropriate. Furthermore, the avoidance of human rights abuse, environmental injustice and enthronement of social justice in the oil-producing Niger Delta should be paramount and ad rem to the MNOCs and the Nigerian government. The MNOCs should not undermine opportunities of the resource-rich region and its natural environment as they strive to meet their own economic needs and benefits. Rather, strong sustainability that talks about a constant natural capital rule and a rule to invest in natural capitals should be a sine qua non for implementation by the Nigerian government. Moreover, both the MNOCs and the Nigerian government ought to know that the oil-producing Niger Delta has rights and entitlements under the capability approach[25] and third generation of human rights.[26] If the MNOCs take seriously their own new mission statements (as elucidated above) they should actively take the role of social entrepreneurs who promote, assist and finance a fresh start to restore the Niger Delta and improve capabilities of its inhabitants. The moral reasons are embedded in PPP,[27] BPP[28] and APP[29] because MNOCs are polluters, they have benefitted and they are highly able to make payments that may counts investments in a better future. MNOCs may also have sound prudential reasons to gain reputation among a global civil society if they act as if they would remorse their past behaviours.

---

[25] Amartya Sen concept of capability approach required the Niger Delta oil-rich to have the freedom to be and to leave the quality of life they want to live in order for them to exercise their functionings which has to do with the issue of ends (intrinsic value) and issue of means (instrumental value). While, the idea of 'dignified livelihood' is the basic though behind Martha Nussbaum capability approach; because human beings (Niger Delta local communities) are essentially rational agents and ought to possess the power of moral choice.

[26] This third generation of human rights addresses, right to development, right to peace, right to self-determination, right to decent environmental conditions, right to natural resources, right to food security, right to safe fresh water, right to unspoiled soils, right against polluters, right to intergenerational equity and sustainability, right to specific goods and access to infrastructures that are crucial for capabilities performance.

[27] See footnote number 6 on the components of Polluter pays principle (PPP).

[28] See footnote number 9 on the constituents of Beneficiary pays principle (BPP).

[29] Ability to pay principle (APP) postulates that taxes ought to be paid based on the amount of the taxpayer's earnings notwithstanding the utilities obtained. APP states that a taxpayer's earnings ought to display the proportion to be given for communal spending; with emphasis on income as the best means for such measurements.

References

Abidde, S.O. 2017. *Nigeria's Niger Delta: Militancy, Amnesty, and the Post Amnesty Environment.* Lanham: Lexington Books.

Abraham, N.M. 2011. Functional Education, Militancy and Youth Restiveness in Nigeria's Niger Delta: The Place of Multi-National Oil Corporations (MNOCs). *African Journal of Political Science and International Relations* 5 (10): 442–447.

Ite, A.E., U.J. Ibok, M.U. Ite, and S.W. Petters. 2013. Petroleum exploration and production: Past and present environmental issues in the Nigeria's Niger delta. *American Journal of Environmental Protection* 1(4): 78-90.http://dx.doi.org/10.12691/env-1-4-2.

Boele, et al. 2001. Shell, Nigeria and the Ogoni. A Study in Unsustainable Development: 1. The Story of Shell, Nigeria and the Ogoni People—Environment, Economy, Relationships: Conflict and Prospects for Resolution. *Sustainable Development* 9: 74–86.

Bowie, N.E. 1999. A kantian approach to business ethics, part I business ethics and normative theories.

Broadstock, D. 2016. *Finding a balance between economic and environmental Sustainability.* South China Morning Post Publishers Ltd.

ECCR. 2010. *Shell in the Niger Delta: A Framework for Change.* Oxford.

Esikot, I.F., and M. Akpan. 2013. The Niger Delta Crisis in Nigeria: Some Moral Lessons. *International Journal of History and Philosophical Research* 1 (1): 1–13.

Essien, E.S. 2008. *Philosophy of Peace and Conflict Beyond the United Nations.* Calabar: University of Calabar Press.

Eweje, G. 2006. Environmental Costs and Responsibilities Resulting from oil Exploration in Developing Countries: The Case of the Niger Delta of Nigeria. *Journal of Business Ethics* 69: 27–56.

Frederick, R. 1999. *A Companion to Business Ethics.* Malden, Mass., Oxford: Blackwell Publishers.

Friedman, M. 1970. The Social Responsibility of Business is to Increase Its Profits. *The New York Times Magazine,* 13 Sept 1970.

Haas, P.M. 1992. Introduction: Epistemic Communities and International Policy Coordination. *International Organization* 46: 1–35.

Halsband, Aurélie. 2016. *Konkrete Nachhaltigkeit. Welche Natur wir für zukünftige Generationen erhalten sollten.* Bade-Baden: Nomos Press.

Hananel, R., and J. Berechman. 2016. Justice and transportation decision-making: The capabilities approach, *Transport Policy*49: 78–85. http://dx.doi.org/10.1016/j.tranpol.2016.04.005.

Heather, M. 2012. Nigeria Mulls Gas Flare Crackdown. *Voice of America.*

Ibeanu, O. 2000. Oil the Friction: Environmental Conflict Management in the Niger Delta, Nigeria. *Environmental Change and Security Project Report,* Issue 6 (Summer 2000).

Institute of Business Ethics. 2006. Reports.

Isiaka, A.B. 2010. Oiling the Guns and Gunning for Oil: Oil Violence, Arms Proliferation and the Destruction of Nigeria's Niger-Delta. *Journal of Alternative Perspectives in the Social Sciences* 2 (1): 323–363.

Kadafa, A.A. 2012. Environmental Impacts of Oil Exploration and Exploitation in the Niger Delta of Nigeria. *Global Journal of Science Frontier Research Environment and Earth Science* 12 (3): 19. (Versions 1.0).

Kibert, C., et al. 2012. *Working Towards Sustainability.* Hoboken, New Jersey: Wiley.

Lodge, G., and C. Wilson. 2006. *A Corporate Solution to Global Poverty: How Multinational Can Help The Poor and Invigorate Their Own Legitimacy.* Princeton: Princeton University Press.

Nigeria National Petroleum Corporation News (2014).

Nussbaum, M.C. 1999. *Sex and Social Justice.* Oxford: Oxford University Press.

Odeyemi and Ogunseitan. 1985. Petroleum Industry and its Pollution Potential in Nigeria. *Oil and Petroleum Pollution* 2 (1985): 223–229.

Odunkoya, A.O. 2006. Oil and Sustainable Development in Nigeria: A Case of Study the Niger Delta. *Journal of Human Ecology* 20 (4): 249–258.

Okorosaye-Orubite, A.K. 2008. Education and Sustainable Development in the Niger Delta: The Role of the Youth. In *Conference Proceedings of International Conference on the Nigerian State, Oil industry and the Niger Delta*, 1002–1013.

Onyemaechi, J.O. 2012. Economic Implications of Petroleum Policies in Nigeria: An Overview. *American International Journal of Contemporary Research* 2 (5): 60.

Ott, K., et al. 2011. *Strong Sustainability as a Frame for Sustainability Communication*. Berlin: Springer Science + Business Media.

Ott, K. 2008. On Substantiating the Conception of Strong Sustainability. In Erschienen ed. Ralf Döring *Natural Capital*. Marburg: Metropolis-Verlag.

Oviasuyi, P.O., and J. Uwadiae. 2010. The Dilemma of Niger-Delta Region as Oil Producing States of Nigeria. *Journal of Peace, Conflict and Development* 16: 10.

Raji, A.Y., and T.S. Abejide. 2013. Shell D'Arcy Exploration and the Discovery of Oil as Important Foreign Exchange Earnings in Ijawland of Niger Delta, C. 1940s–1970. *Arabian Journal of Business and Management Review* 2: 11. (OMAN Chapter).

Ruggie, J. 2008. Protect Respect and Remedy: A Framework for Business and Human Rights. *Publication of the United Nations*.

Saliu, et al. 2007. Environmental Degradation, Rising Poverty and Conflict: Towards an Explanation of the Niger-Delta Crisis. *Journal of Sustainable Development in Africa* 9 (4): 275.

Tamuno, S.O., and S.G. Edoumiekumo. 2012. Nigeria in the Niger Delta: An Allegory of the 'Legs Tying the Hands'. *International Review of Social Sciences and Humanities* 4 (1): 113–120.

The Economist. 2008. Nigeria: Another Deadline Goes Up in Flames. April 3rd 2008. http://www.economist.com/node/10979890.

UNEP. 2016. Nigeria Launches $1 Billion Ogoniland Clean-up and Restoration Programme. http://www.unep.org/newscentre/.

Chapter 19
Niger Delta Environmental Crises and the Limitations of Africanizing Aldo Leopold's Land Ethic: Towards an Earth-Eco-Socialist Model

Philomena Aku Ojomo

Abstract This chapter argues that while Aldo Leopold's land ethic opens a new vista for understanding the complexities of human-nature interrelatedness, his view has not satisfactorily dealt with some germane aspects of environmental problems in Africa. The chapter considers some important problems in environmental degradation in the Niger Delta area of Nigeria, West Africa, which cannot be adequately addressed using Leopold's land ethic as a theoretical foil or normative principle of action. Although Leopold correctly identifies ignorance as one of the problems of land-use, this chapter argues that the economic structure of society is a key determinant to how humans treat the natural environment. Against the view that Africanizing Leopoldian land ethic wholesomely is viable, this chapter proposes earth-eco-socialist theory as a way of improving the land ethic for contextual relevance in Nigeria's Niger Delta. Earth-eco-socialism is defended as a more robust and serviceable ethical paradigm for confronting environmental degradation in the Niger Delta region of Nigeria, and the world by extension.

19.1 Introduction

In his recently edited volume, *African Philosophy and Environmental Conservation*, Chimakonam (2018) identifies ignorance and poverty as the core problems responsible for the abuse of the environment in sub-Saharan Africa. While observing the paucity of environmental ethical thoughts from the African place addressing the preponderance of environmental problems in the continent, Chimakonam (2018: 6) thinks that African philosophers have crucial roles in protecting and conserving the environment in sub-Saharan Africa. He charges that "the battle to protect and conserve the sub-Saharan environment has to be led by African philosophers who have the tools to fight both ignorance and poverty and diffuse the dilemma of survival and conservation." In consonance with Chimakonam's call on African philosophers to

P. A. Ojomo (✉)
Lagos State University, Ojo, Nigeria
e-mail: philoojomo63@gmail.com; philoojomo@yahoo.com

M. Chemhuru (ed.), *African Environmental Ethics*, The International Library of Environmental, Agricultural and Food Ethics 29,
https://doi.org/10.1007/978-3-030-18807-8_19

interrogate environmental problems in Africa, this chapter is an attempt to provide systematic reflection and thorough contextualization of the classic environmental thoughts of Aldo Leopold's land ethic within the prism of Nigeria's Niger Delta environmental crises.

In difference to Chimakonam's emphasis on 'ignorance', which coincidentally finds place, too, in Leopold's understanding of land-use, this chapter shall argue that within the context of the Niger Delta in Nigeria, the root cause of environmental problem owes much not to ignorance nor poverty but to the prevailing greedy capitalist ethos underpinning the economic structure and relationship with the environment. Though Leopoldian land ethic has been espoused in several contexts as the theoretical valve for addressing environmental problems (Meine 1988; Adams and McShane 1992; Callicott 2013; Forbes et al. 2014; Musgrave 2015), this chapter is critically circumspect of a wholesome application of the ideas espoused in land ethic to the environmental problems in Nigeria's Niger Delta.

The Niger Delta environment is under serious threat: climate change, severe gully erosion; coastal and marine erosion; flooding in low-lying belt of mangrove and fish swamps along the coast; uncontrolled logging with inherent problems of the destruction of biodiversity; inappropriate agricultural practices; destruction of watersheds; soil-crust formation caused by loss of water; creation of burrow pits associated with bad mining practices; oil pollution from spillage and gas flaring; industrial pollution; municipal waste generation and urban decay (Fagbohun 2010: 373). Amidst these problems, the key question of interest to this chapter is: what philosophical template can be plausibly used in addressing environmental crises in Nigeria's Niger Delta region?

To answer the above question, this chapter is organised in four sections. The first section exposes the environmental problems in the Niger Delta. This is important not only in setting the background to the rest of the discussions in the chapter, but also to understand the mechanism through which Western Europe had exploited and continues to degrade the Niger Delta's natural environment, exploit the land and the people's economy through unwholesome oil-driven activities of multinational corporations. The second section discusses the tenets, assumptions and moral intuitions salient in Leopold's land ethic. The third part of this paper shows the limitations of Africanizing the Leopoldian land ethic in the context of the Niger Delta in Nigeria. As an alternative, the fourth section articulates earth-eco-socialism as a viable ethical framework and reconstructive ideal to Leopold's land ethic in ensuring environmental conservation in Nigeria's Niger Delta and the world, inclusively. The last section provides some concluding reflections and recommendations.

19.2   Environmental Problems in the Niger Delta, Nigeria

Nigeria has abundant environmental resources. From the mangrove wet land sand rain forests of the South, through the various savannahs and semi-arid ecosystems of the North, to the opulent mineral deposits in the East and Niger Delta, the nations endowed with a rich environment (Fayemi 2016: 364). However, the environmental degradation in the Niger Delta region is particularly pathetic. The description of the Niger Delta region by Nnamdi et al. (2013: 65) is apt:

> The region lies in Nigeria's tropical region where the River Niger empties into the Atlantic Ocean, creating the largest delta in Africa, an area unique for its enviable biodiversity. It also boasts of one of the most biologically unique terrestrial freshwater and marine habitats in the world. It covers an area of 112,110 square kilometres and is inhabited by thirty-one million people according to the 2006 census. Its rural population density is one of the highest in the world with 276 inhabitants per square kilometre. The region confronts a conspicuous menace on a daily basis; its biosphere is being diminished due to a lack of environmental considerations in the business of oil prospecting and extraction.

Historically, when oil was first discovered by Shell-BP in Oloibiri in the Niger Delta in 1956, the economy of Nigeria was buoyant, and the environment was relatively green and unharmed. Few decades after that, Nigeria eventually became one of the largest oil producing countries. Unfortunately, the "Communities in the Niger Delta, where most of Nigeria's oil was found, received little more than token payments after significant extraction got under way in the 1960s, and this accelerated a process of national breakdown" (Maass 2009: 53). The land, water and economic activities that were the source of livelihood to the natives of Niger Delta have now been polluted by the activities of Shell, Chevron, Mobile, Texaco, among others, by the release of toxic wastes into the environment.

Today, the Niger Delta "environment and its human populations are victims of one of the world's greatest ecological tragedies" (Nnamdi et al. 2013: 65). In the same line, LaMonica (2011: 273) articulates that "the Niger Delta Region (NDR) is under tremendous developmental strain; to include environmental degradation, relocation of peoples, affronts to cultural ways of life, and a sudden rise of violent conflict." The negative environmental consequences of nihilistic resource extraction for the people in the area and on the well-being of nonhuman species there are inestimable. An environment that used to be a green settlement systematically turned to one that oil pipelines and gas flaring run through human settlements; oil pollution resulting from spillage and release of toxic waste flood homelands; farmlands and rivers are no longer appropriate for their teleological agricultural purposes; in securing oil installations and expatriates on oil fields, previously peaceful communities have become militarised.

For one, environmental destruction in the form of contamination of water and air pollution has no boundaries. Hence, neighbouring communities also suffer the negative impact of oil-related activities by the multinational oil companies. For the other, the continuing environmental degradation and "the abandonment of ecological stewardship in the Niger Delta by oil-prospecting bureaucracies and the Government of Nigeria" (Nnamdi et al. 2013: 67) calls into question the rationale for the environmental laws and regulations that have turned ineffectual, selective and promotive of environmental injustice. According to Ejumudo (2011: 24):

> The costs of environmental pollution and degradation that is borne by the marginalized, oppressed and pauperized people [of the Niger Delta] as well as the benefits that should flow to them in the form of employment, skill acquisition programmes, educational scholarship

schemes, provision of basic social amenities and other pro-poor life-enhancing programmes
are heavily disproportional so much so, that the principles of fairness and equity that underlie
or underpin environmental justice are impaired with one likely hazardous consequence,
environmental crisis.

Whereas environmental laws which could promote sustainable environmental justice, ameliorate such ecological destruction and inhumane treatment of the biotic life
in the Niger-Delta have become nihilistic and oppressive instruments of cooperation between the Nigerian government and some multinational corporations from
the West to perpetuate sordid environmental damage. Watson (2005: 480–481) is
perhaps correct when he writes that:

> The growing awareness of widening catastrophic conditions is insufficient to bring about
> a response as long as the structures of daily urban-industrial-commodity life are not mate-
> rially challenged. When they confront the various manifestations of the crisis separately,
> communities are left on the terrain of emergency response, demands for technological and
> regulatory reform, and ultimately, "treatment" of an increasingly denuded world.

Various laws and regulations to protect the environment have been put in place by
the Federal Government of Nigeria. The Federal Ministry of Environment (FME),
through National Environmental Standards and Regulations Enforcement Agency
(NESREA), is the regulatory body charged with the function of administering and
enforcing environmental laws in Nigeria. Although the FME has published several guidelines and procedures for evaluating environmental Impact Assessment
reports (EIA reports) the environment-damaging activities have continued relatively
unchecked by relevant government agencies because of corruption perpetrated by
Nigerians and their foreign collaborators. One of such activities is gas flaring. The
Federal government took a step at regulating gas flaring in 1979 when it enacted the
Associated Gas Re-injection Act (Oludayo 2004: 69). Despite the Act, there is still
massive oil exploration and gas flaring in the Niger Delta.

Oil companies in Nigeria flare gases, irrespective of the fact that it is not in consonant with best global environmental practices. Second, the Nigerian government has
failed to implement extant environmental laws, some of which are not potent enough
to prevent environmental degradation by multinational oil companies. In view of the
complicity of the Nigerian state, Maass' remarks about environmental disasters on
a global scale is applicable to the situation in the Niger Delta:

> The world offers a multitude of environmental disasters created by extractive industries that
> dig for oil, gold, silver or other minerals. Calling these events "tragedies" may not be right,
> because the word implies a course of events that went in an unexpected direction, like an
> early death, a sudden landslide, a plane crash. Mineral ecocides have happened often enough
> and predictably enough to be cast as the order of things. In countries too weak to control
> powerful industries that tend to behave responsibly only if they are required to, the invasion
> of bulldozers and other machines of extraction is a disaster foretold. (Maass 2009: 80)

While oil explorations by multinational corporations, such as Shell, in economically developed parts of the world conform to the global best practices in the industry,
this is not the case in Nigeria's Niger Delta. Multinational corporations often receive
no sanctions with environmental assault in the region. This situation has continued

to give rise to agitations, civil disobedience and militancy in the region in demand for environmental justice and sustainable environmental practices, which often, have been repelled and resisted by the Nigerian government with counter state force and power.

Having exposed the environmental and existential conditions of the Niger Delta, I now turn in the next section to a discussion of the essential tenets of Leopold's land ethic.

19.3 Aldo Leopold's Land Ethic

One of the early contributors to theoretical debates about the best way to provide a philosophical basis for tackling environmental problems is Leopold (1949). In *A Sand County Almanac*, Leopold synergises a remarkable range of knowledge—scientific, literary, biological, ecological, poetic, economic, ethical and aesthetic. He traces the problem of environmental degradation to our mistaken conception of "land" (i.e. soils, waters, plants, and animals). According to him, we abuse and misuse 'land' not because of any baseness in our nature but due largely to ignorance and greed. Leopold's land ethic is both eco-centric and non-anthropocentric. This approach extends ethical consideration and respect to all the members of the biotic community intimately connected with the human species: plants, animals, mountains, waters, etc.

Leopold believes that the mistakes we make concerning the environment are due to our perception of land as a commodity belonging to us. He enjoins us to see land as a community of interdependence and interconnectedness to which we belong. With the right perception and understanding of land, he believes, humans would "quit thinking about decent land-use as solely an economic problem" and would begin to use land with love and respect. Thus, he postulates the basic principle of achieving this as: "A thing is right when it tends to preserve the integrity, stability, and beauty of the biotic community. It is wrong when it tends otherwise" (Leopold 1949: 224–225). To justify the idea of a land ethic, Leopold argues that we must develop an ecological conscience which is not guided by economic concerns.

Leopold identified several causes of environmental problems. However, he places all of them under the label 'anthropocentrism'. The causes range from the religious teaching that humans are masters over land, to inappropriate technology, the desire for economic growth and poor educational programmes.

First, Leopold observes that at the root of environmental problems is an economic interest towards land which gives rise to malnutrition of the land. Leopold argues that since most parts of the biotic community lack economic value, they are not cared for. But since the economic parts have become a source of wealth to individuals and government, no recognition is given to land's intrinsic worth. He argues that land-use ethics is still governed wholly by economic self-interest, just as social ethics centuries ago. This economic interest propels human abuse, exploitation and degradation of land. Therefore, it follows that an ethic which guides human relation to land presupposes the existence of some mental image of land as a biotic mechanism. We can be ethical only in relation to something we can see, feel, understand, love, or otherwise have faith in. Leopold believes that education is yet to achieve this aim.

Second, Leopold maintains that prevailing education, whether regarding land use or conservation, has not inspired commitment to land. The predominant education on land use is incapable of promoting ecological stability, integrity and beauty of land. For whereas conservation, in Leopold's conception, is a state of harmony between humans and land, the type of education currently in operation, makes no mention of obligations to land over and above those dictated by self-interest. One way this problem can be tackled, according to Leopold, is to develop an understanding of ecology, and this is by no means co-extensive with true 'education'; in fact, much of higher education seems deliberately geared to avoid ecological concerns. Leopold argues that current educational approach to land-use fails to get to the root of environmental problems such as abnormal floods, loss of soil's fertility and species' death at high rate. In his words:

> The status of thought on these ailments of the land is reflected in the fact that our treatments for them are still prevailingly local. Thus, when a soil loses fertility we pour on fertilizer, or at best alter its tame flora and fauna, without considering the fact that its wild flora and fauna, which built the soil to begin with, may likewise be important to its maintenance. (Leopold 1949: 194–195)

What ecology teaches, which we lack in the dominant land-use ethic or rules, is the ability to perceive that the stability and efficiency of the biotic community rests on the healthy functioning of all its members. This ecological vision produces a dictum: "live and let live," which repudiates self-seeking land use ideologies. Moreover, he also identifies civilization, particularly the use and invention of technological equipment in agriculture, farming, fishing, and so on as another major root of environmental problems.

Leopold notes that the use of machines in industrial farming has long been adopted by our ancestors. Our generation, he argues, has massively and abruptly degraded the environment because of its mechanized cultivation. This has necessitated the destruction of what Leopold calls 'the split-rail value'. According to Leopold, "mechanization offers no cultural substitute for the split-rail values it destroys; at least none visible to me." Leopold holds that there is nowhere mechanization has been so destructive as in its destruction of wilderness and release of chemicals into the atmosphere.

He notes that for the first time in the history of the human species, two changes are now threatening. One is the exhaustion of wilderness in the more habitable portions of the globe. The other is the world-wide hybridization of cultures through modern transport and industrialization. In a factory, for instance, Leopold observes that the labourers seek to conquer land which they see as raw material of production. The wilderness is also seen as a material to devour by civilization through the aid of machines. Consequently, Leopold sees economic interest as one of the motivating bases for technological growth, which has heightened the false consciousness in prevailing conservation notion that land is synonymous to soil:

> Perhaps the most serious obstacle impeding the evolution of a land ethic is that our educational and economic system is headed away from, rather than toward, an intense consciousness of land. Your true modern is separated from the land by many middlemen, and by innumerable physical gadgets. He has no vital relation to it; to him it is the space between cities on which crops grow. (Leopold 1949: 223–224)

For Leopold, our present ecological problems arise due to our attitude and implements. He argues that we are altering the earth's resources with our technology at a rate which harms the well-being of land. The violent use of the biotic community, therefore, lies at the erroneous belief that land is a commodity which can be used and disposed of at will. Accordingly, Leopold rejects conservation that does not allow the land to be valued for its intrinsic worth but as a means for solely human good. This, seemingly, jeopardises the good of nonhuman species. He notes that several conservation efforts are cosmetics. Rather than address the cause of erosion, flood-control dams are constructed. Conservation practices of this kind, though necessary, should not be regarded as a permanent solution.

Leopold argues that the problem with the prevailing conservation formula is that government somewhat takes control of large areas of soil. Due to the economic motive, governments are in charge of large portions of land. But it is doubtful whether government can manage those lands successfully since many species in the biotic community do not have economic value. For this reason, Leopold argues that a system of conservation that is solely based on economic self-interest cannot produce a balanced biotic system.

Leopold's land ethic is based on five fundamental tenets: (1) the principle of independency; (2) the principle of shared kinship; (3) the precept of moral sentiment; (4) the principle of intrinsic value; and (5) duty to preserve the land. These principles are derived from the ecological, evolutionary and philosophical background and their influences on Leopold. It is through these tenets that Leopold puts together a defence of his claim for extending moral consideration to land as a solution to environmental concerns. Most fundamental of all he principles and which all others rest, is the principle of interdependence anchored on Leopold's understanding of ecology.

According to him (1949: 224), "one of the requisites for an ecological comprehension of land is an understanding of ecology." It is through ecology that Leopold seeks to unite natural species, because all-natural species are members of an ecological community. Combining the Darwinian idea of survival of the fittest and the idea of moral sentiment to his conception of natural interaction among species, Leopold proposes that "all ethics so far evolved rest upon a single premise: that the individual is a member of a community of interdependent parts. His instincts prompt him to compete for his place in that community, but his ethics prompt him also to cooperate (perhaps in order that there may be a place to compete for" (Leopold 1949: 203). The land ethic, therefore, rests on the principle of ecological interdependency upon which the notion of community is drawn.

19.4   Limitations of Aldo Leopold's Land Ethic: The Niger Delta Example

Leopold's environmental philosophy has been criticised from different angles. The holistic nature of the land ethic, his communitarian and kinship theoretical standards, his position on intrinsic value, among others have been criticised. Without any doubt, some of the criticisms of the land ethic, either in Leopold's exploration of it, and even the subsequent defence of it by Callicott and others are valid. Some arguments against the land ethic have been refuted by Leopold and his disciples. Several criticisms arose from a misreading or misunderstanding of Leopold's *A Sand County Almanac*. This misreading or misunderstanding is partly due to Leopold's literary style, that Callicott, a well-known exponent of his land ethic, identified as one of the factors that have led to improper grasp of Leopold's position. One other fundamental cause of misunderstanding is inadequate attention to the details of Leopold's theory.

I begin with Tom Regan's criticism of Leopold's land ethic. His criticisms against Leopold's land ethic include: (a) Leopold's land ethic does not protect the right of each experiencing subject-of-life (Regan 1998), and (b) Leopold's land ethic is eco-fascist because it implies that human population could be reduced if they become a threat to the biotic community. As Regan (1983: 362) puts it, "Environmental fascism and the right view are like oil and water: they don't mix." Regan holds that the land ethic is a version of eco-chauvinism and environmental fascism since Leopold did not totally rule out the consumption of animals.

J. B. Callicott argues that Regan's paradigm of 'right-view' is inadequate and creates unjustifiable demarcation among sentient animals. He argues that Regan fails to comprehend the actual meaning of the term 'right' when it is used by environmental ethicists like Leopold. According to Callicott (1985: 368), "'Right(s)' formulations are used to state claims. As opposed to mineral rights, water rights, property rights, civil rights, legal rights, etc., 'moral rights' is used to claim moral consideration—for oneself or for other less articulate beings." Callicott disagrees with Regan's view that because the land ethic is holistic, then it "might be fairly dubbed environmental fascism" (1985: 367). Callicott argues that Regan does not have a robust theory on what should constitute the goal of wildlife management and environmental ethics. He explains further that:

> In the biotic community there are producers and consumers, predators and prey. One might say that the integrity and stability of the biotic community depends upon death as well as life; indeed, one might say further, that the life of one member is premised squarely on the death of another. So, one could hardly argue that our killing of fellow-members of the biotic community is, prima facie, land-ethically wrong. It depends on who is killed, for what reasons, under what circumstances, and how. The filling in these blanks would provide, in each case, an answer to the question about respect. (Callicott 2001: 210)

I believe that Regan is demanding too much from ethics since it appears that everyone would have to protect nonhuman animals even during the periods of famine and hunger. And if such demand is used as a basis for resolving environmental problems, it will fail. This is not the goal of Leopold. While Regan's position in this regard is untenable, Leopold (1998: 121) explores the dialectical struggle and survival of the fittest. Leopold sees ethics as a means of reducing the impact of intense competition among species. All ethical theories or systems so far evolved rest upon a single premise: that the individual is a member of a community of interdependent parts. His instincts prompt him to compete for his place in that community, but his ethics prompt him also to co-operate, perhaps in order that there may be a place to compete for.

As Callicott argues: "Animal right, a la Regan, does nothing if it does not draw some animals (mammals) into a single community with humans" (Callicott 1985: 372). The problem with Regan's view is that it neglects: (a) the community concept and, (b) it introduces a paradigm based on what he calls the "experiencing subject of life" that removes countless number of species which play vital parts in the stability, integrity and beauty of the environment. In this connection, Callicott writes:

> If the case for animal rights would be theoretically restructured to divide animal right holders from non-holders along the domestic/wild axis rather than subject-non-subject of a - life axis, then its reconciliation with environmental ethics could be envisioned. Both would rest on a common concept - the community concept. And, the very different ethical implications of either would be governed by different kinds of communities' humans and animals comprise - the "mixed" human domestic community, on the one hand, and the natural, wild biotic community, on the other. (Callicott 1985: 372)

While the community concept appears to be one of the principles upon which the land ethic is based, it is still debatable whether this concept has been carefully worked out. On a general note, Callicott's reply to Regan's criticism is important. The implication of Regan's position, here is that if taken seriously, it will undermine the interest of many non-sentient species which have contributed to the sustenance of the human and non-human community.

In his reply and defence of Leopold's land ethic, Callicott argues that Leopold does not intend that humans are to be sacrificed as claimed by Regan for the sake of beauty and order in the environment. As Leopold (1998: 117–118) clearly states "the land ethic simply enlarges the boundaries of the community to include soils, waters, plants, and animals, or collectively: the land." He adds: "as the ethical frontier advances from the individual to the community, its intellectual content increases" (Leopold 1998: 124). According to Horn (2005: 413), what this means is that "when human ethics conflicts with environmental ethics, human ethics takes precedence (prima facie)." This is what Callicott (1998: 128) means when he says that "the land ethic has a holistic as well as an individualist cast."

The weakness in Leopold's moral maxim is acknowledged by Callicott, who criticises his ethical doctrine on the ground of erroneous construction of ecology based on the ideology of 'balance of nature'. For Callicott (2002), the 'flux of nature' is what rightly expresses our ecological knowledge. In other words, there is a paradigm shift in the ecology from the 'balance of nature' to that of 'flux of nature'. However, Callicott does not think that this has in any way undermined the strengths of the land ethic as the moral maxim only needs to be reformulated. Hence, it is erroneous to suggest, as Leopold does, that balance of nature is a cardinal value of the land ethic. What is wrong with human activities that alter the natural environment is the degree, frequency and massive rate at which they occur. Consequently, Callicott suggests a new moral maxim thus, "a thing is right when it tends to disturb the biotic community only at normal spatial and temporal scales. It is wrong when it tends otherwise" (Callicott 2001: 216).

Aside from Regan's and Callicott's criticisms, there are other questions that arise regarding Leopold's land ethic. These include the question of how conflict of interest between human and non-humans can be resolved; question of whether the community is a necessary concept for developing a holistic theory on the environment as Leopold has attempted or, whether it is a necessary element of an environmental ethics that is sufficient to create an ethical relation between humans and non-human beings. Put differently, what are the conditions that necessitate a community-based theory and what makes a community communitarian? If Leopold places human ethics above environmental ethics, does this not amount to the same anthropocentrism which he had earlier rejected? Would the defence of what Callicott calls "land ethic as an accretion" not amount to a contradiction of Leopold's main thesis? Put differently, by what parameters can we decide which of the conflicting interests is paramount in the land ethic? To answer these questions would require an in-depth engagement with Leopold's land ethic. While this is a legitimate engagement worthy of further exploration beyond the responses of scholars such as Passmore (1974), Fieser (1992), Horn (2005), Domsky (2006), among others, the immediate and primary concern of this paper is to consider the inadequacy of Leopold's land ethic as a normative principle of action in addressing environmental degradation in the Niger Delta area of Nigeria.

According to Leopold, individuals, rather than governments, are to decide when an action is ethically right. Three fundamental issues are involved here. First, Leopold criticises economic self-interest, but condemns government's management of land. Second, Leopold rejects centralisation, but wants the whole community to protect land. Third, Leopold neglects the challenges of land in the Third World nations, yet he seeks to pursue a healthy-land environmental thesis. Let us address the challenges and strengths of Leopold with respect to these dilemmas. Leopold directly or indirectly finds himself at the centre of capitalist-socialist debate on the one hand, and Western-Developing Countries divide on the other. Let us first attempt a critique of Leopold's criticism of capitalism.

Leopold criticises the continuous intent of government and individuals of seeing land as mere soil that should be valued for its economic worth. Indeed, he demonstrates that this belief has serious setback for land management in the sense that non-human members of the land-community that provide aesthetic values to the environment would have been ignorantly affected. The consequence of this is evident in our societies today. Here, the economic activities of private individuals or government (for instance, land-use law) have serious effects on the ecosystem as a whole. While Leopold's position is invaluable in this respect, he does not identify how the economic motive of either the government or those of private individuals constitutes exploitation of the nonhuman members of the ecological community, as well as the human members, especially those living in the Third World countries. Even if it is correct to assume that environmental restoration can be accomplished by private individuals rather than the government as Leopold thought, I doubt that such can be the case unless it is only private individuals that can be more environmentally responsive and responsible by lessening obsession for economic gain. These two assumptions, which expose the limit of Leopold's theory, deserve further discussion.

Believing strongly that government is always far from land and having observed that government relies more on proceeds from land, Leopold holds that:

> The difficulty is that these communities are usually interspersed with more valuable private lands; the government cannot possibly own or control such scattered parcels. The net effect is that we have regulated some of them to ultimate extinction over large areas. If the private owner were ecologically minded, he would be proud to be the custodian of a reasonable proportion of such areas, which add diversity and beauty to his farm and to his community. To sum up: a system of conservation based solely on economic self-interest is hopelessly lopsided. It tends to ignore, and thus eventually to eliminate, many elements in the land community that lack commercial value, but that are (as far as we know) essential to its healthy functioning. It assumes, falsely, I think, that the economic parts of the biotic clock will function without the uneconomic parts. It tends to relegate to government many functions eventually too large, too complex, or too widely dispersed to be performed by government. An ethical obligation on the part of the private owner is the only visible remedy for these situations. (Leopold 1949: 120)

One may grant that where too much land is controlled by governments that represent minute number of the population of the world, less can be attained if the leadership orientation tends toward economic rather than environmental well-being of humans and nonhumans. On the one hand, individuals that own lands ought to be responsible for how such lands are used. However, the point must be acknowledged that when private properties are owned by individuals, the motive to make profit is paramount. Leopold takes this latter motive for granted, having assumed that individuals will protect their properties (land) and that this will lead to an environmentally friendly world. Today, eco-socialists have shown that this is not always the case because profit motive often hinders such a project.

Given that the developing as well as developed societies are continually experiencing serious climate change, Leopold's assumption that an individualistic environmental management strategy will help resolve environmental hurdles seems to be a weak hypothesis if tested against the reality across the world. Since it has been observed that the "the roots of global ecological problems lie in the disproportionate share of resources consumed by the industrialized countries as a whole and the urban elite within the Third World," it is evident that few people (the rich) control most of the land (Guha 1998: 274). Thus, it will be wrong to argue that individuals can manage better the resources of nature for the society at large since governments represent a fewer percentage of the population.

However, it should be noted that while Leopold presents an invaluable criticism of economic interest which constitutes one of the major causes of environmental degradation, some of his positions may hinder the objective he sets for himself. He demonstrates clearly that it is not an easy task to resolve environmental problems. Arguably, Leopold shows consistently that when one disregards non-human species on the ground that they have no economic interest and relies solely on the belief that only economic aspect of the land is valuable, the psychological mindset of the people works towards environmental destruction. I agree that this is actually the conclusion that one can plausibly draw on the ground that it is only when one takes the worth of something as valuable in itself that he or she would be motivated to protect it resolutely. Leopold should be commended for being able to tie the implication of uninformed economic interest of land-use to other issues such as ecological consciousness, ecological conscience, and ecological actions.

Although Leopold remarks that only private individuals can manage land more effectively for there to be holistic environmental management, it is arguable that most environmental disasters are mostly caused by private corporations. Leopold had identified clearly the negative implications of ignorance in the misuse of land. Nevertheless, the issues at the core of environmental concern in recent years go beyond what he envisaged in his land ethic. From the economic roots of environmental degradation, there is a shift to the issue of imperialism, racism, globalism, regionalism, poverty, and corruption. Dealing with these complex issues requires a theory of justice that can balance the interests of Third World countries with those of the developed nations on the one hand, and the interests of humans with those of nonhuman natural species, on the other.

Excessive exploitation of land and people by multinational corporations stems mainly from economic interest, with little regard for the well-being of the citizens of the Third World countries. As it is today, no company among the perpetuators of environmental degradation in the Niger Delta has been diligently prosecuted by the federal government. The emphasis has always been on the revenue accruing to government. I have already underscored the reasons for the preoccupation with economic considerations in the use of land, which arises from shallow understanding of development as something that emerges from cut-throat competition. More fundamentally it indicates appalling disregard for human life as well as the moral right to live and let live.

Leopold did not address the issue of well-formulated and implementable environmental laws to back a theory that seeks to influence such demands in action. One shortcoming of the land ethic is that as a theory, it fails to address the problem of enforceability of morality. Morality is difficult to enforce unless it is embodied in law. This means that Leopold's land ethic cannot adequately confront the challenges he seeks to address. An environmental ethic will be effective when there is a legal framework for implementing its requirements. By implication, given that government regulates conduct through laws and policies, the government is equally important in environmental management (if not more important than the private individuals who are to use the land).

On the issue of environmental management, the question may be asked: how do we regulate international environmental challenges since environmental problems are global concerns? That question provokes a serious concern on environmental issues, such as transcending the problem of nature versus humans which Leopold's land ethic is centred on, to other fundamental concerns. Such concerns include: Western versus developing countries, political cum economic debate in terms of exploitation, domination, subjugation and underdevelopment of Third World countries. To a considerable extent, pollution of the environment is caused by multinational companies operating all over the world. The exploitation of land in Third World countries as a concern for environmental holism was hardly mentioned by Leopold. Rather, he only stresses that economic interests have negative effects without explaining how global capitalism has affected adversely the environment of developing countries. Leopold's land ethic does not take the issue of poverty and the existential conditions of people across the world into consideration. With particular reference to issue of poverty and weak institutions, especially in Third World countries, Maass (2009: 55) writes:

> Now the world's eighth-largest exporter of oil, Nigeria earned more than $400 billion from oil in recent decades, yet nine out of ten citizens live on less than $2 a day and one out of five children dies before his fifth birthday. Its per capita GDP is one-fifth of South Africa's. Even Senegal, which exports fish and nuts, has a larger per capita income. Nigeria's wealth did not vanish, as in a magic trick. It has been stolen by presidents, generals, executives, middlemen, accountants, bureaucrats, policeman and anyone else with access to it. This is what can happen in a country with weakly enforced law.

Scholars such as Walter Rodney, Michael Parenti, and Frantz Fanon are of the view that the domination of Third World countries and of working peoples across the world is because of the institutionalization of private property rights. It seems clear that Leopold has not identified the dangers of granting property rights to land to individuals with respect to the environment, especially where government's involvement is inefficient and ineffective. Consequently, I suggest that issues such as human versus nonhuman members of the biotic community, capitalists versus workers, and The West versus Third World countries, need to be re-interrogated. By focusing on the human and non-human components of the biotic environment to the neglect of such other issues as racial, class, economic, political and social factors, Leopold's theory has not successfully captured the germane issues in environmental ethics. In the next section, I shall undertake an earth-eco-socialist reconstruction of Leopold's land ethic.

19.5   Earth-Eco-Socialism as a Viable Normative Framework for Environmental Sustainability

Today, environmental matters require decisive approaches—approaches that will match theory with practice. If it can be shown that there are theoretical problems in Leopold's land ethic, then it follows that the theory be reworked. Such reworking will be in the light of practical and more humane conditions that are suitable for addressing contemporary environmental challenges. While it is true that Leopold anticipated some of these issues, I need to stress that one needs to go beyond the land ethic as espoused in *A Sand County Almanac*. I have argued that Leopoldian environmental philosophy contains valuable insights on the very important issue of environmental degradation and its amelioration. But there are some loopholes in Leopold's land ethic which invite a reasoned search for a better alternative. This is important if we are to find a robust and serviceable solution to human-induced environmental problems. As a result, 'earth-eco-socialism' shall be defended here as a more robust alternative for addressing global environmental concerns.

Earth-eco-socialism is a duty-based cum consequentialist ethical orientation that is rooted in evolutionary principles of interdependency, common good and social responsibility. As an evolutionary ethical perspective, earth-eco-socialism enjoins the cultivation of 'care conscience' for the sustenance of the earth, and survival of all inhabitants of the biotic community. Earth-eco-socialism is, indeed, a fundamental way of life that expresses itself in actions, attitudes and policies that focus on maintaining, preserving and sustaining the earth. It emphasises the centrality of concrete actions guided by theory in the effort towards environmental sustainability.

Earth-eco-socialism suggests that our care for the Earth is the first place our ethical deliberation ought to start from. When we do this, we are not concerned with the interest of only humans; the well-being of the entire organisms is also brought under consideration. Moreover, a care for the Earth is not merely a call for taking Earth into ethical consideration. Rather, it is a realistic call for restricting our tampering with the Earth to avoid ecological disequilibrium. In this respect, our call is not restricted to an attempt to seek the interest of the Third World countries at the expense of the West or vice versa. Rather, it is an attempt to provide a moral platform for considering extant environmental issues that affect the global community inadequately considered by Leopold.

Earth-eco-socialism favours socialist theory and takes the issue of environmental justice as fundamental. I agree with Marx that the issue of exploitation, alienation, domination, and subjugation of the workers need to be reconsidered. In this connection, I affirm that the principle of cooperation is urgently needed today. However, I reject the notion that social change is only possible through violent revolution. Instead, I favour a framework that prohibits and *avoids* global war or violence. Accordingly, respectful dialogue and communication across racial, class, economic cultural and religious boundaries are paramount. This can be institutionalised at all the levels of social organisation, and reinforced by the United Nations.

'Socialism' in Earth-eco-socialism emphasises cooperation rather than competition. This, however, does not mean that every socialist system is necessarily cooperative. Now, unless a system or institution—be it, political, economic or educational—promotes cooperation among people it would tend to be oppressive. This is what happens in the capitalist order. The logic of capitalism, which stresses the capacity to out-compete one's rivals, does not in principle, exclude unfair methods or practices. Fierce competition tends to relegate morality to the back burner. For example, the competitions among multinational companies in Nigeria have led to the liquidation of many indigenous Nigerian companies. This is in consonance with the logic of capitalism. The problem lies in the fact that its repercussions are detrimental to the Nigerian people. Against this, socialism, which gives primacy to promotion of cooperation, has a greater chance of promoting holistic survival of human and non-human members of the biotic community. A system which is more likely to promote people's well-being is indeed preferable to one which is less likely to achieve the same goal.

Another ingredient of socialism that makes it more suitable for confronting both economic and environmental challenges is that it tends to reward those who are involved in the production process. In this case, socialists argue that labourers produce more than what they get, and consequently, they should be compensated adequately. The socialist orientation stresses the need to end the exploitation of man by man through a radical re-engineering of the existing unjust capitalist system. Fundamentally, socialism provides a platform for addressing the problem of international trade that arose from the unbridled quest for profit. As I already indicated, the major problem with capitalism is its tendency to subordinate human welfare to the quest for ever expanding profits. This tendency is detrimental to both the human and nonhuman members of the biotic community.

Having justified our preference for a socialist orientation as a humane ideological compass in our attempt to go beyond Leopold's land ethic, I now present earth-eco-socialism as a robust philosophical paradigm that should guide individuals, corporate organisations and governments as they seek solutions to global environmental problems. More specifically, it offers a satisfactory principle for understanding and tackling environmental crisis in the Niger Delta of Nigeria.

Earth-eco-socialism embraces the better aspects of Leopold's land ethic and Marxist philosophy. It is anchored on the ethical maxim that, "an action is environmentally right if it tends to promote the use of natural resources in a manner consonant with the well-being of members of the biotic community that would be affected by the action. Otherwise, it is wrong." This ethical maxim is an improved reformulation of Leopold's land ethic: "a thing is right when it tends to preserve the integrity, stability, and beauty of the biotic community. It is wrong when it tends otherwise" (Leopold 1949: 224–225).

The issue of poverty is significant when discussing environmental crises within a socialist framework. The question of justice is important for understanding environmental problems in the Third World. For instance, in the Niger Delta the issue of injustice to indigenous inhabitants of the area by the Federal Government of Nigeria and multinational corporations such as Shell, Chevron, Exxon Mobil, Texaco, etc. is intimately connected to the environmental crises in that region.

Earth-eco-socialist orientation considers the issue of injustice in the Niger Delta as a misguided act against the people of the region, Nigeria, Africa and the world at large, since all the toxic materials released into the environment due to oil exploration and exploitation contribute to global warming. Against capitalist proclivities, earth-eco-socialist suggests that the first step in the movement towards a better society is to dissolve the systems that permit the exploitation of one group by another. While Marx and Engels were interested in addressing social crises such as the alienation of working people around the world, based on their strong belief that the world is a class society, African political philosophers with strong Marxist orientation like Kwame Nkrumah believe that the socialist agenda for Africa is to confront the racial challenge posed by Western imperialists and capitalists. While I agree that problems of racism and conflict between the bourgeoisie and the proletariat or the rich and the poor are significant and must receive adequate attention, none of them can be isolated from environmental justice issues.

19.6 Conclusion

In this chapter, Leopold's land ethic is conceptually analysed, critically engaged and contextually explored focusing on the Niger Delta, Nigeria. The environmental problems in the Niger Delta are revealing of the complexities of the ecological destruction in many other Delta regions in Africa. However, the moral suppositions, ecological principles and environmental management ideas expressed in Leopold's land ethic are systematically applied within the Nigeria's Niger Delta setting. The discussions in this chapter showed that Leopold's land ethic cannot totally explain the bane of environmental crises in the region nor cogently serve as a serviceable normative framework for effectively addressing environmental destruction in the Niger Delta. Indices of poverty and ignorance, which have become popular in accounting for the root of ecological havoc in the Niger Delta do not sufficiently suffice; rather, the quest for excessive or surplus profit lies at the core of the environmental crises. For this reason, the chapter defended that rather than accepting wholesomely the paradigms of Leopold's land ethic in the management of the Niger-Delta environment, Africa and the world at large, a better alternative is to look in the direction of an earth-eco-socialist theory.

While providing the crux of an earth-eco-socialist theory, the chapter argues that it is an environmental ethical theory that challenges capitalist proclivities while also enjoining cooperative management of the environment anchored on socialist principles of non-exploitation and non-alienation. Developed to address the peculiar environmental crises in Africa, this novel environmental ethical approach is also revealing outside the African context. Earth-eco-socialism affirms the prime importance of matching normative principles with activism, ecological education with ecological consciousness, environmental regulations with national enforcements and international sanctions as binaries in efforts towards sustainable management of the environment in Africa. In resisting further ecological destructions in Africa, it is sacrosanct having collective and concerted efforts by stakeholders involving environmental scientists, environmental ethicists, environmental activists, and environmental legal luminaries that would challenge the unbridled capitalist expropriation of the African environment.

References

Adams, J.S., and T.O. McShane. 1992. *The Myth of Wild Africa: Conservation without Illusion.* New York: W. W. Norton.

Callicott, J.B. 1985. Review of Tom Regan, the Case for Animal Rights. *Environmental Ethics: An Interdisciplinary Journal Dedicated to the Philosophical Aspects of Environmental Problems* 7 (4): 365–372.

Callicott, J.B. 1998. The Conceptual Foundations of the Land Ethic. In *Environmental Ethics: Readings in Theory and Application,* 2nd ed., ed. Pojman, L.P., Belmont: Wadsworth Publishing Company.

Callicott, J.B. 2001. The Land Ethic. In *A Companion to Environmental Philosophy*, ed. Dale Jamieson. London: Blackwell Ltd.

Callicott, J.B. 2002. From the Balance of Nature to the Flux of Nature: The Land Ethic in a Time of Change. In *Aldo Leopold and the Ecological Conscience*, ed. Richard L. Knight and Suzanne Riedel. Oxford: Oxford University Press.

Callicott, J.B. 2013. *Thinking Like a Planet: The Land Ethic and the Earth Ethic*. New York: Oxford University Press.

Chimakonam, J. (ed.). 2018. *African Philosophy and Environmental Conservation*. New York: Routledge.

Domsky, D. 2006. The Inadequacy of Callicott's Ecological Communitarianism. *Environmental Ethics: An Interdisciplinary Journal Dedicated to the Philosophical Aspects of Environmental Problems* 28 (4): 395–412.

Ejumudo, K.B.O. 2011. Environmental Justice, Democracy and the Inevitability of Cultural Change in Nigeria: A Critical Analysis of the Niger Delta Dilemma. *Africana: The Niger Delta* 5 (1): 22–48.

Fagbohun, O. 2010. Environmental Degradation and Nigeria's National Security: Making Connections. In *Law and Security in Nigeria*, 358–383. Lagos: Nigeria Institute of Advance Legal Studies. Available online: http://nialsnigeria.org/pub/OlanrewajuFagbohun.pdf.

Fayemi, A.K. 2016. African Environmental Ethics and the Poverty of Eco-Activism in Nigeria: A Hermeneutico-Reconstructionist Appraisal. *Matatu* 48 (2016): 363–388.

Fieser, J. 1992. Leopold and the Compatibility of Eco-Centric Morality. *International Journal of Applied Philosophy* 7: 37–41.

Forbes, W., K.B. Antwi-Boasiako, and B. Dixon. 2014. Some Fundamentals of Conservation in South and West Africa. *Environmental Ethics* 36: 5–30.

Guha, R. 1998. Radical Environmentalism and Wilderness Preservation: A Third World Critique. In *Environmental Ethics: Readings in Theory and Application*, 2nd ed, ed. Louis P. Pojman. Belmont: Wadsworth Publishing Company.

Horn, E.B. 2005. On Callicott's Second-Order Principles. *Environmental Ethics: An Interdisciplinary Journal Dedicated to the Philosophical Aspects of Environmental Problems* 27 (4): 411–428.

LaMonica, C. 2011. External Challenges to Moving Toward Sustainability in the Niger Delta Region: Why a Critical Assessment of the Classical Epistemologies and Developmental Assumptions of External Actors Matters. *Africana: The Niger Delta* 5 (1): 272–371.

Leopold, A. 1949. *A Sand County Almanac: And Sketches Here and There*. New York: Oxford University Press.

Leopold, A. 1998. Ecocentrism: The Land Ethic. In *Environmental Ethics: Readings in Theory and Application*, 2nd ed, ed. Louis P. Pojman. Belmont: Wadsworth Publishing Company.

Maass, P. 2009. *Crude World: The Violent Twilight of Oil*. New York: Vintage Books.

Meine, C. 1988. *Aldo Leopold: His Life and Work*. Madison: University of Wisconsin Press.

Musgrave, M. 2015. Aldo Leopold and Lessons for African Conservation. *The Musgrave Musings*. http://sustainableafricandevelopment.com/. Uploaded September 25, 2015. Accessed November 19, 2017.

Nnamdi, B.S., O. Gomba, and F. Ugiomoh. 2013. Environmental Challenges and Eco-Aesthetics in Nigeria's Niger Delta. *Third Text* 27 (1): 65–75. http://dx.doi.org/10.1080/09528822.2013.753194. Accessed November 20, 2017.

Oludayo, A.G. 2004. *Environmental Law and Practice in Nigeria*. Lagos: University of Lagos Press.

Passmore, J. 1974. *Man's Responsibility for Nature: Ecological Problems and Western Traditions*. New York: Charles Scribner's Sons.

Regan, T. 1983. *The Case for Animal Right*. Berkeley: University of California Press.

Regan, T. 1998. The Radical Egalitarian Case for Animal Right. In *Environmental Ethics: Reading in Theory and Application*, 2nd ed, ed. Louis P. Pojman. Belmont: Wadsworth Publishing Company.
Watson, D. 2005. Against the Megamachine: Empire and the Earth. In *Environmental Philosophy from Animal Rights to Radical Ecology*, 4th ed, ed. Michael E. Zimmerman, et al. New Jersey: Pearson Education, Inc.

Chapter 20
"Cleanliness Is Next to Godliness": A Theological Reflection on the Solid Waste Problem in Ghana

Afia Ban

Abstract This chapter sets out to explore how the faith community in Ghana can be better involved in addressing solid waste management in the country. In Ghana, most of the principal streets are filled with heaps of trash, principally polythene products. The drains are choked with uncollected garbage causing flooding. The government spends huge sums of money on waste management due to the inhabitants' poor attitude towards waste generation. The aim of chapter is to build a theology of stewardship by proposing advocacy for change of attitude toward God's creation, commitment to purposeful solid waste management strategies, and confronting weaker systems that obstruct solid waste management as three practical ways the church in Ghana can help in dealing with the state's solid waste problem.

20.1 Introduction

The significance of the environment to humankind cannot be underestimated because most human activities depend on the riches and glories of the environment. The impact of the environment permeates many facets of human life ranging from health, business, agriculture, and religion to entertainment, education, finances, and life, in general. Yet, less attention is paid to the sustainability of the environment, which has led to the rise of new and challenging ecological problems. Ozone layer depletion, loss of biodiversity, public health issues, and an increase in solid waste generation coupled with its poor management practices are but a few.

These environmental challenges need immediate attention from all stakeholders of creation care because; neglecting them threatens God's creation. In Ghana, the issues of the collection, management, and disposal of solid waste continue to feature prominently in the main towns and cities across the country. Improper management of solid waste in Ghana has created a variety of problems ranging from the contamination of water bodies, leading to scarcity of potable water and spread of water-borne diseases

A. Ban (✉)
Columbia Theological Seminary, Decatur, USA
e-mail: revafiaban@gmail.com

© Springer Nature Switzerland AG 2019
M. Chemhuru (ed.), *African Environmental Ethics*, The International
Library of Environmental, Agricultural and Food Ethics 29,
https://doi.org/10.1007/978-3-030-18807-8_20

in most rural communities, to environmental pollution from the stench emanating from uncollected and decaying garbage. Too, garbage-choked drains and gutters in the cities lead to uncontrolled flooding. Plastic waste is a menace. Illicit littering of plastic products, such as polyethene bags and sachets are in almost every street in the country and has become difficult to control. This irresponsible disposal of refuse is affecting the aesthetic nature of my beloved country. Has the Ghanaian situation on waste management been like this all the while? What contributed to the deterioration state of Ghana's waste management systems? Toward solution, how can humanity, and especially the church, involve itself in the care of creation considering Ghana's solid waste situation? An attempt to answer these questions will direct the discussion of this chapter.

20.2   Ghana's Solid Waste Situation in Context

Historically, solid waste management was very rudimentary in Ghana until the late nineteenth and early twentieth centuries. Before then, each household was responsible for managing its waste without burdening the whole community or the country at large of their waste. The common practice was throwing the trash into a demarcated place in the city which was known and accessed by the people without a fee. Usually, teenage girls in every family ensured the trash was sent to the dumping sites commonly called a refuse dump. Solid waste management was under control with this system because of the following factors:

1. The government had a strict labour[1] force in place, among whose duties was to ensure total sanitation in every community. This labour force's duty was to ensure total sanitation in every community. They used to visit houses at least once a week and to summon culprits who mishandle solid waste. For example, it was a crime to throw trash on the street or behind your building or otherwise not dump it correctly at the site. These workers were up to their task. The residents, including children, knew them very well. They helped in managing solid waste in various communities with the support from the government and cooperation of the people.

2. Traditionally, there were norms[2] and taboos[3] which served as a means of managing solid waste properly. Communal labour was a common practice in which the

---

[1] The workers of the labour force were under the town council unit. They wear khaki, long sleeves, and pants as their uniform. The inhabitants addressed them as "tankasefo" which meant the workers from the town council unit. These workers used to go around the community on a weekly basis, mostly on Thursday mornings, to ensure total sanity in that particular area.

[2] Norms are the unwritten but agreed upon expectations and rules by which a culture guides the behaviour of its members in any given situation, and they vary widely across cultural groups. An example of such norms on waste management in my community is: The sun must not set on a household's trash.

[3] Taboo is one of the types of norms. It is any behaviour which a culture forbids, and any violation of it attracts fine, punishment, or banishment from the community. The use of taboo is common in

community gathers to tidy up their environment by sweeping around principal streets, draining choked gutters and weeding bushy areas. Families who failed to participate in such activities were fined. It was a taboo to throw trash into water bodies. And it was a taboo for the sun to set on a family's trash in the house. All these were culturally instituted to ensure human discipline and commitment towards waste management. These systems were less harmful to the environment and human life because the system received the needed collaboration from the people, that is, it permitted the treatment of the waste before becoming a nuisance to the community. Unfortunately, when Christianity was winnowing African Traditional religion, some of these norms, customs, and taboos were lost and, to date, have not been replaced with a more environmentally appropriate method of managing solid waste.

3. Solid waste composition was predominantly organic, generated by households and a few market centres. Much of this waste was reused as compost for various farming activities and decomposed quickly on landfills without demanding large areas, unlike today. Factors such as industrialization, cosmopolitanism, population growth, and globalization have affected the waste composition entirely, making the traditional methods ineffective.

Today, house-to-house collection and central collection of garbage are the two most important systems put in place to control solid waste problems in Ghana. These systems are further divided into two parts: larger portion of the waste collection is handled by private contractors, whereas the other is handled by the municipal and sub-metropolitan authorities in all 216 districts.

The privatization of solid waste collection in mid-1990s by the government was related to the economic forces of the 1990s that grew out of the Washington Consensus, a term coined by an English economist, John Williamson to mean a set of ten economic policy instruments forming the basis of recommendations for economic reforms for less developed countries promoted by Washington, D. C.-based institutions such as the International Monetary Fund (IMF), the World Bank, and the United States government (Oxford Dictionary 2017). Those reforms drove countries toward privatization of industries. Even though the government privatized solid waste collection, the public sector still collected half of the city waste. Moreover, in Accra, the collection systems differed between the high-income and low-income residents. Low-income groups cannot afford to pay for proper garbage disposal, and they tend to dump domestic garbage near their houses, in rivers, into sewage drains, and at other illegal sites.

James Fearson and Paul K. Adraki report, "In 1998, 80% of waste was from the low-income residents, 17% came from middle-income residents, and 3% of waste was from high income groups" (Fearson and Adraki 2014: 16–22). Most of the waste generated from the low-income residents in the country is not effectively collected because those residents cannot afford the payment. Before 1995, 60% of waste was collected by the waste management department.

---

the Ghanaian context. A typical example is: It was a taboo to throw trash into river bodies or to throw your trash at night.

In 2006, an 88,000-employee organization called Zoomlion Ghana Limited was set up as a solid waste collection company. It has, over the years, expanded to other related services such as composting and recycling services (Accra Composting and Recycling Plant, ACARP), sewage treatment, janitorial services (Zoom Janitorial Services, Ltd.), landscaping and beautification services, mobile toilet services (Zoom Cabin, Ltd.), and oil waste treatment (Zoil Services Ltd.) (Annepu and Themelis 2013). The company is currently operating in all 216 districts in Ghana. Though the various metropolitan, municipal, and district assemblies have been spending large sums of money to collect, transport, and dispose of solid waste properly, they all prove insufficient. Thus, during the 2012 the president's state of the nation's address, he indicated that he would ensure the country was cleaned by the first one hundred days of his administration with the vision of seeking more advanced ways of managing solid waste problems. That is the state of waste management in Ghana, even though the various departments for waste management are assiduously working toward zero waste sustainability in the country.

20.3   Composition of Ghanaian Solid Waste

Waste composition is defined in this context to mean the sum of the all individual components of solid waste generated. In Ghana, the changes in material consumption patterns and lifestyle which follow economic development and globalization have resulted in an increase of waste generation levels. Organic and inorganic are the primary classification for solid waste composition in Ghana. They are subdivided as including 64% of organic, 36% of inorganic (3% paper, 4% plastic, 1% metals, and 28% glass and other inert materials). Organic waste is generated from food scraps, yard waste (such as leaves, grass, brush), and process residues. It constitutes the highest percentage in Ghanaian waste composition because, unlike, commercial, institutional, or industrial by-products, increase in organic waste rises with an increase in population, which is a natural phenomenon.

20.4   Solid Waste Collection and Disposal in Ghana

In Ghana, Solid Waste is collected using different types of vehicles ranging from manually driven tricycles, donkey carts, small trucks equipped with compactors, large trucks, and large trucks equipped with compactors. Tricycles are used to access areas with narrow lanes. Small trucks are used to access hilly regions with narrow roads, while large trucks equipped with compactors are also employed in places such as vegetable markets and corporate areas which generate large quantities of waste every day. The waste collectors from both the public and the private sectors move around neighbourhoods to collect the waste. The 2010 population census report revealed that 37.7% of households in Ghana dispose of their solid waste in open space at free dumps, and about one-quarter (23.8%) dispose of their solid waste into public containers without going through the proper collection procedure in the country managed by the collectors. Significant proportions of households either have their solid waste collected (14.4%) or burned (10.7%). In the regions, most households dispose of their solid waste at public dumps, either in containers or open space because of inadequate waste bins and the high level of poverty among the residents. However, in the Greater Accra Region, almost half (48.5%) of households have their solid waste collected from their homes. A significant proportion of households in the region (25.7%) dumps their solid waste in containers. The percentage of households which dump their solid waste indiscriminately is highest in the Upper West (36.0%) Region, followed by the Northern Region (26.4%) (Ghana Statistical Service 2012) due to improper management systems.

Over the last decade, the Accra Metropolitan Assembly has used at least seven temporary dumping grounds to dispose of Accra's solid waste. Some of these dumpsites were used for less than two months, while others, like the Oblogo controlled dumpsite, were used for years. All the dumpsites were located inside the city. Residential areas surround some dumpsites, and others are near surface water sources which severely impacts public health, the environment, and quality of life. Such insufficiency of resources, such as land, obstruct the smooth management of solid waste.

20.5 Factors Impeding Solid Waste Management in Ghana

Ghana's solid waste crisis continues to worsen as the days go by because of the uncompromising attitudes of some citizenry towards the management systems in place. Is it because of the incompetency of the management institutions? Or is it that Ghana generates more waste that any country whether developed or developing? Or are there no other strategies and methods that can be adopted to curb the worsening and deteriorating situation? These questions are raised to find out, what technical and practical factors impede the efficient and smooth management of solid waste in the country. According to earlier researchers in this field, there are many factors which jeopardize the management of solid waste. Among such factors include inadequate fiscal support, overpopulation coupled with unregularized consumption pattern, and the rampant propagation of prosperity gospel.

20.6 Financial Constraint in Ghana

It is hard to argue against the idea that inadequate funds are a contributing factor to proper solid waste management. Such reasoning will not be discarded entirely, but let one not also forget that although physical cash does not eat trash, it facilitates the management of trash before it turns into a bane in each community. Due to limited funds, most of the private institutions that manage solid waste continue to lament that they are understaffed. They are not able to attract qualified personnel such as engineers, mechanics, sanitation officers, administrators and even researchers to their company because of poor service conditions and remuneration. At times, it takes them a whole year to pay one month's salary to their workers.

Another effect of insufficient support with funds to their offices is that these management bodies are sometimes handicapped by lack of equipment and other appropriate technologies needed to carry out their activities. This, in turn, limits their provision of waste management services. Due to the lack of sufficient funds for the management of solid waste in the country, there are few skip containers in the country, or even in the cities. Skip containers are large, open- or closed-topped containers designed for loading onto special trucks. Residents empty their waste containers into these skip containers. It is possible to walk more than ten miles within the cities of the country without seeing even a skip container on the road. Because of this, people who wish to take responsibility for their waste find it difficult to do so. It has caused the principal streets in the cities to be swamped with much filth. These heaps of trash on the streets are awaiting trucks to convey them to their disposal sites, but those trucks have broken down along the way, and there are no funds for maintenance or replacement. These institutions also lack funds to run educational campaigns on the residents' involvement in solid waste management.

20.7 Overpopulation

Another unfavorable factor jeopardizing solid waste management is overpopulation. The *Cambridge Advanced Learner's Dictionary* defines overpopulation as "having too many people or animals for the amount of food, materials, and space available." In the Ghanaian situation, the effect of the "too many people" is limited space available for waste disposal strategies. For a more convenient definition that relates to the ecological issue, overpopulation is seen as a term that refers to "a condition by which the population density enlarges to a limit that provokes the environmental deterioration, a remarkable decline in the quality of life, or a population collapse" (Nahle 2003). According to Nasif Nahle,

> The impact of human populations on the environment has been severe. Some animal species have been extinguished or forced to live in inhospitable regions by the advance of urban areas; pollution is a problem that is increasing gradually because of the practice of burning as a means of managing the solid waste we generate. Emerging countries industrialization is not paying attention to environmental issues because of the feeding demands of their ever-growing populations.

The difficulty is humanity cannot live without creating waste. Thus, when population increases, consumption rates also rise. In a more concise form, Jessica McAllister frames the matter with the analogy as, "an inevitable consequence of more consumption is the rapid increase of waste that is produced." Apart from the consumption rate, overpopulation has also increased the speed of urbanization in the country, which has affected the city's waste management. The cities are choked with many people, affecting even human settlement. Places that used to be sites for dumping trash are now occupied by people. Accra, which is the country's capital, is now struggling for a convenient site for the landfill. The picture is almost the same in the other nine major cities of the country.

20.8   Propagation of Prosperity Gospel

While the management of solid waste departments in Ghana are struggling with financial constraints and overpopulation as an impediment to the smooth running of their office, the church is daily compounding the problem by educating the populace on how to generate more waste without recourse to its effect on the environment. One may ask, why do I associate the church as a sacred institution to solid waste issues? How does the church, which is known as the prophetic voice of a state on social issues serve rather as an important cause? One can expect nothing less when, through the pulpit, the blessings of God for his people forms the central idea, and the meaning of this blessing is what informs the content of what I refer to as "prosperity gospel".

The prosperity gospel is a heretical version of the gospel that serves as a "divine lens" through which people seek to amass material wealth irrespective of its consequence on one's environment, and any less thing is a curse. People are blessed from the pulpit with words that threaten the efficient management of solid waste in Ghana. Some of the examples of such blessings pastors invoke on their members include: "May the Lord help you to build ten mansions before you die," "May you be blessed that you can change your wardrobe every week," "May you never use materials that other people have used before," "May you be blessed that you will also drink sachet and bottled water." And there are many others blessings, to which the church members gladly respond, "Amen!"

On the surface, these words may seem not harmful but rather mere words of hope. To critically analyse them environmentally, the prosperity gospel is a danger to the environment. If the country finds it difficult to manage the current 3% of plastic waste, imagine how the country will be if the plastic waste becomes 70% of the solid waste? What happens to the waste from the demolition of these mansions? What do we do with the clothing that is changed weekly? What happens to the materials we purchase but no longer have need of? What will be the implications of this lifestyle on God's creation? These and others are questions this thesis is calling the church to reconsider.

20.9   The Church and Creation Care

Creation care is a term mostly chosen in theological dialogues because of its theo-centric implication since the 1970s, but it simply means to care for God's creation. Other terms such as environmental stewardship, missionary earth-keeping, ecojus-tice, eco-missiology, and evangelical environmentalism represent different ways of understanding what creation care means from different theological perspectives and different fields of study. Pope Francis prefers to use the phrase "care for creation" as a pastoral invitation for ecological conversation. He even uses the phrase as title of his book. Whatever the term, the message of the term is a concern to address environmental issues in a more religious way, to make ecological issues a matter for the faith community. Per Rhoads and Rossing, the concern to care for creation is not an invention in the faith community. Christians have for the past centuries sought for appropriate means to care for creation. From their understanding, there have been several meetings, gatherings, and sessions to find out an effective role of the Church in creation care (Rhoads and Rossing 2010: 123–43). Because creation care is complex, multisensory, and multifaceted, it is still prudent for the Church to continue the search for the more convenient and appropriate ways of addressing ecological problems. Such a movement could, perhaps, help because the concept of creation care, as Harvey Cox puts it, "calls for a profound conversation about values that involves a new understanding of our relation to God's creation, both the earth and its creatures, as well as our fellow human beings," (Francis) though he is not proposing anthropocentrism.

In Psalm 148, about thirty categories of creatures are addressed as members of a cosmic choir that joins humans to praise God. Therefore, any action such as improper management of solid waste that affects the ability and involvement of the cosmic choir to worship the creator is a way of denying the creator corporate worship from all creatures due God. Ultimately, my goal is to demonstrate that failure to take responsibility for the waste we generate (which pollutes the environment in many ways) directly affects our relationship with God in many different ways, as well.

For example, considering the etymology of the word "sin." Among the Akan tribe of Ghana, it simply means something that stenches. Reformed theology views sin as something that causes a separation of us from God, and is biblically affirmed. The prophet Isaiah writes, "Surely the arm of the Lord is not too short to save, nor the ear too dull to hear. But your iniquities have separated you from God" (Isa. 59: 1–2). By implication, in a Ghanaian context, God through the prophet was expressing a concern about not being able to live with the Israelites because of the "stench" emanating from their new way of life, which was against the law.

Metaphorically, God smells things. God has the sense organ for smelling. God reacts to every smell whether good or bad. Smell is supremely a very powerful sense that has divine connotation. It can be argued that God is not human so does not have a nose, which is perceived as the organ for smelling. But what distinguishes God from a god/idol is the sense of smell, not the organ for smelling. The Bible recounts a number of gods that have organs, such as nose, but the organs cannot perform or smell. The psalmist describes it as the impotence of the god or idols:

> Our God is in the heavens; he does whatever he pleases. Their idols are silver and gold, the work of human hands. They have mouths, but do not speak; eyes, but do not see. They have ears, but do not hear; noses, but do not smell. They have hands, but do not feel; feet, but do not walk; they make no sound in their throats[4] (Ps. 115: 3–7).

God smells in diverse ways. Right from Genesis, God started smelling. God receives our sacrifices of worship as fragrance through the sense of smell (Gen. 8:21: Ex. 30: 7–8; Lev. 2:2; Num. 4: 16). God also smells God's children, including Jesus Christ, and our gifts as fragrance (Eph. 5:2; Phil. 4: 18). God, through Jesus Christ's incarnation, commends a woman for pouring an expensive perfume on Jesus Christ to prepare him for his burial (John 12: 3). Not only that, God smells human actions of justice and shows displeasure at the scent of injustice. God punishes disobedience and evil acts with stench (Ex. 7: 18; 16: 20; Isa. 3: 24; Amos 4: 10; Joel 2: 20).

In the same way, solid waste shares a similar property with sin as it produces stench when kept unattended, and makes it difficult and unhealthy for people to stay in such polluted environment. The idea that sin is a repulsive odour caused by something's transformation from health to disease or rot, is a rich metaphor here, not only because of its connection to solid waste (which stinks), but because of the way God smells things throughout history, especially in the scriptures of the Old Testament. What is pleasing to God in the Old Testament, including the pursuit of justice and love of mercy, also, figuratively, smells good to God, which is why the prophets link the pursuit of justice to sacrifices worthy of and desired by God (Amos 5: 21–24). Biblically, anything that is unhallowed, hypocritical, conceded, fraudulent, or illusory in our hearts and our leadership team stenches and could be termed as sin.

The Harper Collins Dictionary of Religion defines sin as an offense (usually deliberate) against a religious or moral law. Generally, different religions have different perspectives on sin. In Judaism, sin is a violation of the stipulation of the covenant with God. There are a number of terms used in the Hebrew Scriptures to signify sin, chief among them *het* (a failure to carry out a duty), *avon* (refers to crookedness or transgression), *pasha* (a serious breach of covenantal responsibility), and *averah* (a general term from the root meaning "to pass over," as found in *Harper Collins Dictionary of Religion*). Sin is "a wrong deed insofar as it transgresses God's will as laid out in divine revelation. Rabbinic Judaism, in line with Genesis 8: 21, holds that people are by nature inclined to sin even though they recognize the two key distinctions of sin—the sin of commission, where one does that which is expressly prohibited, and sin of omission, in which one fails to do what is required.

In Christian theology, sin is any action or habit detrimental to the spiritual progress of the self, or to moral interrelations. The New Testament Greek calls sin *harmartia*, a missing of the mark or a wandering from the path. Theologically, sin is a rebellion against God that results in spiritual regress and harm to self or neighbour. Classical

---

[4]Unless otherwise noted, all scriptural references are from the New Revised Standard Version of the Bible, Oxford University Press, 1998.

theologians, such as Augustine, also define sin as "any transgression in deed, word or desire of the eternal law." *The Oxford Dictionary of the Christian Church* defines sin as "the purposeful disobedience of a creature to the known will of God." Relating the doctrine of sin to creation, *The Oxford Companion to Christian Thought* explains, "Sin denotes human disruption of the relationship between humans and God." Sin is what works against God's intention, presence, and action in creation and salvation. This disorientation in our relation to God causes immediate confusion concerning "truth, reality, and goodness and thereby in our judgments concerning what is good and right, resulting in disorientation in all our relationships: to ourselves, one another and the natural world." The magnitude of sin is that the original sin has affected every humanity and has affected how humanity relates with other creatures of God. The result of sin is partly the cause of the ecological crisis the world is facing today.

Therefore, sin must be understood within the whole ecology of Christian faith. Understanding sin solely in the context of creation could be tempting, but the Christian understanding of creation, the original order, and orientation of the world is inseparable from the eschatological perspective of salvation in Christ. As the Christian creation story asserts, sin is represented as a constant factor in the experience both of God's people and of the world from the first transgression of Adam and Eve in the Garden of Eden (Gen. 3). As a result, the creator, asked them to leave the garden.

My argument is this: If when we sin, it affects our relationship with God, and if the church is consistently empowering people to overcome sin through various theological avenues, then solid waste must also be a matter of concern for the church since, in essence, it mars our relationship with the creator because it affects the creator's creation. In other words, a concern to care for God's creation has more to do with our relationship with the creator, God, than with creation. For that reason, one of the ways in caring for God's creation that I am proposing in this essay is the management of solid waste through the strategy of Christian stewardship. But, how can the church claim Christian stewardship as a strategy for solid waste management in Ghana?

20.10 My Response

In the face of myriad environmental challenges, such as solid waste management problems in Ghana, I propose that voices of Christian ethicists cannot be left out in addressing crucial problems that threaten the safety of the environment. Christian environmental ethicists like Willis Jenkins address environmental issues, such as the solid waste management problem in Ghana, in ways so as to make them intelligible for Christian communities and significant for Christian experience. Jenkins suggests that "religious ethics should focus less on constructing and applying religious worldviews and more on inviting, tutoring, and pressing moral communities to make better use of their inheritance."[5] This inheritance refers to God's creation that God has entrusted to the care of humanity, for which the church has a key role to play. To Jenkins, the church can add her voice on environmental issues, but the impact will greatly depend on the appropriateness of the strategy adopted. That is why I claim the strategy of Christian stewardship be adopted in addressing environmental issues such as solid waste problems.

Stewardship means caring for something that belongs to another, while Christian stewardship entails the idea of preserving the conditions for nature's integrity, stability, and beauty. As Christians, stewardship conveys the notion of looking after all of creation—human and non-human creatures—that belong to God, the creator. According to Evans F. Bernard, stewardship, as applied here, means more than a simple, unattached "watching over." It implies that "we must both care for creation according to the standards that are not of our own making and, at the same, time be resourceful in finding ways to make it flourish." That is, good stewardship conforms to God's will, not nature's order, and Christians discover nature only by participating in God's acts. Most stewardship theologians try to establish and evaluate environmental responsibilities from God's establishment and formation of human responsibilities for the earth.

Using Jesus feeding the crowds as pericope encapsulates much of what the Church's involvement in environmental issues needs to be. The Church, called to imitate Christ, cannot neglect Christ's active involvement in reconciling "all" creation to himself. With reference to solid waste management, the gospel accounts of Jesus' remark regarding the leftover food after the crowd was fed indicate the relationship between solid waste and God's creation.,

All the accounts (Matt. 114: 21; Mark 6: 43; Luke 9: 17; John 6: 12) reveal that, at Jesus command, the disciples gathered twelve baskets full of the left over. I wish to explore three key ways by which the Church can adopt the strategy of stewardship to address Ghana's solid waste problem. The strategies are advocacy for change of attitude, commitment to proper solid waste management practices, and confronting systems that impede waste management. Collectively, they are the "Three C's": change, commit, and confront. The "Three C's" convert the already existing management strategies of "4R's": reduction, reuse, recycle, and recovery into more theological terms for the community of faith. The essence is to make the solid waste management matter a case for religious consideration.

20.11 Advocacy for Change of Attitude

The term "attitude" has been subjectively constructed as beliefs, feelings, evaluations, and response predispositions. However, I will focus on two definitions of attitude based on theoretical and contemporary views from the "*Encyclopaedia of Psychol-*

---

[5] Willis Jenkins, *The Future of Ethics: Sustainability, Social justice, and Religious Creativity* (Washington, DC: Georgetown University Press 2013).

ogy." Theoretically, attitude refers to a "hypothetical construct, namely a predisposition to evaluate some objects in a favourable or unfavourable manner" (American Psychological Association 2000). Within contemporary psychological research this means "a relatively general and enduring evaluation of some object, person, group, or concept along a dimension ranging from negative to positive." These definitions work well with this chapter because my vision is to call for an insightful and purposeful change of attitude of the Ghanaian community towards solid waste management, moving from waste generation to waste disposal. I anticipate such a change through attitudinal advocacy. Attitudinal advocacy is a technique for changing attitudes by inducing people to engage in behaviour that has implications for their attitude.

Attitudes are formed and changed on the basis of cognitive, affective, and behavioural processes. Cognitive attitudes are based on how people form beliefs about the characteristics of entities in their environment. The action of individual residents in a given community has impact on the mindset and choices of other peoples' lifestyles, which can positively or negatively affect the individual or a community as a whole. Therefore, the church can make an impact on the solid waste situation of Ghana if it starts the changing process, which in this instance can be developed through commitment and engagement.

What is the current attitude which the church must seek to change? There are two attitudes that I propose the church address: (1) people's mindsets concerning "holiness and sacredness" and (2) people's perception of waste as something without any worth.

Even though about 70% of the Ghanaian population is Christian, their attitudes towards solid waste portray an error in the church's understanding and application of "holiness or sacredness" as expounded in Christian theology. Why else could they allow filth to cover the beauty of a Christian populated country? As the profound English proverb says, "Cleanliness is next to godliness." In other words, sanitation is next to holiness or sacredness. But the solid waste problem in Ghana and the population of Christians question the rationality of this English proverb. Because it seems to me the greater the number of Christians, the more the solid waste problem worsens—though other factors contribute to the menace. Yet, I think the church could do better if proper attention is paid to the holiness code of the country.

Holiness, in Hebrew (*kodhesh*) means "separation" or "cutting off." It simply means a separation from "uncleanliness," from anything recognized as ceremonially, religiously, morally, or ethically unclean. The theological reason for our call to holiness is based on our relationship with God. God is holy. Therefore, believers are also to be holy. "For I am the LORD your God; sanctify yourselves therefore, and be holy, for I am holy (Lev. 11: 44). Accordingly, in Leviticus 19: 1–2, "The LORD spoke to Moses saying, speak to all the congregation of the people of Israel and say to them, "You shall be holy, for I the LORD your God am holy." Likewise, the invitation to holiness continues in Leviticus 20: 26: "You shall be holy to me; for I the LORD am holy, and I have separated you from the other peoples to be mine." It is in God's nature to deal with anything that defiles holiness. From the Garden of Eden to today, God is still in the business of dealing with the filth and uncleanliness of creation. If the church claims to be bound by the holiness code of God, then it must noticeably reflect that code in relation to solid waste management.

In biblical times, the unclean were separated from the camp until they had been ceremonially proven clean by the priest. Now that God, as spirit, dwells in us (1 Cor. 3: 16), how do we sell at market places full of filth? Why do we litter our communities with plastic waste to create an unclean environment with no consideration for its effects on the holy God's creation? The Church must revisit its teaching notes on holiness and the implication of Christian worship on God's creation. As Mayam posits, "Holiness does not mean bodily or ritualistic purity alone; it involves moral and ethical quality as well because pollution such as solid waste can degrade the clean to unclean" (Mayam, 110).

Holiness must, therefore, be taught as a virtue that benefits both creator and creation. The one who is taught from the pulpit to abstain from fornication must equally be taught from the same pulpit to abstain from any behaviour that leads to improper management of solid waste. It is unethical for the faith community to "clean the chapel" and throw the trash in a nearby drain, stream, or street. The urgency of this call is as a result of the devastating rate at which the filth enters the chapel, presumed to be a sacred place for God. People eat and drink from plastic containers and leave the trash on and under pews. The worst is those who stain the pews with bubble gum. The church, both as human bodies and structure, is losing its sacredness. Churches close a day's program and the vicinity turns into a dump. The church must reclaim the old interpretation of holiness as "separation," and dissociate itself from anything that supports the illicit generation and disposal of waste.

Finally, the church must advocate a change of people's perception towards waste. The perception of waste as the valueless product of human consumption fans the flame of throwaway culture and impedes solid waste management. The throwaway culture is partly problematic to solid waste management strategy because all waste is considered as "valueless" and therefore must be discarded in any form convenient to us which affects the space of landfills available.

An alternative use of waste can be promoted by the church, which might be called to consider waste as resource. "Waste" is a relative concept, and waste management practices differ. One person's waste could be another person's resource, provided it is something a person needs at a given time.

The caution here is people should not hide behind "usefulness" of waste and turn other people's communities into refuse dump. If the waste material cannot be reused for any meaningful thing again, then it must be properly disposed. I have seen goods other countries have exported to Ghana become waste scattered on Ghana's streets and in its market squares. However, a change in the perception of waste as a resource will influence other positive management strategies. For example, people must be made to understand that for effective recycling and composting, there has to be proper sorting of the waste material. The duty of the church is to continually announce the need to sort our waste for proper waste management. The inorganic and organic waste can be reused if I start the process from my home as a Christian by packing them in separate containers.

20.12   Commitment to Management Systems

Another aspect of solid waste management in which the church can involve itself is actively committing to the waste management systems put in place by the state. As part of the management strategies practiced by the management departments, these departments provide waste bins and skip containers, organize monthly communal clean up exercises, and run seminars and education programs through the media. These systems are good on paper but receive little cooperation from the populace. Moreover, due to insufficient resources available to the management departments, they are not able to provide enough waste bins, skip containers, and tricycles or trucks to convey the trash to its appropriate management unit, either to the assembling point, treatment site, or disposal site.

What can the church do about such a situation? Since churches are widely spread in the country, especially in the state's capital and areas where solid waste is poorly managed, I propose that the church decide on helping to improve the system by suppling waste bins or skip containers at their area of residence. Promote the idea of at least "one church, one community waste bin or skip container."

In terms of education, the church can support the waste management systems' media from the pulpit. At least the church can add proper management of solid waste to its announcement schedule. Religious Ghanaians bestow much trust and respect on the office of pastor and elder. They are receptive audiences for information delivered by the church. The church can organize creation care-oriented programs and invite the waste management units to educate the members on creation care with particular attention to solid waste problems and their remedies. At such programs, church members can be given the opportunity to express themselves regarding why they are not willingly supporting the existing solid waste management systems and they turn their neighbour's backyard, gutters, streets, and market centres into their personal refuse dump. The ethical and religious implication of such attitudes can be explained to them at such programs.

The church can organize communal labour for their communities. The objective of this organization is to form a group that brings all faiths under one umbrella to champion the cause of "clearing the air of the stench," thereby cleaning the communities to facilitate proper management of solid waste. In this way, all the religious bodies in the country can fully participate in dealing with the solid waste problem. The exercise will also serve as a platform for interfaith mission. For example, such gatherings will create an opportunity for Christians to reach out to Muslims, or involve the palace in dealing with social issues.

20.13 Confront Systems that Hamper Proper Management of Solid Waste

The third "C" which the church can apply as a strategy for managing the country's solid waste problem is to confront and challenge weaker conceptual systems that hamper the effective management of solid waste. Prominent among those weaker systems is materialism. The *Oxford Dictionary of Economics* defines materialism as "a tendency to consider material possessions and physical comfort as more important than spiritual values." In other words, materialism is the situation of craving for creation in all means without consideration of its implication for the relationship with the creator or other creatures. Materialism breeds negative characteristics such as greed, covetousness, and jealousy, all of which, in turn, fuel injustice in the world. A materialistic person or nation cares little about the good of other people or nations. Materialistic people are more selfish because of the intense inner desire of craving for more. Materialism steals our consciousness of stewardship for creation, and cunningly replaces it with a sense of exploitation.

One thing that makes materialism dangerous and a threat to the sustainability of the environment is its strong attachment to material possession. If a person is hard-working and can pay for everything he/she wants, what is wrong with that? Something is wrong with that, both in a religious and ethical sense. Waste generation is an unavoidable product of materialism. How the waste is handled and its effects on God's creation determine whether materialism only ends with ability to buy.

Materialism conveys three hidden motifs—ability to pay, ability to deal with the addictive qualities of its character, and ability to pay for its product and effects. For instance, if one is driven by materialism to buy a new vehicle, what that force is seeking to do is, after buying that vehicle, then one desires to buy another vehicle. This means treating the old vehicle as waste. How do we discard the so-called old goods that we no longer want or need? These are some of the reasons why the church must confront and challenge this system. It is deadly.

Both the Hebrew and Greek words for covetousness (*pleoneksia* and *batsa*, respectively) signify "the desire for more in a greedier manner." Many identify covetous people of the Bible, such as Achan (Josh. 7), Saul (1 Sam. 15: 9, 19), Judas Iscariot (Matt. 26: 14–16), and Ananias with his wife (Acts 5: 1–11), who were rebuked and punished. Covetousness and greed, which are fuels for materialism, are considered as very grave and gross crimes. As the writer of the Epistle to the Ephesians states, "But fornication and impurity of any kind, or greed, must not be mentioned among you, as is proper among saints" (Eph. 5: 3). Biblically, materialism, which manifests itself as covetousness or greed, is one of the first sins the early Church had to deal with because it draws believers away from the faith (Acts 5). Therefore, the Church is called to dialogue with the ruling classes on the general effect of materialism on the country's environment and ecology. If the authorities' interest is to import goods to satisfy the government's material gains, the church must counsel the state regarding such actions and the implication on solid waste management.

20.14   Conclusions

Creation care would note that human beings are created to steward creation by maintaining it through daily upkeep by tilling and keeping the ground. We are gardeners that spend our time and energy pruning and encouraging growth. We are composters who help organic waste return to its original forms to nourish new life. We are caretakers of creation. Yet, we have let things decay and moulder where they should not, creating a stench of death and disease where we ought to be cultivating life and hope.

Therefore, this thesis proposes a Christian stewardship that is a way of living on the land that cares for the land. It offers a strategy the Church must adopt to help in managing the solid waste situation in Ghana through advocacy for change of attitude, commitment to realistic management strategies, and confronting weaker systems that impede effective management of solid waste.

References

Books

Clement of Alexandria. 1994. Quis Dives Salvetur 33. In R.B. Tollinto, Clement of Alexandria: A Study in Christian Liberalism, vol. 1 London: Williams and Norgate.
Louisville: Westminster/John Knox. 2010. Shibu. R. Mayam. *Zero Waste Management: Theological Insights for Urban Sustainable Waste Management.* India: Christian World Imprints 2016.
Rhoads, M. David. and R. Barbara. Rossing. 2010. *A Beloved Earth Community: Christian Mission in an Ecological Age.* In ed. Kalu Ogbu, Vethanayagamony and Chia Kee-Fook. Edmund.

Articles

Annepu, Ranjith. and Nicholas R. Themelis. 2013. *Analysis of Waste Management in Accra, Ghana and Recommendations for further Improvements*, Columbia University, Earth Engineering Center, March 2013.
Fearson, James, and Paul K. Adraki. 2014. Perception and Attitudes to Waste Disposal: An Assessment of Waste Disposal Behaviors in the Tamale Metropolis. *Journal of Environment and Earth Science* 4.

Websites

Nahle, Nasif. 2017. *Overpopulation.* Biology Cabinet Organization (Biol.), Nov 2003. http://biocab. org/Overpopulation.html. Accessed on 27 Feb 2017.

Reports

Ghana Statistical Service. 2012. *2010 Population and Housing Census: Summary Report of Final Results*. Ghana: Sakoa Press Limited.